CAMBRIDGE SOUTH ASIAN STUDIES

LAND TENURE IN VILLAGE CEYLON

CAMBRIDGE SOUTH ASIAN STUDIES

These monographs are published by the Syndics of Cambridge University Press in association with the Cambridge University Centre for South Asian Studies. The following books have been published in this series:

GOPAL, S., *British Policy in India, 1858–1905.*

PALMER, J. A. B., *The Mutiny Outbreak at Meerut in 1857.*

OBEYESEKERE, G., *Land Tenure in Village Ceylon. A Sociological and Historical Study.*

LAND TENURE IN VILLAGE CEYLON

A SOCIOLOGICAL AND HISTORICAL STUDY

BY

GANANATH OBEYESEKERE

Lecturer in Sociology, University of Ceylon

CAMBRIDGE
AT THE UNIVERSITY PRESS
1967

Published by the Syndics of the Cambridge University Press
Bentley House, 200 Euston Road, London, N.W. 1
American Branch: 32 East 57th Street, New York, N.Y. 10022

Library of Congress Catalogue Card Number: 66–16664

Printed in Great Britain
at the University Printing House, Cambridge
(Brooke Crutchley, University Printer)

FOR

RANJINI, INDRAJIT AND NALINIKA

CONTENTS

MAPS

PREFACE

The following work is a revised version of a thesis, submitted as part requirement for a Ph.D. degree at the University of Washington in 1964. I have used in the spelling of Sinhalese technical terms a consistent phonetic transliteration. When Sinhalese names have to be written in the plural I either retain the Sinhalese singular form, or for purposes of convenience add an 's' in the English manner. Sinhalese place names and personal names are, however, used here as they are generally written by English-speaking Sinhalese or as represented in official documents. Many of the personal names have been changed so as to maintain the anonymity of informants. However, I tried as best I could to maintain the flavour of the original names. Thus a name like Charles could easily be converted into David or James; and a name like Appu Singho could be converted into Podi Singho, or Singho Appu. For purposes of convenience I have often abbreviated the surnames of informants, a practice adopted by informants themselves. For example, a person named Pahala Madagama Gamage Jinadasa may sometimes be referred to as P. M. G. Jinadasa. I have also used two bibliographic abbreviations for convenience sake: 'A.R.' refers to 'Administration Report'; 'S.P.' refers to 'Sessional Paper'.

The present study is largely based on field work undertaken by me in 1961 in the village of Madagama (pronounced *Mädagama*, 'middle village'), Southern Province, Ceylon. We were in the village sporadically from January to July, 1961. Our stay involved only about three months of continuous and intensive field work. Field work was made possible by a generous grant given by the Asia Foundation in Ceylon, for which I thank them. The grant given to me was for field work in Madagama and for the training of Sociology students in the University of Ceylon in techniques of field work. Several students participated in the project for short periods—Tissa Fernando, P. Gamage, M. Cooray, and J. C. de S. Jayasinghe. I owe a special debt of gratitude to two students, Sarath Amunugama and P. A. S. Saram, who continuously and actively participated in the field project, not only in the collection of data, but also in provocative discussions. Mr K. P. Wimaladharma of the Galle Kachcheri assisted me in collecting data from the Government Land Registry. Mr P. Weerasekera, Divisional Revenue Officer, Hinidum Pattu in 1961, not only went out of his way to help us, but also, with characteristic generosity, put his house at our disposal. Special mention must be made of three major informants—Mr I. M. G. Sarnelis, Mr P. M. G. Charlis, and Mr J. G. George—who were helpful to us in innumerable ways. They exemplified a general characteristic of Madagama society, and the more traditional Sinhalese low country villages—a warm hospitality and courtesy almost impossible for the field workers from the city to reciprocate. I express, therefore, my gratitude to the good people of Madagama.

My original intention was to study religion in Madagama from a sociological and psychological point of view. Though I spent some time on this in the field, I was soon impressed by the importance of land tenure in the social structure of the village. Land was a major topic of village conversation. Moreover, a few weeks after I had started field work I received a copy of Leach's *Pul Eliya*. This stimulated my interest in land tenure further so that for a period of about two months we concentrated our efforts more or less exclusively on land tenure. Neither field work on land tenure nor the present thesis would have been undertaken by me but for the stimulation provided by Leach's study. I have not hesitated to borrow ideas or terms from *Pul Eliya*, for I must admit that, not being a kinship specialist, I view my own work as a novice's job. Any professional touch that may exist is largely due to what I have learned from my friends and teachers—Professors Melford E. Spiro, Kenneth E. Read and Edward B. Harper—not only in the classroom, but also, more importantly, over the coffee table. Other writers have also influenced this work and if I have not always indicated the source of my ideas it is because I believe that these ideas are a part of our common anthropological knowledge. However, I must mention that I have been influenced by David Schneider for the manner in which the problem is formulated in Chapter III, and by Robert Merton's essay on the 'role set' in Chapters VI and IX. I am aware of the shortcomings of this study, especially the short period of field work that went into it. I had originally planned to include chapters on the tenure of garden lands and the spread of the *taṭṭamäru* system in the Southern, Western and Sabaragamura Provinces; unfortunately, I was not able to carry out the necessary research. Nevertheless

I am convinced that this study is worth presenting to a professional audience.

In April 1964 I was awarded the first Esperanza Fellowship of the Royal Anthropological Institute to work in association with colleagues at Cambridge University for a period of six months. This gave me an opportunity to revise my thesis for publication, and I greatly profited by the critical comments of three Cambridge colleagues—Dr Edmund R. Leach, Mr B. H. Farmer and Dr S. J. Tambiah. I thank the trustees of the Esperanza Trust for providing me with this opportunity.

When I came back to Ceylon in October 1964 I visited Madagama several times to cross-check some of my data. During these visits Mr D. Amarasinghe, the present Divisional Revenue Officer, was most hospitable. The Government Agent, Galle, and the Registrar General were good enough to give me access to the Grain Tax registers and marriage records respectively. My friend Mr R.K.W. Gunasekera, Principal of the Ceylon Law College, kindly read through the whole work and corrected several legal *faux pas* I had made; any remaining ones are largely due to my own lack of legal sophistication combined with the necessity to simplify legal facts for the purposes of the present study. Mr K. Kumarasamy typed this book, Mr E. V. Christian prepared the maps, and Mr E. E. Reynolds made the index. Miss Maya Wijesekera assisted me in preparing the typescript. The Cambridge University Press was kind enough to tolerate an inconsistent author inexperienced in correcting proofs! The Esperanza Trust and the Radcliffe-Brown Memorial Fund of the Royal Anthropological Institute granted generous subsidies for the publication of this book. My sincere thanks to the individuals and institutions mentioned above.

G.O.

Department of Sociology
University of Ceylon
24 April 1964

CHAPTER I

INTRODUCING MADAGAMA

The village (*gama*) of Madagama is located in the northern tip of the Southern Province, one of the nine provinces of Ceylon. The Southern Province is part of what is in common parlance called the low country, or the Maritime Provinces. In Ceylonese historical writings a distinction is made between the low country or Maritime Provinces and the up-country or Kandyan Provinces. This distinction is based on historical experience. The Maritime Provinces are those areas along the coast that were occupied by the Portuguese (1505–1658), the Dutch (1658–1796) and the British (1796–1948). The Kandyan Provinces (consisting largely of the contemporary Central, North Central, Uva and Sabaragamuva Provinces) were up to the British conquest of 1815 under Sinhalese rule. The distinction between the two areas has significance for contemporary law. The residents of the Maritime Provinces marry according to the Roman-Dutch law, introduced by the Dutch and implemented by the British. The residents of the Kandyan Provinces have the option to marry under traditional Sinhalese law known today as Kandyan law.

Each province in Ceylon is divided into several administrative 'districts', under the charge of a Government Agent, a prestigious civil service office modelled after the traditional feudal *disāva* or governor. The Southern Province consists of a land area of $2146\frac{1}{4}$ square miles and consists of three revenue districts: the Galle District ($652\frac{1}{4}$ square miles), the Matara District ($481\frac{1}{4}$ square miles) and the Hambantota District ($1012\frac{3}{4}$ square miles). The Galle District in which Madagama is located is composed of the following six Divisional Revenue Officers' (D.R.O.'s) Divisions: (1) Bentota-Walallawita Korale (168 square miles); (2) Wellaboda Pattu ($79\frac{7}{12}$ square miles); (3) Four Gravets ($31\frac{1}{4}$ square miles); (4) Talpe Pattu ($99\frac{3}{4}$ square miles); (5) Gangaboda Pattu ($139\frac{2}{3}$ square miles) and (6) Hinidum Pattu (134 square miles) (see Map 1). Each D.R.O.'s Division is divided into village Headmen's Divisions, the Hinidum Pattu being the smallest of these containing only fifteen Headmen's Divisions, all the other D.R.O.'s

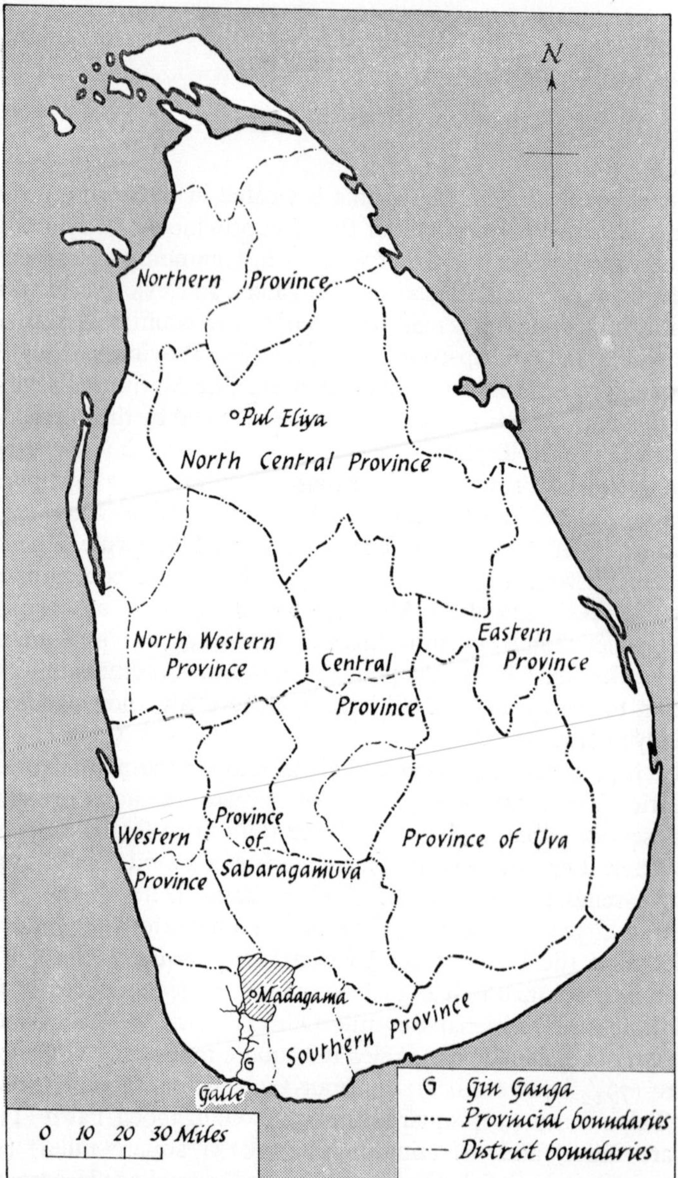

Map 1. Ceylon, showing Provincial and District Boundaries, the location of Madagama, Hinidum Pattu (shaded area) and Pul Eliya.

Divisions containing about twice the number or more. For administrative purposes each Headman's Division is divided into several villages. Madagama was in the Headman's Division of Neluva consisting of six villages—Danawala, Koswatte, Lelwala, Mavita, Neluva and Madagama. The whole Pattu contains ninety villages and hamlets. The headman of the Neluva Division in 1961 was a resident of Lelwala; he was directly responsible to the Divisional Revenue Officer (D.R.O.) whose office was in Hiniduma Town; the D.R.O. in turn was responsible to the Government Agent in Galle (see Map 2). Before the office of the D.R.O. was established by the British the revenue officer was called a Mudaliyar, a native office continued by the Dutch and the British. The first D.R.O. for Hinidum Pattu assumed duties in 1941.

The Hinidum Pattu is the northernmost D.R.O. Division in the Galle District in the upper reaches of the Gin Ganga, a river which rises in the Rakwana Hills beyond the Sinharaja Forest, the largest area of virgin tropical forest in Ceylon. Madagama is one of the northern villages of the Pattu bordering this forest. The Pattu is interesting ecologically. It consists of undulating hills and valleys rising gradually as one proceeds north (see Map 2). Madagama itself is at an elevation of 470m.s.l. It is in a heavy rainfall area of 150–200 inches per year. These ecological facts have several implications for land tenure. (*a*) Hinidum Pattu is ecologically sharply contrasted with 'dry zone' villages like Pul Eliya (Leach 1961) lying in a dry, flat country with scarce rainfall and dependence on a tank. As Leach points out this sets the stamp on its land tenure arrangements. The stretches of paddy field (*yāya*) are dependent on the tank for their existence. (*b*) It is also contrasted with most other low country 'wet zone' villages along the coast with their flat terrain, which permits the cultivation of large stretches of paddy land (*yāya*). Hinidum Pattu permitted the cultivation of small *yāyas* of about fifteen to twenty acres in the valleys and the formation of small human communities associated with such a *yāya*. The country was not as steep as the central Kandyan Hills, so there is no terraced cultivation of paddy.

Practically up to the 1930's Hinidum Pattu was considered a remote, inaccessible area. In population and consequently in agricultural (paddy) output it was extremely small when compared with other Divisions in the Galle District. According to a population estimate in 1878 the whole Pattu contained 4291 people.

Even making allowance for considerable under-enumeration it is markedly contrasted with two other Divisions in the Galle District with almost the same area: Gangaboda Pattu was estimated to have a population of 23,214 and Bentota-Walallawita Korale a population of 36,758 (A.R. 1878:13). According to the censuses of 1946 and 1953 the population of the Hinidum Pattu was 11,946 and 14,603 respectively, about half the population of each of the two other *pattus* seventy years ago!

The area under paddy cultivation was also low. In 1869 and 1870 according to the Government Agent of the district the area under cultivation, calculated in terms of 'sowing area', was about 70 and 120 bushels respectively for the Maha season; the next lowest Division was Bentota-Walallawita Korale which had a sowing area of 160 and 200 bushels (A.R. 1870:127). In 1877 and 1878 the sowing area in bushels computed by the administration for taxation purposes were as follows (A.R. 1888:19):

	Maha 1877	Maha 1878	Yala 1877	Yala 1878
Hinidum Pattu	585	436	3331	3333
Bentota–Walallawita Korale	998	1102	8430	8644
Gangaboda Pattu	9271	7489	12752	14308

Though the administration bewailed the fact that it was a poor area with few fields, the small area under cultivation, at this date at any rate, was largely due to the demographic factor.

Early Administration Reports often make reference to the remoteness and inaccessibility of the region. A Grain Tax Commissioner's report of 1890 is typical of these comments:

A part of this district used to belong to the Kukulu Korale, and the villages in that part pay a tax of one-fourteenth instead of one tenth... The people subsist chiefly on Kurakkan and sweet potatoes; the paddy grown is insufficient, arecanut and garden produce are plentiful.

There is not a school in the district, and few people can read or write. The chief headman is called a Mudaliyar and the way he treats his people he is more like a rate mahatmaya. Not a single road is passable for carts, and in wet weather there must be some difficulty for foot passengers—The *pattu* shows no signs of advancement and it is where it was half a century ago (S.P. XIII, 1890:2).

Things were only slightly better in 1939. The Administration Report of that year reads: 'The progress and prosperity of the people of Hinidum Pattu are retarded by lack of communication and the absence of education. The economic condition of the people of this division is poor' (A.R. 1939:4C). Even in 1939 there was still no hospital; no major road communication to Galle (the major road from Galle ended in Udugama twelve miles from Hiniduma); no telecommunication facilities; only a few schools scattered sporadically in the *pattu*. After 1940 things took a turn for the better with the construction of new roads, a hospital, good schools, and a police station. However, even today there is not a single town in the whole *pattu* supplied with electricity. A heavy shower of rain still floods the causeway on the Udugama–Hiniduma road either bringing motor traffic to a virtual standstill or causing traffic to take a tedious circular detour back through Akuressa in the Matara District, and thence to Hiniduma. Government servants abhor the work in the area, and generally higher administrative officers like the D.R.O., the Medical Officer and Inspector of Police are young, though responsible, men serving their first 'sentence'! Most villages of the *pattu* are still inaccessible by car. Madagama itself is over a mile off the main road; other villagers are accessible only through jungle footpaths, or suspension bridges; less fortunate ones are stuck in the Sinharaja Forest and one has to reach them through ingeniously constructed native cane 'suspension bridges' (*kolave*) perilously poised over the rapids of the Gin Ganga; or a plain tree trunk (*edaṇḍa*) over a stream. The remoteness of the region combined with its heavy rainfall made it unattractive for European rubber plantations, so that the region, especially the northern part, was singularly unaffected by a plantation economy. However, there are a few small tea and rubber plantations, and plumbago and gem mines all owned by Ceylonese. Today many villagers have small plots of rubber and tea or coconut grown on *badu iḍam*; that is, land given by the government on 'permanent lease'. This constitutes a major subsidiary source of income for the people.

Before British times a northern portion of the Hinidum Pattu, known as the *yakavala kottāsaya* consisting of about fifteen villages, belonged to the Disavany (district) of Sabaragamuva which in turn was part of the Kandyan Kingdom (D'Oyly 1929:20–9). In British times this part of Sabaragamuva was incorporated into the Southern Province permanently. This fact had some relevance for law. The villages, including Madagama, that belong to *yakavala kottāsaya* were permitted to marry according to Kandyan law. As far as we know, this is the only part of the low country where citizens are permitted to marry according to either Kandyan or the General (Roman-Dutch based) Law. Twenty-six marriages of Madagama males and females are recorded in the Kandyan marriage register between 1875 and 1919, about half of them *binna*, or uxorilocal marriages. After 1919 no Kandyan marriages are recorded though the register continued to exist. The reason for this is quite simple. The privilege of marrying according to Kandyan law was granted to only a few villages; the rest of the *pattu* married according to the General Law. Since most marriages are contracted between residents of both types of villages, they must be registered under the General Law. There was also official discouragement of these marriages in order to have a uniform system of marriage registration for the whole low country. As such the Kandyan register, which only permitted marriages between a small number of villages, became gradually defunct.

Not many sociological conclusions could be derived from the formal registration of marriages under Kandyan Law in this part of the *pattu*. While some marriages were being registered under Kandyan Law, other marriages were being registered under the General Law simultaneously (1863 onwards). The earliest marriages registered (1848) were in an entirely different register—palm leaf records based on the Dutch *thombos* (registers) and continued by the British. The formal law governing these early registrations is Roman-Dutch! The really significant sociological conclusion that can be drawn from these totally divergent registers is the following: it seems clear that the traditional (pre-British) law of Madagama (and probably the whole Pattu) was Kandyan (Sabaragamuva) law. It is very likely that people acted according to these jural norms irrespective of the formal mode of registration practised. This is entirely confirmed by genealogies, which provide a sociologically far more satisfactory source of information.

The relative isolation of Hinidum Pattu and its absence of 'progress' makes it an excellent region for anthropological field work, specially as a 'baseline' for ascertaining traditional modes of behaviour and culture and an assessment of change. Such a task is practically impossible in most other Divisions of the low country owing to radical changes they have experienced. 'Every evening', say Madagama villagers, 'we can hear the beating of drums from our village.' This is almost literally true for traditional exorcistic ceremonies and ritual are still consistently performed. There are plenty of Buddhist temples in the region, and the dominant ethos is Buddhist. A Catholic Church started about half a century ago is barely struggling for survival. Culturally, then, there is in Hinidum Pattu a great deal of traditional belief and practice. From the point of view of social structure, too, considerable 'tradition' prevails. For example, in many villages traditional modes of organizing land tenure still prevail. However, it is important not to minimize the changes that have come over the *pattu*. The changes are considerable and in some areas of social action, radical. Yet this is a region where both tradition and change, which is the subject-matter of this book, could still be successfully studied.

The village of Madagama consists of an area of about a hundred acres, forty of which are paddy lands. It is in the land tenure of paddy lands we are interested in this work. The agricultural year is divided into two seasons. A government monograph on paddy statistics gives an accurate account of the agricultural year in Hinidum Pattu. The year commences with the *maha* season (*mās mōsama*): the main sowing period is from the second week of October to the first week in November; the main harvesting period is from the fourth week of January to the second week of February. The sowing period for *yala* commences about the second week of March to the second week of April; the harvesting period is from the fourth week of July to the second week of August (A Report on Paddy Statistics, 1956:21, 24). Agricultural activity preliminary to sowing commences a month or even two months before the sowing period. The technology is primitive; the seed is 'broadcasted', the labour employed in ploughing, harvesting and threshing is largely manual. Forty years ago several villagers owned buffaloes which were used for ploughing; but probably owing to the radical changes in land ownership resulting in 'absentee landlordism' the use of buffaloes was discontinued. Still some of the more wealthy occasionally hire buffaloes for ploughing and muddying the fields. The area sown is calculated not in terms of acreage but 'sowing area', i.e. the amount of seed that could be broadcasted in a particular field. The smallest unit of paddy measure is a *kurini* (k); roughly about 8 k makes a bushel; 10 k makes one *pāla*, another unit of measure; four *pāla* make one *amuna*; a sowing area of 14 k roughly constitutes an acre. The yield (*asvänna*) is extremely poor and has remained constant from 1889 to the present day—four- or fivefold (A.R. 1889: 1 E). Since most villagers cultivate small units, each person works at his own plot often assisted by an individual or individuals with whom he has an *attan* relationship; that is, where an individual *X* assists in the cultivation of *Y*'s fields gratuitously while *Y* reciprocates by assisting *X*. The few owners of large units of cultivation may employ a *kaiya*, where a group of villagers assemble for a day to assist the owner to cultivate his fields gratuitously. It is obligatory for the owner to provide the *kaiya* group with breakfast, lunch and tea.

The techniques and economics of agriculture presented above have no direct relevance for the subject-matter of this work. We are also not concerned with land use or agricultural ritual. Ours is a sociological study of land tenure in relation to tradition and change in the village of Madagama. This village in 1961 consisted of about 289 people forming 47 nuclear families. But these demographic facts are also of little relevance for this work. Some of the present inhabitants of Madagama are outsiders planted on the outskirts of the village by the government through its village expansion programmes. Others more significant from our point of view have left the village to reside elsewhere. The subject-matter of our work then is not a study of the social system of Madagama village. It deals with the study of its land tenure system from its very inception till the present day. In fact it deals with two land tenure systems: (*a*) the land tenure system of Pahala (lower) Madagama, and (*b*) that of Ihala (upper) Madagama. Lower and upper refer to the two sections (hamlets) that constitute the village of Madagama. One system (Pahala Madagama) is functioning on the basis of a traditional 'plan'; the other system has practically disintegrated and its end is imminent. The second represents to us the kind of end that this type of system will eventually be confronted with. What we have done in our study is to describe the natural history of a land tenure system from its founding to its predictable disintegration or demise. The period is from 1790 to 1961; the data therefore have considerable diachronic depth.

When we collected our data for Madagama in 1961 we were struck by the discrepancy between the cognitive plan that individuals had and the actual facts of land tenure. It seemed to us quite clear that the cognitive plan of land tenure was geared to empirical conditions that prevailed 'traditionally'. Such a traditional cognitive plan called for certain conditions in the kinship system and the inheritance laws of the society. These conditions did not prevail in 1961. That they did prevail traditionally is clear from the early British works in Sinhalese (Kandyan) law, like Sawers (1826), D'Oyly (1929), *Niti Niganduva* (1880), Armour (1860). Thus we had a 'baseline' for the 'typical' manner in which the traditional land tenure system operated in (*a*) the cognitive plan of land tenure, and (*b*) in the traditional inheritance laws of pre-British Sinhalese society.

In chapter 2 we have converted the cognitive plan which exists in the minds of (Pahala) Madagama informants into an indigenous or ideal model. The model is *our* construction based on the informants' cognitive plan, and differs from such a subjective cognitive map in at least two major respects. First, informants would verbalize how they should ideally or actually organize the tenurial arrangements of the society. These statements are rephrased abstractly by us as part of the process of anthropological conceptualization, rather than the conceptualization (cognitions) of informants. Lévi-Strauss would call such an abstraction a mechanical model (Lévi-Strauss 1953:528–31). Secondly, ours is an idealized construct in which complicating variables that inhibit the optimum functioning of the system are eliminated. The methodological utility of such an idealized type will be discussed at the concluding chapter of this work. For the present we could state that the normative referents of our ideal model are more or less isomorphic with the traditional cognitive plan of informants, and thus provide a baseline for the study. Moreover, since the ideal model has no complicating variables we could place the empirical facts in which complicating variables always occur against the ideal so that these variables stand out in relief. The variables could then be isolated and analysed.

The ideal model requires for its optimum functioning patrilineal inheritance and a patrilocal aggregation of kinsmen. In chapter 3 we inquire whether these conditions are met by examining the traditional laws of inheritance and marriage of the society. These are available in the works of British civil servants mentioned earlier. We assume that these Kandyan laws were traditionally applicable to Madagama also. We have pointed out earlier the basis for this assumption.

In chapter 3 we therefore deal with the main principles of Kandyan law. Since we have no grounds for assuming that land tenure determines inheritance or vice versa, we have presented a formal description of traditional inheritance and marriage rules. Though the long-range operation of the rules is consonant with the requirements of the ideal model, they are by no means isomorphic with it. In this chapter we have attempted to explain why some of the inheritance laws 'deviate' from the requirements of the ideal model. Like chapter 2, chapter 3 is also a baseline—it tells us what the inheritance rules of the society were before British contact, so that we have further means of controlling the changes in inheritance and marriage laws that have occurred since then.

Chapter 4 presents the detailed empirical facts on inheritance for Pahala Madagama hamlet from its founding till 1961. When these facts are placed against the ideal model and the traditional inheritance laws of the society the factors of change can be isolated. These factors—the loss of the structural prerequisite of the system, the grain taxes of the late nineteenth century, the introduction and implementation of the bilateral Roman-Dutch laws of inheritance—are discussed in chapter 5. The operation of these factors of change produces the empirical conditions of 1961. The rest of the book deals with the analysis of some of these empirical conditions:

(*a*) The most impressive feature of the empirical system in 1961 is the minute fractioning of shares. This is most evident in Ihala Madagama hamlet: we present the land tenure data for that hamlet in chapter 6. The proliferation of shares creates a share-market. In chapter 7 we examine the structure of the share-market and the nature of share speculation.

(*b*) The existence of a multiplicity of shares and share owners renders the application of the traditional scheme of land tenure difficult. In chapter 8 we show how the traditional cognitive plan is implemented in the organization of tenure in 1961, and the kind of strain involved in its application.

(*c*) In both hamlets a large number of shares are owned by outsiders (non-residents). The types of contractual relationships between absentee share owners and resident villagers are discussed in chapter 9. These outside share owners belong to a single kin group, the *peläntiya*. *Peläntiyas* are treated as status groups formed on the basis of a traditional feudal ideology. The nature of this ideology and its contemporary relevance are discussed in some detail.

(*d*) The changes in the land tenure system noted in 1961 have resulted in changes in the strategy of marriage and in residence alignments. These have resulted in the radical reorganization of the traditional hamlet structure. These problems are discussed in chapter 10. Chapter 11 is the concluding chapter which discusses the methodology involved and the place of our study of Madagama in the tradition of anthropological writing.

CHAPTER 2

THE IDEAL MODEL OF LAND TENURE

SOME PRELIMINARY DEFINITIONS: VILLAGE, 'PRAVĒNI', 'VĀSAGAMA', AND SUBCASTE

The word *gama* has several connotations which require elucidation. *Gama* is used by both peasants and government officials to mean 'village'. But while the Administration limits itself to this meaning, the villagers use it to designate other social units also. As a 'village' Madagama largely consists of kinsmen related affinally or consanguineally to each other, but is not a 'clearly defined structural entity' (to use Srinivas' words). There are few bonds other than kinship sentiments of varying intensity that bind its members together; any cohesiveness that exists is a function of 'mechanical' rather than 'organic' solidarity. Of late Madagama village has organized (in conjunction with several adjacent villages) a Rural Development Society and a Women's League, both having the support of the Central Government. In 1960 the village organized its own 'grade school'. It is as if the Government's recognition of Madagama as a 'village' for administration purposes, for the granting of aid, social benefits, etc., has forced the villagers to think of themselves in some sense as Madagama folk, and to act collectively in their own interests.

Traditionally and up to about two or three decades ago, Madagama as a 'village' was of little sociological significance. What was important then, and to a lesser extent even now, were the segments of the village, also called *gama* but here translated as 'hamlet'. If the basis of solidarity of Madagama is largely one of kinship sentiment, the ties that previously united the 'citizens' of the hamlet were of a more viable character based upon economic interdependence; specifically, a joint economic interest in the paddy and garden lands of the hamlet by, ideally, an agnatically related body of kinsmen. The hamlet was then a much more clearly defined structural unit, within which were articulated some of the major social relationships of the group. It is this unit, the major focus of our analysis, which we shall now attempt to describe.

The Ideal Model of Land Tenure

The 'village' of Madagama is divided into two hamlets called Pahala Madagama and Ihala Madagama. Each contained a stretch of paddy land (*maḍa iḍam*) and high ground (*goḍa iḍam*) or garden land on which were built the houses of its citizens. The lands of the hamlet are called *pravēni*, 'ancestral lands', which according to the prevalent myth were originally owned as one estate (*gama*) by a patrilineal ancestor (*mutta*) who founded it.

These meanings of *gama* and *pravēni* are entirely consonant with the etymology of the words. In Sanskrit the word *pravēni* denotes a 'braid of hair'. Definition of rights in terms of hair is not unusual in Sanskrit where *anulōma* (hypergamy) means 'in accordance with the direction of the hair' and *pratilōma* (hypogamy) is 'against the hair'. In Pali the term 'braid of hair' is given a metaphorical twist so that *paveni* (the Pali for *pravēni*) meant 'series, succession, line; tradition, custom, usage'. In Sinhalese these several meanings are combined so that the dictionary gives the meaning of *pravēni* as *santatiya* ('ancestry'), *parapura* ('pedigree'), both having connotations of linearity. In Madagama the term *pravēni* traditionally meant primarily agnatically derived ancestral rights in an estate (*gama*), or to define it loosely in a manner applicable also to the present situation, 'rights having an agnatic frame of reference'. Thus *pravēni iḍam* meant ancestral lands; *pravēni pangu*, or *pravēni koṭasa* meant 'shares' (rights) in an ancestral estate derived, most often, from an agnatic source. If *pravēni* refers to ancestral rights, *gama* refers to the estate in which these rights are embodied or enshrined. Thus the sum of shares held in *pravēni* by villagers constitutes the *gama* or total estate. This is in agreement with one of the etymological and dictionary meanings of *gama* (Sanskrit, *grāma*; Pali, *gama*) 'a collection of land holdings'. It is desirable then to isolate the several meanings of *gama* held by Madagama folk.

(1) The primary meaning of *gama* is an estate, owned originally by a founding ancestor. Ideally agnatic descendants of this individual have *pravēni* (ancestral) rights in the estate. Thus villagers continually make statements of the following order: '*Maṭa gamen aṭen panguvak aiti*—I own $\frac{1}{8}$ share of the *gama*.' It is clear that in this context a villager is thinking of *gama* as 'estate' in which he has rights in the form of 'fractional shares' (*pangu*). For the purposes of land tenure this is the most important meaning of *gama*. Hereafter, in order to avoid confusion we shall avoid the popular

English translation of *gama* as 'village' in this context. We shall use the indigenous terms *gama* (estate), *pravēni* (ancestral rights), *pangu* (fractional shares).

(2) *Gamēminussu* (people of the *gama*) refers to the people who live, in a physical sense, within the bounds of the *gama*. Thus *gama* is often used to designate the estate and the people living in it—the territorial and demographic aspect of the estate. I shall use the English term 'hamlet' to describe this territorial and demographic unit.

(3) *Gama* is used for a collection of contiguously located hamlets loosely related by a web of cognatic and affinal kinship. Thus Ihala Madagama and Pahala Madagama are two contiguously located hamlets which form the village of Madagama. I shall employ the English term 'village' to refer to such administrative units, and in reference to our village, may simply use the name of the village, that is, 'Madagama'.

One notes then that the core meaning of the term *gama* as 'estate' is 'constant': first *gama* simply means estate in its legal sense as a parcel of rights, secondly *gama* (hamlet) means estate in its physical sense plus the people (groups) who live therein (that is, the collectivity) and, thirdly, *gama* refers to a plurality of such collectivities designated for administrative purposes as 'village'. Incidentally, it is the meaning of *gama* as estate that is also important in understanding some of the technical aspects of words like *gabaḍā-gama* (*gama* of the king), *ninda-gama* (*gama* of a lord), *vihāra-gama* (*gama* of a Buddhist vihara), *devālagama* (*gama* of a temple of the deities) of Kandyan feudalism.

Theoretically there is no reason why the *gama* and *pravēni* (ancestral rights in the *gama*) should be associated with unilinearity; these concepts are congruent with any mode of inheritance. But empirically we believe that traditionally in the Kandyan and Maritime provinces the patrilineal devolution of *pravēni* rights was the statistical norm, as we shall show later. Even today the ideology of agnation is strong. It is in relation to the patrilineal *mode* of transmission of property rights that the next concept of *vāsagama* assumes importance. Literally *vāsagama* means *vāsa* ('residence') and *gama* ('estate'), that is, those who reside in, enjoy rights in, a common estate. But the *gama* or estate in the hamlets in our area originally belonged to a patrilineal ancestor; thus members of the *vāsagama* are the descendants of the ancestor in the male line. In an ideal scheme it is they who have residence rights in the *gama* and constitute *ideally* the human collectivity of the hamlet. The *vāsagama* is prefixed to the personal name of each individual of the line, and hence constitutes an individual's 'surname'. An examination of an individual's full name will give us more information as to what constitutes a *vāsagama*.

Take the case of a person from the hamlet of Pahala Madagama whose personal name is Jinadasa. I ask Jinadasa what his full name is and he tells me that it is 'Pahala Madagama Gamagē Jinadasa'. His surname or *vāsagama* is 'Pahala Madagama Gamagē' and his personal name is Jinadasa. This means that he is a member of the Pahala Madagama Gamage *vāsagama*. Further examination shows that the *vāsagama* has two structural components.

(1) Pahala Madagama, which is the name of the hamlet and estate.

(2) *Gamagē*, which is the name of what I call a *subcaste*. Thus a person's name consists of a personal name (*nama*), and his *vāsagama*, the name of his 'patriline', which in turn includes the name of the estate in which he has *pravēni* rights and the name of the subcaste to which he belongs. A person's *vāsagama* name then is a combination of the names of his hamlet or estate and of his subcaste.

The subcaste *gamagē* in this particular instance is a subcaste of the larger *goigama* ('cultivator') caste. The several subcastes of the *goigama* caste can be classified on the basis of their relationship to the soil, that is, the nature of their involvement in the agricultural production process.

(*a*) *Goigama subcastes that own the soil but do not directly cultivate it* ('*feudal aristocracy*'). These typically are represented by the *radala* subcastes, the great feudal aristocracy of the Kandyan Kingdom, who owned large estates cultivated by tenants. Below the *radala* are the less affluent subcastes of smaller feudal officials like the *liyanagē* (subcaste of scribe), or *kariyakaranagē* (subcastes having hereditary 'official' duties to perform). In the feudal economy these subcastes had estates given over to them which were probably cultivated, partly at least, by peasant tenants or share croppers. In contemporary Hinidum Pattu, there are no longer any *radala* subcastes, though there has arisen since British times a new bureaucratic officialdom wielding many of the accoutrements and symbols of the old *radala*. The feudal official subcastes have for all practical purposes lost all their importance in the contemporary social structure, except for a few *vāsagamas* which have managed to preserve their status by retaining official positions in the new bureaucracy. These constitute a very small minority, but are important in the power structure of Hinidum Pattu.

(*b*) *Subcastes who own the soil and directly cultivate it* (*'free peasants'*). These subcastes constituted the bulk of the *goigama* caste in Hinidum Pattu, and probably in most of the western and southern provinces. Traditionally their numbers probably diminished as one approached the central provinces where feudalism showed its most intense development and where large feudal 'fiefs' prevailed. These subcastes of free peasants had to perform feudal services (*rājakāriya*) in both the Kandyan Kingdom and under Dutch rule, but were not under obligation to cultivate their lord's *muttеṭuva* (special fields), an act which defined the lowest status of subcastes.

This relationship to the soil could be formulated in terms of the following proposition: the higher the status of the subcaste the lesser its dependence on the soil and the agricultural production process; that is, direct cultivation of the land and the performance of physical labour. The degree of ownership of the soil is the important factor: the total lack of ownership of the soil is the hallmark of the traditional slave (*vahalla*), a person who has lost or sold his *pravēni* rights completely. Forms of 'slavery' are still present in contemporary Ceylon though the word *vahalla* is rarely used: indigent villagers all over Ceylon may still occasionally sell their children or themselves as 'slaves' to wealthy landowners and members of the bureaucratic officialdom. Euphemistically addressed as domestic servants (*väḍakārayo*), they are a category of persons with practically no *de facto* rights and similar in status to the *vahalla* of Kandyan times. In many respects their position, particularly those of females, is much worse than that of the traditional *vahalla*.

The people of Madagama belonged traditionally to one of the subcastes of free peasants in Hinidum Pattu. There were several named isogamous subcastes in the area, for example, *gamagē*, *goḍagē*, *heṭṭigē*, *dasiligē*, of which the first two were the most common. Marriages occurred either within the subcaste or between isogamous subcastes. Each subcaste was divided into exogamous *vāsagamas*, which had property rights in their common estate and lived in patrilocal aggregations in hamlets. However, as will be shown later, these *vāsagamas* were in no sense corporate unilineal descent groups of the type found in Africa. *Vāsagamas* of the kind described here are, or were, found typically in the Sabaragamuva, Western and Southern Provinces of Ceylon: their structural counterpart in the Kandyan Provinces is the *gedera* (Tambiah 1958). They are practically of no importance in the Dry Zone of Ceylon (Leach 1961). They are also probably of little sociological significance among the non-agricultural castes like the Karavas (Raghavan 1961).

(*c*) *Subcastes who do not own the soil, and are in some sense tied to it* (‘*peasant tenants*’). These would typically be the peasant tenants of the *radala*. These castes are no longer important in the area owing to the contemporary absence of feudalism, but their present *vāsagamas* still carry the taint of their earlier status. Some of the *goigama* shamans of contemporary Hinidum Pattu come from these ‘low subcastes’. Marriage with them is frowned upon by members of the higher class of subcastes.

THE IDEAL MODEL OF LAND TENURE

The ideal model of the land tenure system is beautifully simple in structure. The traditional model is, however, no abstraction divorced from reality but, as Leach points out for Pul Eliya, is important in the present operation of the system, and would have been even more important before the socio-economic changes that have come over Madagama in recent years. The traditional ideas pertaining to land tenure are based on an important assumption that has no validity in contemporary Sinhalese law, namely the availability of land with few legal restrictions. In theory a hamlet comes into existence when a man, a founding ancestor, leaves his hamlet of origin, and with the permission of some traditional authority demarcates a space of forest or waste as his *gama*. A part of this space is cleared and converted into paddy lands (*maḍa iḍam*, mudlands), the other part into *goḍa iḍam* or highlands (gardens). It is in the *goḍa* that the houses of the founder and his descendants are built. This area is simply called *goḍē*. The rest of the *goḍa* is converted into fruit and vegetable gardens and grazing grounds for cattle.

Pangu

Theoretically, then, the original 'owner' of any *gama* is its founding ancestor. On a kinship chart the founder would be at the apex of a triangular scheme. At his death his sons would inherit the patrimonial estate equally, but there is no physical partitioning of the estate. On the contrary, the founder's sons will have equal shares or *pangu* of the estate. The characteristic of *pangu* is that like stock market shares they are not 'fixed', or attached to any single area of property or land; the shares are 'floating'. Thus a descendant who works a share does not work a fixed partitioned area of the estate; rather he works on a rotation basis, so that every year he moves to a new area, till the whole length of the field is covered. This is based on the equalitarian ideology governing the concept of shares or *pangu*: one has shares in the *gama* as a whole, hence one must have access through a period of years to the total area of land, ensuring an equitable distribution of both fertile and infertile land among the respective shareholders. Shares or *pangu* are defined as fractions of the total area of land. It follows that with the increasing number of heirs at every descending generation from the founding ancestor, the number of shareholders would increase resulting in an increased fractioning of the estate.

Fractioning into many shares makes the rotation scheme unworkable or unwieldly; hence according to the traditional ideal scheme of land tenure, though rarely in practice, there is a fixed upper limit on the number of shares. A *gama* can hold only a limited number of shares for the land tenure system to work, depending on two important variables—the size of the *gama*, and the number of shareholders. Translated into demographic terms this means that there is a population limit for each hamlet. When this limit is reached, there has to be emigration to other areas; people will have to move out of their hamlets of origin and found new estates for themselves and their descendants. Thus new hamlets are born. It is obvious that for such a system to work new land must be relatively easily available.

Taṭṭumāru

The scheme of rotation of plots spoken of earlier is known in Sinhalese as *taṭṭumāru*, literally *taṭṭu* or 'tray', hence 'plot' and *māru* or 'exchange', 'shift' hence 'rotation'. Let us consider how a hypothetical ideal scheme of *taṭṭumāru* works. Assume that a founding ancestor (FA^1) of some hamlet had two sons, who on his death, inherited equally the total stretch (*yāya*) of paddy land. These two sons had in turn three sons each, with a perfect symmetry in reproduction. Thus in the third generation (generation FA^3) the estate is divided into six equal shares, each individual working four acres of paddy land, assuming that the total consisted of twenty-four acres. How does the *taṭṭumāru* scheme operate in this situation?

For purposes of *taṭṭumāru*, the total stretch of paddy land is treated as a single contiguous unit, though in fact it does not possess this kind of symmetry. The total stretch of *yāya* is divided into two equal parts—*ihala kaṭṭi* (upper section) and *pahala kaṭṭi* (lower section). The division is not based on area or acreage, but on yield, each section having individual fields (*kumburu*) containing *in toto* a yield of paddy that equals the total yield in the other section. This division into *kaṭṭi* is a permanent division having a genealogical reference which could be graphically represented thus.

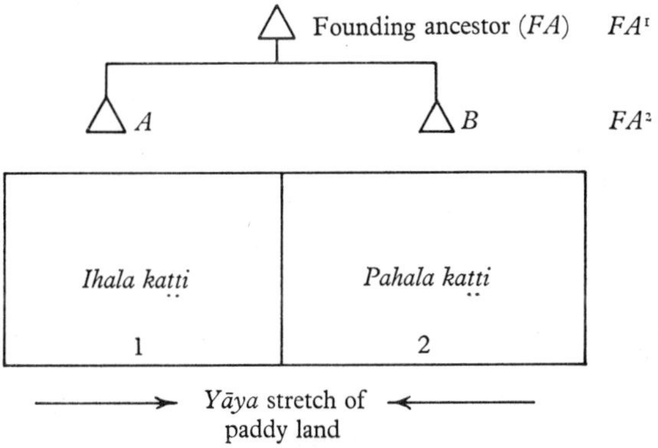

Fig. 1.

At this point the *taṭṭumāru* scheme would work with beautiful simplicity. If *A* works the fields in section 1 for the two agricultural seasons—*maha* and *yala*, which constitute a calendar year—and *B* works section 2, the scheme will be reversed (*māru*) in the next year with *A* working section 2 and *B* working section 1. This scheme of alternating sections is never changed, even though, in the next generation, the proliferation of descendants makes *taṭṭumāru* much more complicated. *A* had three sons, we said (*C*, *D*, and *E*), and *B* also had three sons (*F*, *G*, *H*) who were the heirs of their respective estates. For *taṭṭumāru* each set of siblings was treated as a single unit, each sibling unit assigned to a single *kaṭṭi*. Thus the principle of the division of the *yāya* into two equi-proportional alternating sections is not changed, though the simple

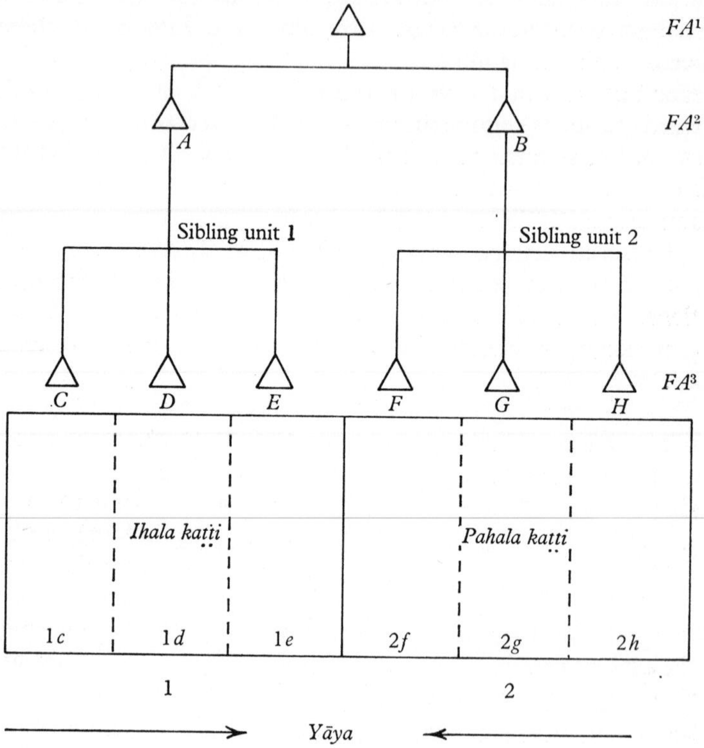

Fig. 2.

temporal scheme of alternation on an annual basis in generation FA^2 has to be altered because of the arrangements *within* each *kaṭṭi among* the individuals that constituted each sibling unit. Thus in generation FA^3, each *kaṭṭi* would be subdivided into three equal parts (also called *kaṭṭi*), genealogically represented as in Fig. 2.

Since each 'subsection' is also called *kaṭṭi*, I shall refer to these in English as 'subsections', reserving the Sinhalese term *kaṭṭi* to the larger dichotomous sections. In generation FA^3 the *kaṭṭi* were rotated, only after the subsections within each *kaṭṭi* had been rotated, that is, there had to be *taṭṭumāru* among the subsections within each *kaṭṭi* before there could be *taṭṭumāru* between the two *kaṭṭi*. Each subsection is worked by a shareholder for a year, and then he moves over to another *kaṭṭi*. Thus *F* may work 2*f* for a year and move over to subsection 2*h*; *H* would move over to subsection 2*g*, and *G* would move over to 2*f*. A reciprocal arrangement would occur in *kaṭṭi* 1, so that at the end of the three years, each person would have traversed the length of a single *kaṭṭi*—which includes both fertile and infertile fields. At this point the two *kaṭṭi* themselves are rotated, and sibling unit 1 moves over to *kaṭṭi* 2, and sibling unit 2 moves over to *kaṭṭi* 1. There is a neat genealogical fit here.

However, with an increase in population the *taṭṭumāru* arrangement becomes more and more complicated in descending generations. A point is reached where further fractioning of the *gama* becomes impracticable and unworkable, depending obviously on the size of the *gama* and the number of heirs at a given time. The *taṭṭumāru* scheme has therefore to be 'frozen' on the basis of some pragmatic criterion. Assume that our hypothetical hamlet possessed paddy land to the extent of twenty-four acres. There are six co-sharers of the *gama*; each has an area of four acres. If four acres per family is regarded as a satisfactory holding, and if a further fractioning of such a small *gama* was considered unworkable and cumbersome, then the *taṭṭumāru* scheme would be frozen at this point. The formal structure of *taṭṭumāru* depends on the extent of the *gama* and the number of co-partners. If our hypothetical *gama* had an area of forty acres instead of twenty-four, then it would be feasible to extend the *taṭṭumāru* arrangement to the next generation. Or, alternatively, if the founding ancestor had three sons instead of two, the formal structure of the *taṭṭumāru* would be different: the *gama* would then be divided into three equal *kaṭṭi*, and the rotation of plots would take place once every three years, instead of two, in generation FA^2. This would in turn involve more complicated *taṭṭumāru* arrangements in the following generation owing to the greater number of sibling units involved. Thus while the formal structure of the *taṭṭumāru* may vary in this manner, the inner logic of the scheme as a system of plot rotation would be the same.

The empirical translation of the ideal scheme

Any ideal scheme of norms, such as the one delineated above, has to meet the empirical reality of social living. The complexity of social living may create difficulties in the implementation of the ideal scheme. As was suggested earlier, the fundamental structural prerequisite of the system was the availability of land for expansion when the *gama* surpassed an optimum population load. The availability of land, even in pre-British times, varied considerably from area to area. For example, in an area which was under the control of a feudal governor, there were several obstacles pertaining to protocol that had to be overcome. Or again if the nature of the terrain was geographically unsuited for paddy cultivation, and the population was large, as was generally the case in the immediate vicinity of Kandy, the capital of the Sinhalese kings, then the availability of land for expansion would be strictly limited (assuming of course that the kind of ideal scheme delineated by us has relevance for the area under consideration). Thus, there could always have been demographic, geographical, political and even idiosyncratic (for example, a bad governor or corrupt officials) factors that militated against village expansion. In such a case, a proliferation of co-sharers at each descending generation would have resulted in the fractioning of the original estate into increasingly smaller shares. When the ideal scheme could not be implemented, what alternative adaptations were possible?

One thing is explicit: the freezing of the *taṭṭumāru* scheme at a certain generation level, which permits the easy working of plot rotation, is not affected by the scarcity of land and the proliferation of co-sharers. Fractioning of shares is certainly possible and all co-sharers have their legitimate rights in *pravēni*, but any further fractioning below the point of 'freezing', are private arrangements between individual co-sharers and not part of the publicly accepted *taṭṭumāru* structure. In other words, after a certain point, the *kaṭṭi* (including 'subsections') arrangements are permanent and fixed though the number of shares or *pangu* may be multiplied indefinitely. The operation of the *taṭṭumāru* system is in no way affected by the multiplication of shares (*pangu*) after the structure has been frozen. Ideally of course there should be no further fractioning of the *gama*—excess descendants of those in generation FA^3 in our example should migrate elsewhere, or found new villages. But, as we said earlier, it is doubtful that land would have been readily available for expansion in every single case. If we apply such an empirical possibility to our example, the descendants of members of FA^3 generation will remain in the village and there will be an increase in shareholders and consequent fractioning of the estate at generation FA^4. Assume that *G* in Fig. 2 had three heirs, and *H* had four heirs—in such an instance the subdivision of the inheritance of *G* and *H* would be a purely private arrangement between the respective groups of heirs in no way affecting the *taṭṭumāru* scheme. These private arrangements may be of various sorts, though two types of arrangement are commonly recognized in the area.

(1) If the inheritance of *G* is large enough, then the heirs may cultivate the land jointly every year and divide the harvest; or if the sibling groups are not very co-operative they may divide the land and each sibling cultivate an individual plot. If *G*'s heirs cultivate subsection 2*f* in one year as one sibling unit, they would in the next cultivate subsection 2*h*, and in the following year 2*g*: thus the *taṭṭumāru* scheme of rotation operates independently of the fractioning of shares at FA^4 generation.

(2) The second type of 'private' arrangement is known as *karamāru*, literally meaning 'change of shoulders', or rotation of persons as against the rotation of plots in *taṭṭumāru*. This type of arrangement is feasible when the fragmentation of the patrimonial estate is such that it does not seem economically feasible for all the shareholders to cultivate the land jointly. In which case each shareholder cultivates the total plot for a specified period (say, one season, or one year) while the others take their turns alternatively in the following periods. In terms of Fig. 2, the *karamāru* may well run as follows—*G*'s heirs no. 1, may work their father's inheritance in subsection 2*f* in one year; in the next year, according to *taṭṭumāru*, *G*'s share moves to subsection 2*g*, which according to *karamāru* will be worked by *G*'s heirs no. 2; in the following year *G*'s heirs no. 3 will work subsection 2*h*. *Karamāru* arrangements were not very common in Hinidum Pattu, however. Once again the *karamāru* arrangement in no way affects the *taṭṭumāru* system.

There is another empirical difficulty with which the ideal scheme has to contend. The ideal scheme requires a neat fit between genealogy and the division and rotation of plots (*taṭṭumāru*), but the symmetry of the *taṭṭumāru* scheme cannot obviously be duplicated in the genealogical series owing to the unpredictability of the latter. So that in translation of the model into action, one important problem is to relate the symmetry of the *taṭṭumāru* scheme to the asymmetry of the genealogical series. Let us see how these complications are resolved in the land tenure system of Pahala Madagama hamlet.

According to the ancestral myth the hamlet of Pahala Madagama was founded by a man who resided in the neighbouring village of Mavanana. None of the present villagers know his name or any significant details pertaining to his life. This founding ancestor owned initially the whole hamlet, that is, the *gama* belonged to him. The founding ancestor had two sons, Babappu and Mathes. All that the informants' statement 'had two sons' implies is that only Babappu and Mathes had *pravēni* rights in their father's estate; it does not imply that they were the only children born to the founding ancestor. How is the ideal model translated into action at this point? In translation the ideal model has both a genealogical and geographical reference.

Genealogical reference: this is quite simple and at this point there is a perfect fit between the facts of genealogy and the ideal model. The two sons have equal shares (half shares) in the *gama*. Geographically this would mean that the total stretch, treated for *taṭṭumāru* as if it were a rectangular stretch, would be divided into two equal parts or *kaṭṭi*—in this case *ihala kaṭṭi* (upper section) and *pahala kaṭṭi* (lower section). This is on the one hand an allocation of shares to two individuals on the basis of the ideal scheme. In this sense there is no fixed geographical area allocated permanently to each individual, for since shares are floating, each individual works the *kaṭṭi* on an alternating basis. But the description of the *kaṭṭi* as *ihala* and *pahala* has permanent topographical reference, for the *pravēni* fields are divided into two equal parts permanently as *ihala* (upper part) and *pahala* (lower part). Thus *kaṭṭi* has two technical connotations in the idiom of land tenure—first as rotating shares having genealogical reference and secondly as a geographical division of the fields into two equal parts *ihala kaṭṭi* and *pahala kaṭṭi*. In the present instance if Babappu works the *pahala kaṭṭi* for one year and Mathes the *ihala*, the position would be reversed in the next year. The equalitarian norms underlying the ideal *taṭṭumāru* scheme are fully translated into action at this point in the genealogical series.

It is obvious that at the generation immediately below that of the founding ancestor (FA^2), there would inevitably be a perfect fit between the model and the facts of genealogy, for the division into equal *kaṭṭi* would simply be based on the number of male descendants at this level, the only variation being that the larger the number of descendants, the longer the period for an 'individual' to traverse the length of the estate. Complications arise at the next generation (FA^3), for if this model is to be fully translated, one of two sets of sociological facts have to be realized at this level. There has to be a radical rearrangement of the *kaṭṭi* system, so that all the descendants of the men of generation FA^3 should have equal shares in the *total pravēni*. Thus in our hamlet Babappu had three sons, and Mathes had one, forming a total of four males in generation FA^3. What could be done in terms of the above alternative is to ignore the bisection of the estate into two *kaṭṭi* in generation FA^2, and rearrange it at FA^3 level into four equal shares. Thus each descendant of the founder in the third generation would have a fourth share of the *gama*: the total length of the *gama* would be covered in four years. This scheme is only a logical possibility; it is not an empirical possibility in the Sinhalese social structure. Such an alternative might have been possible empirically if the Sinhalese had patrilineal corporations, whose members had equal rights in the total estate, but the facts of Sinhalese social structure are otherwise. The procedure would violate Sinhalese norms, for, according to Sinhalese inheritance rules, the sons have rights in their father's estate only, rather than in a patrilineal corporation. A rearrangement of the kind mentioned above, would, for example, diminish the rights of Mathes' only son, and enhance the rights of Babappu's three sons in *pravēni*. Sinhalese kinship, as will be demonstrated later, recognizes individual rather than lineage rights in property.

A second logical possibility exists, but this is dependent entirely on a symmetrical genealogical devolution in generation FA^3. So that either all the fathers in FA^2 generation would have an equal number of sons in the next generation; or the fathers by prior arrangement should see that only an equal number of sons inherit a particular *gama*, the others being given no rights in the ancestral estate: for example by a rule of ultimo or primogeniture. Thus assume that Babappu and Mathes had three sons each (sociologically speaking), then each of the two *kaṭṭi* will be divided into three equal parts, and at the end of three years the *kaṭṭi* would be 'changed'. However, it is difficult to imagine this symmetrical arrangement being realized except under exceptional and fortuitous circumstances. The genealogical symmetry required by the ideal type can only rarely occur in nature. As for any rule of inheritance that restricts the number of heirs, this again is contrary

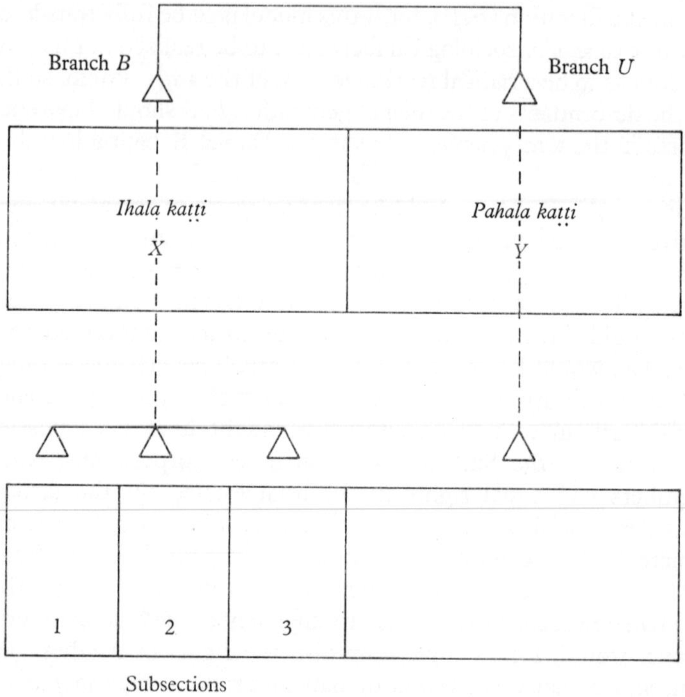

Fig. 3.

to Sinhalese values which clearly stipulate the rights of all sons equally in the father's estate.

Babappu had three sons, Lokuappuve, Balappuve and Dingi Appu while Mathes had only one son, Upeappu. Since the villagers make a clear distinction between the two sets of kinsmen and their descendants, and since this distinction is crucial to the operation of the *taṭṭumāru* system, I shall refer to these as two branches—branch *B* and branch *U* respectively. At this generation then there is in our empirical case a lack of symmetry between branches *B* and *U* but this in no way involves difficulty in the empirical translation of the model. For the sibling group Dingi Appu-Balappuve-Lokuappuve would divide *ihala kaṭṭi* (*X*) into three parts, whereas the single son Upeappu would retain *pahala kaṭṭi* (*Y*) as a single unit (Fig. 3).

Subsections 1, 2, and 3 will be rotated among the sibling unit Dingi Appu-Balappuve-Lokuappuve for a period of three years during which time Upeappu of branch *U* would work *kaṭṭi Y*, which of course does not require division into subsections. At the end of this period the sibling group Dingi Appu-Balappuve-Lokuappuve would move into *kaṭṭi Y* which will now be divided into three subsections; and Upeappu would move into *kaṭṭi X*. We have no evidence as to how Upeappu worked this large tract of paddy land, whether he worked as much as he could and left the rest fallow, or whether he gave a portion on a sharecropping (*andé*) basis, or what. What we can be certain, however, is the easy empirical translatability of the norms governing the ideal model at this generation. In terms of proprietorship Balappuve, Lokuappuve and Dingi Appu each owned $\frac{1}{6}$ share of the *gama*, while Upeappu owned $\frac{1}{2}$ share.

The *taṭṭumāru* scheme was frozen at this point for branch *B*, but not for branch *U*. This simply meant that branch *B* considered a tripartite division of their *kaṭṭi* as the most feasible and practicable arrangement; obviously such a division was impracticable for branch *U* which had only a single heir, Upeappu. However, Upeappu had four sons, Adiriyan, Elias, Hin Hamy and Babappu, each owning $\frac{1}{8}$ share: the *kaṭṭi* belonging to branch *U* was divided into four subsections (Fig. 4). Thus the *taṭṭumāru* scheme was frozen at two different generational levels, based undoubtedly on pragmatic and practical considerations.

This is the scheme that operates even today for *taṭṭumāru* purposes: further subdivision was considered unrealistic and unworkable, for the task of operating the land tenure scheme. All other arrangements would be *private* arrangements between the individuals involved, and these arrangements have to be accommodated within the *publicly* recognized scheme delineated above. How these accommodations are effected is the subject matter of a later chapter of this book.

The lack of genealogical symmetry between branches *B* and *U* resulted in the 'distortion' of the ideal model in actual practice, for the one *kaṭṭi* had to be divided into three equal parts (subsections) while the *kaṭṭi* belonging to branch *U* needed four subsections. But the principles that govern the ideal model are applied in this case too, so that the several subsections within each *kaṭṭi* are rotated, before the *kaṭṭi* themselves are alternatively rotated. But in this case it takes four years for each subsection in branch *U* to traverse the length of the *kaṭṭi*, while it takes only three years for branch *B*. How was the dilemma resolved in Pahala Madagama? Since the ideology states explicitly that the whole length of the *gama* has to be traversed in order to ensure an equitable allocation of good and bad fields (plots), it was decided to use a four year period as

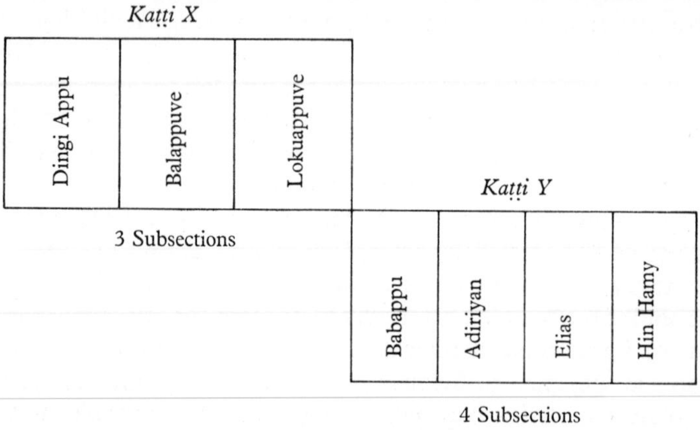

Fig. 4.

the norm, which would permit an equitable rotation of subsections in branch *U*. But this arrangement when applied to branch *B* involves a discrepancy for since it takes only three years to rotate these subsections, it is inevitable that, in this situation, the fourth year for branch *B* would be a repetition of the subsection arrangements of the first year. Thus 'owners' of the fields belonging to the subsections must cultivate in the fourth year the very same fields that were cultivated in the first. This would certainly upset the egalitarian norms underlying the ideal scheme. Assume, for example, that subsection *A* allocated to Lokuappuve in the first year contained infertile fields, and subsection *C* given to Dingi Appu contained some fertile ones. In the fourth year Lokuappuve would be burdened with the same lot of poor fields he had had in the first year. However, concession is made to egalitarian norms by initially selecting the subsections on the basis of the drawing of lots, so that those who draw the 'fertile lots' in the first year are lucky enough to cultivate them again in the fourth year. It would be seen that the Pahala Madagama case clearly illustrates the lack of 'fit' between the normative model and the actual on-going system. This lack of fit does not make the 'model' inapplicable, remote, or divorced from reality. On the contrary, the actual system is a translation of the model in terms of the complexities of on-going social life.

Further empirical complications arose in respect of branch *B*. According to informants Lokuappuve, son of Babappu, 'lived with' his brother Balappuve, and had 'no children of his own'. Thus for all practical purposes Lokuappuve and Balappuve were a single unit owning $\frac{2}{6}$ shares of the *gama*. The statements 'lived with' and 'had no children of his own' strongly suggest a polyandrous union (polyandry and polygyny were historically well established in the area) and implies an attempt to conserve and consolidate the patrimonial estate through this form of plural marriage (see Leach 1959:104–13). This link-up between the brothers did not involve a distortion of the model, for the subsections were rotated *as if* there was no such link-up. But according to the logic of the scheme complications were bound to arise in the next generation, for it is too much to hope that the sons of Lokuappuve-Balappuve would continue the amicable and co-operative relationship that existed between their 'fathers'. The sibling pair Lokuappuve-Balappuve had three sons, Odiris, Juan Appu and Adonis who were thus entitled to $\frac{1}{9}$ share each of the *gama*. How did this complication at level 4 affect the *taṭṭumāru* scheme in respect of branch *B*?

For purposes of *taṭṭumāru*, the section is divided into the three subsections 'owned' by Lokuappuve, Balappuve and Dingi Appu of FA^3. Lots are drawn as to how these 'owners' should be placed, for as we have seen, the arrangement has to be repeated in the fourth year. With the drawing of lots Dingi Appu's share of the *kaṭṭi* is 'kept aside'. The two remaining sections belonged to the 'polyandrous' Lokuappuve-Balappuve. This is now divided into three equal 'parts' constituting shares of $\frac{1}{9}$ of the total estate. Lots are drawn again and the shares of Odiris, Juan Appu and Adonis 'arranged' on this basis (represented in broken lines on the chart). The following year the fields are rearranged. Dingi Appu's share is once again separated, but since the rule is that he cannot 'work' the same section as the year before, he moves to another subsection. Then the rest are again divided into three parts and allocated, through lots, once again to Odiris, Juan Appu and Adonis. The procedure is repeated for the third year, the logic being that while

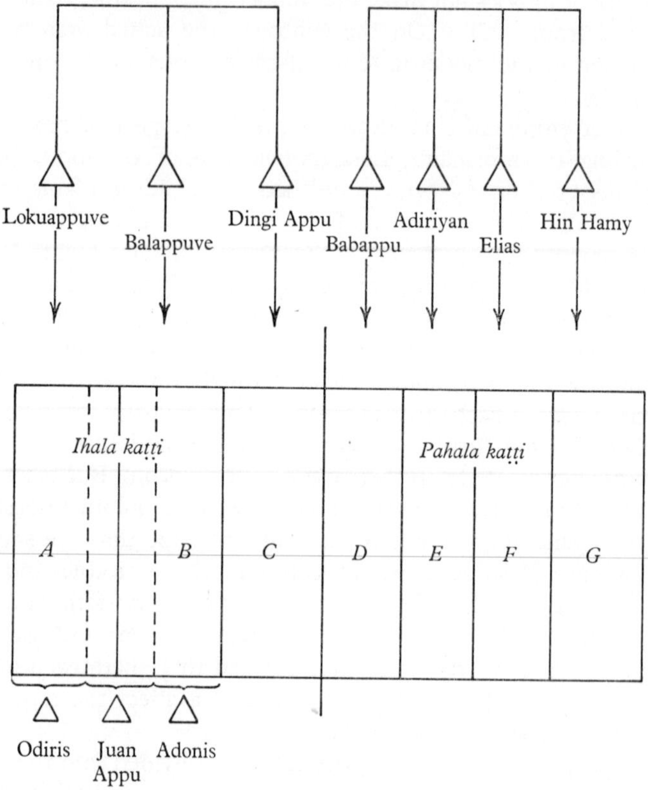

Fig. 5.

Dingi Appu's heirs traverse the whole length of the *kaṭṭi* once during the period, the sibling group Odiris-Juan Appu-Adonis would have traversed it twice. This once again is an attempt to meet egalitarian norms, for though the *individuals* that constitute the tripartite sibling group may not have traversed the length of the *kaṭṭi* as single individuals, the sibling unit as a whole would have to traverse the whole *kaṭṭi* twice. Egalitarian norms which state that the whole *kaṭṭi* has to be traversed *in toto*, so that 'shareholders' work both good and bad fields are maintained in principle. Once every three years Dingi Appu traverses the *kaṭṭi* once, while Odiris-Juan Appu-Adonis *as a unit* traverse it twice. The number of times traversed obviously does not affect the principle of equality. What does upset it is the fact already mentioned, namely owing to the asymmetrical arrangement of subsections in the two branches, branch *B*, in the fourth year, has to return to the *taṭṭumāru* arrangements of the first year.

The *taṭṭumāru* arrangements in respect of branch *B* could be better seen through a specific illustration. Assume that the rotation scheme had commenced with the allocation of shares on the basis of 'lots' (see Fig. 5).

First Year. Assuming that Dingi Appu's (that is, his heirs) work *C*; then Odiris-Juan Appu-Adonis would work *A* and *B*.

Second Year. Dingi Appu's heirs now work *A*. Odiris-Juan Appu-Adonis work *C* and *B*.

Thus at the end of the second year subsection *B* is worked twice, *A* once, and *C* once by the sibling unit Odiris-Juan Appu-Adonis.

Third Year. Dingi Appu's heirs now have to work *B* while Odiris-Juan Appu-Adonis work *A* and *C*.

At the end of the third year Odiris-Juan Appu-Adonis have worked *B* twice, *A* twice and *C* twice. This means that this sibling unit as a whole has traversed the field twice, while Dingi Appu has done it once in three years. In the fourth year, the egalitarian principle is upset for shareholders revert to the arrangements of the first year.

TAṬṬUMĀRU IN IHALA MADAGAMA

Ihala Madagama hamlet had been subject to considerable social change resulting in radical alterations in the patterns of land ownership, as pointed out in chapter 1. We felt that originally *taṭṭumāru* here was based on an eight-subsection system which was much more complex than the contemporary four *kaṭṭi* system. We do not know when the eight-subsection system changed to the present one. It is highly probable that this was due to a large number of *pangu* falling into the hands of outsiders (non-villagers and non-kinsmen) in this *gama* so that it was not possible to utilize the genealogy of FA^2 generation for *taṭṭumāru* purposes. In any case the present mode of *taṭṭumāru* is a four *kaṭṭi* arrangement based on the genealogy, actual or fabricated, advanced by the dominant outside shareholders of the estate. According to this genealogy the *taṭṭumāru* scheme is based on the *pravēni* rights of the four sons (FA^2) of the founder who owned ¼ share each. Though there is considerable conflict and confusion regarding the genealogies of early ancestors of this hamlet most informants are agreed that there were in fact four *kaṭṭi* ancestors. Some informants state that two of them were descended from a man from Giguruwa and the other two were from a man from neighbouring Mavanana. Once settled in Ihala Madagama, one informant stated, they considered

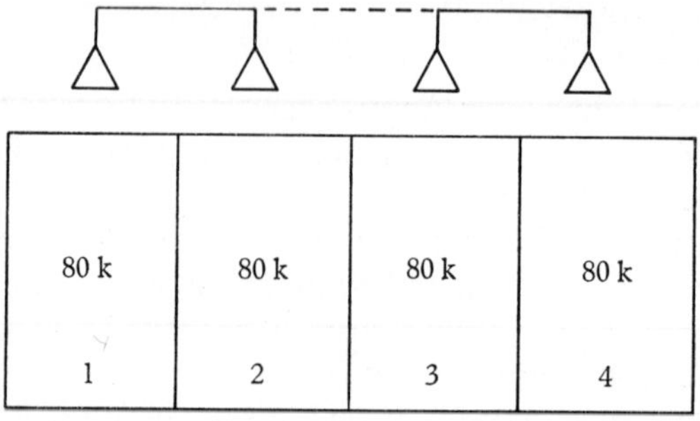

Yāya, 320 k

Fig. 6.

themselves as brothers (*sahodarayo*). The explanation we feel is an entirely plausible one, for what is important for *vāsagamas* is not the fact but the ideology of common descent. For purposes of convenience we shall refer to the four descendants of the 'founder', or founders as *A*, *B*, *C*, and *D*. The reader is referred to chapter six for their actual names and discussion of Ihala Madagama genealogies.

The entire *yāya* consisted of a sowing area of 320 k in theory, i.e. for purposes of *taṭṭumāru* computation. It is divided into four, theoretically equal, named *kaṭṭi*, each consisting of a sowing area of 80 k allocated to each ancestor of FA^2 generation as in Fig. 6.

Each *kaṭṭi* consisted of several distinct fields or plots of varying size and sowing area. The name of the *kaṭṭi* is simply the name of one of its fields. It is obvious that the Pahala Madagama *kaṭṭi* names of *ihala* (upper) *kaṭṭi* and *pahala* (lower) *kaṭṭi* are impossible in this four *kaṭṭi* system.

Fig. 7 indicates the names of the *kaṭṭi*, the names of the fields and their sowing areas. However, since we are interested here only in the formal operation of the model we shall simply refer to the *kaṭṭi* as 1, 2, 3, and 4.

According to the formal model of *taṭṭumāru* each *kaṭṭi* is worked for a period of two years; and the length of the *yāya* is traversed in eight years, thus:

If group *A* (i.e. the present share owners of the original *kaṭṭi* ancestors ¼ share) work *kaṭṭi* 1 for two years, group *B* will work

A	*B*	*C*	*D*
Alabodaliyadi kaṭṭiya	Okanda kaṭṭiya	Atagoipola kaṭṭiya	Dangahakumbura kaṭṭiya
Iriyagahaliyadde (10 k)	*Panniti Okanda* (12 k)	*Atagoipola* (60 k)	*Dangahakumbura* (60 k)
Dikliyadde (10 k)	*Korosvalmandiya pahala kaṭṭiya* (10 k)	*Delgahakumbura* (15 k)	*Kahambiliyawalakada kumbura* (24 k)
Mahakumbura (10 k)	*Bammekumbura* (20 k)		
Korosvalmandiya (10 k)	*Okande kaṭṭiya* (30 k)		
	Velendehenedeniya (10 k)		
Mahabamma (16 k)			
Alabodaliyadde (16 k)			
Ambagahaliyadde (10 k)			
1	2	3	4

Fig. 7.

kaṭṭi 2, group *C* will work *kaṭṭi* 3, and group *D kaṭṭi* 4. At the commencement of the third agricultural year in September–October (Maha season), *taṭṭumāru* occurs and group *A* will move over to *kaṭṭi* 2, group *B* to *kaṭṭi* 3, group *C* to *kaṭṭi* 4, and group *D* to *kaṭṭi* 1. In the fifth year group *A* will move over to *kaṭṭi* 3, group *B* to *kaṭṭi* 4, group *C* to *kaṭṭi* 1, and group *D* to *kaṭṭi* 2. In the seventh year group *A* will move over to *kaṭṭi* 4, group *B* to *kaṭṭi* 1, group *C* to *kaṭṭi* 2, and group *D* to *kaṭṭi* 3. This will last till the end of the eighth year. In the following (ninth) year everyone will revert to the *taṭṭumāru* arrangements of the first year. Thus during a period of eight years each group has traversed the whole length of the *yāya* fulfilling in principle the egalitarian norms underlying the *taṭṭumāru* schemes. In practice all sorts of arrangements could be made *within* each *kaṭṭi* by the contemporary shareowners. Such internal manipulations of *kaṭṭi* are facilitated by the fact that each *taṭṭumāru* period of two years consist of four agricultural seasons, so that in principle each section could be split into four equiproportional parts as in Fig. 8.

There could be an internal rotation of the four parts during the four seasons that constitute the two-year *taṭṭumāru* period. This scheme of *taṭṭumāru* within *taṭṭumāru* is sometimes referred to as *kaṭṭi māru*. It introduces a great deal of flexibility in the actual

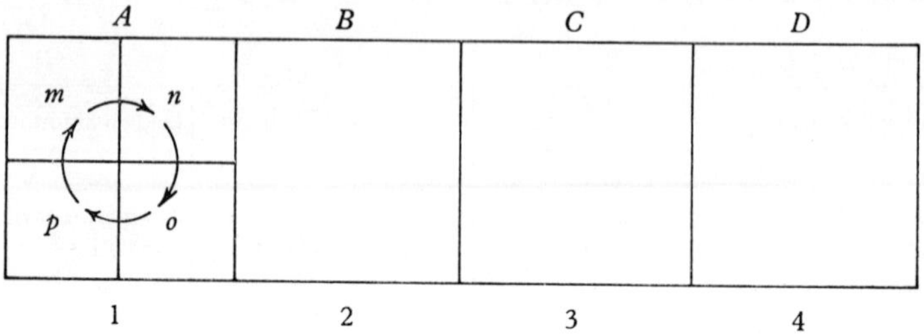

Fig. 8.

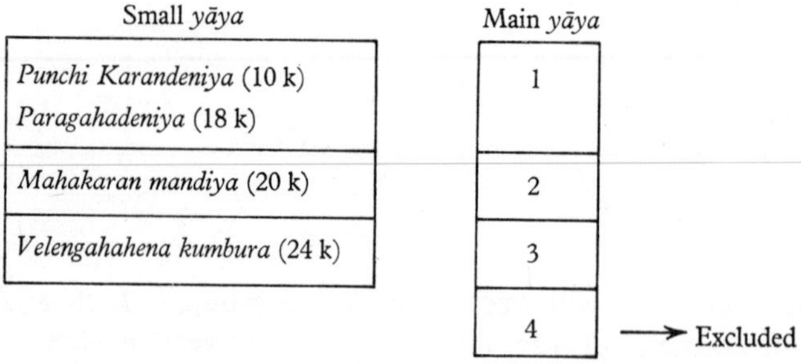

Fig 9.

contemporary operation of *taṭṭumāru* in Ihala Madagama where a large number of shareholders exist.

In addition to the main *yāya* of 320 k the Ihala Madagama hamlet also contained a small *yāya* of 50 k. This stretch was probably not part of the traditional scheme and was not involved in the current partition suit. This *yāya* which is extremely infertile is geared to the actual operation of the main *taṭṭumāru* system, so as to reinforce the egalitarian ideology of *taṭṭumāru*. The *dangaha-kumbura kaṭṭiya* (*kaṭṭi* 4) of the main *yāya* contained extremely fertile fields. As a result the small *yāya* of 50 k was used to compensate those who worked the other three *kaṭṭi*. It was therefore divided into three parts as in Fig. 9. This is entirely a means for compensating the owners of *kaṭṭi* 1, 2 and 3. Thus at the commencement of the *taṭṭumāru* cycle groups *A*, *B* and *C* work one part each, excluding *D* who would work *kaṭṭi* 4. In the following three periods the same principle of organization operates. Those who work *kaṭṭi* 4 are excluded, the three parts rotated, and at the 4th *taṭṭumāru* period (7th year) one reverts to the arrangements of the first year. There is no drawing of lots here because the fields are extremely infertile and no one evinces a great desire to cultivate this *yāya*. What in fact happens is that one person gets permission from a majority of shareowners and cultivates the whole stretch for a nominal rent or token acknowledgement of the latter's rights.

TAṬṬUMĀRU 1 AND TAṬṬUMĀRU 2

The kind of land tenure arrangement we have described in our model as *taṭṭumāru* is found, as far as we know, in the whole of the Hinidum Pattu. It is a system of rotation of plots in an undivided tract of paddy land so that access to the whole stretch is made available to all shareholders during a fixed period of time. However, in legal, governmental and administration reports the term *taṭṭumāru* is associated with another set of meanings. Since the latter is the currently accepted meaning of *taṭṭumāru* it is important to distinguish between *taṭṭumāru* 1 (the meaning in Hinidum Pattu) and *taṭṭumāru* 2. The two meanings of the term *taṭṭumāru* were stated by D'Oyly as early as 1827. 'Tattoo Maroowa—alternation —where an estate is too small to be divided among the Heirs or Coparceners, or where it comprises several fields of various degrees of productiveness, the possession is so arranged by compact that each in his turn either enjoys the whole land, or by rotation cultivates the more and the less fertile portions' (D'Oyly 1929:65).

Taṭṭumāru 2 refers to a practice previously described by us as *karamāru*. This meaning of *taṭṭumāru* was given formal explication by Justice Phear in 1880.

Sometimes the enjoyment of the property is by *taṭṭa māru* succession. The subject is supposed to be divided into as many equal parts as will just admit of the proportionate share of each coparcener being represented by an integral number of these parts; and then instead of an actual division being made accordingly, and every sharer obtaining his proper number of *parts*, each takes his *entirety* for the same number of seasons as he is entitled to parts, giving it up at the end of such period of time to the sharer who stands next in the rota in order that he may similarly hold it for his own number of seasons; and so on for all the shareholders in turn. Thus if *A*, *B*, and *C* were jointly entitled to a paddy field in undivided shares proportionate to 2, 3 and 4, i.e. to a 2/9th, 1/3rd, 4/9th share of the whole respectively, then by this method of enjoyment *A* would take the whole field for two years, after him *B* for three years, and after *B* again *C* would take it for four years; and then the set of turns would be repeated in the same order, for successive periods of nine years, until some sharer should insist on having an actual partition of the field. (Phear 1880:203–4)

The people of Hinidum Pattu do not employ the term *taṭṭumāru* in this sense. However, it is characteristic of Sinhalese culture that the same term may be used to denote several things. A danger therefore lies in uncritically identifying a term like *taṭṭumāru* with a specific custom. One doubts the accuracy of government agricultural statistics which list the extent and prevalence of *taṭṭumāru*, when the term may refer to different things. An operational procedure for investigating customs is required if reliance is to bc placed on official statistics.

In principle the two meanings of *taṭṭumāru* are closely related. Both conditions arise in situations where land is a valued asset: *taṭṭumāru* 2 arises in situations of extreme land scarcity, whereas for *taṭṭumāru* 1 there has to be greater availability of land. We noted that in *taṭṭumāru* 1, a stretch of paddy land is divided into *kaṭṭi* and subsections which are rotated; if and when a large number of persons own shares in each *subsection* various devices have to be employed in order to ensure the smooth *internal* operation of each subsection. *Taṭṭumāru* 2 is one such device; other devices are described by us in chapter 8. *Taṭṭumāru* 2 can also arise in any instance where a *small* plot is owned by a large number of individuals. However, such instances generally arise in conditions of great land scarcity where the traditional modes of land tenure are breaking or have broken down. In our work we shall reserve the term *karamāru* to describe *taṭṭumāru* 2 type arrangements. The term *taṭṭumāru* will hereafter refer to *taṭṭumāru* 1 type land tenure arrangements only.

CHAPTER 3

THE TRADITIONAL LAWS OF INHERITANCE

In any social system which allows individuals or groups of individuals to own land, there must be provision for disposing of this property when an individual owner or a member of a group of owners dies. Such 'rules of inheritance' are related to the kinship system of a society. In the Madagama system land should ideally remain with the agnatic descendants of a common ancestor or group of ancestors who held the land during part of their lifetime. This would logically mean that married women of the *vāsagama* and widows of its members would not be able to alienate permanently to non-agnates any of the patrilineal lands. Furthermore, if the norms stipulate that male agnates should work their own land, then the rule that will fully implement the norm would be rule of patrilocal residence for males and virilocal residence for females, for any other residence rule would militate against a residential aggregation of male patrilineal kinsmen. These two norms we saw govern the ideal type: hence the rules of inheritance and residence most consonant with the ideal type and directed towards its optimum functioning must perforce be patrilineal and patrilocal.

We shall start off by formulating one of the 'functional tasks', in the Parsonian sense, of any kinship system. This would be the allocation of the rights to individuals, families and lines in respect of property. However, the allocation of rights involves certain problems, for viewed in the abstract, the unilinear structure of the line is opposed to the bilateral structure of the family, and in turn these are opposed to the ego-focus of the individual. We could formulate an axiom to deal with this issue. The axiom is as follows:

The allocation of rights to the individual, the family and the line in respect of a given piece of property tend to be inversely proportional, the rights of the one diminishing the rights of the others.

Thus *Axiom* 1*a*:

The rights of the individual diminish the rights of the line and that of the family.

And *Axiom* 1*b*:

The rights of the family diminish the rights of the individual and that of the line.

These axioms pertaining to the allocation of rights are applicable to any kinship system in which both lines and families are present. We have to see how this functional task of allocation of rights is performed in the system under consideration.

In the Sinhalese kinship system we are interested in the allocation of *pravēni* shares in the *gama*. From the point of view of the optimum functioning of the model, shares should not leave the *vāsagama* (the line). One would therefore expect a jural rule which states that individuals cannot alienate *pravēni* shares to outsiders. However, though there were non-jural norms disapproving alienation to total outsiders, these norms had no traditional jural validity. On the contrary alienation to non-*vāsagama* persons could occur under two major circumstances. First, the importance of the family is such that in default of male heirs, females could inherit. The offspring of females marrying in what is known as a *binna* marriage could also inherit *pravēni* shares. In both circumstances the shares would devolve on non-*vāsagama* kinsmen. Secondly, individuals had the right in law to alienate property to total outsiders, though such actions were viewed as morally undesirable. We shall examine the traditional inheritance rules of the society to explicate further the manner in which shares were allocated.

Axiom 1*a*

The rights of the individual diminish the rights of the line and that of the family.

One of the characteristics of land ownership in Ceylon is the individual rather than the corporate ownership of property, whatever be the nature of that property. In respect of our ideal type it should be noted that, though the soil in theory belongs to a common body of agnatically related kinsmen, the respective rights to the soil are held by individuals in terms of fractions of an original estate held by a single ancestor (or a group of patrilineally related kinsmen descended from a common ancestor). Ownership was absolute, and alienation *inter vivos* was left to each owner's discretion. Says Sawers: 'It is stated unanimously by the chiefs, who have been consulted, that a person having the absolute possession of real or personal property, has the power to dispose of that property unlimitedly, that is to say, he or she may dispose of it, either by gift or bequest, away from the heirs at large' (Sawers 1826:4; see also Armour 1863:94, and Turnour 1826:109). Though there were undoubtedly strong pressures against alienation to outsiders by a person's agnates and potential heirs, we have evidence that such alienation did sporadically occur. Among the 790 pre-British deeds and mortgages translated by Lawrie in his Central Province *Gazetteer* (Lawrie 1898), a large number refer to alienation of land to outsiders. It is also evident from these deeds that such actions were considered unusual and extreme. For example, cases in which a son was disinherited were reported to result from the son's gross neglect or cruelty to the father. Other reasons for alienation were extreme indigence, indebtedness and the absence of male descendants. In the latter case, the property may be given to an affinal kinsman, or non-agnate like daughter's husband. The evidence of the Central Province *Gazetteer* suggests that alienation to non-agnates was very real. These documents often contain imprecations against persons who may obstruct and hinder the owner from enjoying his rights. (For example, Lawrie, vol. I, 1898:10, 19, 24, 25, 37, 44, 46, 55, 65.)

The fact that land could be alienated at the will of the owner—however scarce actual occurrences were—is important for understanding the Sinhalese system of kinship and land tenure. This means that the 'line' we spoke of is not a corporate descent group, in the classical sense of Fortes (Fortes 1953). The line does not own the property: individuals own land and could alienate it at will; in order to do this consultation with a person's agnates or heirs is not even required (Armour 1860:94; Sawers 1826:4). Though the ideology that property should ultimately revert to the source whence it came, namely an agnatic source (Hayley 1923:330 ff.; Armour 1860:42 ff.), is well established in Sinhalese custom, the importance attached to individual ownership and alienability may sometimes result in land moving away from the agnatic source. Hence initially we could say that the rule of patrilineal inheritance one would have expected of the ideal type is contravened by the rule that grants individual owners the right to alienate land absolutely *inter vivos*. Note, however, that some kinds of property, namely movable items which could be classified as ancestral property (Hayley 1923:450) such as insignia flags, copper plates given by kings, heirlooms, etc., could not by definition be alienated by a single individual, since the right of each individual to a specific object was qualified by the rights of other patrilineal kinsmen to the same object, unless of course a prior division of these objects among co-owners vesting each owner with absolute rights on a specific object had been effected. Such problems, however, would arise in 'noble' families, and would be of little significance for the land-owning agricultural subcastes we are concerned with. In summary we could say that the legal right of the individual to sell his *pravēni* property to outsiders *inter vivos* absolutely diminishes the shares of the family in the same property, for members of the family have no legal power of preventing such alienation. It also weakens the *vāsagama* (line), because property which should ideally remain in the *vāsagama* could leave it permanently.

Axiom 1b

The rights of the family diminish the rights of the line and that of the individual.

If the unity of the line, and the unity of the family are in principle opposed, pure unity of one type is inconceivable without the radical elimination of the other. Empirical approximations of such radical elimination are for example the traditional Nayars of South India where the family is eliminated, and the modern nuclear families in industrial societies where the line is eliminated. In these situations the values of the society emphasize the solidarity of the line and the solidarity of the family respectively. Sinhalese society emphasized both the family and the line, but we have to see the relative jural weightage given to them, that is, the allocation of rights, obligations, privileges in respect to each system.

The primary intention of this work is to describe the natural history of a land tenure system, rather than of the family, though it is not possible to understand the former without an awareness of the latter. Fortunately for us, there is one crucial variable that links the system of land tenure with that of the family—once again, the laws of inheritance and succession. The laws of inheritance determine the *manner* in which property shall devolve *inter vivos* or in terms of intestate succession. In so far as it applies to the land tenure system it influences the structure of that system. But the law of inheritance of any society also involves members of the family—positively by prescribing the rights and privileges members tend to inherit, or negatively by denying some members rights and privileges which are the exclusive preserve of others.

It is very likely that in peasant societies succession *inter vivos* would be more the exception than the rule; the typical mode would be intestate succession. By the time a man is old, the effective ownership of the property is in the hands of his heirs, so that at his death intestate succession would follow easily. In Sinhalese society, an aging person is *de facto* dependent on his offspring, but the latter is *de jure* dependent on the former. An ageing person is most often *de jure* owner of his property. This serves as an effective means of control over sons who 'neglect' their parents: they could legally be disinherited by the father. Moreover, all authorities agree that transfer of property, whether in written or oral form was always *conditional* upon the 'good faith' of the transferee, so that all deeds and related transactions were revocable by the grantor. A person could at any time revoke the property he had made in advance to his heirs, by written or oral deed, so that a recalcitrant heir could be 'controlled' in this manner. The concept of 'assistance' is crucial to Sinhalese ideology and, as we shall show later, springs from strongly cathected familial norms (Hayley 1923: 347, 356, 456; Sawers 1826: 10). Thus a man may alienate his property to a non-heir who may have rendered him 'assistance', that is, acted as a member of the family according to familial norms.

Fundamental to Sinhalese rules of intestate inheritance are two principles. First, as Hayley (1923: 330–1) states, equality of division among *all* children is a cardinal point of the Sinhalese system of inheritance. Secondly, the principle felicitously phrased by Sawers, and in agreement with other authorities, that property should ultimately revert to the source from which it came. It seems clear that the two 'principles' enunciated here seem, on the surface, contradictory, for while the first emphasizes the strictly *bilateral* character of Sinhalese inheritance, the second emphasizes its 'unilinearity'. The first principle is based on family norms, the right of a man's family of procreation against all others. 'When a man dies intestate', says Sawers, 'his widow and his children are his immediate heirs...' (1826: 21). The second principle is not simply an injunction that in the absence of heirs, property should revert to the source of its origin, which in fact rarely happens; but that the governing principle of succession and inheritance is that *pravēni* should not leave the source, this being in Sinhalese society, an agnate source (*vāsagama*). How does Sinhalese custom resolve this seeming contradiction? Or rather, how is it possible to reconcile the 'rights' of the family with the 'rights' of the line? For it is obvious that if women married, and were permitted to inherit absolutely, the property would leave the 'source from which it came' and become attached to another man's estate.

This problem has been ingeniously resolved in Sinhalese custom by an important distinction made between temporary and permanent rights in *pravēni*. Males (and in some cases females) who are the carriers of the patrilineal name (the Kandyan *gedera* or low country *vāsagama*) will enjoy permanent rights in an intestate's *pravēni*; while females who will breed heirs that will be carriers of *another* person's patrilineal name will have only temporary rights in a deceased intestate's *pravēni*. Thus while all members of the family are a man's immediate heirs, the rights of some heirs are restricted in a manner that will ensure the continuity of the ancestral line, and the convergence of property among a body of agnatic kinsmen. Sawers therefore immediately qualifies the statement earlier quoted: 'but the widow although she has the chief control and management of the landed estate of her deceased husband, *has only a life interest in the same...*' (Sawers 1826:4, italics mine). And then:

> Daughters, while they remain in their father's house, have a temporary joint interest with their brothers in the landed property of their parents, but this they lose when given out in what is called a *deega* marriage, either by their parents, or brothers after the death of the parents. It is however reserved for the daughters, in the event of their being divorced from their *deega* husbands, or becoming widows, destitute of the means of support, that they have a right to return to the house of their parents and then to have lodging or support and clothing from their parents' estate—but the children born to a *deega* husband have no rights of inheritance in the estate of their mother's parents.
>
> (Sawers 1826:5; see also Armour 1860:20, 24, 54; *Niti Niganduva* 1880:62 ff.)

We are once again confronted with the concept of 'assistance': any member of the nuclear family must be supported by the other members in case of destitution or similar circumstances, even if the former has no permanent interest in the patrilineal estate. A *dīga* (Sawers' *deega*) or virilocally married daughter, would be entitled to family support if she divorces her husband (a common enough occurrence) or is destitute, unless she has violated in some manner the 'status honour' of the family (Armour 1860:33; Hayley 1923: 379; Sawers 1826:7; *Niti Niganduva* 1880:53–4). Similar rights are available to the widow.

The rules of inheritance, in their actual operation, we said, involve certain restrictive qualifications regarding the permanent or temporary character of an individual's rights. These restrictive qualifications pertain to marriage. In traditional Sinhalese law, and in contemporary Kandyan law, there are two types of marriage, *dīga* and *binna*. *Dīga* marriages are those in which the woman leaves her paternal home and resides virilocally with her husband. *Binna*, where a man lives uxorilocally in the village of the wife's father. Hayley put the matter succinctly:

> When the daughter marries and leaves her father's house, the *mulgedera*, she passes into the family of her husband and severs her connection with her father's people. Whatever claim she has to a share of her property is satisfied by her dowry, and neither she nor her children have henceforth any claim in competition with brothers and sisters who may have not so left the family abode. But the name may be perpetuated by artificial means, by adoption and by the *binna* marriage.
>
> (Hayley 1923:166)

As far as the rules of inheritance go, the issue of a *binna* marriage is entitled to the maternal grandfather's estate, whereas the issue of a *dīga* marriage is not. Conversely the issue of a *binna* marriage is not entitled to the paternal grandfather's estate, whereas the issue of a *dīga* marriage is so entitled (Hayley 1923:169; Sawers 1826:6; Armour 1860:60–5). The *dīga* married daughter gets a dowry (*dāvadda*) which both Hayley and Leach (Hayley 1923: 331–6; Leach 1961:135–6) point out correctly is an advance on her inheritance, or a conversion of her interest in the landed property into cash, jewelry and other movable and non-*pravēni* property. The dowry then legally and symbolically, and sometimes economically, gives validity to the marriage as *dīga*, restricting the rights of issue from such a marriage in the mother's paternal *pravēni*, in preference to certain classes of patrilineal heirs. In early British court decisions the dowry was sometimes used to define the rights of a daughter to her father's property in cases of intestate succession.

All authorities are agreed that *dīga* is the preferred, the ideal marriage. *Binna* has low prestige and is a disfavoured kind of marriage. The purpose of *binna* marriage is to raise heirs artificially in the absence of males to perpetuate the 'line': this kind of marriage is arranged by a wealthy man for his daughter. Even if such a 'wealthy' man has sons, but not enough to work the family estate, he may arrange a *binna* marriage for his daughter so that his son-in-law may assist in cultivation (Sawers 1826:34). Finally of course, *binna* marriage may well be arranged for purely idiosyncratic motives—if, for example, the father loved the daughter so much that he wanted her to reside near him. The inferior status of the male in *binna* marriages is easy to understand: for if ideally marriage should be of the *dīga* type, then a rule which is the contradiction or opposite of the ideal must perforce be negatively evaluated. The *binna* husband (son-in-law) as Leach and our authorities all recognize is by definition a poor, or landless individual having an almost servant status in his father-in-law's household. In a society where land (*pravēni*) ownership is an index of status and poverty a 'sin', *binna* marriages would carry the stigma associated with landlessness. 'The husband married in *binna* has no privileges in his wife's house. He has no power over her property; he may be expelled or divorced by the wife or her parents at any moment' (Sawers 1826:37). Sawers also quotes the well-known Sinhalese proverb that the *binna* husband should constantly have at the door of his wife's room, a walking stick, a *talipot*, and a torch, so that he would be in readiness for eviction at a moment's notice (1826:37). He has no rights in his children's (*pravēni*) property acquired through their mother, though he may succeed to their non-*pravēni* property. The *binna* married husband is a sociological (and sometimes psychological) female, and the *binna* wife a sociological (and sometimes psychological) male. The *binna* man is a 'consort' of his wife, strictly parallel to the Queen and her consort in the British monarchy, in respect of inheritance and succession. The children of a *binna* marriage may sometimes take the mother's *vāsagama* name.

It should be noted that *binna* and *dīga* in Sinhalese kinship refer to types of marriages rather than rules of residence, for the mere fact of uxorilocal or patrilocal residence for males or females cannot make a marriage *dīga* or *binna*. The critical factor involved here is a mode of inheritance. Hayley was surely right when he said that the meaning of *dīga* or *binna* is dependent on the intention of the parties and their parents rather than on formal ceremonies (Hayley 1923:194); and the chiefs summoned by Sawers were explicit that the children of a *binna* marriage were entitled to the maternal grandfather's estate, only if recognized as heirs presumptive by the latter which may involve 'situational' factors like residential propinquity, patterns of visiting and the fundamental concept of 'assistance' (Sawers 1826:10). Armour also mentions the possibility where both parents of a woman may have large estates and the *binna* husband brought to reside in the estate of the wife's mother (Armour 1860:61). Thus, though *binna* in most instances involves uxorilocal residence for males, the rule of residence is not the defining criterion for this kind of marriage. Rather it is a question of rights associated with the two forms of marriage. Moreover, the terms *binna* and *dīga* apply to both male and female; a *binna* marriage refers to the marriage of both husband and wife, and so does *dīga*. This is given linguistic recognition in Sinhalese. For example, the word *dīga genāva* (brought in *dīga*) and *dīga gēnava* (will bring in *dīga*) is used if a male is speaking; *dīga giya* (went in *dīga*) and *dīga yanava* (will go in *dīga*) if a female is speaking.

It will be evident from the above discussion that though in theory the rules of inheritance to *pravēni* are bilateral, the long run consequence of the rules would result in the aggregation of agnatic kinsmen in a localized area, and the preservation of *pravēni* in the agnatic source. Hence *dīga* marriage is the ideal. On the basis of this evidence we could formulate an ideal typical statement pertaining to marriage and inheritance that will be consonant with our indigenous model of land tenure. *Dīga* marriage, with its consequence in the clustering of agnatic kinsmen, and the associated norm which stipulates the land should not leave the agnatic source, is geared to the optimum efficient functioning of the land tenure model. However, in so far as the individual rights are absolute, the possibility of land leaving the *vāsagama* always exists.

We notice then that Sinhalese laws of inheritance attempt a reconciliation between the 'rights' of the line and the family, by making a distinction between temporary and permanent rights, in respect of members of an intestate's family. But, it should be noted, Sinhalese law places a primary emphasis on descendants as against collaterals and ascendants, so that when the choice is between *pravēni* leaving the family *or* the ancestral line, clear recognition is given to the priority of the former over the latter. Our

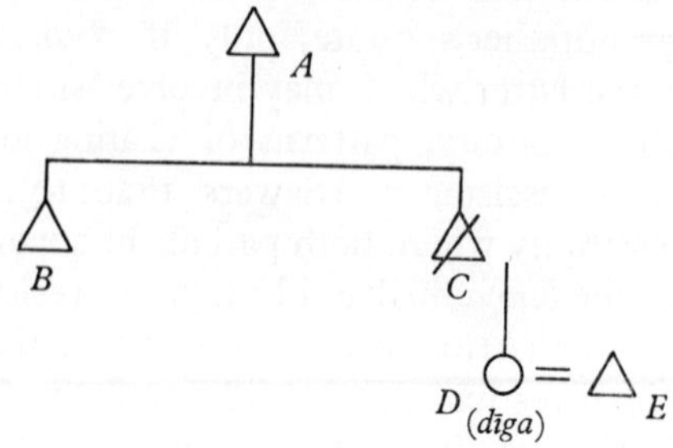

Fig. 10.

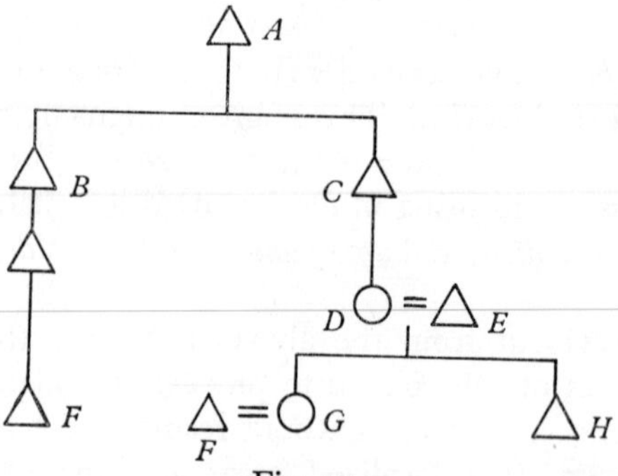

Fig. 11.

authorities all agree that while the preference is for male descendants, over females, *yet in the absence of male heirs, female descendants inherit absolutely, in preference to ascendant or collateral male patrikin* irrespective of the fact that these female heirs are married in *dīga* or *binna* (see Sawers 1826:6; *Niti Niganduva* 1880:59, 73). This is shown in Fig. 10.

On the death of *C*, *D* inherits absolutely to the exclusion of *A* and *B*. It is obvious that this feature of the law is based on the solidarity of the family *contra* the line. All authorities agree to this (Sawers 1826:2; Armour 1860:45; *Niti Niganduva* 1880:59, 73; D'Oyly 1929:104). It is evident that in such a situation ancestral property will leave the 'source' unless it can be recouped partly or wholly, in the next generation through classificatory cross-cousin marriage of the type shown in Fig. 11.

If *G* inherits completely (*inter vivos* or intestate) the mother's estate, the recoupment would be complete. In the above example, the woman *D* will inherit, either *per capita* or *per stirpes*, even if she had half-brothers by her father's second wife. These rules of intestate succession for females in default of male heirs is fundamentally in contrast with similar rules in societies containing unilineally organized property owning corporations.

Rights of grandchildren

After one's immediate descendants, those of the second descending generation have priority over ascendants and collaterals. However, the principle of property devolution in this instance is not *per*

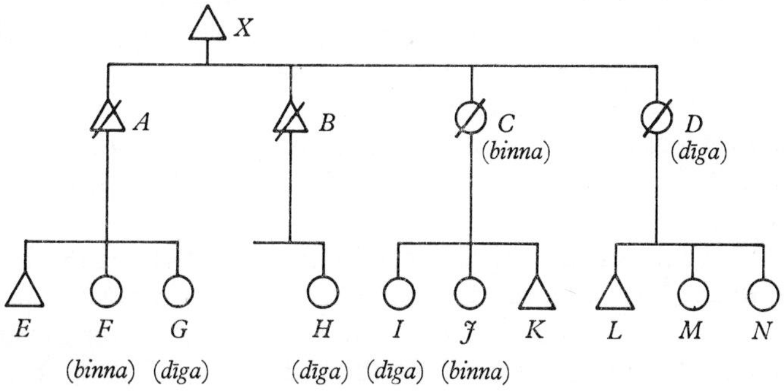

Fig. 12.

capita but *per stirpes*. But the right to inherit, as Hayley puts it will 'depend on the principle of representation', the general rule being that children represent their parents and take *per stirpes*, so that grandchildren inherit through their deceased parents (Hayley 1923:343–5). Fig. 12 (example based on Hayley, Sawers and Armour) illustrates this.

If *A*, *B*, *C* and *D* have predeceased *X* their father, the grandchildren would, in terms of each sibling unit, represent their father: the rights of each sibling within each unit will be dependent in turn on the type of marriage contracted. Accordingly *L*, *M* and *N* have no rights whatever in the grandfather's estate, because their mother, whom they represent, has already been given a dowry and married *dīga*. Of the children of the *binna* married daughter, *I*, *J* and *K*, the *binna* married girl *J* and the son *K* inherit equally, but not *I* who having married *dīga* would not inherit the *pravēni* property of her mother. The daughter of *B*, named *H*, will inherit her father's share *in toto*, since in default of male heirs, she solely represents her father. But our authorities recognize (Sawers 1826: 4; Armour 1860:62–3, 73, 79) that if the girl was given in marriage by her grandfather, who would have provided her dowry, she would lose her rights in preference to collaterals—for the 'dowry' diminishes the estate. What is most pertinent to our discussion is that in both the first and second descending generations, the familial rights take priority over lineal ones, even if this means property leaving the ancestral source and attaching itself to another man's estate. It is only when a man has no descendants, that the ancestral property reverts to his parents, and on their death to their male children and *binna* married females, that is, the intestate's brothers and sisters. This again is based on the principle of representation, that children represent their parents and that parents represent their children. Both principles are based on a familial (bilateral) rather than in a unilineal ideology. In so far as this is the case, the possibility once again exists for *pravēni* shares to move out of the *vāsagama*.

We have illustrated the major principles of traditional Sinhalese inheritance law: a more exhaustive discussion is contained in the textbooks. Most of our authorities are agreed on those fundamental principles, the disagreement is on the details of application. Hayley and other writers have tried to fit Sinhalese law into a systematic framework of rules, and to invest it with the systemic rigour it lacked. While most writers recognize the lack of 'rigour' in Sinhalese law, they nevertheless attempt, quite naturally, to give this body of norms the character of 'legal rules' which are inflexible in application. Thus in judicial decisions, as well as in expositions of Kandyan law (as, for example, in Hayley 1923 and Modder 1914), deductions are made from first principles quite rigorously, which is quite contrary to the spirit of Sinhalese law. For example, the contemporary legal position in Kandyan law, as a result of judicial decisions made through deductions from first principles, is that widows have no life interest over *pravēni* (Hayley 1923:353–4), something which though logically consistent with the principle that land should not leave the agnatic source, is inconsistent with the notion of family solidarity, and that members of the family are always entitled to support. The British system of judicial administration required the law to have a systemic rigour which Sinhalese law lacked. Several British administrators were puzzled by the lack of agreement among chiefs over matters of detail; for example, the suggestion was made that the difference in the laws of Sabaragamuva from the rest of the country was due to the fact that some chiefs had wilfully tried to introduce legal concepts prevalent in the Maritime Provinces. The fact of the matter is that traditional Sinhalese courts, like other traditional ones, did not give judgement on interpretations of the rules *per se*, but rather on a combination of legal principles with the situational aspects of any particular case. Thus the concept of assistance, deriving from family ideology, so important in Sinhalese law, was underemphasized in later judicial decisions in British times. In Sinhalese 'law' any person who had rendered assistance to an intestate was 'entitled' morally to a share of the intestate's estate, even if the person so entitled was a non-agnate or outsider. While cases involving 'assistance' would have been judged situationally by the traditional Sinhalese courts of chief and the King (*mahanaḍuva*) such situational judgements (quite different from legal 'precedents') were inconsistent with the procedures of 'modern' courts instituted by the British. Sawers in several places intersperses his statement of general principles with qualificatory notes emphasizing the importance of 'assistance' which may in certain situations override first principles. For example, Sawers says that a *binna* married daughter, quitting her parents' house, to live subsequently in *dīga*, forfeits her patrimonial inheritance, but adds in a note that:

> Some of the chiefs are of the opinion that the daughter previously married in *binna* may preserve for herself and her children her own and their claim in her parent's estate, by visiting him frequently and administering to his comfort, especially being present, nursing and rendering him assistance in his last illness. (1826:6)

The concept of assistance and the situational character of the law

Both the *Niti Niganduva* (1880: 41, 48–51, 53–5) and Armour pay considerable emphasis to the concept of familial assistance and the situational character of the law and its implications for inheritance.

Armour's examples are very instructive and worth consideration for they illustrate the strong familial norms involved.

(*a*) A father could bequeath a major part of his estate to one son in recognition of assistance received from him, and give another son only a small portion. Such a deed need not contain an explicit clause of disinheritance; but a birth of another son automatically annuls the deed (Armour 1860: 102).

(*b*) Assistance received from a relative could result in land leaving the agnatic source.

If the father had received debts and being aged and infirm required assistance, and if he was disregarded and neglected by his children, and he did therefore avail himself of assistance and support by some friendly relation—and if he did bequeath his estate, including even *all* [italics Armour] his lands, to that relation...such bequest will be perfectly valid, although the donor had not reserved any portion of his lands for his children and did not expressly disinherit them—it being premised that the donor's children were adults, and had wilfully neglected their duty to their said parent. (Armour 1860:105–6)

(*c*) Armour lists four reasons for the revocation of deeds by a donor, of which the last two are related to the concept of assistance. 'If because of neglect or ill usage on the part of the Donee, the Donor resumed possession of the land specified in the deed and refused to receive assistance from the said Donee any longer' (Armour 1860: 92). Or, 'if having cause to be dissatisfied with the treatment he received from the Donee, he the Donor quit of his own accord the said Donee's premises and did afterwards take up quarters elsewhere...In such case the deed or gift will become perfectly null and void' (Armour 1860: 92).

(*d*) Armour has several cases which illustrate the point that 'assistance' may in certain situations override the formal rules of inheritance.

If the father left a son and a daughter, minors by one wife, and a son and a *deega* married daughter by another wife, if that *deega* married daughter came back and attended and assisted her father during his last illness, and if the father had therefore on his deathbed expressed his will, that his *deega* daughter should have a share of his lands, notwithstanding her being settled in *deega*; in that case the *deega* daughter will be entitled, by virtue of such nuncupative will, to participate equally with her uterine brother and their parental half-brother and half-sister, in the father's estate. (Armour 1860:65–6)

However, it should be noted that simply returning to the parental home does not give her *pravēni* rights: the marriage must be converted from *dīga* to *binna* or there must be assistance rendered to the father.

The rights of widows

The greatest area of disagreement in the textbook writers and among the chiefs ('assessors') interviewed by the early magistrates, relates to the rights of widows. However, all our writers—Armour, *Niti Niganduva*, D'Oyly and Sawers—are agreed on one thing—that widows have no absolute interest in the *pravēni*, whatever their rights may be in respect of acquired property. All are agreed that *pravēni* property should ultimately revert to the familial source.

The differences pertain to whether the widow has temporary possession or usufruct of a portion of it (Armour 1860:17–18) or whether the woman has managerial control over all of it in some instances (*Niti Niganduva* 1880:27, 28). All writers are agreed that the unity of the family is maintained by giving the wife temporary interests of some sort in the husband's estate if she does not remarry *dīga* and leave the family premises. Thus there is no fundamental difference in *principle* among the writers mentioned. All are agreed that the widow has no absolutely *permanent* interest or prescriptive rights in the *pravēni*; she cannot dispose of it at will to outsiders. Historical sources disagree as to whether on the death of a man, his sons and *binna* married daughters take over the *pravēni* at once or whether their rights remain in 'abeyance' until the death or *dīga* marriage of the widow. But once again the likelihood was that these 'issues' were judged situationally, either on the village level, or that of the traditional courts, rather than through rules deduced from first principles.

Regarding acquired property, however, there are some differences of opinion among our authorities. The *Niti Niganduva* is of the opinion that the widow will have only temporary rights to land, either acquired or *pravēni*, and permanent rights only to movables (1880:27, 90). Sawers says that a widow, *if a cross-cousin*, was entitled to *fee simple* in respect of all acquired property of her husband next to full brothers (1826:24–5). Hayley thinks this incorrect, but this would be quite consonant with our view that *cross-cousin* marriages would often be contracted without a dowry, and the wife in such cases, would be entitled to special privileges. Controversy exists as to the rights of the mother regarding acquired property, for Armour, contrary to D'Oyly and Sawers, says that the mother is heiress to all acquired property of a man.

In conclusion it seems clear that females (wives, mothers and daughters) married in *dīga* do not acquire permanent rights in *pravēni*, except under exceptional circumstances. However, familial obligations are recognized, by giving them temporary rights in the estate of the husband or parents, or both, as the case may be. Widows and mothers in several instances can inherit acquired property absolutely, since such property is not associated with the patrilineal ideology of the society. In summary we may say that while males are given preference in respect of *pravēni* property, females (mother, widow) are given preference over males regarding acquired property. The managerial and usufructual control of *pravēni* to widows and their right over acquired property give recognition to the importance of the 'family tie'; the importance of the lineal tie is recognized by denying them the right to inherit *pravēni* absolutely.

The law of Sabaragamuva

The authorities so far considered are basically agreed on the general principles of traditional Sinhalese law. However, there is one glaring and serious exception in Turnour's *Memorandum on the Laws of Sabaragamuva* (1826: 107–9). Turnour's short compilation was based on information given to him by six prominent chiefs (acting as 'assessors' for the government) from the Sabaragamuva province. While the Sabaragamuva chiefs agreed in the main with the principles of Kandyan law as enunciated by the chiefs from the other Kandyan provinces they differed radically in respect of the rights of widows. The Sabaragamuva law of inheritance differed from other Kandyan areas in the following respects:

(1) 'The legal wife of a landed Proprietor succeeded to the whole of the husband's estate if he died intestate and without issue, although he might have left Brothers or other kin' (Turnour 1826: 107).

(2) Another difference is also fairly important. 'Children who survived both parents equally shared their family estates. If the children were of the two marriages, each family inherited the exact

half of the property, whatever the number of children might be' (Turnour 1826:107). That is, division of property was *per stirpes* rather than *per capita*.

(3) The widow's rights were restricted if there were children to the husband by a former marriage in which case one-half of the estate would go to the latter and the other to the surviving widow of the second marriage (Turnour 1826:107).

(4) If the widow had children she had full managerial control of the husband's estate, Turnour implies; but the children could institute proceedings against her for a division of the estate in which case 'they were adjudged the exact half of the lands she might be possessing' (1826:107).

(5) The portion allotted to the widow could be alienated by her in any way she liked, but this right she loses if she contracts a subsequent *dīga* marriage. But it is fully within her power to dispose of her share of the property *before* contracting a *dīga* marriage (Turnour 1826:108).

The rights of the widow then are very great in Sabaragamuva. The reason given by the chiefs is that these rights in the husband's estate are compensation for the loss of a woman's rights in her own paternal *pravēni* due to *dīga* marriage. If a woman married *binna* she is treated as if she were a male, so that if she had contracted two successive *binna* marriages, her estate is divided *per stirpes* according to the rule of intestate succession for males. Turnour is silent on the *binna* married husband's rights in the wife's estate.

The case of Sabaragamuva is of considerable importance for the study of the land tenure system of Madagama for, as we have shown in our introductory chapter, the village is adjacent to and has had considerable contact with the Sabaragamuva province. Are we to assume that the laws pertaining to the rights of widows were the same as those prevailing in Sabaragamuva? Though we cannot be certain about this, we feel that it is methodologically desirable to take a clear stand and specify a baseline, so that we shall treat the pre-British jural rules of Hinidum Pattu *as though* they conformed with Sabaragamuva in this respect. One should note, however, that after the British conquest this recognition of a widow's right to the husband's estate was 'repealed' and Sabaragamuva was brought under the general rubric of Kandyan law, which gave the widow almost no rights in *pravēni*, temporary or permanent. What explanation can we give for the importance given to widows in Sabaragamuva?

The early British administrators were singularly piqued by this legal aberration and suggested that the people of Sabaragamuva had wilfully adopted the legal rules of the Maritime Provinces, which they assumed were the Roman-Dutch law. But this view meets with serious objections. First, the people of Sabaragamuva hardly came under the rule of the Dutch. In the absence of coercion it is doubtful that they would have adopted the law of their enemies. Secondly, we have already shown that it was unlikely that the Roman-Dutch law prevailed even in the Maritime Provinces and still less likely that it influenced Hinidum Pattu, enshrouded as it was at that time in dense tropical jungle, inaccessible and remote. Thirdly, while the right of widows had some superficial resemblance to the Roman-Dutch law of the marital 'community of goods', there are considerable differences, especially the division *per stirpes* in the instance of the intestate having had two families. Finally, it is highly doubtful whether the Roman-Dutch law would have influenced the rights of widows, whereas the other aspects of the legal system so offensive to Roman-Dutch law, like polyandry, *binna* marriages, etc. remained unaffected.

If the influence of the Roman-Dutch law was nil or negligible, how could one explain the important difference in the traditional law of Sabaragamuva and the rest of the Kandyan provinces? We are strongly tempted to speculate on the lines of analysis conducted earlier in this chapter. We suggest that the Sabaragamuva case represented an intensification of a condition that prevailed in Ceylon generally, the conflict between bilateral familial rights and the unilateral rights of the line. If this is correct can we then infer that the strength of the family and marital ties in Sabaragamuva (and the Maritime Provinces) were stronger than in the other Kandyan provinces, and/or that there were certain conditions prevailing there which were consonant with the granting of substantial inheritance rights to widows. We suggest that these widow rights are consonant with the existence of a strong ideology of wifely devotion in Sabaragamuva and in the Maritime Provinces. Evidence for this comes from three sources. First, contemporary society in Madagama accords a great deal of formal respect to the wife. The strength of the marriage tie is emphasized, divorce and desertion are quite rare. One of the reasons is that divorce according to current Roman-Dutch derived law is practically impossible for villagers in the Maritime Provinces, but the villagers of Madagama had always an option of marrying according to Kandyan law, where divorce was easy. This opportunity was rarely used. We suggest that the strength of the marriage ties and an ideology of wifely devotion to the husband is not simply a function of change but a continuous ethical value in the society. The second bit of evidence comes from a mythological source in the worship of the cult of the goddess Pattini. The Pattini cult was historically the major cult of the region, both in Sabaragamuva and the Maritime Provinces. In the Kandyan areas the cult was much less systematized, whereas in the former areas elaborate ritual dramas were enacted in honour of the goddess. The major theme of the ritual dramas is the devotion, chastity and fidelity of the wife, and the fickleness and moral weakness of the husband. Chastity endows a woman with supernatural strength and may lead to her deification. The main seat of the goddess Pattini is Navagamuva in the Sabaragamuva province. Finally the existence of the custom of 'blood evidence' among high status families on the day after the nuptial night is another indicator of the importance attached in this area to virginity and chastity in women. This custom is totally absent in the Kandyan areas.

MARRIAGE RULES AND THE IDEAL TYPE

The ideal model of land tenure requires for its optimum functioning patrilineal inheritance and patrilocal residence. If we 'place' the data on inheritance rules presented in this chapter against the ideal model, one major point of difference emerges—namely, the rule of *binna* marriage and uxorilocal residence for males, plus females inheriting in the absence of male heirs, which contradict the ideal of patrilineal inheritance and patrilocal residence. In this section we shall attempt to explain this contradiction between the ideal and the actual systems.

The ideal model of land tenure based on a criterion of optimum functioning required a hypothetical homeostatic condition, land and labour equitably balanced in terms of some criterion of optimum efficiency. Thus, if the criterion of efficiency requires three acres per family, and each family consisted exactly of three males and three females, and the hamlet consisted of ten families then the hamlet would require an optimum cultivable area of thirty acres.

As far as the actual working of the land is concerned *any* rule of residence would do, as long as the estate had the ideally requisite number of males and females to 'manage' it. In fact the model, we noted, is associated with a preference for males inheriting, managing and residing in the patrimonial estate. Thus the ideal model contains an ideal norm of *dīga* marriage involving virilocal residence. In such a situation the sex ratio in respect of the pure conditions postulated in the model would remain constant. With every female who moves out of the family at marriage, another would move in to marry a male permanently resident in the village. Given the equitable distribution of land and labour in the ideal type, there is no economic incentive for any form of marriage other than the *dīga* ideal. Given the prestige associated with land as part of the patrimonial estate there is no 'prestige' incentive for any other form of marriage and residential arrangement. We have then the following paradigm of pure conditions in the model.

Ecology	Demography	Residence
Land	People	*Dīga* marriage
3 acres per family	3 males, 3 females	Virilocal residence

What we have in the model is a pure homeostatic condition of balanced resources. Empirically one never has ideal families. The most one could expect is a consistent pattern of ejection of females from the group through *dīga* marriage. But the decision as to whether females are to be ejected or not does not lie with the line (*vāsagama*); it is a matter for the family. Elementary families (*pavula*) resident in single households are major structural units in this society. A share in the *gama* owned by any individual is worked by the family as a whole, and contributes to their support and welfare. The problem of residence choices have to be seen in relation to the interests of the family.

The upsetting of the pure conditions depicted in the model can arise from two conditions: when there are too many males, such that the shares allocated to them are insufficient to maintain the family; or alternatively, when there are a few or no males but only females in a family so that cultivation of the family estate becomes difficult. In terms of the ideal model, in a condition where there is a population excess, the solution would be the founding of a new *gama*. But this is not always a feasible proposition for several reasons:

(*a*) lack of land in the vicinity of the parent hamlet;

(*b*) lack of permission from the requisite government authorities; and, most important,

(*c*) the practical difficulty for any family to muster personnel and resources to found a new hamlet and *vāsagama*.

Alternatively, a solution would be to siphon off excess males to a situation where there is a short supply of males. To illustrate, consider two hypothetical families belonging to two *vāsagamas*: family *A* in which there are five males and no females, and family *B* in which there are two females but no males. Family *A* has inadequate land for its males and family *B* has enough land but no males to cultivate it. The solution to the problem would be for family *A* to eject its excess males, and family *B* to bring in males from the outside. In such a situation *dīga* marriage (with its rule of virilocal residence for females) would exaggerate the problem—the males in family *A* will have to remain in family *A*, the females in family *B* will have to leave family *B* and deplete its human resources further. The Sinhalese solution to the problem is for family *A* to 'eject' at marriage the two excess males who will be 'received' as husbands for the women in family *B*, and would reside in the latter hamlet. This is exactly what happens in *binna* marriage.

Binna marriage, viewed in relation to traditional land tenure, can be seen as an alternative to founding a new *vāsagama*. Ejection of males from one family and their reception into another brings the empirical system close to the homeostatic condition of balanced resources postulated in the model, never of course equalling it, for equilibria exist only in models of social systems, not in their empirical (statistical) dimensions. Empirically, ejection and reception of males mean that both the ejecting group and the receiving group are economically better able to manage their estate after the marriage relationship has been established than before. *Binna* marriage is viewed by us as essentially a phenomenon of the traditional social structure: contemporary cases of uxorilocal marriage are in our opinion both structurally and functionally quite different. The difference could be summed thus: traditionally *binna* marriage was between a group without adequate land and having excess of males and a group with adequate land but inadequate males to manage it. This arrangement could operate efficiently only when there are adequate land resources. Contemporary uxorilocal arrangements are, as will be shown in a later chapter, *a phenomenon of universal land shortage*. There is a shortage of land everywhere, and uxorilocal residence is one of many residential alternatives to cope with the problem. It is interesting that Madagama citizens are quite aware of the traditional meanings of *dīga* and *binna* and have contracted such marriages up till 40 years ago, though none use these terms to describe contemporary marriage arrangements.

Formal paradigm of binna and dīga marriage and land tenure

Our view of the relation between traditional *dīga-binna* marriage arrangements and land tenure can be presented in a formal paradigm. We said that the ideal model contained a homeostatic condition of balanced resources—land and the people to operate it are perfectly balanced. There is an ideal rule of *dīga* marriage with *virilocal* residence. Empirically we suggested that some families may have scarce resources while others abundant resources; families with scarcity of land and excess males siphon off the excess males to groups in need of males, equalizing the land/population (male) ratio in the process. In the ideal model we have a pure balancing of resources; empirically we have *scarcity* of resources (below optimum) and *abundance* of resources (above optimum) both of which pertain to *imbalance* of resources. These terms are entirely relative in character. They 'upset' the ideal scheme and produce a set of combinations, thus:

scarcity of land	scarcity of people (males)
abundance of land	abundance of people (males)
scarcity of land	abundance of people (males)
abundance of land	scarcity of people (males)

(1) *Scarcity of land, scarcity of people.* The term 'scarcity', we noted, implied 'relative scarcity'. The paradigm here refers to empirical situations where there is a scarcity of land, combined with a scarcity of males per family. Similarly:

(2) *Abundance of land, abundance of people.* This represents the polar extreme of (1). However, in both situations the disparity between land and labour is evened out; in one because both are scarce, and in the other because both are abundant, thus approxi-

mating more or less to the ideal model of balanced resources. The closer the approximation to the ideal type the greater the incidence of *dīga* marriage and virilocal residence. The dominant pattern or normal trend of residence in such situations would be virilocal. In so far as 'scarcity' or 'abundance' is relative and *some* disparity exists between land and labour, there will be cases of non-virilocality—in the traditional Sinhalese situation this would mean uxorilocal residence. Neo-local residence would be rare in a predominantly agrarian economy, where agricultural work requires kinship co-operation. Thus the greater the disparity between ecology and demography, the greater the rise in *binna* marriage and uxorilocal residence. This leads us to:

(3) *Scarcity of land, abundance of people.* If there is a scarcity of land and an excess of people, the alternatives for ego (male) are of two types: either (*a*) he stays with his own group and lives in poverty or scarce resources, or (*b*) he moves away from his group and lives elsewhere. An extreme traditional example of the latter was slavery, where indigence compels the individual to sell himself as bondsman to another. If such an individual marries this would be a case of 'neo-local' residence, but the factor that precipitates such action is indigence, specifically lack of land. Pure neo-local residence would be unusual, for kinship assistance for cultivation may not be easily available. Another traditional alternative would be to found a new hamlet and *vāsagama*. If this alternative is also unavailable, impracticable, or undesired, the practical alternative is to move away from one village through *binna* (uxorilocal) marriage, thus easing the land/population ratio. Hence we could say that where there is a scarcity of land with an abundance of people (males) there will be a drift away from virilocality, and a trend towards *binna* marriage and uxorilocality. The greater the disproportion between the two—the greater the scarcity of land and the greater the abundance of people (males)—the greater the incidence of *binna* marriage. But such a situation is feasible only if the 'husband receiving group' has enough land to spare for the 'husband ejecting group'. Which leads us to the fourth combination:

(4) *Abundance of land, scarcity of people.* If the group has abundance of land, but not enough males to cultivate it, one could leave the land fallow, or bring in outsiders to help cultivate it. Leaving the land fallow is not an economically feasible proposition,

for, if there is a 'family' without steady male help to cultivate it, it may mean indigence or starvation, given the traditional economic importance of rice. Thus one has to bring in outsiders to the group on terms of temporary or permanent contract. If permanent, it is either slavery or *binna* marriage, facilitated maybe by cross-cousin marriage. A male in a situation falling into category (3), is brought into a situation falling into category (4). Hence empirical instances that involve situation (3) must also involve situation (4). Thus where you have an abundance of land and a scarcity of people, the greater will be the tendency to contract *binna* marriage for females of the group.

CHAPTER 4

THE DIACHRONIC DEVOLUTION OF THE SHARE SYSTEM

In this chapter we propose to deal with the devolution of shares or *pangu* in the Pahala Madagama *gama* from the date it was founded till the time of field work—1790 to 1961. The founding of the village has been computed from early marriage registers, while the devolution of shares is from data in our genealogies and records of land transactions kept in the provincial capital in Galle. The devolution of shares is an extremely tedious, factual account of share inheritance and mortgage transactions. The share devolution for the two branches of the *vāsagama* are treated separately. The details are almost impossible to follow without reference to the genealogical charts (Figs. 13 and 14) of the two branches. A summary of the data is presented in the tables at the end of the chapter.

Since *pangu* are fractional shares in a single estate, the estate can be treated as unity, in the mathematical sense. The original owner of the estate could be seen as owning a share of one. Those who inherit shares later own fractions of one. It follows then that if the shares are added up at each generation they should constitute one; the shares of each branch at any generation level should add up to one-half. All the shares in 1961 when added up should be unity. We have demonstrated this in the present chapter.

However, this chapter is not simply a display of arithmetical virtuosity. The detailed facts presented have central methodological relevance. Methodologically, the 'statistical facts' described here have to be placed against the ideal model of land tenure. The ideal model serves two purposes. First, it is constructed on the basis of optimum functioning *in the absence of complicating variables*. Secondly, it serves as a baseline which features how the land tenure system would ideally have worked before the social changes of the nineteenth and twentieth centuries had taken place. The raw empirical facts depicted in this chapter, when placed against the ideal model, bring into relief the *complicating variables* that occur in the empirical system. It is therefore possible to isolate these complicating variables, and analyse them in subsequent chapters. Further 'control' over the 'complicating variables' is established through the description of traditional inheritance rules in chapter 3. Changes in inheritance rules and in the structure of the land tenure system are brought into 'relief' through this methodological procedure.

THE FOUNDING OF THE HAMLET

Dating the founding of Pahala Madagama hamlet has been facilitated by the existence of early marriage registers. Two types of registers are extant.

(*a*) Dutch type *thombos*—where the marriages were entered on a palm leaf record. These are now available in the Galle Kachcheri. Originally they were probably kept in Hiniduma. The Dutch recorded marriages of those (Christians) who were willing to register, and when the British took over in 1795 they continued these records. The earliest extant marriages from Pahala Madagama recorded in these *thombos* are in December 1848. The last one is on 29 August 1863.

(*b*) The second set of records come from the marriage registries in the Hinidum Pattu and reflect British bureaucratic principles, for government-appointed marriage registrars recorded these on standard forms. There are two types of such records: (i) records of marriages based on the general law, and (ii) records of Kandyan marriages in the *yakawala kottāsaya* of the Hinidum Pattu. The first Pahala Madagama marriage registered under the general law is 4 November 1867, and under the Kandyan Law, 17 June 1875.

Thus it is obvious that between 1863 and 1867, the old Dutch system of recording marriages became superseded by a new system introduced by the British.

The thombo marriages

Two marriages were registered on the same day—December 11, 1848.

A *thombo* entry records that Pahala Madagama Gamage Baron married Hewasam Ganewatlege Babanona of Halvitigala. The entry immediately following reads that (Pahala Madagama) Gamage Baron pige Adonis of Pahala Madagama married Galgoda

Liyanage Babona of Habarakada. 'Baron *pige* Adonis' means 'Adonis, son of Baron'; thus it is obvious that father and son were 'married' on the same day! We have identified these people with Balappuve (or Lokuappuve) of our genealogies and his eldest (?) son Adonis. Identifying Adonis was quite easy for the names coincided. Furthermore, though none of our present informants knew the name of his wife (not surprising in people who sometimes forget the names of their own children), they were agreed that he married from Habarakada, which fits with the evidence from the marriage record. Adonis' father according to our genealogies is Balappuve (living in polyandry with Lokuappuve). Here the difficulty was that none of our informants knew the personal names of those in Balappuve's generation. Thus Dingi Appu, Balappuve and Lokuappuve simply meant 'the youngest gentleman', 'the younger gentleman' and the 'oldest gentleman', an age classification. However, they knew that Balappuve married a woman from Halvitigala, which once again fits the *thombo* evidence. Further clinching evidence for the identifications suggested above comes from a marriage record of 29 August 1863 of the *thombo*. It reads that Pahala Madagama Gamage Baronge Juan (widower) married Banagala Vanasinge Abeyhamy of Banagala. 'Baronge Juan' means Juan, son of Baron, and our genealogies confirm that Juan is indeed son of Balappuve (Baron) and that he did marry from Banagala. Thus we are practically certain about the marriage registration of Balappuve (Baron) and two of his sons Adonis and Juan.

On the same day that P. M. G. Juan got married to Banagala Vanasinge Abeyhamy of Banagala, an entry reads that Banagala Vanasinge Adiriyan married Pahala Madagama Gamage Baru Hamy of Pahala Madagama. These were easy to identify in the genealogies as Dingi Appu's daughter Baru Hamy and her husband Vanasinge Adiriyan. But the marriage records also suggest brother-sister exchange, for example, P. M. G. Juan and P. M. G. Baru Hamy are classificatory brother and sister: they 'marry' Banagala Vanasinge Abeyhamy and Banagala Vanasinge Adiriyan on the same day, the latter *vāsagamas* also suggesting they were brother and sister (actual or classificatory).

Six Pahala Madagama marriages are recorded in the *thombos*. We have accounted for four, but the identifications of the remaining two marriages are difficult. An entry of 18 December 1848 reads that Goigama Gamage (literally: Gamage of Goigama caste) Uporis of Pahala Madagama married Goigama Gangoda Liyanage Nonne of Pahala Panangala. We could only guess at Uporis' identity through a process of elimination. The following are the logically possible identifications:

(1) Dingi Appu, since his brother has already registered his marriage;

(2) Odiris, son of Balappuve (Baron) since two of his siblings are registered;

(3) Upeappu (branch *U*);

(4) Hin Hamy, son of Upeappu.

Of these four possibilities we can eliminate Odiris (2), for our genealogies state that he married from Banagala and subsequently from Neluva and not Pahala Panangala as the *thombo* states. His second marriage which was registered give his name clearly as Odiris and not Uporis. We exclude Dingi Appu, for we know that he too married from Neluva. This leaves us with Upeappu (Branch *U*) and his son Hin Hamy. We have registration records for Upeappu's sons—their marriages are recorded in the new registers; Hin Hamy's marriage is registered on 17 June 1875. This leaves us with the father—Upeappu is probably Uporis of the *thombos*. There is a further basis for this identification. The name Upeappu, unlike Balappuve, etc., has no age connotation, but simply means 'gentleman Upe'. 'Uporis' is a respectable and formal version of 'Upe'. Furthermore our genealogies indicate that Upeappu did indeed marry from Panangala—which tends to confirm Uporis of the *thombo* as Upeappu of our genealogies.

The other marriage we cannot easily account for is *thombo* entry of 26 January 1863, where Mavita Gamage Lodivisge Mathes of Ambelegedera married Mavanana Pahala Madagamage Dano of Mavanana. The identification here is not very important, for this female is sociologically irrelevant at this point in the generation series. Anyhow, one is tempted to guess. The records translated state 'Dano of Pahala Madagama Gamage *vāsagama* resident at Mavanana'. This last detail gives us a clue. We know that P. M. G. Odiris (and his father Balappuve too) resided at Mavanana—thus Dano could very well be one of Odiris' sisters, or daughters. The former seems more feasible in view of the date.

From the new register the following selected information was obtained. In these registers the ages of the persons are included.

(1) The marriage registration of four sons of Upeappu (Uporis). On 13 December 1867 P. M. G. Babappu (age 28) married Ganekande Kankanange Ano (age 17) of Panagoda—the latter is obviously Kananan Gamage Babahamy of our genealogies. On 18 July 1870 P. M. G. Elias (age 28) married Mutuhetti Gamage Babahamy (age 22). On 11 July 1870 P. M. G. Adiriyan (age 29) married Neluva Liyanage Madduhamy (age 25). One marriage is recorded in the Kandyan register: P. M. G. Hin Hamy married I. M. G. Indo Hamy on 17 June 1875.

(2) P. M. G. Juanis (widower, age 30), son of Juan Appu, married Korelegama Patirage Hinni Hamy (age 16) of Korelegama on 31 December 1890. Witness to the marriage was his brother Agoris.

(3) P. M. G. Elaris (age 28), son of Babappu, married Tavalama Pahala Gamage Nonnohamy (age 16) on 25 December 1901. Witness was his mother's brother Adris.

In spite of the impressive documentary evidence of 'marriages' of early patrilateral ancestors of the present members of the Pahala Madagama Gamage *vāsagama*, the evidence is not always of a sociologically meaningful kind. It is obvious that the formal registration of marriages is no indication of the actual date of marriage—witness the 'marriage' of father and son on the same day. However, several conclusions can be drawn from the data.

(1) That from 1848 onwards people were becoming increasingly motivated to register their marriages. The reasons for this will be discussed later.

(2) The actual dates of marriages are different from the registration date: it would also be reasonable to assume that this discrepancy would diminish as we descend the generation series.

(3) Thirdly, the actual dates of registration fall into certain patterns; for example, the months during which registrations occur

Table 1. *Thombo marriages*

Year	No. of marriages		Total	Period
	Pahala Madagama	Ihala Madagama		
1848	3	6	9	December
1863	3	3	6	January (4), August (2)

are roughly during the June–July–August spell, or the October–November–December–January spell. They fall into several distinct years not only in Pahala Madagama, but in the adjacent hamlet Ihala Madagama.

An interesting conclusion can be drawn from the above table, particularly from the old register. There was a mass desire to get registered and group registration was practised, not only in Pahala Madagama but also in Ihala Madagama and probably in the whole of Hinidum Pattu. Furthermore, both Ihala and Pahala folk had their marriages registered on the same day, as the following classification of marriages of the old register indicates. Thus it is

Table 2. *Thombo marriages*

Date	No. of marriages	
	Pahala Madagama	Ihala Madagama
11 December 1848	2	2
18 December 1848	1	4
23 January 1863	0	2
26 January 1863	1	1
29 August 1863	2	0

obvious that in the years 1848 and 1863 and after, the villagers of Madagama were taking crucial decisions regarding registrations; so that in generations FA^3 and FA^4 in the charts there are only two members of the line of whose 'marriages' we have no record.

The major difficulty in dating the actual founding of the village is the obvious discrepancy between marriage and the registration of the marriage. We have to calculate roughly the date of the actual marriage from the registers. In order to do this we assume that the discrepancy would decrease as we descend the generation series. Assuming that individuals in the new registers could guess their ages accurately and that their actual marriages and registration would be roughly coincident, we could compute an average age of marriages for those in generations FA^4 and FA^5. This average is 28·5 years approximately. Assuming again that people in the earlier generations would have married younger we deduct 2·5 years from the average, which leaves us with 26 years as a rough, but conservative average for working purposes.

If we are certain of the identifications of individuals in generation FA^5, and if we could pick out the eldest born child in each branch, our task would be relatively easy. But we cannot be certain of the latter, and hence we have to use cruder methods. We shall assume that P. M. G. Adonis, the eldest son in generation FA^4 of branch *B*, in fact married in 1848, the same year as the registration of the marriage. In making such a decision we can err only on the conservative side, for the only possibility is that the actual marriage would be earlier, and not later than the date of registration. On this basis P. M. G. Adonis' father Balappuve alias Baron would have married in 1821. His own father the head of branch *B* would have married sometime *before* 1794, since we know that Balappuve was not the eldest in the family. Taking 1794 as a conservative date for the marriage of the founder of branch *B*, the founder of the whole *vāsagama* would have married before 1767 (if the *vāsagama* was indeed founded by a single ancestor).

To move over to branch *U*. If P. M. G. Babappu was twenty-eight years in 1867, he would have been born in 1839. If he was the first born (for which we have no evidence) his father Upeappu or Uporis may have actually married about 1838, revealing a discrepancy of ten years between marriage and registration. Assuming that Upeappu was the first born (and here it is very unlikely since Upeappu was an only son, and there could conceivably have been older girls in the family), Upeappu's own father, the founder of branch *U*, would have been married *before* 1811. Thus according to our calculations the two sons of the founder of the *vāsagama* married sometime before 1794 and 1811, and the founder himself before 1767. The date of marriage is no accurate indication of the actual founding of the village. Assuming that the founding ancestor needed the help of grown up sons we may roughly estimate the founding of the village as 1790, a highly conservative estimate. The chances are that the village was founded much earlier.

According to the origin myth of the group, the hamlet was founded by the ancestor who was a chief (*bandāra*) who fled Sinhale (the Kandyan provinces) and lived in Mavanana, to escape punishment for a crime. From there he founded the hamlet of Pahala Madagama. While there is strong evidence that the founder was originally from Mavanana there is no evidence that he was a chief from Sinhale. The myth in this respect is typical of myths of lower status groups in a caste stratified society, where a common theme is that of a founder of aristocratic or royal birth who was considered *déclassé* owing to some heinous crime. Thus the untouchable Rodiyas believe that their caste was founded by Ratnawalli, a royal princess, outcaste for eating human flesh; or according to the ancestral myth of Rambadeniya (a village in the Central Province where we once worked) the village was founded by a prince who had cohabited with a Rodiya girl; and the origin myth of the Veddhas state that they spring from the union of the first Sinhalese King Vijaya and Kuveni, a demoness. The function of the myth is on the one hand to validate the low status of the group (the polluted or *déclassé* hero) and on the other to bolster the self-esteem of the group, by stressing the purity and grandiosity of its origins. For example, Rodiyas would proudly talk at length about their royal antecedents, so strikingly contrasted with their actual degradation. The myth of eating human flesh expresses not only their traditional sociological position as disposers of corpses but also their fantasies of oral rage against the world. The higher castes believe that the Rodiyas should be given anything they beg for, because a Rodiya's curse could result in sickness, harm or death to a person. Similarly in our hamlet, belonging to the middle range of independent cultivating *goigama* subcastes, the founding ancestor is a *déclassé* aristocrat, belonging originally to the upper range of *goigama* (*radala*) subcastes. Our villagers too insist on the purity of their origins. A major goal of status striving in the villages in the area is to achieve some of the highly cathected goals of the traditional feudal aristocracy, typically, as we shall show later, not through subcaste mobility, but by enhancing the 'status honour' of the family. Thus the idea of aristocratic origins has psychological relevance for contemporary Madagama, for upwardly mobile individuals have as a major goal retrieving the lost purity and prestige of the line.

Irrespective of the fictional or non-fictional character of the aristocratic antecedents of the founding ancestor, there is some evidence that the early ancestors of the group were from Mavanana, an adjacent village, within easy walking distance from our hamlet. Even today Madagama villages have close consanguineal and affinal kin ties with Mavanana folk. Madagama villagers are *dayakayas* (congregation) of the Mavanana temple, which they, together with Mavanana folk, were instrumental in building. We also know that P. M. G. Odiris, who, though owning shares in

Pahala Madagama and a member of its *vāsagama*, resided in Mavanana. It was his son P. M. G. Abaran who actually decided to reside in Pahala Madagama. We also know that two sons of P. M. G. Adonis of branch *B* inherited their father's *pravēni* shares in Mavanana, while the youngest son Nikulas inherited alone the Pahala Madagama *pangu*. A girl, P. M. G. Dano, whom we guessed to be a sister of P. M. G. Odiris, got married in 1863, and the *thombo* includes her residence as Mavanana. The evidence strongly suggests that:

(*a*) some of the ancestors of the group actually resided in Mavanana;

(*b*) some of them had *pravēni* rights in Mavanana.

There is some further evidence for the latter. There is a stretch of paddy land in Mavanana which is today called the Pahala Madagama field. Several members of our hamlet have *pravēni* rights in this field, which they vaguely state belonged to their ancestor (*mutta*). The Grain Tax register of 1882, available in the record room of the Galle Kachcheri, also shows that several Pahala Madagama folk owned paddy lands in Mavanana. The evidence is strong that the hamlet was founded by people who were originally residents of the village of Mavanana.

THE DIACHRONIC DEVOLUTION OF SHARES

As we have already seen the village was 'owned' by a single founding ancestor who had two sons, Babappu (branch *B*) and Mathes (branch *U*), who each owned half of the village. The following account will describe the devolution of the inheritance of these two ancestors among their respective descendants through a systematic examination of the genealogy (*pelapata*) of the two branches. How did the original half shares belonging to each ancestor devolve on their descendants down to the present day? We shall first examine the fate of branch *B* in diachronic perspective.

BRANCH 'B'

Babappu as we have seen had three sons, Lokuappuve, Balappuve and Dingi Appu, each having one-sixth share of the Pahala Madagama estate. Lokuappuve, however, 'lived with' Balappuve and thus jointly Lokuappuve-Balappuve owned two-sixths of the *gama* while Dingi Appu owned only one-sixth.

THE INHERITANCE OF LOKUAPPUVE-BALAPPUVE

The sibling pair, Lokuappuve-Balappuve, had three sons and one daughter. Adonis, Juan Appu, Odiris were the sons in order of birth. None of my informants remember the name of the daughter: they only know that she married virilocally (*dīga*) to a man from the village of Udugama, about fifteen miles away. There are 'no connexions' (*kisi sambandayak nä*) between Pahala Madagama folk and the offspring of this woman and their descendants. This female was not given any of the ancestral property according to informants, whereas each son had equal shares of $\frac{1}{9}$ *pravēni* from their 'father'.

P. M. G. Adonis, $\frac{1}{9}$ share

Adonis Appu had three sons Odan, Odanis and Nikulas and two daughters. He gave his share of the Pahala Madagama *pravēni* to Nikulas, a carpenter; the other sons were excluded. Instead they inherited property their father possessed in the village of Mavanana. The girls did not inherit *pravēni* rights at all.

Nikulas who inherited $\frac{1}{9}$ share, married a wealthy heiress from Ambelegedera village and settled down uxorilocally. He had two sons and two daughters, residents of Ambelegedera, to whom he transferred *inter vivos* his share in October 1916. The government record reads: 'Transfer of planter's undivided half-share of Ambagaswatte madde-watte in extent one acre and undivided $\frac{1}{6}$ of the remaining trees and of soil share trees and of soil of the above'.

The cryptic and enigmatic language of the land registry department requires some elucidation. Note that Nikulas is claiming $\frac{1}{6}$ of the *gama* as his share when in fact he is only entitled to $\frac{1}{9}$—the reason for such enhanced claims will be stated later on in our analysis. Nikulas had planted fruit trees in a half-acre plot of *goḍa iḍam* named *ambagaswatte madde watte* (literally the garden in the middle of the garden named 'mango garden'). In the transfer he is not only specifying his share of *pravēni* but also specifying the area of garden land he would expect his descendants to enjoy. 'Soil share trees' are those trees planted by an ancestor to which Nikulas has rights; also those trees that grow wild or naturally on the soil and belong to all. Thus if there was a jak tree that existed in the *goḍa iḍam* from the time of the founding of the village, Nikulas would have $\frac{1}{9}$ (or according to his claims, $\frac{1}{6}$) share of the produce of that tree. 'One-sixth...of soil of the above' refers to his *pravēni* rights in the total estate. *On the very day this transfer was made*, the same property was mortgaged by Nikulas' sons and daughters (and the husbands of the daughters) jointly to P. M. G. Semaris of Miguntenna, a patrilateral kinsman from branch *U* for Rs. 100. What is the significance of this curious deal? Nikulas had wanted some cash urgently and had made plans to sell his share of the *gama*. His children dissuaded him from this course of action which would result in the loss of their patrimony. They persuaded Nikulas to transfer his rights to them, and they raised the cash required by Nikulas by mortgaging the property to P. M. G. Semaris, 'with right of possession in lieu of interest'. The mortgage bond was discharged in 1925.

In December 1926 one of Nikulas' daughters, P. M. G. Karlina (together with her husband), living in the government colony at Tinnewala transferred her share of $\frac{1}{36}$ (which she claimed as $\frac{1}{24}$) to her daughter P. M. G. Podi Nona and her son-in-law as a gift, subject to the grantor's 'life interest' (*prāna buttiya*). Since none of these shareholders are residents of the hamlet, they have given out their shares of the property to Pahala Madagama residents on a share-cropping (*andē*) basis or on lease.

P. M. G. Juan Appu, $\frac{1}{9}$ share

P. M. G. Juan Appu had three sons and one daughter and lived at Madagama. As usual the daughter did not get any *pravēni* share, her name and whereabouts are 'not known' and 'no connexions' are maintained with her descendants. These three sons, Agoris, Juanis and Karo Appu, inherited each equally $\frac{1}{27}$ of the *pravēni*.

P. M. G. Agoris, $\frac{1}{27}$ share

Agoris had two sons and one daughter, P. M. G. Singho Appu, P. M. G. Theris and P. M. G. Hinni Hamy. In this generation (FA^6) women get to share equally with the men and hence each child gets $\frac{1}{81}$ share of the *pravēni*. Hinni Hamy who married *dīga* to Talangalle sold her $\frac{1}{81}$ share to Korale Hevage Karu Hamy, a 'new speculator in shares' for Rs. 40 in spite of the fact that her brother wanted to buy it himself. This caused a severance of relationship between them. This share is worked by Karu's sons, Karunadasa and Andreas. The transaction is not recorded in the government register of deeds. Singho Appu sold his $\frac{1}{81}$ share to D. L. S. Weerawardene, Registrar of Marriages of Neluva, for Rs. 200 since he wanted the money urgently for litigation. However, he sold only his paddy shares. He had hoped to buy it back, but Weerawardene refused to sell. This transaction is also not recorded in the government register. Theris, married to Godapita Gamage Sisily Hamy, lives in Pahala Madagama. Theris has eight children ranging from ages thirty to three. His share is worked by his eldest son, Ariyapala (age 26).

P. M. G. Juanis, $\frac{1}{27}$ share

Juanis married a woman in *binna* (1915) from Korelegama and resided uxorilocally; he sold his share to two speculators:

(1) $\frac{1}{54}$ to Korale Hevage Karu Hamy, mentioned earlier;

(2) $\frac{1}{54}$ to Vanniacchi Kankanage Somaris.

There are no official records of these transactions. However, the property was enjoyed by these two people and their heirs. On 25 November 1957, Somaris transferred his $\frac{1}{54}$ share to his daughter Somawati of Mavanana (as part of her dowry). Karu Hamy died intestate and his six heirs, Somapala, Karunadasa, Andreas, Piyasena, Lilawati and Jinadasa, own through this inheritance $\frac{1}{324}$ share each of the *gama*.

P. M. G. Karo Appu, $\frac{1}{27}$ share

Karo Appu married from Udugama and resided uxorilocally, and like his brother sold half of his ancestral property to two persons, on 20 September 1910.

(1) $\frac{1}{2}$ of $\frac{1}{54}$ of his share to Edirisinghe Andiris, a newcomer to the village of Madagama, who thus owned $\frac{1}{108}$ share of the village. This is now 'enjoyed' by Edirisinghe's widow and worked by the youngest son, Edirisinghe Sumanapala.

(2) $\frac{1}{2}$ to P. M. G. Podi Singho of Pahala Madagama, an 'adopted' member of the *vāsagama* (branch *U*).

On 18 August 1926 Karo mortgaged the remaining $\frac{1}{54}$ share to P. M. G. Podi Singho, to whom he had sold $\frac{1}{108}$ in 1910. Government records state: 'Mortgage of undivided $\frac{1}{6}$ share of soil and trees of Ambagahawatte in extent five acres, and undivided $\frac{1}{54}$ of the remaining soil share trees of the above for Rs. 50 with right of possession in lieu thereof'. This was later 'bought' by P. M. G. Podi Singho though no government record of this transaction exists. Thus $\frac{1}{27}$ share of Karo devolved on Podi Singho who owned $\frac{3}{108}$ and E. Andiris, $\frac{1}{108}$. On 4 April 1961 Podi Singho transferred '$\frac{1}{2}$ of $\frac{1}{54}$ + $\frac{1}{2}$ of $\frac{1}{36}$ parts of the soil, trees of the above', that is, the *gama*, to his youngest son David.

P. M. G. Odiris, $\frac{1}{9}$ share

Odiris, who owned $\frac{1}{9}$ of the *gama* and lived in Mavanana, married twice: once from Banagala, and on the death of his first wife he married from Neluva in 1902. From his first marriage he had two children, Abaran, a male, and Kalingu Hamy, who married from Kalubovitiyana. From his second marriage he had one son, Diyonis, and several females. As usual with this generation level, daughters did not inherit *pravēni* and the patrimonial estate was split equally between the two half-brothers, each having $\frac{1}{18}$ share of the *gama*. Abaran had two daughters and two sons, P. M. G. John and P. M. G. Uruveris, both alive. The latter sold his share of $\frac{1}{36}$ to Epa Seneviratne, a shopkeeper. However, he only sold his paddy land. One daughter married *dīga* from Tavalama, and had one son. The males have 'no connexion' with this sister and her husband, who are now both dead, and their sons, regarding whose whereabouts the maternal uncles professed 'ignorance'. At first this seemed quite strange to the anthropologist since Tavalama is only a few miles from Madagama. Still more strange when we consider that John maintains contact with his other sister married *dīga* at Panangala, which is about twelve miles away, and even acknowledges formal recognition to the descendants of his father's sisters' children married into 'distant' villages. In any case the females did not get any *pravēni* property, which devolved on the two sons who thus had $\frac{1}{36}$ each. If Abaran did not 'give' *pravēni* shares to his daughters, this certainly was not the case with his half-brother Diyonis whose two children, a male, Derenis, and a female, P. M. G. Podi Nona, inherited equally $\frac{1}{36}$ share each of the *pravēni*. In fact, however, Derenis enjoys his sister's share of the property too. The reason given is that the share was mortgaged by the father and he, Derenis, redeemed it. The facts of the case are as follows: On 17 January 1917 Diyonis mortgaged his share of *pravēni* to Senanayake Dasilige Theris, a speculator from Mavanana, for Rs. 30. On 24 March 1919 he mortgaged the same property to Edirisinghe Samel Appu of Ambelegedera for Rs. 35, and on 14 July 1923 to Senanayake Dasilige Theris for Rs. 50. No official records are available regarding the redemption of the mortgages by Diyonis. On 23 December 1933 S. D. Theris 'assigned' the mortgage to Mavanana Hettige Appu Singho of Mavanana for Rs. 50. On 17 December 1957 Derenis, son of Diyonis, redeemed the mortgage from Appu Singho for Rs. 50. Thus Derenis either works the $\frac{1}{18}$ share himself or gives it on lease.

INHERITANCE OF DINGI APPU, $\frac{1}{6}$ PRAVĒNI SHARE

Dingi Appu owned one-sixth of the Pahala Madagama *pravēni*. He had two daughters, Loku Hamy and Baru Hamy, who, in the absence of sons, each inherited $\frac{1}{12}$ of the patrimonial property. Loku Hamy married *dīga* in 1875 and lived with her husband at Batuwangala. Her share was bought jointly by Abaran and his wife's brother (*massinā*), Don Davith of Batuwangala (there is a deed for this transaction according to Abaran's son John). Thus Abaran owned $\frac{1}{24}$ and Don Davith $\frac{1}{24}$ of Pahala Madagama *pravēni*. Don Davith's share devolved upon his sons and daughters, who had no use for this share; so they sold it to their father's sister's son's sons (Piyasena and Ariyasena), that is, sons of their cross-cousin John. The money was provided by the mother (John's wife), but John the father is 'manager' of this share too. The share of $\frac{1}{24}$, bought by Abaran, devolved on John and his brother Uruveris. The latter sold his portion of $\frac{1}{48}$ to Epa Seneviratne, a boutique owner from Neluva.

Dingi Appu's second daughter married Vanasinge Adiriyan of Banagala and lived virilocally. She, however, died childless and her husband remarried a woman from Mapalagama. There were three children by this marriage, two sons, Emanis and Lairis, and a daughter. Thus theoretically each person here stood to inherit $\frac{1}{3}$ of $\frac{1}{12}$, that is, $\frac{1}{36}$ share of Madagama *pravēni*. But the woman's share was 'ignored'. Vanasinge Adiriyan, in November 1914, sold his share of paddy land (and half of the garden he had planted) to his two sons Vanasinge Lairis and Vanasinge Emanis, and the daughter's prospective share to a speculator who had previous interests in the hamlet, Kariyavasam Godage Arnolis de Silva of the neighbouring village Mavanana, for a 'consideration' of Rs. 100. It is interesting to note here that it is not as if the daughter was not legally entitled to inherit: her prospective share was 'put aside' and sold to an outsider, giving covert recognition to her prospective rights in the estate. Thus each person had $\frac{1}{36}$ *pravēni* right to paddy land.

Vanasinge Emanis (married *binna* in 1904 to Ihala Madagama Gamage Duli Hamy) mortgaged his share to another wealthy speculator, Panangala Liyanage Peter from neighbouring Lelwala village, for Rs. 55 in July 1921; in July 1923 he sold this share outright to the same person for Rs. 100. On 17 September 1946 P. L. Peter transferred this share to his son-in-law Senanayake Dasilige Boris of Mavanana, but the records 'mistakenly' put the share as $\frac{1}{32}$ (rather than $\frac{1}{36}$). The sociology of these mistakes will be made clear in the analysis. The other son Vanasinge Lairis mortgaged his share in December 1921 to Senanayake Dasilige Pitchoris of Mavanana (a close *vāsagama* kinsman of Senanayake Dasilige Theris) and to the speculator mentioned earlier, Panangala Liyanage Peter. In August 1931 the share was mortgaged to a man from Lelwala (Don Samel Madarasinghe Siriwardene); in September 1950 the offspring of Lairis (two females and a male) sold their $\frac{1}{36}$ share to Madarasinghe Aron of Mavanana. Note that Lairis' heirs did not sell their property to P. L. Peter or S. D. Pitchoris—for now there is competition among speculators.

BRANCH 'U'

The Founding Ancestor's second son's son Upeappu, who 'owned' half of the Pahala Madagama *gama*, had four sons, Babappu, Elias, Hin Hamy, and Adiriyan, and several daughters who did not inherit *pravēni* and thus as usual fade out of the picture. Each 'son' inherited $\frac{1}{8}$ of the *gama* on the death of the father.

P. M. G. ADIRIYAN, $\frac{1}{8}$ OF GAMA

On 2 June 1888 the government records read that Pahala Madagama Gamage Adiriyan sold his share to Kariyawasam Godage Arnolis de Silva of Mavanana for Rs. 80. 'Transfer of $\frac{1}{8}$ of high and low ground of the above property together with the wattled tile house of 9 cubits standing thereon.' A few years later Adiriyan's second son, James, earned enough money to buy back the land for his father. Government records do not mention this transaction, though none of my informants had the slightest doubt that it did take place. It certainly *must* have taken place for a government entry of 3 June 1901, three years later, reads that P. M. G. Adiriyan has transferred his share of $\frac{1}{8}$ to seven of his children, including both females and males. But the persons selected were quite interesting. P. M. G. Adiriyan married twice. From his second marriage in 1895 he had two females, Wimala Hamy and Dingiri Hamy. In his deed of transfer he excluded the female from his first marriage, but included the only children, two females, from his second. Thus his action is analogous to Dingi Appu's in branch *B* of the earlier generation, who 'gave' his property to his two daughters in the absence of male heirs—in Adiriyan's case, in the absence of male heirs from his second marriage. Such a position would be totally consonant with traditional rules of inheritance which state that in the absence of male heirs from any marriage, females inherit. However, in this instance, the division of property was *per capita* rather than the traditional division *per stirpes*. In appreciation of the fact that his second son was instrumental in buying back the patrimonial inheritance, Adiriyan transferred one-half of his $\frac{1}{8}$ share to James, and the rest equally among the males from his first marriage—Anada Hamy alias Andiris, Owinis, Semaris and Appu Singho—and the females Wimala Hamy and Dingiri Hamy from the second. Thus, James had $\frac{1}{16}$ share of the estate while the rest had $\frac{1}{96}$ each.[1]

P. M. G. James, $\frac{1}{16}$ share

P. M. G. James mortgaged his share of $\frac{1}{16}$ with right of possession in lieu of interest to his brother P. M. G. Semaris of Miguntenne on 10 December 1916. On 15 November 1922 P. M. G. Semaris in turn mortgaged this same property, which he does not own, to a speculator Don James Rubasin Gunawardene of neighbouring Lelwala—explicitly excluding his own share ($\frac{1}{96}$) of the *pravēni*. P. M. G. James in turn mortgaged $\frac{1}{32}$, that is, half of his *pravēni* right for Rs. 40 to Senanayake Dasilige Pitchoris of Mavanana on 23 July 1923, and again in 1929 this same portion was mortgaged to the same man. On 8 August 1942 Dasilige Boris assigned the James mortgage of 1929 to his cousin Dasilige Sumanapala. On 15 June 1944 James discharged the mortgage from Sumanapala. (On 13 December 1943 James mortgaged $\frac{1}{32}$ share to his son P. M. G. Francis Appuhamy for Rs. 50.) In 1954 James died at the age of 78 and his share of $\frac{1}{16}$ devolved on seven children who each inherited $\frac{1}{112}$ share of *pravēni*.

P. M. G. Hovis, $\frac{1}{112}$; *P. M. G. Baby Nona*, $\frac{1}{112}$; *P. M. G. Francis*, $\frac{1}{112}$; *P. M. G. Eddin*, $\frac{1}{112}$

These several shares were cultivated by Hovis, since P. M. G. Francis and Eddin work in Colombo and live there permanently, and Baby Nona is married to a worker in the Colombo Railway workshop and lives in Ratmalana, a suburb of Colombo. In March 1959 Hovis persuaded his siblings, Baby Nona, P. M. G. Francis and P. M. G. Eddin, to sell their shares with his own to Senanayake Dasilige Sumanapala. The shares sold to Sumanapala amounted to $\frac{4}{96}$ according to the deed of transfer, but in fact what was effectively transferred was probably these four shares of $\frac{1}{112}$ each.

P. M. G. Podi Nona, $\frac{1}{112}$ *share*

Podi Nona married a classificatory cross-cousin Godapita Gamage Diyonis from the adjacent village Mavanana, and lived uxorilocally with her husband. However, 'uxorilocality' has not the conventional structural significance of *binna*, because Podi Nona's *goḍa iḍam* is located on the boundary of her husband's village, Mavanana. Uxorilocality permits her husband to make use of his wife's property, on which they have built a house, and also control his own patrimonial land a few hundred yards away in Mavanana. This action led to antagonism between G. G. Diyonis and his brother-in-law Hovis, so that there was a severance in kin relationships.

P. M. G. Seetin, $\frac{1}{112}$ *share*

Seetin lives in government *badu iḍam* in nearby Neluva and cultivates his own land at Pahala Madagama. He periodically enjoys his brother P. M. G. Jinadasa's share of $\frac{1}{112}$. Jinadasa ($\frac{1}{112}$) works in the Colombo harbour and lives permanently in Colombo.

P. M. G. Owinis, $\frac{1}{96}$ *share*

Owinis married a woman from Gonagala and lived there uxorilocally. He has no interest in Madagama, since he has a comfortable income at Gonagala. James' son Hovis claims to have bought this share—probably a 'lie', as there is no evidence for this transaction.

P. M. G. Appu Singho, $\frac{1}{96}$ *share*

Appu Singho married from Opata and lived there uxorilocally. On 20 December 1953 he mortgaged his share to P. M. G. Gunadasa, a classificatory parallel cousin for Rs. 50. The statement in the government records is interesting: 'Mortgage of the *right title claim* and demand in and to the above for Rs. 50 with right to possess in lieu thereof.' This share of $\frac{1}{96}$ was bought by Hovis, without the knowledge of Gunadasa, from Appu Singho's widow and children.

P. M. G. Semaris, $\frac{1}{96}$ *share*

Semaris married *binna* from Miguntenna in 1903 and now belongs to a respected family owning plumbago mines in the village. Hovis, his classificatory 'son', proclaims to the villagers that he has bought this share and indeed enjoys it—but Hovis denies this when interviewed. He says that Semaris owns and enjoys it. The actual position is that Semaris owns the share, but P. M. G. Seetin, Hovis' brother, enjoys it, since the former is not interested in actually working a small share. Hovis has to proclaim that he has bought it, to prevent others buying it.

P. M. G. Andiris, $\frac{1}{96}$ *share*

P. M. G. Andiris married from Porevegama and had three daughters—Sumana, Katrina and another daughter, and one son, Pediris Singho who all inherited intestate $\frac{1}{384}$ *pravēni* share. Sumana married Korala Hevage Munis from Halvitigala, who resided in the wife's village. They had one son Sirisena; soon afterwards the husband deserted her. Sumana then had two 'illegitimate' children, K. H. Piyadasa and K. H. William Singho. Pediris Singho married and settled in Pahala Madagama, but on his death the family scattered no one knows where. Katrina ($\frac{1}{384}$)

married at Mavita and her sister ($\frac{1}{384}$) from Habarakade. None of them are interested in the paddy land, but periodically visit the village to pick a few coconuts and jak fruit. Effectively Andiris' $\frac{1}{96}$ paddy share is worked by the sons of Sumana who reside in the village, and work the land on a *karamāru* basis. Sirisena, Sumana's eldest son, married a classificatory cross-cousin, P. M. G. Nandiris' daughter; but Sirisena died a few years ago by falling from a coconut tree during a *gam maḍuve* (religious) festival—this 'share' is worked by his father-in-law Nandiris. Nandiris wanted to get his daughter remarried to Piyadasa, Sirisena's brother, leviratically, but the former was not willing. Some controversy whether Nandiris has a 'right' to work Sirisena's share exists but no one contests either the legality or morality of the case. In any case Nandiris is an influential man who could have his way in this instance.

The children of Adiriyan by his second marriage

Dingiri Hamy, $\frac{1}{96}$ share. The case of Dingiri Hamy is a sad one and illustrative of another social trend in villages—the export of women as 'servants' and prostitutes. Adiriyan's son James took her out of the village as a servant to Colombo—her fate was the fate of thousands of other women in overcrowded villages. As far as the hamlet was concerned she 'died' and her share devolved on her sister Wimala Hamy. Once again, no one was sure what the custom was, though both Hovis and Wimala Hamy's son, Don William, admitted that the property should devolve on all the children of Adiriyan equally.

Wimala Hamy, $\frac{1}{96}$ share. Wimala Hamy married her father's brother's wife's brother's son—a classificatory cross-cousin, Kankanan Gamage Siyadoris in 1907. Siyadoris is dead but Wimala Hamy is alive. She has two sons and two daughters; the property is managed by her eldest son K. G. Don William. But both Don William and Wimala Hamy are agreed that the mother's property should ultimately devolve on the four children equally.

BABAPPU, $\frac{1}{8}$ OF GAMA

Babappu, another son of Upeappu Gamarala, married Kankanan Gamage Baba Hamy from Panagoda. For some reason or other, Babappu wrote his share to his wife's brother K. G. Adris Hamy, probably in the 1880's. After Babappu's death, K. G. Adris Hamy transferred the *pravēni* share for a 'consideration of Rs. 100' to the following, on 1 August 1914.

(1) Kankanan Gamage Anohamy (or Babahamy)—Babappu's wife and Adris' sister.

(2) P. M. G. Girigoris—son of deceased.

(3) P. M. G. Elaris—son of deceased.

(4) P. M. G. Nonno—daughter of deceased.

(5) Kankanan Gamage Andoris of Panagoda.

Each obtained $\frac{1}{40}$ share of *pravēni*. The last named was a son of Adris, who was a religious recluse (*upasaka*) and died childless—his share of $\frac{1}{40}$ devolved once again on Adris, his father.

Kankanan Gamage Adris, $\frac{1}{40}$ *share*

On 26 October 1916 K. G. Adris transferred $\frac{1}{80}$ share of the *gama* to his son K. G. Siyadoris. For the first time the deed of transfer is executed in an unusual manner—the share in paddy land is clearly separated from the share in high lands. Thus two deeds were written for Siyadoris—one specifying one-eightieth share in paddy land and the other an eightieth in high land.

On 26 February 1919 K. G. Siyadoris mortgaged this share to his cross-cousin P. M. G. Girigoris with 'right of possession in lieu of interest'. On 5 May 1924 Siyadoris transferred this share permanently to Girigoris for Rs. 60. In September 1926 P. M. G. Girigoris sold this $\frac{1}{80}$ share to Senanayake Dasilige Pitchoris, a speculator mentioned in earlier transactions. Siyadoris meanwhile owned three shares of $\frac{1}{80}$ each which he had bought from P. M. G. Nonno. Siyadoris was getting old and before he died he transferred these shares (September 1952) to the following: his favourite daughter Kankanan Gamage Podi Nona $\frac{1}{80}$, his son K. G. Don William, $\frac{1}{80}$. On 12 September 1954 he transferred $\frac{1}{80}$ to his third child K. G. Podi Hamy, wife of P. M. G. Gunadasa. There is still $\frac{1}{80}$ share coming from Adris which remains. Legally, according to contemporary bilateral inheritance it should devolve on all Siyadoris' siblings, but in fact it is diffused among Siyadoris' three children living in the village, and is actually enjoyed by Don William, Siyadoris' son.

P. M. G. Elaris, $\frac{1}{40}$ share

This is the most controversial share among the descendants of Babappu. According to K. G. Don William, this $\frac{1}{40}$ share was bought by E. W. Thevonis of Neluva, father-in-law of I. M. G. Kartelis, a village leader of Madagama, and by Senanayake Dasilige Ernolis. The transaction is not included in government records. According to P. M. G. Hovis, who has another version, the story is as follows: Elaris married from Tavalama (25 December 1901) and lived in Madagama. The wife died childless and he remarried from Mavita, but the woman deserted him. Later on Elaris 'married' a woman from Talangalla and had a son P. M. G. Arnolis. Soon after Elaris died the rest of the family went back to Talangalla. The crux of the question was to whom was Elaris *legally* married—according to Thevonis and Ernolis, to his second wife who deserted the husband. So they bought the $\frac{1}{40}$ share from her. According to Hovis, the second marriage was not registered and the 'legal owners' are the offspring of the third 'wife'. So he got a deed from Elaris' son at Talangalla, P. M. G. Arnolis, for the astonishingly low price of Rs. 50 on 2 November 1957 for $\frac{1}{40}$ and $\frac{1}{120}$ shares of *pravēni*. Note: (*a*) that the land was effectively owned and operated by E. W. Thevonis and S. D. Ernolis, but Hovis was banking on a partition suit in the future; (*b*) Hovis took no chances; he persuaded P. M. G. Arnolis to give him $\frac{1}{40}$ share owned by Elaris and also a $\frac{1}{120}$ share. What was this? Remember that Elaris' mother had also been given $\frac{1}{40}$ share by Adris and this was claimed by Nonno. Hovis was smart enough to take a chance that this was not given on a deed to Nonno—in which case theoretically the share would devolve through intestate sucession to her three children, Elaris, Girigoris and Nonno who would have $\frac{1}{120}$ each. This was the share he was after. He transferred this controversial share of $\frac{1}{120}$ to Hettigamage Jinasoma, his mother's eldest brother's son on 17 September 1959 and mortgaged the $\frac{1}{40}$ share to Panangala Liyanage Upalis in 1960 for Rs. 100 'to deliver $\frac{1}{2}$ bag paddy in lieu of interest at 12% per annum'. The only evidence we have about Elaris' marriage is that he married *dīga* in 1910 to a woman from Mavita. Thus Hovis' speculation must ultimately come to nothing.

P. M. G. Nonno, $\frac{1}{40}$ share of gama

Nonno married virilocally and had little interest in Pahala Madagama *pravēni*. She owned $\frac{1}{40}$ of the *gama* and her mother 'gave her' the latter's share of $\frac{1}{40}$ before dying—or so it is said for there is no legal evidence for the $\frac{1}{40}$ share transaction.

On 5 June 1926 Nonno mortgaged $\frac{3}{80}$ share to Panangala Liyanage Uporis. The entry reads as follows: 'Mortgage of undivided $\frac{3}{80}$ share of the above with undivided $\frac{1}{8}$ of half of the planter's share of the plantation made on undivided Ihalagederawatte by P. M. G. Elaris for Rs. 50 with right of possession in lieu of interest at 18% per annum.' We fail to understand yet why Nonno should be entitled to $\frac{1}{8}$ of Elaris' share—probably this was included at the suggestion of P. L. Uporis, as an act of speculation. In any case, on 28 July 1942 Wimala Hamy, wife of Siyadoris, got the mortgage assigned to her for Rs. 50, and became effective owner of the shares. On 17 July 1943 Nonno transferred the $\frac{3}{80}$ shares to Siyadoris for Rs. 70.

Note that Nonno still has $\frac{1}{80}$ share, entitling her to citizenship claims at Pahala Madagama. For all intents and purposes the effective owner of this share too is Siyadoris' son, Don William.

P. M. G. Girigoris, $\frac{1}{40}$ share of gama

Another highly controversial share. Girigoris owned $\frac{1}{40}$ of the *gama*. (Later on in 1926 he bought $\frac{1}{80}$ from K. G. Siyadoris, his cross-cousin. This gave him three shares of $\frac{1}{80}$.) He was married three times. His first wife from Porevegama died childless; he had two daughters from the second marriage who married virilocally. From his third marriage he had seven children, four sons and three daughters. The sons do not refer to the two daughters from the second marriage; as far as a public façade of appearances are concerned they do not 'exist'. Girigoris mortgaged his $\frac{1}{40}$ in 1926 to Senanayake Dasilige Boris. He died soon afterwards. According to his eldest son Gunadasa his father gave him on a deed $\frac{1}{80}$ share, though there is no legal or documentary evidence for this. The rest of the family got the remaining share, equally, entitling each individual to $\frac{1}{480}$ share. These shares, says P. M. G. Gunadasa, are of no use to his siblings, so he enjoys them, since he resides in the village.

Gunadasa's marriage with his classificatory cross-cousin was a strategic merger for his wife stood to own $\frac{1}{80}$ of *pravēni* too. Girigoris' son Gnanadasa gave a slightly different but erroneous version. According to him Girigoris owned $\frac{1}{64}$ of the village. He sold half of this to an outsider (whose name he does not know) and the remainder to be divided among seven, that is, $\frac{1}{128} \div 7$. He says all this is worked by P. M. G. Gunadasa, who won't give even a 'cent' to him. However, he, as well as his sister, own *koraṭu* (enclosures) in the high land. However, Gnanadasa's evidence is unreliable for in spite of his name which means 'brainy', he is practically an idiot.

On 18 February 1946 Gunadasa made an 'unusual' transaction with one of his half-sisters, P. M. G. Pelensina, married virilocally, and otherwise 'forgotten'. Pelensina transferred 'her share'—which Gunadasa would deny she owned anyway—of both high and low land to him. The government register reads: transfer of undivided $\frac{1}{2}$ of $\frac{1}{2}$ of $\frac{1}{5}$ of $\frac{1}{8}$ or $\frac{1}{160}$ part of all the soil and soil share trees of the above, that is, the paddy lands. A separate deed was written for the high lands. What are Gunadasa's motives for buying shares from a woman whose patrimony, and indeed existence, he denies? Gunadasa imagines that the daughters of his father's second marriage are entitled through intestate succession to one-half of his father's *pravēni* rights on a division of his estate *per stirpes* rather than *per capita*. They would be entitled to $\frac{1}{2}$ (*per stirpes* division) of $\frac{1}{5}$ (the five people to whom Kankanan Gamage Adris wrote Babappu's estate in 1914, one of whom was P. M. G. Girigoris) of $\frac{1}{8}$ (the original share owned by P. M. G. Babappu and sold to K. G. Adris). Thus Pelensina, one of the daughters of Girigoris' second marriage, would be entitled to half of this. The whole involved arithmetic is faithfully recorded in the deed—thus Pelensina transfers $\frac{1}{2}$ of $\frac{1}{2}$ of $\frac{1}{5}$ of $\frac{1}{8}$ or $\frac{1}{160}$ share to her far-sighted half-brother P. M. G. Gunadasa! Once again one gets some insight into the mind of the village share speculator.

HIN HAMY, $\frac{1}{8}$ OF GAMA

Hin Hamy, one of the four sons of Upeappu, the founder of branch *U*, held $\frac{1}{8}$ of the *gama*. He married *dīga* a woman from Ihala Madagama (registered 1875). He quickly faded out of the picture for he sold his property and settled in distant Baddegama. One-sixteenth of his *pravēni* was sold by him to Panagala Liyanage Suaris in the 1880's. This share was given by P. L. Peter (Suaris' son) to his son-in-law Dasilige Boris. This share of $\frac{1}{16}$ is now worked by Piyadasa, a Pahala Madagama resident for *bin havula*. The other share of $\frac{1}{16}$ was sold to Habarakada Ihalamadde Opisara who was P. M. G. Agoris' (branch *B*) wife's mother's brother. This share was given by deed of gift to Laiso, Agoris' wife, by her uncle. Ultimately it devolved on Laiso's three children—P. M. G. Singho Appu, P. M. G. Theris, P. M. G. Hinni Hamy. They thus owned, in addition to their shares of $\frac{1}{81}$ in the *B* branch, $\frac{1}{48}$ share each of the *gama* from branch *U*. P. M. G. Hinni Hamy sold her share to K. H. Karu Hamy. P. M. G. Singho Appu sold the paddy share to D. L. S. Weerawardene. P. M. G. Theris' share is retained by him and enjoyed by his son P. M. G. Ariyapala.

ELIAS, $\frac{1}{8}$ OF GAMA

The case of Elias' inheritance is the most complicated of the shares and illustrates the anomie that prevails in respect of land tenure in Ceylon. There are several conflicting claims and overt antagonisms between the descendants of Elias; also a conflict in genealogies which illustrates the point to be developed later in our analysis, that in this type of system *a genealogy is a charter of rights*. It also illustrates, even more poignantly than the other cases in our hamlet, the conflict between indigenous and introduced legal norms—so that individuals act in terms of the system that is profitable in any given circumstance. Owing to the confusion and conflict that prevails among the claimants to their shares, what I shall do here is to give a straight genealogical description of the situation and state some of the legal complications involved.

Elias married Muttuhetti Gamage Hin Hamy in 1870 at the age of 28. From this marriage he had two sons, P. M. G. Jayaweera and Eranolis. Elias died probably about five years after his marriage. His widow remarried an outsider from a neighbouring village, Habarakada—the husband lived uxorilocally in Pahala Madagama. From this marriage there were three sons and a daughter, Vyanti Hamy. Present informants agree that only the first marriage was 'registered' and indeed government records confirm the first but no mention is made of the second. The children of both marriages were minors and grew up together. However, interestingly enough, the children of the second marriage did not adopt the *vāsagama* of the father, but of their mother's first husband—Pahala Madagama Gamage. The reason for this action, we guess, is that according to traditional Sinhalese law the offspring of a *binna* married man could take the mother's *vāsagama* and inherit her paternal property. The present marriage was not a *binna* type in the conventional sense though it may have been classified as *binna* by the villagers. The *Niti Niganduva* clearly recognizes this type of marriage as *binna*. When a woman's husband dies, says the *Niti Niganduva*, she could contract a *binna* marriage in the husband's premises with the consent of her late husband's relations, in order to care for his infant children. The marriage will not be vitiated as a result of her action and her children (by the first marriage) cannot refuse the mother suitable maintenance from their father's estate (*Niti Niganduva* 1880:31).

It is doubtful whether there was traditional precedence for such an action, for the *Niti Niganduva* is explicit that the widow who brings a man in *binna* to reside in her first husband's premises cannot transfer to the children of the second marriage the property which belonged to her dead husband (*Niti Niganduva* 1880:32). Moreover, according to the traditional law of Sabaragamuva, which we suggested applied to our village, a woman stood to inherit one-half of her husband's property on his death. She loses this if she contracted a *dīga* marriage—but we noted that the woman married *binna* the second time. One can be certain that the 'adoption' of Hin Hamy's children into the Pahala Madagama *vāsagama* was motivated by the mother's wish to give her children *pravēni* claims in the *gama*.

In any case, this did not work out satisfactorily, for the sons of Elias, on their maturity, assumed control of the estate of their father. The sons, P. M. G. Jayaweera and P. M. G. Eranolis, each controlled $\frac{1}{16}$ share. Of the two brothers, Eranolis resided uxorilocally at Panagoda and the effective ownership of the property devolved on his brother Jayaweera. It is interesting that present informants attribute the disinheritance of Hin Hamy's sons to the fact that the second marriage was not registered, and hence, they assume incorrectly, not legal. This is admitted by P. M. G. Podi Singho, one of Hin Hamy's sons, resident in the hamlet.

Then there arose a new complication. An outsider Kariyawasam Godage Nikulas, brother of K. G. Arnolis, speculator from

Gigummaduva, left his paternal village and opened up a boutique in Madagama. He wished to acquire hamlet citizenship and married Vyanti Hamy, the daughter of Hin Hamy's second marriage. Vyanti Hamy's stepbrother, Jayaweera, gave her half of his inheritance—that is, $\frac{1}{32}$ of the Madagama *pravēni*, as dowry. It is more likely that K. G. Nikulas, who was a wealthy boutique keeper, bought the share for his wife Vyanti Hamy—later transactions support this. In any case the government entry of 12 November 1904 reads that P. M. G. Jayaweera transferred to P. M. G. Vyanti Hamy the following: 'the planters half of the plantation planted by the grantor's father near Ibbagahawatte and $\frac{1}{8}$ of the soil and remaining trees of the above land'. Thus *in fact* he has sold not only his own share but also his brother's totalling $\frac{1}{8}$! He has sold his total *effective* ownership in Madagama.

Here is a problem: legally Jayaweera has transferred a share ($\frac{1}{8}$) of Pahala Madagma *pravēni* which in fact he does not 'legally' own; but effectively he has transferred only $\frac{1}{32}$, and continued to 'enjoy' a share of $\frac{1}{32}$, and also his brother's $\frac{1}{16}$, since the latter was not a resident of the hamlet.

Of the offspring of Hin Hamy's second marriage, the only persons remaining in the village were Vyanti Hamy, married to K. G. Nikulas, and P. M. G. Podi Singho, married to his cousin Muttuhetti Gamage Karlina, Podi Singho's mother's brother's daughter.

Vyanti Hamy and her husband K. G. Nikulas effectively owned only $\frac{1}{32}$ of the *pravēni*; on 29 March 1920 the two of them jointly transferred half of this ($\frac{1}{64}$) to their daughter K. G. Rancho Hamy. Meanwhile on 30 August 1918 the second son of Elias, who was residing uxorilocally in Panagoda mortgaged his share of $\frac{1}{16}$ to P. M. G. Podi Singho, his stepbrother, who thus became effective owner of $\frac{1}{16}$ share of the *gama*. On 4 February 1924 P. M. G. Jayaweera mortgaged his share of $\frac{1}{32}$ to P. L. Peter of Lelwala. On 17 September 1928 P. M. G. Eranolis mortgaged again his share of $\frac{1}{16}$ to P. M. G. Podi Singho and Senanayake Dasilige Nandoris of Mavanana.

Meanwhile other events had taken place. Vyanti Hamy had died —she had two daughters, K. G. Hin Hamy and K. G. Rancho. The younger girl Hin Hamy had married P. M. G. Nandiris (about 1925), her classificatory cross-cousin, her mother's stepbrother's (Jayaweera's) son. This created the alliance between the kinsmen of Hin Hamy's two marriages. Moreover, the marriage was a strategic one and could have resulted in the consolidation of property. We saw that Jayaweera transferred $\frac{1}{32}$ of his share to Vyanti Hamy. Vyanti had two daughters, who would inherit $\frac{1}{64}$ each plus anything else that the industrious K. G. Nikulas may buy. Thus through the marriage of Nandiris with K. G. Hin Hamy one-half of the share he had given to his sister would be brought back into Jayaweera's family through his son.

But things did not work out this way. We have seen that K. G. Nikulas and his wife Vyanti Hamy had already transferred $\frac{1}{64}$ to their eldest daughter Rancho Hamy. This was in 1920. Soon after her second daughter's marriage, Vyanti died and her husband Nikulas, now an old man, married H. K. Katrina Hamy, an attractive woman previously living in sororal polygyny with a man in an adjacent village. Meanwhile, Rancho had also died and her share of $\frac{1}{64}$ effectively devolved on her father, Nikulas. Ten years after his marriage with Katrina, Nikulas transferred to her as a gift $\frac{1}{32}$ share of high land (that is, the total amount of high land owned by his former wife and including the deceased Rancho's share, and the prospective share of his second daughter Hin Hamy), and $\frac{1}{64}$ of paddy land. It is very likely that the remaining $\frac{1}{64}$ of paddy land was reserved by him for his daughter Hin Hamy, but Nikulas died soon after, and this share too reverted to his wife Katrina. This was to create enduring bitterness between Katrina (and her son Amarapala) and Hin Hamy and her husband P. M. G. Nandiris.

Meanwhile Jayaweera had died intestate and the $\frac{1}{32}$ share he effectively owned devolved on three daughters who had married *dīga* and two sons, P. M. G. Nandiris living in Pahala Madagama, and P. M. G. Jainoris living on a *badu iḍam* in Lelwala. Thus, each person effectively should own $\frac{1}{160}$ of *pravēni*. A whole host of questions arise at this point:

(*a*) if indeed Jayaweera had legally sold his total share to Nikulas in 1904, there is nothing for his heirs legally to own intestate;

(*b*) alternatively, they could say since Jayaweera was in effective ownership of the land they were legally (prescriptively) entitled to it;

(*c*) let us assume that Jayaweera's heirs were legally entitled to $\frac{1}{32}$ of *pravēni*, each owning $\frac{1}{160}$. Nandiris' claims that his father gave the property to him exclusively, since he was the only one to live in the hamlet—his daughters received dowries and the other son had *badu iḍam* in Lelwala. This may well have been the case though no deed was given to Nandiris to this effect. But legal and moral rights have at this generation level been confused, so that those not morally entitled to land were using their legal rights for monetary gain.

On 23 January 1946 P. M. G. Eranolis, who had mortgaged his share earlier to P. M. G. Podi Singho, his maternal stepbrother, double-crossed the latter and sold his share outright to Ihala Madagama Gamage Nandoris and Ihala Madagama Gamage Kartelis of the adjacent hamlet for the handsome sum of Rs. 600, and political pressure. On 11 December 1950 P. M. G. Nandiris mortgaged $\frac{1}{32}$ which he legally does not certainly own, to Dasilige Boris of Mavanana; later he 'sold' this same share to D. L. S. Weerawardene of Neluva. Nandiris gave a deed to Weerawardene for this but the deed was never registered in the government files for the very good reason that Weerawardene knew it was legally invalid! But interestingly enough, D. L. S. Weerawardene is the effective owner of this share—which he has given to Nandiris once again on lease.

Let us sum up the state of affairs so far. Elias owned $\frac{1}{8}$ of the *gama*. His two sons inherited $\frac{1}{16}$ each. One of these shares owned by Eranolis was mortgaged to Podi Singho and later sold to I. M. G. Nandoris and I. M. G. Kartelis. The rest was owned by Jayaweera ($\frac{1}{16}$). Of this, $\frac{1}{32}$ went to Vyanti Hamy, who in conjunction with her husband gave $\frac{1}{64}$ to her daughter, Rancho. Rancho died and Nikulas gave the $\frac{1}{32}$ share to his second wife Katrina. The other share of $\frac{1}{32}$ devolved effectively on Jayaweera's son Nandiris, who sold it to D. L. S. Weerawardene.

SUMMARY OF DATA

Table 3. *Shareholders of branch B*

Generation	Name of shareholder	Pangu	Comment
FA[2]	P. M. G. Babappu (m)	$\frac{1}{2}$	Son of Founding Ancestor
	Total	$\frac{1}{2}$	
FA[3]	P. M. G. Dingi Appu (m)	$\frac{1}{6}$	—
	P. M. G. Lokuappuve (m) jointly with P. M. G. Balappuve (m)	$\frac{2}{6}$	—
	Total	$\frac{1}{2}$	
FA[4]	P. M. G. Loku Hamy (f)	$\frac{1}{12}$	Sold share to P. M. G. Abaran and his brother-in-law Don Davith
	P. M. G. Baru Hamy (f)	$\frac{1}{12}$	'Inherited' by husband Vanasinge Adiriyan, who sells to sons Lairis and Emanis and an outsider, K. G. Arnolis
	P. M. G. Adonis (m)	$\frac{1}{9}$	—
	P. M. G. Juan Appu (m)	$\frac{1}{9}$	—
	P. M. G. Odiris (m)	$\frac{1}{9}$	—
	Total	$\frac{1}{2}$	
FA[5]	P. M. G. Abaran (m)	$\frac{1}{24}$	—
	Don Davith (m)	$\frac{1}{24}$	Sold to P. M. G. John's wife. John, P. M. G. Abaran's son, is effective owner
	V. Lairis (m)	$\frac{1}{36}$	Sold to Madarasinghe Aron
	V. Emanis (m)	$\frac{1}{36}$	Sold to P. L. Peter

Generation	Name of shareholder	Pangu	Comment
	K. G. Arnolis (m)	$\frac{1}{36}$	—
	P. M. G. Nikulas (m)	$\frac{1}{9}$	—
	P. M. G. Agoris (m)	$\frac{1}{27}$	—
	P. M. G. Juanis (m)	$\frac{1}{27}$	Sold $\frac{1}{54}$ to K. H. Karu Hamy and $\frac{1}{54}$ to V. K. Somaris
	P. M. G. Karo (m)	$\frac{1}{27}$	Sold $\frac{1}{108}$ to E. Andiris and $\frac{3}{108}$ to P. M. G. Podi Singho of branch *U*
	P. M. G. Abaran (m)	$\frac{1}{18}$	—
	P. M. G. Diyonis (m)	$\frac{1}{18}$	—
	Total	$\frac{1}{2}$	
FA[6]	P. M. G. John's wife (f)	$\frac{1}{24}$	Bought on behalf of her two sons
	P. M. G. John (m)	$\frac{1}{48}$	—
	Epa Seneviratne (m)	$\frac{1}{48}$	Bought from P. M. G. Uruveris, Abaran's son
	Madarasinghe Aron (m)	$\frac{1}{36}$	—
	K. G. Arnolis' son Senaratne (m)	$\frac{1}{36}$	—
	P. L. Peter (m)	$\frac{1}{36}$	Transferred to S. D. Boris
	P. M. G. Karaneris (m)	$\frac{1}{36}$	—
	P. M. G. Hitcho Hamy (f)	$\frac{1}{36}$	—
	P. M. G. Karlina (f)	$\frac{1}{36}$	—
	P. M. G. Punneris (m)	$\frac{1}{36}$	—
	D. L. S. Weerawardene (m)	$\frac{1}{81}$	Share sold by P. M. G. Agoris' son, P. M. G. Singho Appu
	P. M. G. Theris (m)	$\frac{1}{81}$	—
	K. H. Karu Hamy's heirs	$\frac{1}{81}$	Share sold to Karu Hamy by P. M. G. Agoris' daughter

Generation	Name of shareholder	Pangu	Comment
	K. H. Karu Hamy's heirs	$\frac{1}{54}$	Each of six heirs has $\frac{1}{324}$
	V. K. Somawati (f)	$\frac{1}{54}$	Transferred to his daughter by father V. K. Somaris
	P. M. G. Podi Singho (m)	$\frac{3}{108}$	—
	Edirisinghe Sumanapala (m)	$\frac{1}{108}$	Son of deceased Edirisinghe Andiris, now effective owner
	P. M. G. John (m)	$\frac{1}{36}$	—
	Epa Seneviratne (m)	$\frac{1}{36}$	—
	P. M. G. Derenis (m)	$\frac{1}{18}$	Includes his sister's share
	Total	$\frac{1}{2}$	

Table 4. *Owners of Pahala Madagama shares in branch B, 1961*

Name of share owner	Share
P. M. G. Karanelis	$\frac{1}{36}$
P. M. G. Hitcho Hamy	$\frac{1}{36}$
P. M. G. Karlina	$\frac{1}{36}$
P. M. G. Punneris	$\frac{1}{36}$
P. M. G. Theris	$\frac{1}{81}$
P. M. G. John	$\frac{1}{36}+\frac{1}{24}+\frac{1}{48}$
Epa Seneviratne	$\frac{1}{48}+\frac{1}{36}$
P. M. G. Derenis (includes sister's share)	$\frac{1}{36}+\frac{1}{36}$
P. M. G. Podi Singho	$\frac{3}{108}$
Edirisinghe Sumanapala	$\frac{1}{108}$
K. H. Karu Hamy's heirs	$\frac{1}{54}+\frac{1}{81}$
V. K. Somawati	$\frac{1}{54}$
D. L. S. Weerawardene	$\frac{1}{81}$
S. D. Boris	$\frac{1}{36}$
K. G. Arnolis' son Somaratne	$\frac{1}{36}$
Madarasinghe Aron	$\frac{1}{36}$
Total	$\frac{1}{2}$

Table 5. *Shareholders of branch U*

Generation	Name of shareholder	Pangu	Comment
FA^2	P. M. G. Mathes (m)	$\frac{1}{2}$	Son of Founding Ancestor
	Total	$\frac{1}{2}$	
FA^3	P. M. G. Upeappu (m)	$\frac{1}{2}$	Son of son of Founding Ancestor
	Total	$\frac{1}{2}$	
FA^4	P. M. G. Adiriyan (m)	$\frac{1}{8}$	—
	P. M. G. Babappu (m)	$\frac{1}{8}$	Sold to brother-in-law Adris Hamy
	P. M. G. Hin Hamy (m)	$\frac{1}{8}$	$\frac{1}{16}$ sold to Panangala Liyanage Suaris and $\frac{1}{16}$ to I. Opisara
	P. M. G. Elias (m)	$\frac{1}{8}$	—
	Total	$\frac{1}{2}$	
FA^5	P. M. G. James (m)	$\frac{1}{16}$	—
	P. M. G. Andiris (m)	$\frac{1}{96}$	—
	P. M. G. Owinis (m)	$\frac{1}{96}$	—
	P. M. G. Semaris (m)	$\frac{1}{96}$	—
	P. M. G. Appu Singho (m)	$\frac{1}{96}$	Sold to Hovis
	P. M. G. Wimala Hamy (f)	$\frac{1}{96}$	—
	P. M. G. Dingiri Hamy (f)	$\frac{1}{96}$	'Died', and share devolved on sister, Wimala Hamy
	P. M. G. Girigoris (m)	$\frac{1}{40}$	—
	P. M. G. Elaris (m)	$\frac{1}{40}$	Sold to E. W. Thevonis and M. Aron
	P. M. G. Nonno (f)	$\frac{1}{40}$	Sold $\frac{3}{80}$ to K. G. Siyadoris
	K. G. Anohamy (f)	$\frac{1}{40}$	On death devolved on daughter Nonno Hamy
	K. G. Adris (m)	$\frac{1}{40}$	Effectively devolved on son Siyadoris, who sold $\frac{1}{80}$ to P. M. G.

Generation	Name of shareholder	Pangu	Comment
			Girigoris who in turn sold it to Senanayake Dasilige Pitchoris
	P. L. Peter (m)	$\frac{1}{16}$	Given to S. D. Boris
	Ihalamadde Opisara (m)	$\frac{1}{16}$	Given to P. M. G. Theris, Agoris and Hin Hamy
	P. M. G. Jayaweera (m)	$\frac{1}{16}$	$\frac{1}{32}$ sold to P. M. G. Vyanti Hamy
	P. M. G. Eranolis (m)	$\frac{1}{16}$	Sold to I. M. G. Nandoris and I. M. G. Kartelis
	Total	$\frac{1}{2}$	
FA[6]	P. M. G. Hovis (m)	$\frac{1}{112}$	Sold to S. D. Sumanapala
	P. M. G. Seetin (m)	$\frac{1}{112}$	—
	P. M. G. Francis (m)	$\frac{1}{112}$	Sold to S. D. Sumanapala
	P. M. G. Jinadasa (m)	$\frac{1}{112}$	—
	P. M. G. Eddin (m)	$\frac{1}{112}$	Sold to S. D. Sumanapala
	P. M. G. Podi Nona (f)	$\frac{1}{112}$	—
	P. M. G. Baby Nona (f)	$\frac{1}{112}$	Sold to S. D. Sumanapala
	P. M. G. Hovis (m)	$\frac{1}{96}$	—
	P. M. G. Sumana (f)	$\frac{1}{384}$	—
	P. M. G. Pediris (m)	$\frac{1}{384}$	Effective owner Sumana
	P. M. G. Katrina (f)	$\frac{1}{384}$	Effective owner Sumana
	P. M. G. Katrina's sister (f)	$\frac{1}{384}$	Effective owner Sumana
	P. M. G. Semaris (m)	$\frac{1}{96}$	—
	P. M. G. Hovis (m)	$\frac{1}{96}$	Originally mortgaged by Appu Singho to P. M. G. Gunadasa; later sold by Appu Singho's heirs to P. M. G. Hovis

Generation	Name of shareholder	Pangu	Comment
	P. M. G. Wimala Hamy (f)	$\frac{2}{96}$	Legal owner is Wimala Hamy who also 'obtained' her sister Dingiri Hamy's share. Son Don William works it for mother
	P. M. G. Gunadasa (m)	$\frac{1}{80}$	—
	P. M. G. Hendrik (m)	$\frac{1}{480}$	—
	P. M. G. Vimaladasa (m)	$\frac{1}{480}$	—
	P. M. G. Gnanadasa (m)	$\frac{1}{480}$	—
	P. M. G. Karunawati (f)	$\frac{1}{480}$	—
	P. M. G. Lilawati (f)	$\frac{1}{480}$	—
	P. M. G. Gunawati (f)	$\frac{1}{480}$	—
	M. Aron (m)	$\frac{1}{80}$	—
	E. W. Thevonis (m)	$\frac{1}{80}$	—
	P. M. G. Nonno (f)	$\frac{1}{80}$	Originally $\frac{1}{40}$ share of P. M. G. Nonno and $\frac{1}{40}$ of Ano Hamy her mother which former 'obtained'
	K. G. Podi Hamy (f)	$\frac{1}{80}$	—
	K. G. Podi Nona (f)	$\frac{1}{80}$	—
	K. G. Don William (m)	$\frac{1}{80}+\frac{1}{80}$	—
	S. D. Pitchoris	$\frac{1}{80}$	—
	Senanayake Dasilige Boris (m)	$\frac{1}{16}$	Given by P. L. Peter to son-in-law Boris
	D. L. Weerawardene (m)	$\frac{1}{48}$	Sold by P. M. G. Singho Appu
	K. H. Karu Hamy's heirs	$\frac{1}{48}$	Sold to K. H. Karu by P. M. G. Hinni Hamy
	P. M. G. Theris (m)	$\frac{1}{48}$	—
	K. G. Amarapala (m)	$\frac{1}{32}$	Sold by P. M. G. Jayaweera to half-

Generation	Name of shareholder	Pangu	Comment
			sister P. M. G. Vyanti Hamy, on whose death husband K. G. Nikulas took over. Gave $\frac{1}{64}$ to second wife. Effective owner son K. G. Amarapala. Also claims remaining $\frac{1}{64}$. Total $\frac{1}{32}$
	Either		
	P. M. G. Jainoris (m)	$\frac{1}{160}$	Controversy around these shares. Nandiris claims $\frac{1}{32}$ for himself but this is contested by his sibling group
	P. M. G. Nandiris (m)	$\frac{1}{160}$	
	P. M. G. Pelansina (f)	$\frac{1}{160}$	
	P. M. G. Laisina (f)	$\frac{1}{160}$	
	P. M. G. Alpina (f)	$\frac{1}{160}$	
	Or		
	P. M. G. Nandiris (m)	$\frac{1}{32}$	Sold to D. L. S. Weerawardene by Nandiris
	I. M. G. Kartelis (m)	$\frac{1}{32}$	Bought from P. M. G. Eranolis
	I. M. G. Nandoris (m)	$\frac{1}{32}$	Bought from P. M. G. Eranolis
	Total	$\frac{1}{2}$	

Table 6. *Owners of Pahala Madagama shares in branch U, 1961*

Name of share owner	Share
P. M. G. Seetin	$\frac{1}{112}$
P. M. G. Podi Nona	$\frac{1}{112}$
P. M. G. Jinadasa	$\frac{1}{112}$
P. M. G. Hovis	$\frac{1}{96}+\frac{1}{96}$
P. M. G. Semaris	$\frac{1}{96}$
P. M. G. Sumana	$\frac{1}{384}$
P. M. G. Andiris	$\frac{1}{384}$
P. M. G. Katrina	$\frac{1}{384}$
P. M. G. Katrina's sister	$\frac{1}{384}$
P. M. G. Gunadasa	$\frac{1}{80}$
P. M. G. Vimaladasa	$\frac{1}{480}$
P. M. G. Gnanadasa	$\frac{1}{480}$
P. M. G. Hendrik	$\frac{1}{480}$
P. M. G. Karunawati	$\frac{1}{480}$
P. M. G. Lilawati	$\frac{1}{480}$
P. M. G. Gunawati	$\frac{1}{480}$
P. M. G. Nonno	$\frac{1}{80}$
P. M. G. Theris	$\frac{1}{48}$
Either	
P. M. G. Jainoris	$\frac{1}{160}$
P. M. G. Nandiris	$\frac{1}{160}$
P. M. G. Pelansina	$\frac{1}{160}$
P. M. G. Laisina	$\frac{1}{160}$
P. M. G. Alpina	$\frac{1}{160}$
Or	
D. L. S. Weerawardene	$\frac{1}{32}(+\frac{1}{48})$
K. G. Don William	$\frac{2}{96}+\frac{2}{80}$
K. G. Podi Hamy	$\frac{1}{80}$
K. G. Podi Nona	$\frac{1}{80}$
K. G. Amarapala	$\frac{1}{32}$
I. M. G. Nandoris	$\frac{1}{32}$
I. M. G. Kartelis	$\frac{1}{32}$
S. D. Sumanapala	$\frac{4}{112}$
S. D. Pitchoris	$\frac{1}{80}$
M. Aron	$\frac{1}{80}$
E. W. Thevonis	$\frac{1}{80}$
K. H. Karu Hamy's heirs	$\frac{1}{48}$
S. D. Boris	$\frac{1}{16}$

Table 7. *Non-resident, non-vāsagama members (outsiders) holding shares in Pahala Madagama*

Branch *U*	
D. L. S. Weerawardene	$\frac{1}{32}+\frac{1}{48}$
I. M. G. Kartelis	$\frac{1}{32}$
I. M. G. Nandoris	$\frac{1}{32}$
H. Jinasoma	$\frac{1}{120}$ (this is only a claim)
S. D. Pitchoris	$\frac{1}{80}$
M. Aron	$\frac{1}{80}$
E. W. Thevonis	$\frac{1}{80}$
K. H. Karu Hamy's heirs	$\frac{1}{48}$
S. D. Boris	$\frac{1}{16}$
S. D. Sumanapala	$\frac{4}{12}$
Branch *B*	
K. H. Karu Hamy's heirs	$\frac{1}{54}+\frac{1}{81}$
V. K. Somawati	$\frac{1}{54}$
D. L. S. Weerawardene	$\frac{1}{81}$
S. D. Boris	$\frac{1}{36}$
Madarasinghe Aron	$\frac{1}{36}$
K. G. Arnolis	$\frac{1}{36}$
Epa Seneviratne	$\frac{1}{48}$

About 40 per cent ($\frac{2}{5}$) of the Pahala Madagama *gama* is owned by non-resident non-*vāsagama* shareholders.

Table 8. *Total number of Pangu in 'market', Pahala Madagama, 1961*

Branch *B*: $\frac{1}{36}+\frac{1}{36}+\frac{1}{36}+\frac{1}{81}+\frac{1}{36}+\frac{1}{36}+\frac{1}{24}+\frac{1}{48}+\frac{1}{48}+\frac{1}{36}+\frac{1}{36}+\frac{1}{36}+\frac{1}{36}+\frac{3}{108}+\frac{1}{54}+\frac{1}{81}+\frac{1}{54}+\frac{1}{81}+\frac{1}{36}+\frac{1}{36}+\frac{1}{108} = \frac{1}{2}$

Branch *U*: $\frac{1}{112}+\frac{1}{112}+\frac{1}{112}+\frac{1}{80}+\frac{1}{96}+\frac{1}{96}+\frac{1}{384}+\frac{1}{384}+\frac{1}{384}+\frac{1}{384}+\frac{1}{480}+\frac{1}{480}+\frac{1}{480}+\frac{1}{480}+\frac{1}{480}+\frac{1}{480}+\frac{1}{80}+\frac{1}{48}+\frac{1}{32}$ (or $\frac{1}{160}+\frac{1}{160}+\frac{1}{160}+\frac{1}{160}+\frac{1}{160}$) $+\frac{1}{48}+\frac{2}{96}+\frac{2}{80}+\frac{1}{80}+\frac{1}{80}+\frac{1}{32}+\frac{1}{32}+\frac{1}{32}+\frac{4}{112}+\frac{1}{96}+\frac{1}{80}+\frac{1}{80}+\frac{1}{80}+\frac{1}{48}+\frac{1}{16} = \frac{1}{2}$

CHAPTER 5

FACTORS OF CHANGE

THE STRUCTURAL PREREQUISITE OF THE SYSTEM

Any empiricial system of land tenure has to have almost by definition one structural prerequisite—namely, land itself. In terms of our ideal type, there should be, for the optimum functioning of the system, a demographic balance between land and people, in terms of some intra-cultural criterion of adequacy of land per person or family, or larger group. When this balance is upset then theoretically in the context of Sinhalese cultural values, there has to be a fissioning of the group and the founding of a new one, or, in the reverse direction, a recruitment of new people into the group. Thus in terms of our model, the prerequisite is the availability of land for expansion when the *gama* or estate cannot 'take in' more people. Since pure conditions do not obtain in nature an ideal population/land balance would be a rarity, but if the system is to continue functioning, an 'adequate' availability of land would be a structural prerequisite. *Permanent* unavailability of land involves a loss of the structural prerequisite: when this condition obtains the system is doomed, and it is matter of time for its eventual disintegration and demise. In our analyses we shall consider the loss of the structural prerequisite as a major factor in change; we shall also treat as factors other processes that accelerated the change, and we shall isolate these 'factors'. Modes of coping with the changes will also be examined in detail.

The Crown Lands Encroachment Ordinances

The loss of the structural prerequisite for any single hamlet or a number of hamlets in a region does not necessarily lead to the disintegration of the system of land tenure, for movements of population to areas with an abundance of land could occur, once again equalizing the population/land ratio. But if *all* villages lost their structural prerequisites, then the disintegration of the old system would commence. The possibility of this condition being realized lay in several ordinances passed by the British after 1840 to prevent encroachment on Crown Lands. The more important of thesc laws were respectively: Ordinance No. 12 of 1840, 'To prevent encroachment upon Crown Lands' (The Crown Lands Encroachment Ordinance), and amended by the Order in Council of 11 August 1841; Ordinance No. 1 of 1897, 'An Ordinance related to claims to forest, chena, waste and unoccupied lands' (Waste Lands Ordinance) as amended by No. 1 of 1899, No. 5 of 1900, and No. 6 of 1903; and Ordinance No. 16 of 1907, 'An ordinance to consolidate and amend the law relating to forests and the felling and transport of timber' (The Forest Ordinance). Since these ordinances were instrumental in bringing about radical changes in the social structure of Sinhalese villages, we shall examine the content and implications of these laws. Substantively most of these laws were embodied in the Crown Lands Encroachment Ordinance of 1840 (C.L.E.O.), the major principle of policy in all these laws being the assumption that all uncultivated land is Crown Land. Section 6 of C.L.E.O. gave expression to this policy:

> All forest, waste, unoccupied and uncultivated lands shall be presumed to be the property of the Crown until the contrary thereof be proved, and all chenas and other lands which can be only cultivated after intervals of several years shall, if the same be situated within the districts formerly comprised in the Kandyan provinces (wherein no thombo registers have been heretofore established), be deemed to belong to the Crown and not to be the property of any private person claiming the same against the Crown, except upon proof only by such person of a sannas or grant for the same, together with satisfactory evidence as to the limits and boundaries thereof, or of such customary taxes, dues or services having been rendered within such period for similar lands being the property of private proprietors in the same districts and in all other districts in this Colony such chena and other lands which can only be cultivated after intervals of several years shall be deemed to be forest and waste lands within the meaning of this clause.
>
> (C.L.E.O. Section 6)

Section 1 amended by Order in Council of 1841 empowers the District Court to evict persons encroaching on Crown land unless presumptive right for a period of five years and upward is proved, though Hayley says that summary proceedings under Section 1 appear to have become obsolete after a few years (Hayley 1923: 270).

The Waste Lands Ordinance which repealed C.L.E.O. is

essentially the same except that it specifies procedures and personnel for declaring lands as belonging to the Crown. Such authority was vested in the Government Agent or his assistant, or 'one or more Special Officers for the whole Island, who may for the purposes perform, do, and exercise in any province or district all or any of the powers, duties and functions vested in the Government Agent or Assistant Government Agent under this Ordinance' (Section 28). If no claim was made within three months of the official notice, land is declared 'Crown'. If a private claim was made the officer could under Section 3 inquire into it and make the following decisions:

(*a*) make an order declaring the land to be the property of the Crown;

(*b*) admit the whole or part of the claim;

(*c*) enter into written agreement with the claimant for the purchase of the whole or any portion of the land which is the subject matter of such claim and embody the agreement in an order (Report of the Land Commission 1958:21). These Ordinances began the process of what was later called Land Settlement, that is, the process of investigating and declaring whether land belongs to the Crown or to private parties. The Forest Ordinance is sociologically not especially relevant for our study: its aim is to put a stop to the illicit use of Crown forest, which includes felling of timber, and pasturing of cattle, and to 'regulate or prohibit the cutting of or setting fire to Chenas...' (Section 21). It put another obstacle against village expansion, and introduced a class of officers (Forest Officers) to implement the provisions of the Ordinance.

These enactments have little sociological significance unless it can be shown that they were, in fact, implemented. The actual implementation of these laws occurred in two ways. Negatively, by alienating vast tracts of Crown land to European capitalists, so that villages in the Kandyan areas were gradually hemmed in by large tea estates, and in many parts of the Western, Southern and Sabaragamuva provinces by rubber plantations. This *effectively* caused the loss of the structural prerequisite of land tenure systems for a majority of Sinhalese villages in these areas. But this factor was not important in areas which had not become submerged under a plantation economy, and since Hinidum Pattu was one of these areas, we have to see the extent to which the laws were *positively* implemented, that is, the effective enforcement of the provisions of these Ordinances as far as Madagama and similar villages were concerned.

It is obvious that in these areas, there would still be large tracts of uncultivated land. Action for encroachment in Crown land could not easily be taken, unless a delimitation of Crown lands had been effected. The area was controlled by a Sinhalese Revenue Officer, the Mudaliyar who also had police duties, and he was assisted by the village headmen of the several villages. The upshot of the whole scheme was to enhance the power and influence of these officers, for villagers were permitted to cultivate their chenas, and probably found new hamlets, if they paid homage to these officials in the traditional manner. The situation permitted these officers to adopt easily the roles of the traditional feudal aristocracy.

The positive implementation of the provisions of these enactments were made all over the low country by special officers appointed by the Governor for the purpose of 'land settlement'. The culmination of the work of these officers resulted in what is known as the Final Village Plan which gave a rough thumbnail description of the village ('Final Report') and a 'Register of Settlement' containing a list of the lands which were (*a*) declared Crown; (*b*) admitted private; and (*c*) sold to villages. As far as Madagama was concerned several notifications appeared in the government gazettes between 1909 and 1913 specifying the lands adjoining Madagama which were to be settled and inviting the presentation of claims before the Commission. These claims were subsequently heard and the final order made in March 1914. The Final Village Plan was completed on 24 April 1915. This definitely, and as far as the Government of the period was concerned, irrevocably decided the limits of the village clearly specifying and demarcating private and Crown lands. In other words, if in certain areas the growth of plantations virtually restricted the growth of the village and 'prescribed' its limits, in this non-plantation area the village limits were analogously prescribed by the government in the manner stated above. There were several areas where the C.L.E.O. was not implemented, as in Nuwarakalawiya District where Pul Eliya is located. But as far as the Sinhalese low country was concerned the provisions of the Ordinance were more or less effectively implemented.

Pahala Madagama in 1909

The Final Village Plan (F.V.P.) gives us brief but interesting clues regarding Madagama village. It is evident from census records and the F.V.P. that for government purposes both Ihala and Pahala Madagama were treated as a single village. The F.V.P. gave it concrete recognition by treating both hamlets as a single unit and settling lands on this basis. In other words, a 'village', Madagama, was officially created. We know from the F.V.P. that the chenas were cultivated with *kurrakkan*, *amu*, *mineri*, *polayal*—all subsidiary crops and the 'gardens' contained coconut, arecanut, jak, breadfruit, mango, lime, orange, pineapple, plantain and gauva. Of these only arecanut was sold as a 'cash crop' in the market. The paddy fields were cultivated in both Yala and Maha, the yield no better than it is today: that is, fivefold. There was a government school in Tavalama six miles away, and a Roman Catholic school in Mavanana (destined to close down soon afterwards). The village had fourteen children of school-going age which meant that some of our present informants were going to school. Medical facilities were provided in a government dispensary in Hiniduma Town, ten miles away, in charge of an 'apothecary'. The Office of the Registrar of Marriages, Births and Deaths was in Lelwala, the village to the east of Madagama; a 'Receiving Post Office', at Hiniduma, was also the headquarters of the Village Committee or *gansabāva*. The Mudaliyar resided at Hiniduma, the Vidane Aratchi at Neluva and the Police Officer at Lelwala. We are also told that the villagers were Sinhalese Buddhists of the *goigama* caste. The population according to the census of 1911 contained seventy-nine people, forty-four males and thirty-five females, belonging to twenty-one families. There were seven head of black cattle and seventeen buffaloes.

Using the 1911 census as a baseline what inferences could we make about the social structure of Pahala Madagama hamlet? By 1911, the *vāsagama* members of generation FA^4, who were all 'married' before 1870, would be dead, or very old: their children (FA^5), however, would be adults, most of them married. Since this is the sociologically significant generation how many families in this generation resided in Pahala Madagama, excluding men married uxorilocally and females virilocally? As our chart indicates there were fourteen families (approximately) of which there was only one

(Jasin Gamage Vilian Singho's) in which neither husband nor wife belonged to the *vāsagama*, though connected with it affinally (see Fig. 15). We know that several shares were owned by outsiders, and those marrying out probably considered themselves owners of shares, but the likelihood is that then, as now, the villagers actually

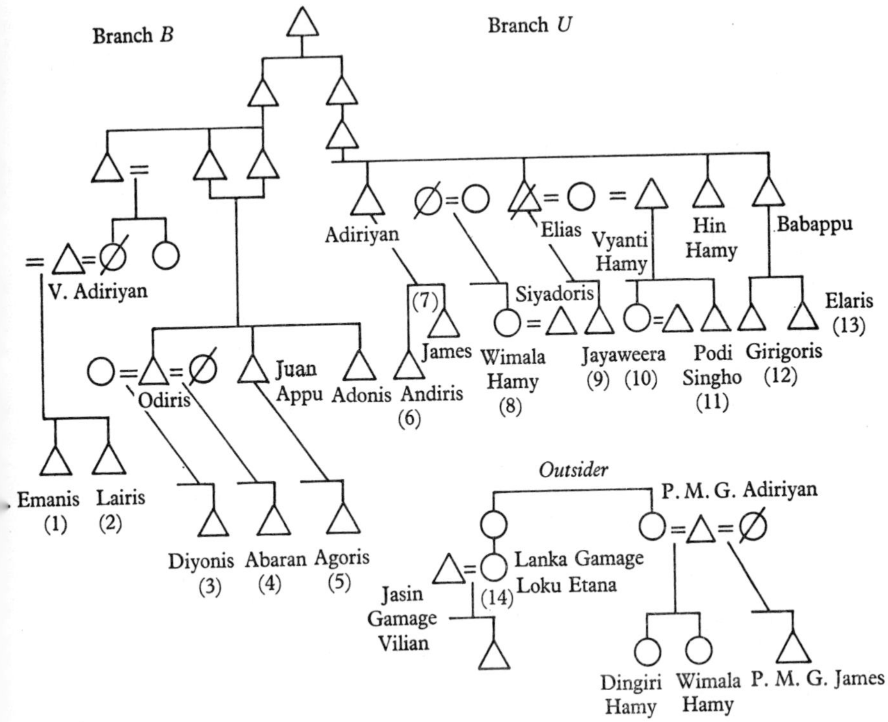

Fig. 15.

cultivated the paddy fields on formal *andē* lease. Thus fourteen families cultivated an area of about 18 acres, which gives each family an average of over an acre, or a sowing area of about 19 k each. This is hardly enough for subsistence. Even the wealthiest member of the *vāsagama* today (P. M. G. John) cultivates only 34 k, which is not adequate to support his family for a season. Therefore during this period one would expect land pressures to create extra-village residential alignments among the males of the group. This expectation is confirmed, for at least seven male shareholders contracted uxorilocal marriages and left the village; this is more than half the number of males of this generation in the *vāsagama*. Land pressures existed in other villages too, for two women lived patrilocally (that is, their husbands uxorilocally) and one new family entered the hamlet. Thus, though the hamlet in 1911 showed a solid residential aggregation of patrilateral kinsmen of a single *vāsagama*, land pressures were causing changes in traditional residential preferences, so that many *vāsagama* members were being ejected from the hamlet, and non-*vāsagama* persons received into the hamlet.

Though an average of 19 k per person was inadequate for subsistence, there were plenty of garden lands and chenas for the cultivation of subsistence crops and hence fourteen families could probably subsist in the Pahala Madagama estate. The 'register of settlement' gives us an indication of the extent of land traditionally claimed by both hamlets. This amounted to about 700 acres of land consisting of paddy lands, *deniyas* (potential or abandoned paddy lands, or flat sandy stretches), chenas and gardens. After the settlement, Madagama village was left with its present lands amounting to about 100 acres: a contraction of the estate to one-seventh of its original size. There was no serious contraction of paddy land but chenas and *deniyas* were eliminated and the gardens radically diminished in size. More importantly, no further expansion of paddy lands was possible. The Final Village Plan settled finally the size of the *gama* for both Ihala and Pahala Madagama so that encroachment was now detectable. Chenas continued to be cultivated both surreptitiously and on permits issued by the government, but the latter were severely restricted owing to the policy of the government to discourage chena cultivation. Sporadic encroachment on Crown land by chena cultivators did occur. This again enhanced the power of village headmen whose responsibility it was to report such occurrences. As far as garden lands were concerned hardly any encroachments occurred between 1910–61, except a few square yards of 'intrusion' into Crown land by the more enterprising villagers through skilful displacement of boundary marks. No new paddy land was illegally *assveddumized* (brought under cultivation) after 1910. One inference, however, can be clearly drawn: the settlement of the villages made the founding of new *gamas* an almost impossible task. We know of several hamlets founded after 1910, but these were located in the heart of the dense Sinharaja forest, out of the official sight. Moreover, these new hamlets were situated in areas unsuitable for paddy cultivation: the main occupation of these hamlets were the tapping of *kitul* trees (*caryota urens*) for making toddy, treacle, and jaggery. No traditional hamlets centring on a stretch of paddy fields were founded in Hinidum Pattu, as far as we know, after 1910. The structural prerequisite was effectively undermined.[1]

FACTOR OF CHANGE: LAND SALES

The effective undermining of the structural prerequisite of the system due to the implementation of the Crown Lands Ordinances probably commenced in Madagama about 1909, when a special Commissioner was appointed to 'settle' the village. However, important changes in the land tenure systems of Ihala and Pahala Madagama had occurred prior to that date. So that while it would be true to say that the loss of the structural prerequisite would entail the eventual collapse of the system, events that occurred prior to this are important for understanding the nature of the changes and the accelerated pace of change.

According to our model the ideal operation of the land tenure system requires among other things a patrilineal aggregation of male kinsmen, constituting a *vāsagama*, having rights in an estate. The rules of inheritance of the society would in the long run result in this situation, though the possibility of land falling into the hands of outsiders existed owing to the right of individual alienability of shares. But shares are perforce rights to the soil, which is owned by the shareholders as a whole. The organization of tenure —the allocation of the soil to the shareowners—is on the basis of the *vāsagama* genealogy. Thus, if a hypothetical total outsider *X* had bought $\frac{1}{8}$ of the estate belonging to P. M. G. Hin Hamy of branch *U* and had worked in the hamlet, he would say that he 'owns' or 'works' Hin Hamy's share. But assume that all four subsection ancestors of branch *U* had sold their shares to outsiders *W*, *X*, *Y* and *Z*: then the genealogy as a framework for the organization of rights would be a 'fiction' which would have no anchorage in the kinship system. Thus it would seem that if the system were to operate efficiently, the residents of the estate have to be largely patrilateral kinsmen of the *vāsagama*: total outsiders without kinship obligations and allegiances to the *vāsagama* could impede the proper operation of the system, for the co-operation of the shareholders with differing kinship allegiances might be difficult to obtain. But this in turn would depend upon who the 'outsiders' were—if the 'outsiders' were residents of the hamlet connected to the *vāsagama* by matrilateral or affinal ties, tenurial co-operation might be easier to obtain than if they were non-resident outsiders with no such kinship connexions and no cultivation interests in the soil. The position would also be different if outsiders who bought shares were like the Pul Eliya traders without vested interests in the soil, in which case the shares would once again devolve on the *vāsagama*. We shall therefore deal with land sales to 'outsiders' as another factor of change in the system. Since most of the land sales to outsiders are from the Ihala Madagama estate we shall primarily consider the changes in that estate: the Pahala Madagama estate where comparatively few sales of this sort occurred would provide a means of control to assess the degree of change qualitatively.

Land sales to outsiders up to 1909: Ihala Madagama

In considering land sales we shall mainly consider sales to total outsiders in order to eliminate kinship (sentimental) variables and postulate economic necessity as the motive on the part of villagers for selling land (shares) and speculative activity on the part of outsiders buying them. The list of sales are as follows:

Grantor (seller)	Grantee (purchaser)	Date of sale	Size of share
I. M. G. Ades Hamy	Elias Gunawardene	1865	$\frac{1}{16}$
I. M. G. Ediriappu	Don David Rubasin Gunawardene	1888	$\frac{1}{32}$
I. M. G. Davith	Panangala Liyanage Suaris	1881	$\frac{1}{56}$
I. M. G. Lokuappu	Elias Gunawardene	1877	$\frac{1}{8}$
I. M. G. Lokuappu	P. L. Suaris	1883	$\frac{1}{24}$
I. M. G. Lokuappu	A. Gunawardene	1879	$\frac{1}{12}$
I. M. G. Edirihamy	Maddegama *Muladāniya*	*c.* 1884	$\frac{1}{8}$
		Total	$\frac{1}{2}$ approx.

Sale between kinsmen: I. M. G. Mathes to Wickremaratne Diyonis 1886 (?), $\frac{1}{6}$.

One impressive fact that emerges from this is the clustering of sales within a definite period. The first sale to an outsider of which we have evidence, and which is acknowledged by villagers, is 1865 and the last sale to an outsider prior to 1909 is in 1888. Another impressive fact is that of all these sales only one reverted back to the villagers. This is due to the kinship relationship between Mathes and Diyonis who were brothers-in-law. All the other transactions were permanent ones, which, during a span of twenty-three years, resulted in about half the *pravēni* shares leaving the *vāsagama* to total outsiders for good. If our assumption is correct that land sales to total outsiders would be due to economic necessity, two questions arise: was the 'economic crisis' an isolated one felt by Ihala Madagama hamlet, or a dispersed one felt by Sinhalese society at large? That the economic crisis felt by Ihala Madagama hamlet during this period is not an isolated phenomenon is seen by comparison with all the land sales in Pahala Madagama during this period.

Pahala Madagama land sales up to 1909, branch U

(1) P. M. G. Adiriyan to Kariyawasam Godage Arnolis de Silva (about 1888)—$\frac{1}{8}$ share. We have only the registration date for this transaction—the actual sale would have occurred earlier. Anyway this share was bought back by Adiriyan's son James, a few years later.

(2) P. M. G. Babappu sold his share of $\frac{1}{8}$ to his brother-in-law Kankanan Gamage Adris, in the 1880's. He (in 1914) split it among his and Babappu's heirs.

(3) P. M. G. Hin Hamy who owned $\frac{1}{8}$ of *pravēni* sold half ($\frac{1}{16}$) to Panangala Liyanage Suaris (who also bought Ihala shares) and the other half to Ihalamadde Opisara of Habarakada also about the same period. The latter portion once again devolved on the *vāsagama* since Ihalamadde Opisara was P. M. G. Agoris' wife's mother's brother.

Thus it is clear that this period was also one of economic hardship for Pahala Madagama, but though $\frac{3}{8}$ of the *pravēni* were sold by its members, only $\frac{1}{16}$ left the line permanently: the rest were recouped through kinship links. No land sales occurred in branch *B* during this period. It is no accident that of the two branches, *B* is the more viable one today, and of the two hamlets, Pahala

Madagama as against Ihala is more viable in respect of land tenure.

Since the 'economic' crisis was not something uniquely felt by Ihala Madagama but also affected Pahala Madagama the question arises whether it was an even more dispersed phenomenon. We also note that all these sales took place between the period 1865–88, a period of only twenty-three years, when about $\frac{7}{16}$ of the estate left *vāsagama* ownership. A further question immediately enters—whether the country as a whole suffered a period of economic crisis about the period 1865–77. We suggest that this indeed was the case and the economic crisis could be identified with the taxes imposed on paddy and grain by the Colonial government prior to and during this period.

The Grain Taxes: 1840–92

The tax on agricultural products, based on a 'tithe' or share of the produce was a feature of Dutch Administration in Ceylon, but we have little evidence of how effective the mode of collection was or how extortionate the taxes themselves were. The British continued these taxes and introduced many others after the occupation. Several of these taxes, like the Coconut Tax, were very unpopular and led to public outcry and revolt in 1807. Other non-agricultural taxes like the Joy Tax (1800), a tax levied on the wearing of ornaments, the Bazaar Tax (1807) on articles sold by retail in public bazaars, all led to serious public opposition and had to be abolished. A subsequent tax, the Gun Tax, was the immediate provocation for a minor rebellion which was so sternly and brutally suppressed that questions were asked in the British Parliament and led to the recall of the Governor Lord Torrington (Perera, n.d.:34, 51, 101; Bertolacci 1817:322–97). After 1824, most taxes on agriculture were repealed, except the tithe or tax on grain amounting to a portion of the produce of grain grown on low lands, chena and high lands.

We know that there were various kinds of tenure in the Dutch-occupied territory, each associated with a tax or tithe payable in kind to the government. Bertolacci, a government accountant, gives a good account of the various types of tenure prevalent in the Dutch territories at the time of the British occupation and the share payable to government as tax (1817:277–98). The British by a proclamation of 1801 continued to levy these taxes; in addition they imposed a general rate of one-tenth or one-fifth of the produce on all lands so far held free of tax. Section 5 of the proclamation reads thus:

On and after the first day of May in the year of our Lord One thousand eight hundred and two next ensuing, all obligations to serve on tenure of lands throughout these settlements shall cease, and lands held duty free at this present time on account of such service shall on and after the said day pay to Government one-tenth of their produce if high lands and one-fifth of their produce if low lands, excepting only such lands as were formerly Mallapalla, Nellapalla, Ratninda or Ande which will continue...to pay one-fourth of their produce to Government.

(Proclamation of 3 September 1801)

In fact, however, different rates of taxation for the various types of tenure were implemented.

The mode of collecting the taxes in the Maritime Provinces by the British up to 1818 is stated in Bertolacci's account (1817:304 ff.). Part of the revenue from the Grain Tax was directly collected by Government by its own officers; 'the rest is farmed out to renters, who give, each of them good securities for the due payment of the amount of the purchase of the farm, and the performance of the conditions attached to it'. The property, movable and immovable, of the renter and his 'securities' become bound to Government by this act. These renters in turn divide the rents among sub-renters who with *their* securities are in turn bound to the principal renter. The 'farms' (i.e. the right to collect the taxes for the government) were sold in the following manner. Sometime before harvest, Harvest Commissioners, who were government civil servants, were employed by the Government to form an estimate of the quantity of grain likely to be realized at harvest for each field. Emoluments for the Commissioners were also included in the estimates. After the completion of these estimates the 'farms' are put up for public sale and granted to the highest bidder (1817: 304). At one time apparently the 'rents' of several villagers were farmed together, but later on an attempt was made to sell the rents of each village separately on the spot so as to give an opportunity for the villagers themselves to 'redeem' the tax. It was, however, doubtful whether this latter goal was satisfactorily realized. If the offers for the purchase (by renters) or redemption (by villagers) of the 'tithe' (government share) or tax were too low, public officers directly collected the government share. Bertolacci states further that in general half the revenue is directly collected by government officers, while the other half is collected by renters and sub-renters (1817:307).

As early as 1817 Bertolacci was highly critical of the whole renting system. He points out several defects of a procedural sort. (*a*) There was sometimes collusion between renters and villagers so that the government did not get its due share. (*b*) Young and inexperienced British civil servants acting as Commissioners could vex and harass cultivators. (*c*) Renters, particularly those who paid a high price for the 'farms', extorted from the villagers. A favourite technique of extortion was by delaying to be present at the time of harvest. The crops then cannot be removed, and may be destroyed; hence proprietors and cultivators have to bribe the renter to be present. (*d*) 'For the years 1810, 11, 12 the average number of executions in revenue cases which arose between the different parties (namely Government, the renters, the sub-renters, the securities and the proprietors or cultivators) amounted, in the district of Colombo alone to seven or eight hundred annually' (Bertolacci 1817:309).

After the fall of the Kandyan Kingdom to the British in 1815, the renting system was extended to this area too, by the proclamation of 21 November 1818. The tithe was, however, less variable here and was generally one-tenth or one-fourteenth of the yield at harvest (Blue Book 1888:147). In 1840 the renting system was formalized for the whole island by Ordinance No. 14 of 1840 entitled 'For securing the due collection of the duties or tax upon paddy and dry grain.' Briefly the Ordinance attempted to formalize the renting system by specifying the various procedures to be adopted by the cultivator, the renter and the Government; the mode of ascertaining the tax due (assessment), penalties imposed on the cultivators for harvesting without due notice, and penalties (fine or imprisonment) for non-payment of tax. The reader is referred to the Ordinance for further details.

The renting system formalized under the Ordinance of 1840 was subject to severe criticism both at home and in England. Government-appointed 'assessors' calculated in advance the probable value of the crop, and a return of the amount liable in every field was made to the Government Agent. Then the farming of the tax for each district was sold by public auction. The peasant was required to give the renter five days' notice of his intention to harvest; two days' notice if the necessity to postpone harvesting arose. If the crop could not, owing to adverse circumstances, be threshed on the expected date further notice had to be given to the renter. The renter could sue the peasant in the District Court for any omission or irregularity. Tennant appointed to head a committee in 1848 to inquire into the Island's revenue, favoured the abolition of the grain tax and a substitution of a General Land Tax. He was unsparing in his criticism of the renting system in his Report of 1848:

> It would be difficult to devise a system more pregnant with oppression, extortion and demoralization than the one here detailed. The cultivator is handed over to two successive sets of inquisitional officers, the assessors and the renters; whose acts are so uncontrolled that abuses are inevitable, and the intercourse of the two parties is characterized by rigour and extortion on the one side, and cunning and subterfuges of every description on the other. Every artifice and disingenuous device is put in practice to deceive the headmen and assessors as to the extent and fertility of the land and the actual value of the crops and they, in return resort to the most inquisitorial and vexatious interference, either to protect the interest of the Government, or privately to further their own. Between these demoralizing influences, the character and industry of the rural population are deteriorated and destroyed. The extension of cultivation by reclaiming a portion of waste land only exposes the harassed proprietor to fresh visits from the headman, and a new valuation by the Government Assessor, and where annoyance is not the leading object recourse is had to corruption in order to keep down the valuation.
>
> But no sooner than the cultivator got rid of the assessor than he falls into the hands of the renter, who, under the authority with which the law invests him, finds himself possessed of unusual powers of vexation and annoyance. He may be designedly out of the way when the cultivator sends notice of his intention to cut; and if the latter, to save his harvest from perishing on the stalk, ventures to reap it in his absence, the penalties of the law are instantly enforced against him. Under the pressure of this formidable control, the agricultural proprietor, rather than lose his time or his crop in dancing attendance on the renter, or submitting to the multiform annoyance of his subordinates, is driven to purchase forebearance by additional payments... (Tennant 1848:68)

It should be noted that these were substantially the same criticisms made by Bertolacci thirty-one years before.

In spite of continuing criticisms the government for many years did not introduce a substantial change. Voluntary money commutation was sporadically introduced into various areas between 1829–1831 but without success (S.P. VIII, 1890: 5–7). The government position was that the tax constituted a major source of revenue and could not be abolished, while a General Land Tax would adversely affect European plantation interests and would require cadastral surveys involving prohibitive costs and delay. The government maintained that the tax was in principle fair; though the procedure (i.e. the renting system) may be subject to abuse. In order to correct this the government introduced the principle of voluntary commutation through two Ordinances—Ordinance No. 29 of 1865 entitled 'An Ordinance to amend the Ordinance No. 14 of 1840', and Ordinance No. 5 of 1866, 'An ordinance to facilitate the collection of moneys due as commutation of the paddy tax, and of the performance of labour'. With voluntary commutation the temptation was great for peasants to get rid of the burdens of the renting system by a long term agreement with the government on a fixed rate per bushel. However, it was a mixed blessing in a society where money was not readily available, for once committed to voluntary commutation there was no getting out of it. In fact it is ironical that villagers of the maritime provinces, who were more acquainted with a cash economy could sense the dangers of voluntary commutation and refused it (A.R., Western Province, 1868: 10). Voluntary commutation was adopted by villagers who had less involvement in a cash economy and no ability to weigh rationally the probable outcome of their projected action. These were in Kegalle and Sabaragamuva Districts and in parts of the Central Province. The actual consequences of voluntary commutation were disastrous.

In 1877, the Government appointed a Commission to inquire into the workings of the Grain Tax. Their views, which run into a few pages, plus the evidence supplied to them and relevant statistical and historical information and past sessional papers were issued in the form of a large Sessional Paper in 1877 (S.P. XVI, 1877). The Commission recommended the abolition of the renting system and the introduction of compulsory commutation for a fixed money payment. In the following year their recommendations were formulated in Ordinance No. 11 of 1878, 'An Ordinance to make provision for the better collection of the Tax, Duty or share due to the government upon grain grown on this Island'. This Ordinance was implemented within a period of five years in all the Provinces of the Island except the North Central, (where Pul Eliya is located), the North-western and Northern Provinces where the old renting system combined with optional commutation prevailed.

The consequences of the implementation of this Ordinance were so disastrous that agitation in Ceylon and in England sought to have the grain tax abolished. A committee of the Ceylon National Association, consisting of prominent Ceylonese political leaders was formed to seek its abolition. The Cobden Club in England (a doctrinaire Free Trade group founded in 1866 a year after Cobden's death) took up the case in England and in the English Parliament. Hundreds of polemical tracts were written by the abolitionists and non-abolitionists. The local papers took up the cause. George Wall, editor of the *Independent*, fought on the side of the abolitionists, while Ferguson, editor of the *Observer*, pointed out the serious consequences to revenue if the tax were abolished, and the impossibility of a Land Tax. Sometimes the polemics descended to a level of extraordinary *naïveté*. Ferguson following a popular view stated that the 'only way to raise revenue in an oriental land is to tax some of the two or three articles which are indispensable to the masses'. The 'pinching of the stomach' is morally good because it will induce peasants to work in the plantations (Ferguson 1890:41–2).

In view of the mounting criticism a committee consisting of prominent Ceylonese and Europeans was appointed in 1890. The evidence supplied to this committee with its report was published as Sessional Paper XVII of 1890. In spite of the heavy weight of evidence against the tax, the committee reiterated the old formula—the tax was a good one, but procedural matters have to be changed. Fortunately in 1890 Havelock was appointed Governor. Havelock consistently advocated the abolition of the Grain Tax. In his *Dispatches* to Lord Knutsford, Secretary of State for the Colonies, he summed up his position:

> The conclusion I have arrived at is that the paddy tax is an obnoxious tax. It is a tax that presses on one particular class of cultivators and on one particular industry. It is a tax the collection of which costs much, incites to fraud and falsehood, and tempts to oppression. I think it should be abrogated... (S.P. III, 1892:5)

Lord Knutsford agreed that the tax, 'a painful chapter in the agricultural history of Ceylon', caused 'unmerited suffering' to the peasants and ordered its abolition (S.P. III, 1892:144).

CRITICISMS OF THE GRAIN TAXES UNDER VOLUNTARY AND COMPULSORY COMMUTATION 1866–92

In the following pages we shall attempt to make certain criticisms of the grain tax under voluntary and compulsory commutation and a rough assessment of its impact on Sinhalese social structure. The subject calls for monographic treatment, impossible for us to attempt here. Ever since 1822 there have been consistent accounts by Government Agents of these taxes in their annual reports, and hundreds of government papers have been published on the subject. Our criticisms are largely based on these Administration Reports and Sessional Papers. Unfortunately much of the evidence is not comprehensive enough, or sociologically meaningful. Our major concern will be the Ordinance of 1878 which introduced compulsory commutation. The reader is referred to the appendix for the relevant sections of this crucial piece of legislation. Here one only need state that this ordinance introduced two kinds of commutation—'annual' and 'crop commutation'. In 'annual commutation' a fixed money payment is to be made annually whether the field yields a crop or not. In 'crop commutation' the payment is made only when a crop is produced. Peasants could choose either one, though the latter involves a larger sum as tax. It should also be mentioned that though the tax was called a 'Grain Tax', the taxation of 'dry grain' grown in high lands had become largely obsolete, except for one-fourth of produce on grain grown in chenas in the Kandy and Kurunegala Districts, one-fifth in the Badulla District (S.P. XII, 1880). Under the Ordinance of 1878 one brand of paddy, *älvi*, grown in high land was classed as a grain to be taxed everywhere. However it is doubtful whether in fact dry grain of any sort was taxed except sporadically. Systematic taxation was on low-grown paddy only.

(1) The Grain Taxes were criticized by the abolitionists on the ground that they violated the very principle of taxation. I. S. Leadam of the Cobden Club stated that it was contradictory to the principle that taxation should be proportionate to wealth and that taxation

should be certain (in Ferguson 1890:11). By contrast in Ceylon since 1824 the produce of all lands was exempted from taxation in order to encourage capitalist plantation enterprises except the tax on grain which affected the poorest section of the population living on a subsistence economy (S.P. III, 1892:90).

(2) Several provisions of the Ordinance designed to protect the interests of the peasant were a dead letter. 'The provision exempting crop commuted lands from the tax in the event of failure to realize a crop of three-fold has in my experience been a dead letter' (S.P. III, 1892:33). Governor Havelock said that 'under compulsory commutation, payment is enforced, whether there be a good crop or a bad crop or no crop at all...' (S.P. III, 1892:6). Similarly the powers given to Grain Commissioners under Section 7 'to determine the mode in which the grain tax shall be payable', and under Section 8 pertaining to the amount of annual commutation and the final determination of the ownership of land, were all ineffectual, for the regular administrative procedure was to obtain the advice of the Mudaliyar, who in turn depended on the village headman (appointed originally on his recommendation). Effectively, procedural matters under the Ordinance were determined by village headmen, who were in most instances the *de facto* 'assessors'. Thus one of the main criticisms of the Ordinance of 1878 and the tax in general related to the power of headmen, who, moreover, in the Kandyan provinces, by Sections 22 and 23 of the Proclamation of 21 November 1818 were exempt from all taxes, including the paddy tax. Governor Havelock noted:

> It is upon information supplied by chiefs and headmen holding office that the assessment of the paddy tax is mainly based. And these chiefs and headmen, not only in the Kandyan Provinces but also in the Maritime Provinces, are the collectors of the Paddy tax and receive a commission on their collections amounting in the aggregate to about Rs. 50,000 or 5% of the proceeds of the tax. (S.P. III, 1892:3–4)

In fact the village headman became an indirect kind of renter. As an unpaid official, he had vested interests in the retention of the tax. The accusation was also levelled that lands sold under auction were often bought by headmen or by others on behalf of headmen. A constant theme in Administration Reports was that peasants themselves were using the misery caused by the grain tax to defraud co-owners. Administration Report of 1887 for Uva gives a dismal account of corruption and injustice in the Commutation Register of 1878. The government Agent (Aelian King) states further that the assessors and writers of registers 'effected a balance in their figures by adding to one man's tax what was taken off another's' (A.R. 1887:214A).

(3) The plight of the *goiya* (peasant) in a subsistent economy was spotlighted by the abolitionists. Panabokke in his evidence before the grain tax committee of 1890 estimated that the expenses for cultivating a field of two acres in the Kandyan area was Rs. 107/96, leaving no profit to the peasant (S.P. VII, 1890:144). A. R. Dawson in the same report showed the unequal incidence of the tax on fields of varying degrees of fertility and the unjust and evil effects thereof (S.P. VII, 1890:145).

In the Kandyan highlands the peasants had an opportunity to sell home-grown coffee or work for wage labour in the coffee plantations, but with the coffee crash of 1869 this avenue too was closed. In Sabaragamuva, the Government Agent who was no abolitionist pointed out that the yield of paddy was fivefold (as it is today). He said that in 'Sabaragamuva and elsewhere, where money is little used and transactions are generally conducted on the barter system, the inconsiderate institution of the fixed annual payment in money, for the previous mode of payment of a tax in kind has carried inconvenience, and brought condemnation of the tax not actually deserved as a tax' (Government Agent, Sabaragamuva in S.P. III, 1892:35). From information gathered in his conversation with Sinhalese leaders, Governor Havelock nicely highlighted the plight of the *goiya*. The grower of the paddy is the consumer of his own produce; rarely has he a margin of profit or outside source of income. 'If (1) he has a good crop, if (2) when the paddy tax falls he has reaped his crop, if (3) he has a fair sale for that portion of his crop which he may not need for his own sustenance, he is probably able to meet his liability to pay the tax without serious difficulty.' But if one or more of these conditions fail 'and failure of one or more is a frequent occurrence—his problems begin' (S.P. III, 1892:22). It seems quite clear that in a subsistence economy, a tax of one-tenth or more of the produce compulsorily commuted into a money payment on the judgement of unsympathetic assessors would be a great blow to peasant cultivators.

(4) When assessment was based on information provided by village headmen with vested interest in the tax, and by British

civil servants with little knowledge of peasant society, gross over-assessment is only to be expected. George Wall pointed out an example of such over-assessment in the four districts of the Central Province in the years 1862 and 1888.

	1862	1888
Uva	Rs. 21,790	Rs. 54,207
Nuwara Eliya	Rs. 11,485	Rs. 22,270
Matale	Rs. 10,638	Rs. 22,667
Kandy	Rs. 24,277	Rs. 54,924
	Rs. 68,190	Rs. 154,068

The tax has been more than doubled though the area of land cultivated and the production of paddy in the region was the same for the two years (S.P. III, 1892:95). Ashmore, an able civil servant, was asked to reassess the Udukinda taxes (Uva Province) in 1887 owing to complaints of over-assessment. The original assessment was Rs. 29,002; Ashmore's revision was Rs. 17,136, a 41 per cent reduction! Ashmore gave two reasons for the over-assessment:

(1) over-estimation of the value of paddy;

(2) mistake as to the English equivalents of the native measurements.

'It appears that in the Udukinda division of Uva the assessing officer thought that an *amunam* was the equivalent of two acres whereas it was there the equivalent of one' (S.P. III, 1892:127). Ashmore goes on to say that by contrast with the over-assessment of peasant estates, those of the rich were under-assessed.

> The lands of chiefs and of the richest class of cultivators have been found to be greatly underestimated in extent, and rated as too low an order of fertility. This is to be attributed to the corruptibility of the native assessors, whom the Revenue officers responsible for the early commutations had insufficient leisure to check. (S.P. III, 1892:128)

Herbert Wace, Assistant Government Agent of Sabaragamuva, in his report of 1888 mentions several commonly made criticisms of the tax. (*a*) Calculations are made in terms of sowing area, not of surveys of land (which do not exist). Hence every Grain Commissioner follows his own scheme guided by his own assessor's opinion of extent and yield, subject to his own personal inspiration and revision. (*b*) One rate is generally made for a whole *koralē* (administrative division) as the price of paddy, no allowance being made for advantages possessed by one village over another regarding adjacency to a market, facilities for transport, favourable rainfall, relative fertility of the soil, etc. (A.R. 1888: 11, 12A). That these conditions could result in severe cases of miscalculation is pointed out by Ashmore.

Ashmore points out that in the Talpe Pattu, Galle District (Southern Province), the rate of taxation assumes that one acre yields twenty bushels of paddy; in Gangaboda Pattu of the same district, which possesses the same type of soil, the assessment is seventeen per acre. By contrast Gampaha of the Uva Province, which is far less in fertility than the earlier mentioned area, is assessed as follows (S.P. II, 1892:3):

Year	1840	1864	1871	1878	1887
Bushels per acre	30	31·3	34·5	35·7	36·8

In other instances very basic information has been incorrectly calculated. A. R. Dawson, Government Agent of the Western Province, mentions in his report of 1890 that his predecessor, in the previous year's administration report, states that of the 44,000 acres of paddy land in the Negombo District, over 38,000 acres pay either one-fourth or one-half of the crop as tax to government. Dawson says that in fact there are only 15,000 acres under cultivation in the area, of which 8,331 acres are taxed at a tenth, 6,300 acres at a fourth, 369 acres at a half. The previous Government Agent had not been able to account for his error. Dawson concludes by saying that he hopes, in the following year, to tax the district at a fair and uniform rate of a tenth of the produce (A.R. 1889:5B).

(5) Dawson's account highlights an important problem, namely the existence of different rates of taxation in the same district, based on the conditions of tenure at the time of the capitulation of the Maritime Provinces over eighty years ago. These conditions of tenure were hardly applicable to the 1880's, yet according to the Blue Book of 1892 the following tax rates prevailed: $\frac{1}{2}$, $\frac{1}{3}$, $\frac{1}{4}$, $\frac{1}{5}$, $\frac{1}{8}$, $\frac{1}{10}$, $\frac{1}{14}$, $\frac{1}{20}$ of the produce. We noted that in 1889 in Negombo 6300 acres were taxed at a fourth, and 369 acres at a half. In Hevagam Korale in the Western Province 880 acres were taxed at a half and 3039 at one-fourth in 1880 (S.P. XXXIV, 1880). In the Salpiti Korale in 1880 (Western Province) 377 acres were taxed at a half and 1747 acres at one-fourth (S.P. XL, 1880:3). In the Siyane Korale

354 acres were taxed at a half, 5269 at a fourth and 549 at a third in 1881 (S.P. III, 1881:21). The Government at several times attempted to induce peasants to 'redeem' these high rates by a money payment and bring them down to one-tenth, but 'redemption' was in many areas a failure, as the above facts collected at random from the reports of Grain Commissioners suggest. It is needless to say that such rates of taxation in a peasant economy, with increasing population and a constant area of land for cultivation, would have had disastrous results.

(6) The over-assessment and miscalculation had one consequence at least—sales of land by government for default of tax. Where gross miscalculations occurred the sales and the consequent 'evictions' would be greater. Two glaring cases of such evictions come from Udukinda Division (Uva) and Walapane Division (Nuwara Eliya District).

Udukinda 'evictions'

The reassessment of Udukinda by Ashmore came about as a result of the fantastic land sales that occurred here during the period 1882–5. According to Fisher's report on these evictions, $22\frac{1}{2}$ per cent of the total area of land was sold during this period. When sold the amount realized was 22 per cent in advance of the tax due upon them! This is actually not unique to Udukinda but true more or less of practically every area where land was sold for default of tax. These sales deprived 2930 heads of households representing 14,650 persons (about 49 per cent of the population of the division) of a means of livelihood. Of these persons 599 (20 per cent) were compelled to leave their homes; 2000 cultivated the fields of others as tenants; 127 were absolutely destitute. Of the 3244 fields sold 985 were bought by villagers; 2259 passed out of their hands. Of the latter 694 were purchased by low-country people, 446 by Moors and Tamils, 670 by headmen, while 145 infertile fields bought by the Crown were returned to the owners in the Jubilee year (S.P. IV, 1891. Detailed statistics for each village in the Division are available in S.P. IV, 1891:5–12).

Walapane 'evictions'

Le Mesurier points out that serious evictions took place in Walapane between 1882–6. The total number of fields in the Division was 18,848. Of this 2889 or 15 per cent of the fields were sold for default of payment of tax. Of those sold 1900 fields were recultivated by their new owners, while the rest were abandoned. Among the original owners of these fields 1048 were dead, and 382 with their families had left the district. The fields were bought by the following: 1001 were purchased by resident Kandyans, 1260 by Low Countrymen and Moors, 628 by the Crown (A.R. 1886). It was complained that the detailed statistics regarding these evictions were 'lost' by the Government.

The Walapane evictions were a great public scandal. It resulted in public criticism of the Government in Ceylon and in England and several tracts were written on the 'Ceylon Starvation Question'. The Government appointed R. W. D. Moir, Government Agent, Central Province, to inquire further into these allegations. Moir, a supporter of the tax, rejected the statistics given by Le Mesurier on the deaths in Walapane, but admitted the gravity of the problem. He reduced the number of persons who died during this period to 573. He stated further that the land sales were only indirectly due to the tax. There was first the failure of coffee, secondly the depletion of the fertility of the land owing to the opening up of new plantations, and thirdly over-assessment of the fields for taxation purposes. As a result people had no cash to pay the tax—hence the land sales (S.P. XXIX, 1889: 2–6). Actually none of these latter arguments are denied by Le Mesurier.

LAND SALES UNDER THE GRAIN TAX

In the preceding account we made certain criticisms of the tax under the Ordinances of 1866 and 1878 in order to give the reader some impression of its social consequences. For our purposes even more crucial are the land sales that occurred under the Grain Tax. There is practically no statistical evidence of land sales previous to 1866; more evidence is available for the period of compulsory commutation (1878–92), though even here the statistical evidence is incomplete and not always sociologically meaningful.

(1) Between 1880 and 1888 in six of the nine provinces where the Ordinance of 1878 was implemented there were 29,899 sales of paddy land by the Crown in default of payment of tax. We do not know the extent of these lands except that most of them were less than ten acres each. Dawson, Principal Assistant Colonial

Secretary, commenting on these sales states: 'It should be explained that these were sales of defined and separate parcels of land in only some instances, and were, I should say, in a majority of cases sales only of undivided shares in a parcel of land' (S.P. III, 1892: 9). Many of these were probably sales of shares (*pangu*) in an estate (parcel of land): but this highlights the serious disruption of the traditional *pangu* system whereby shares may leave the estate for good. It should also be noted that these sales do not account for lands sold to private parties to raise money for tax payment, which may amount to a much greater number, such as land sold to kinsmen in Pahala Madagama, and to speculators willing to pay ready cash.

(2) The following statistics are available for the Central Province for the years 1881–5, when 3607 parcels of paddy land and 6486 of high land amounting to 10,093 parcels of land were sold by the Fiscal on the orders of the court for the recovery of private debts. The likelihood is that most of these debts were incurred in attempting to pay the paddy tax. During the same period there were 3770 sales by the Crown in default of the tax, so that in a period of five years in the Central Province alone there were 13,863 sales of parcels of land. According to the census of 1881 and 1891 there were in this province 54,387 and 56,009 adult cultivators respectively. Assuming that each cultivator represented a family, one in about four families lost a 'parcel' of land. This again is a conservative estimate since we have no data on private sales which may have accounted for a much larger number. Once again, if each sale represented a share in a common estate the consequence of these sales no doubt seriously altered the structure of traditional land tenure systems (S.P. III, 1892: 113–15).

(3) We have no evidence for all Island Sales. However, the Grain Tax Committee Report of 1890 has a table giving the sales of land for certain areas in the five Provinces where the Ordinance of 1878 was implemented. The following table is constructed from the table given in their report (S.P. VII, 1890: 213). The sales are incomplete for they do not account for the years 1899–92, and it excludes sales under the Ordinance of 1866. It also (judiciously, from the Government point of view) excludes several areas where drastic land sales occurred, for example Udukinda in the Uva District and Walapane in the Nuwara Eliya District.

Table 9. *Land sales for select areas in five provinces*

Province and District	Total area under cultivation in acres	No. of acres sold under Ordinance of 1878 for default up to 31 December 1888	No. of acres remaining sold on 31 December 1888
Western			
Colombo	47,484	593	174
Kalutara	45,273	3100	1725
Negombo	14,932	45	45
Central			
Kandy	19,130	141	141
Southern			
Galle	45,641	3442	1592
Matara	45,997	1386	1205
Hambantota	20,118	325	212
Eastern			
Batticaloa	75,690	3452	2304
Sabaragamuva			
Ratnapura	26,539	2027	1382
Kegalle	21,408	108	108
Total	362,212	14,619	8888

The facts in columns 2 and 3 mean that about one in every twenty-six acres was sold. However, according to the government 5731 acres was gratuitously returned to the owners, or were redeemed by the owners themselves leaving a sum of 8888 acres remaining sold on 31 December 1888. We doubt the accuracy of these 'redemptions', but even from this 'doctored' account roughly about one in forty-one acres permanently changed hands. It should be noted that this too is an extremely conservative estimate, since it does not account for (*a*) certain areas like Uva and the Nuwara District, where drastic land sales occurred; (*b*) it omits sales of land of the Fiscal on the orders of the Court for the recovery of private debts; (*c*) it, naturally, gives no account of private sales during this period.

(4) Crucial for our work are the land sales in the region in and

around Madagama. Madagama is located in the Southern Province in the District of Galle. On its eastern side is the District of Matara (also in the Southern Province), on its west is the District of Kalutara (Western Province) and on its north the District of Ratnapura (Sabaragamuva Province). Since it is possible that related land tenure systems existed in these areas it will be interesting to consider the statistics on land sales for default of tax in *three* of these areas (Galle, Matara and Kalutara Districts) for which some evidence is available.

Table 10. *Land sales: Galle District 1883–91*

	Year	No. of lots sold to private parties	Bought by Crown
	1883	283	72
	1884	390	232
	1885	291	468
	1886	167	504
	1887	222	385
	1888	458	461
	1889	441	No information
	1890	204	No information
	1891	62	No information
Total		2518	2122

Total of sales in default of tax 4,640
Total of lots 31,384

Proportion of sales to lots $\frac{4,640}{31,384} = \frac{15}{100}$

i.e. about 3 in every 20 lots changed hands during this period.

The above evidence could be collected from Administration Reports of 1888 and 1891, which provide some information about land sales in the Galle District of the Southern Province to private parties and the Crown for default in the payment of the tax. Since this is the province where Madagama is located the evidence is of interest to us (see A.R. 1877:16A; A.R. 1880, Section E; A.R. 1891:7E). The following evidence is available for the Kalutara District from Administration Reports (A.R. 1886: 135A; A.R. 1886:133A; A.R. 1888:8B–9B; A.R. 1891:5B).

Between 1881 and 1886, 1716 lots approximating 2075 acres were sold by the Crown or to private parties in default of tax. No evidence regarding acreage is available for 1887. However 344 lots (i.e. plots) were sold in that year and since each lot in this district averages slightly over an acre we shall take the acreage sold for the year as 360. Between 1887 and 1891, 724 acres were sold. Thus a total of about 3143 acres were sold between 1881 and 1891. The total acreage under cultivation for the district according to the first commutation register is 48,103 acres. In the Kalutara District 3,243/48,103 (6·6 per cent) were sold during the period. In all the three districts under consideration a small proportion of infertile lands sold to the Crown were redeemed by the owners, but we do not know the exact proportion.

Table 11. *Land sales: Matara District 1883–91*

Year	No. of lots sold to private parties	Bought by Crown
1883	Tax not implemented	—
1884	100	48
1885	289	113
1886	126	75
1887	197	51
1888	300	93
1889	308	Information not available
1890	182	Information not available
1891	122	Information not available
Total	1624	380

Total of lots sold for default 2,004

Total number of lots in the district according to grain register 27,994

Proportion of sales to lots $\frac{2,004}{27,994} = \frac{7}{100}$

i.e. about 2 in every 28 lots changed hands during this period.

The evidence is clear that in the district in which Madagama is located and two adjoining districts to the west and east of Madagama serious land changes had taken place under the Ordinance of 1878, according to government statistics which can err only on the conservative side. The extent of these changes in land ownership become even more impressive when we realize that it does not consider land sold by peasant cultivators themselves in order to pay the tax. It should be remembered that in Madagama there were no cases of land sold by government for non-payment of tax. All the Madagama transactions were regular deeds of transfer from one person to another. There is therefore warrant for inferring that this type of sale—to kinsmen, or shareowners, or outsiders—constituted a very important category of land sales, probably even more important than government sales. If so, the changes in land ownership during this period must have been of the most radical character, altering considerably traditional land tenure arrangements and the power structure of the society. To sum up, the evidence is strong that Madagama was no isolated case: similar consequences were felt in other areas of the Southern Province and all parts of the Island where the Ordinance of 1878 was in force.

As far as the Western and Southern and parts at least of the Sabaragamuva Provinces were concerned these sales were in undivided shares. The Government Agents and their assistants in these provinces in their administration reports often refer to two things. (*a*) A constant reference to 'subdivision of property' and the *taṭṭumāru* system. The term 'subdivision of property' obviously refers to 'fractional shares' in our sense. *Taṭṭumāru* refers to our *karamāru* but may also refer to *taṭṭumāru* of our usage owing to a failure to understand its significance. (For example see A.R. 1877:15A and A.R. 1887:33A for Sabaragamuva; A.R. 1886:78A and A.R. 1885:87A for Southern Province; A.R. 1890:18B for Kalutara District in the Western Province). (*b*) The parcels sold were in undivided shares, and this was one factor responsible for their sale (another was infertility of the soil). For example, if one share owner did not pay the tax the whole field was sold, while in other cases there was deliberate fraud by co-owners. That most of the sales were in 'undivided parcels' is true, for the government published details of the last twelve (or eight) sales in several districts in the Grain Tax Report of 1890 (S.P. VII, 1890:149–60). A summary of this fascinating document is given in Table 12. Some of the fractions were extremely minute. For example, in the Matara District there was a parcel of land of 30 k sowing area which was divided among eighteen shareholders in fractions with a denominator of 224! Our own opinion is that much of this account is misleading. According to the *taṭṭumāru* system, a group of individuals work a whole *yāya* viewed as an estate; one field may be worked in rotation by one individual or a few. If the latter is sold for default one of two things must happen. (*a*) The persons who worked the field must lose their concomitant share in the whole estate. In which case government sales must not be in terms of 'parcels of land' but shares; otherwise people who worked the field must be persuaded to renounce their rights to other plots. (*b*) A piece of land is put up for sale. The individual(s) who worked the plot for that *taṭṭumāru* season or year are not the 'owners' of the plot. All persons who own shares in a *gama* have claim to that plot. Hence these claims would be asserted during sales, accounting at least for some of the share fractions in the lists presented in the Grain Tax Report.

Table 12. *Summary of last twelve/eight sales under Ordinance of 1878*

District	More than one owner	No. of sales
Colombo	8	12
Negombo	8	12
Kalutara	7	12
Kandy	6	12
Galle	9	12
Hambantota	6	12
Batticaloa	8	12
Trincomalee	0	12
Ratnapura	9	12
Kegalle	1	8
Uva	5	8

In either case these sales must have resulted at least in changes in hamlet structure and 'a revolution in the ownership of property' (to use Le Mesurier's words in A.R. 1887:83A), which in turn would have had drastic consequences in *any* land tenure system based on undivided shares in land. It also seems clear from Administration Reports that such undivided ownership of property was the norm in most parts of Sabaragamuva, Western and Southern Provinces. That it was even more widespread is evident from the list of the last twelve sales in the several districts mentioned above. More research on the Grain Tax would show, we think, that its effects, when combined with the loss of the structural prerequisite would have been analogous to that of the enclosure movement in England.

A rather detailed account of the Grain Tax was necessary since no scholarly analysis of this important episode is available. We have adequately shown its serious consequences on Sinhalese social structure in general. This has significance for anthropological methodology which in general is not equipped to handle change, a point we shall take up in our conclusion. Our account was prompted by the necessity to show that the land sales in Madagama were caused by the operation of the Grain Tax. We have certainly not proved this, but there is considerable justification for such an inference. Five of the eight sales in Ihala Madagama took place during the period of the 1878 Ordinance (applied in Madagama in 1882). The other sales occurred at the end of the period of the renting system: they may also have arisen as a result of the non-payment of taxes (in kind). We do not agree with commentators on the tax that payment in kind (tithe) under the renting system had little adverse effects. The following comments are relevant. (*a*) The failure to pay the tithe was peculiarly suited for land sales to private parties. If *X* cannot pay the tax, *Y* would do so, putting *X* under *Y*'s debt. A consequence of this would be indebtedness, and mortgage with possible eventual sale of land. This exactly fits with traditional accounts of mortgage and indebtedness among peasants in Kandyan times (D'Oyly 1929:61–4). (*b*) We believe that while few land sales would have occurred in the earliest period of the tax, increasing population combined with a lack of increase in the cultivated area of land would result in an inability to pay such a high tax in produce or in cash. The Ordinance of 1878 merely enhanced an existing trend. Whether the tax was commuted or not land sales would have occurred, though probably in less drastic fashion. (*c*) In an economy where alternative modes of employment were not available or were devalued, and land was a valued asset, sales would not normally occur (especially to outsiders) except under economic hardship. These sales were concentrated in a period of twenty-three years; hence the 'crisis' could not have been a fortuitous one. It seems reasonable to identify it with the Grain Tax, where similar effects were demonstrably felt elsewhere.

For the most sceptical reader we can at least show that land sales *did* occur in Madagama, and altered the traditional modes of land ownership and tenure. We can also demonstrate that drastic land sales occurred in three districts environing Madagama. In all these areas land was held in undivided shares, and some form of 'taṭṭumāru' prevailed. Even if the land sales in the two cases were caused by totally unrelated factors (which we deny) the end result is the same—changes in the ownership of property and land tenure systems. Thus the kind of effects that land sales had in Madagama land tenure may have occurred in the other areas mentioned.

Finally, we can adopt a reverse procedure in order to assess the importance of the Grain Tax. One of the major criticisms of the Grain Tax by the abolitionists was that village *pravēni* lands went into the hands of speculators and headmen. If this assertion was correct for the country at large, it should also be manifest in the Madagama land sales. This again is indeed the case, for the lands sold were to headmen and their kinsmen.

(1) Elias Gunawardene ($\frac{1}{16} + \frac{1}{8}$) and Amarawickreme Gunawardene ($\frac{1}{12}$), father and son, were related to the Mudaliyar of the time.

(2) Maddegama Opisara ($\frac{1}{8}$) as the name suggests was the village headman of Neluva. The village headman was known in Sinhalese as police *muladāniya* because he was sole police officer (*opisara*) for the area.

(3) Don David Rubasin Gunawardene ($\frac{1}{32}$) was village headman and later Registrar of Marriages.

(4) Panangala Liyanage Suaris ($\frac{1}{24} + \frac{1}{56}$) was Rubasin Gunawardene's brother's wife's brother.

Elias Gunawardene sold $\frac{1}{8}$ of the share he bought to P. L. Suaris in 1892; and after 1909 all shares owned by Elias Gunawardene and Amarawickreme Gunawardene were sold to the Rubasin Gunawardenes and the Panangala Liyanages. We present this relationship in Fig. 16.

Don David Rubasin Gunawardene was village headman of the adjacent village Lelwala during the Grain Tax period. His brother married Panangala Liyanage Suaris' sister. Suaris and his *massina* (cross-cousin, brother-in-law) David R. Gunawardene not only bought shares in Ihala Madagama, but also in Lelwala itself. In the next generation this alliance was cemented when P. L. Suaris' daughter married David Rubasin Gunawardene's son. Moreover these land speculations combined with a marriage to a headman enhanced Suaris' family honour, so that his son P. L. Uporis himself became a village headman of Neluva. During this generation the lands bought by Elias Gunawardene and Amarawickreme Gunawardene passed into the families of the Rubasin Gunawardenes and Panangala Liyanages.

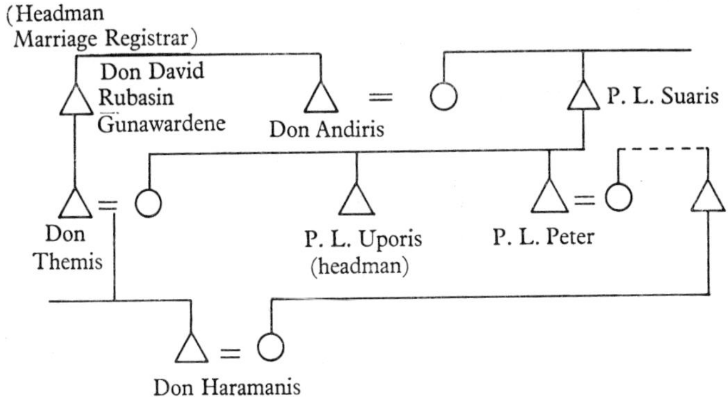

Fig. 16.

In the third generation the alliance was continued when Don David's son's son, married Panangala Liyanage Peter's *massina's* daughter. The implications of these alliances will be discussed in a subsequent chapter. For the present the evidence is clear that lands were indeed sold to headmen and wealthy speculators. If so the criticisms of the abolitionists that similar trends occurred all over Ceylon may be substantially correct.

FACTOR OF CHANGE: THE ROMAN-DUTCH LAW AND THE TREND TOWARDS BILATERAL INHERITANCE

Some of the major social changes brought about by British rule sprang from the introduction of the Roman-Dutch law of marriage, inheritance and divorce to the Sinhalese 'Maritime Provinces'. The introduction of this legal system sprang from a missupposition by the British that the prevailing law of the land during Dutch times was the Roman-Dutch law. That the Dutch 'introduced' the Roman-Dutch law to Ceylon is certain. Dutch civil and *landraads* existed in the Island, but the question is, as Jayawardene puts it, what law applied in the courts (Jayawardene 1901:4). It seems reasonable to assume that by and large the Roman-Dutch law applied only to Dutch residents of Ceylon and to converted Sinhalese Protestants, while the majority of the citizens were governed by their traditional laws. Instructions issued by the Governor-General of India to the Governor of Ceylon in 1656–65 states: 'Justice is administered to the Dutch according to the laws in force in the Fatherland and the statutes of Batavia. The natives are governed according to the laws of their country if these are clear and reasonable, otherwise according to our laws' (Pieters 1908:117). The Moslems were permitted to use their own laws unhampered by the Dutch. As far as the Hindus of the north were concerned the Dutch actually codified their customary law as the 'Tesavalamai Code'. It therefore seems quite unlikely that the Sinhalese Buddhists were made an exception and were forced to accept the Roman-Dutch law. Hayley says that the 'customs of the country were enforced in each *koralē* by the native *Mudaliyar* of the *koralē*, subject to an appeal to a senior civil servant of Colombo, who was given the native title of Disave' (Hayley 1923:23). Jayawardene after surveying some of the evidence available concludes that the 'Roman-Dutch law of succession inheritance and *fidei commissum* does not seem to have been imposed on the Sinhalese' (Jayawardene 1901:5).

After their conquest of the Maritime Provinces the British by the proclamations of 1799 and 1801 gave the Sinhalese the right to use their own laws and customs. A proclamation of December 1802 states, that where a native dies intestate the shares are to be divided according to the laws and customs of the deceased caste and class (Proclamation of 30 December 1802). Marshall writing in 1848 says that no doubt had ever been entertained 'that the native inhabitants of the Maritime provinces were entitled to be governed and had always been governed...by their respective usages and customs, except when they had been abrogated or altered by positive law' (in Hayley 1923:27). In 1835 a case from Kalutara, Western Province, was sent back by the Supreme Court to be decided 'after consultation with those best acquainted with the Sinhalese law of inheritance' (Jayawardene 1901:7–8). But between 1803 and 1833 the Roman-Dutch law was sporadically applied in several cases where the parties were Sinhalese. The reason for this lack of consistency in the application of the law seems to have been due to the assumption by several judges that the Roman-Dutch law was preserved by the act of capitulation; or that since a proclamation of 23 September 1799 restored temporarily Dutch courts (*landraads*) it was assumed by others that the Dutch law was automatically applicable to the Sinhalese (Balasingham, vol. I, 1929:149–50). A drastic change was introduced by the charter of 1833 which repealed the right of the Sinhalese to be governed by their own laws; henceforth they were to be governed by Roman-Dutch law. By 1861, the Roman-Dutch law was fully accepted as the general law of the country, so that Justice Thomson could state unequivocally in his *Institutes of Ceylon*:

> The Roman-Dutch law modified by statute and the introduction of English law, and of modern equity, forms the law of the maritime provinces, and is extended to every inhabitant of the island, except in those instances in which such an inhabitant is by privilege under the sanction of another form of law... (Thomson, vol. II, 1866:12)

Jayawardene summed up the situation well when he said that the Dutch introduced the Roman-Dutch law into Ceylon but the British established it among the Ceylonese (1901:6).

The features of the Roman-Dutch law of marriage and inheritance relevant for our purposes are the following: (*a*) community of property at marriage, (*b*) the strictly bilateral rules of inheritance, and (*c*) the relative inflexibility of its divorce procedures.

(*a*) Under Roman-Dutch law community of property comes into effect soon after marriage. Once introduced it is a permanent arrangement which can come to an end only with the decease of one of the spouses, or with divorce. All goods possessed by the married pair at the time of marriage and acquired after marriage through whatever means (except *fidei commissum* and gifts by husband to wife which are considered *causa nuptiarum*) and all profits and losses incurred are included in the community. Debts whether incurred before or after marriage have to be met out of the community. At the death of either husband or wife community of property ceases *ipso fine*. The common property is divided into two parts, one part is given to the surviving spouse, and the other to the heirs of the deceased. Generally after the death of a spouse community of property exists between the surviving parent and the children (but not between survivors and collateral heirs). However, this law was never adopted in Ceylon (Pereira 1913:13). The children could however ask for an inventory to be taken and a division of property made (Pereira 1913:240). The female spouse is considered to be a jural minor in respect of the community of goods. Her husband is her curator. She has no power to appear in court or enter into any contract without the knowledge and consent of her husband and is bound and liable for the debts of her husband (though not the husband for his wife's debts). The husband had absolute power of disposing of common property without her consent and even against direct opposition of his wife. The wife is, however, permitted to dispose of her property as she pleases by last will without the consent of her husband (Pereira 1913:237–48).

(*b*) Regarding intestate succession the Roman-Dutch law is strictly bilateral in character. The law of North Holland as well as that of the South is unambiguously clear in this regard. Let us consider briefly the law of North Holland, which according to some authorities was the general law of Ceylon before the Ordinance of 1876 (Lee 1953: 403). According to Lee the main principles of intestate succession are as follows:

Descendants: children excluding grandchildren, grandchildren excluding greatgrandchildren, etc.

Ascendants: two surviving parents equally; one surviving parent solely; in default of parents, grandparents (on both sides or on one side) equally; a single surviving grandparent solely; and so on to the exclusion of collaterals.

Collaterals: brothers and sisters of the whole or of the half blood equally to the exclusion of nephews and nieces; collaterals of the third or remoter degrees equally without representation (Lee 1953:94). For other aspects of the law of intestate succession the reader is referred to Lee (1953). For our purposes the examples given above illustrate the strictly bilateral orientation of the law introduced into Ceylon.

(*c*) Marriage is dissolved in Roman-Dutch law by either death or divorce. Divorce is granted only on two grounds, adultery and malicious desertion, and granted by a decree of court. Any other cause for divorce is insufficient under Roman-Dutch law unless it can be brought under the rubric of the above. Some authorities, by an extensive interpretation of the texts, include sodomy and perpetual imprisonment as causes for divorce (Lee 1953:85). The law of Ceylon which is based on the Roman-Dutch law gives three grounds for divorce (Act No. 19 of 1907), viz. adultery subsequent to marriage, malicious desertion, and incurable impotency at the time of marriage. The last according to Roman Dutch law renders a marriage voidable (Lee 1953:94).

It seems clear that these features of the law, especially the extreme jural inferiority of the woman and her jural subordination to the husband; the idea of the community of goods, the under-emphasis of the rights of a person's father, especially that of a woman's; the strictly bilateral inheritance rules; and the inflexibility of the law of divorce seem totally contradictory to the more 'liberal' features of Sinhalese customary law outlined in chapter 3. From 1833 to 1876 there was no question about the relevance of these laws for case decisions were generally based on them. However, the first major substantive enactment of a law of marriage and inheritance was in 1876, Ordinance No. 15. 'An Ordinance to amend the law relating to the matrimonial rights of married persons with regard to property and the law of inheritance.' The first part of the Ordinance dealing with matrimonial rights altered substantively the Roman-Dutch law on the subject, and brought the law closer to the English civil law. The main motive here was to help English residents in Ceylon, rather than from interest in the Sinhalese population (Balasingham, vol. II, 1933:486). The major change was the abolition of the community of property and the enhancement of the jural status of women. The immovable property of a woman married after the Ordinance belongs to her separate estate. She is not liable for the debts of her husband. She has liberty to dispose of her property and enter into a mortgage contract, with the consent of her husband. A woman's wages and earnings are considered to be her separate property, even though she was married before the Ordinance. All jewels, personal and household ornaments, clothes, etc., as well as what she has acquired as gifts from her husband belong to her. She could alienate these *with the consent of her husband*, or without his consent by last will. However, all movable property other than those enumerated above belongs to the husband absolutely. This included the dowry (Balasingham, vol. II, 1933:487). The Ordinance No. 18 of 1923 changed the law still further by enhancing the jural status of women bringing the law in line with English law on the subject. The married woman is now treated as a *feme sole*. According to contemporary law a woman has complete autonomy over her property so that marriage has practically no effect on her property rights.

Part III of Ordinance No. 15 of 1876 specifies the laws of intestate succession, which are once again substantively the ones current today. It is almost entirely based on Roman-Dutch law. For our purposes the most relevant aspects of the law of inheritance are:

(*a*) On the death of a spouse the property is divided in two halves, one-half belongs to the surviving spouse and the other half is divided equally among the children *per capita*, or grandchildren *per stirpes*.

(*b*) Males and females, irrespective of the type of marriage contracted or residence arrangement, share equally in either parent's estate.

Trend toward bilaterality

We noted that traditional Sinhalese rules of inheritance were in theory bilateral, but the distinction between temporary and permanent rights in *pravēni* combined with marriage preferences produced a major trend towards unilinearity and a patrilineal residential aggregation of males. This in turn facilitated the operation of the *taṭṭumāru* system of land tenure. If we place the data presented in the preceding chapter against the ideal model of land tenure, two important features appear in relief, viz. the clear patrilineal trend in the devolution of *pravēni* rights from generation FA^1 to FA^5 (inclusive) and the equally clear trend towards bilaterality from FA^6 downwards. The former trend is conducive to efficient functioning of the model, the latter is not. Thus one of the crucial changes that has occurred in the *empirical* system pertains to the direction of inheritance trends from unilinearity to bilaterality, so that at generation FA^6 the inheritance rules were both in theory and practice bilateral.

Up to generation FA^4 and inclusive of it there is only a single case of females inheriting property: otherwise females are consistently excluded. The rule of residence is consistently virilocal. The exception is however totally consonant with the traditional inheritance laws, for this is a case of two daughters inheriting the patrimonial estate in the absence of male heirs (see Fig. 17).

Dingi Appu had no male heirs: he died intestate and his property devolved on his two daughters, Baru Hamy, whose husband resided uxorilocally in Pahala Madagama, and Loku Hamy who lived virilocally in Batuwangala. At generation FA^5, however, an interesting feature could be noted: a considerable number of females of both branches inherit property *inter vivos* but there is still not a single case of intestate succession for females. At generation FA^6 a radical shift has occurred: most of the females

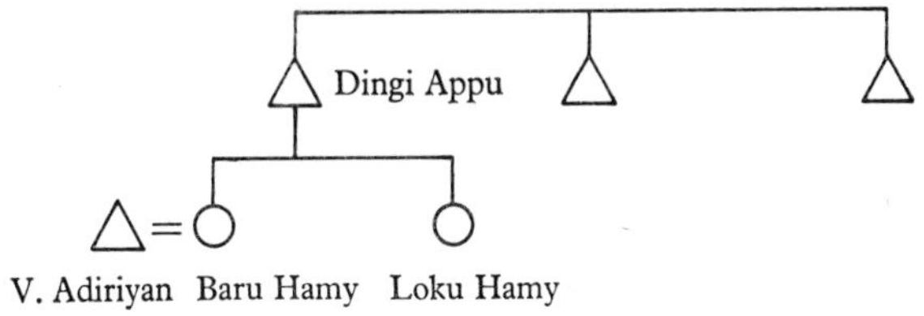

Fig. 17.

of this generation inherited *pravēni* on intestate succession. It is therefore clear that a change in inheritance rules has occurred and either:

(*a*) members of generation FA^5 were making crucial decisions regarding the inheritance rights of their children, or

(*b*) members of generation FA^6 were insisting on rights they did not traditionally claim, irrespective of the wishes of their parents in FA^5. Since no person in generation FA^6 denies the legal right of females to inherit the paternal estate, the trend towards bilaterality would very probably have commenced in generation FA^5. In this generation females were also inheriting property *inter vivos*. This implies that villagers of that generation were beginning to make decisions that gave females more property rights than were traditionally in vogue. Let us consider the trend towards bilateral inheritance from generation FA^5 and after.

Inheritance in 1909 (generation FA^5) and after

We had noted that in 1909, there were about fourteen families of generation FA^5 resident at Pahala Madagama. Regarding the inheritance rule of this generation we notice that women for the first time have inherited *inter vivos*. All three cases of such inheritance in branch *U* have to do with an unusual set of circumstances.

In case *A* according to traditional intestate succession Adiriyan's property should go to the males by the first marriage and the females by the second *per stirpes*. But Adiriyan we saw had to sell his property to an outsider K. G. Arnolis de Silva in 1888; James the second son recovered it. Thus the father gave James the large share, and the rest were divided among all the males of the first marriage and females of the second *per capita*. The female from the first marriage, who was already given in *dīga*, is explicitly excluded, suggesting still the importance of traditional norms. The females of the second marriage are given property *per capita*,

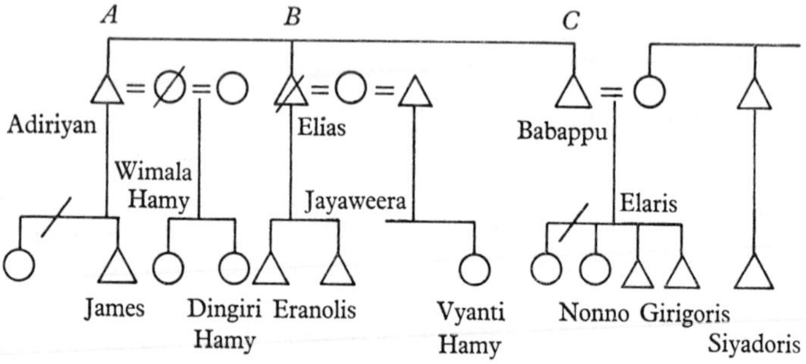

Fig. 18.

rather than *per stirpes*; for the latter mode of division would have curtailed the rights of James who was instrumental in recovering the property.

Case *B* has been discussed on page 86. Briefly stated, Vyanti Hamy probably 'bought' the share from her uterine stepbrother, with her husband Kariyawasam Godage Nikulas' money.

In case *C* Babappu was forced to sell his share to his brother-in-law Adris, probably due to the evil effects of the Grain Tax. Adris retained part of this for himself and his son Siyadoris and transferred the rest to the two sons and a daughter of Babappu. Once again it is interesting to note that the unmarried daughter was given a share, but not the married one.

All these cases of inheritance *inter vivos* are due to special exigencies. There are no cases of succession *inter vivos* in branch *B*, the more stable branch of the *vāsagama*. In generation FA^6, bilateral inheritance in intestate succession is the rule. This is due to the fact that the Roman-Dutch law has become by this time the accepted law of the low country. However, from the sociological point of view what is important is not merely the formal law as interpreted in courts but the perception of the law by villagers. It is in terms of the latter that social action takes place. For this to happen the formal law must reach the village in some way and the villagers in turn must be motivated to accept or reject it. We know that in generation FA^6 aspects of the formal law had been accepted by the villagers. But the time lag is great: for ever since 1833 the Roman-Dutch law was the law of the state—yet up to and inclusive of generation FA^5 (till about 1909) people were acting generally in terms of traditional law. What are the channels of diffusion whereby the formal law of the state reached the village, and was accepted, with reinterpretations, by the villagers themselves?

Channels of diffusion: the courts

One of the primary sources of diffusion of the new legal ideas are the courts themselves. The judicial decisions of the courts would be communicated to the village through litigation. With an increasing scarcity of land and a rising population, litigation in respect of land would increase. Though no accurate statistics are available, a running theme in administrative reports of government agents is the problem of land litigation. Jayawardene in the preface to his monograph on the registration of deeds states that 90 per cent of litigation in Ceylon concerns title to immovable property, that is, generally land (Jayawardene 1919). A specially noteworthy form of litigation was partition litigation, which involved large numbers of people in court action. Partition litigation required a clear statement by the plaintiff(s) of the ownership of the property to be partitioned. In these 'plaints' or 'libels' cognizance has to be taken of the devolution of property according to Roman-Dutch law. Through litigation the villagers also come into contact with lawyers ('proctors', or *perakadōru* as they were called in Sinhalese), who become a direct source for the diffusion of legal ideas. The legal sophistication of 'chronic litigants' can be quite considerable, so that practically in every village there are a number of people who are called *goḍa perakadōruva*, or 'village proctor' owing to their familiarity with the law. For example, P. M. G. Hovis in Pahala Madagama is a *goḍa perakadōruva*.

Notary Publics and the registration of documents

Ever since British rule, land transfers, mortgages, wills and other types of contracts required to be written as notarial deeds and registered. It is evident from the data presented in chapter 4 that a large number of transfers of land were in the form of notarial deeds after 1910. The role of the entrepreneurs is important here; for educated entrepreneurs buying land would be eager to follow strict legal procedure in order to ensure security of title. This in turn would compel the villager to take cognizance of the law. Furthermore, the legal provision requiring the notarial execution of deeds brought the village in contact with the Notary Public. Certain lawyers (proctors) are *ipso jure* notaries, but there were, all over Ceylon, notaries who were not lawyers. They were members of the educated Sinhalese intelligentsia with a licence to execute notarial deeds. There were notary publics in practically every small town in the Maritime Provinces. *Notāris Rālahami* as they were called, they were highly respected and influential in local politics. They were generally Sinhalese-speaking villagers, often indistinguishable from ordinary villagers in dress, directly in touch with village life and thus an important source for the diffusion of legal ideas.

Marriage registration and Registrars of Marriages

Up till the Ordinance of 1876, there was no serious enactment which contained a positive substantial statement about marriage and inheritance, yet after 1833 it was generally assumed that the Roman-Dutch law should apply to residents of the Maritime Provinces. However, for some unaccountable reason there were several Ordinances and Enactments regarding the registration of marriages. The obsession with registration commenced with the preamble to Regulation No. 9, 1822, which stated 'that for the want of sufficient and exact regulations the Registers of the marriages and births of the natives which were established by the former government of the United Province had in several districts become wholly inefficient, and greatly subject to corruption and fraud' (Regulation No. 9, 1822). The reference was to Dutch marriage registers or *thombos* which recorded the marriages of Sinhalese and Dutch Protestants. This regulation made government schoolmasters in each division marriage registrars *ex officio*. No marriage contracted after 1 August 1822 was to be considered legally valid unless registered. Ordinance No. 6, 1847, specified prohibited degrees of marriage, ages of parties, and grounds for divorce as known in Roman-Dutch law.

Several subsequent ordinances were enacted to ensure the registration of Christian marriages, but Regulation 9, 1822, applied to non-Christians. The policy of enforced registration was apparently a failure, for Ordinance No. 13 of 1863 repealed Regulation 9 of 1822. However, the Sinhalese were getting used to registration, for it was noted in 1871 that there were 9605 registered marriages which included only 2081 Christian marriages (S.P. XVI, 1959:173). We noted in an earlier chapter a number of registrations as early as 1848 for Madagama. It is likely that these were registrations under the Ordinance of 1822. Ordinance No. 2 of 1895 reintroduced the requirement of registration as a prerequisite of the legality of marriage, but this was again repealed in the following year. The law from this time onwards was that evidence of a valid marriage consisted of (*a*) registration, or (*b*) 'custom'. Regarding marriages by custom proof of customary rites may be required.

> Where it is proved that the parties who have lived together as man and wife had gone through a form of marriage according to caste and thereby shown the intention to be married, those who seek to establish the marriage between them are not bound to prove that all the necessary ceremonies had been performed.
>
> It will be presumed in the absence of evidence to the contrary that all the necessary ceremonies were performed.
>
> (Balasingham, vol. II, 1933:471–2)

Presumption is strongly in favour of marriage; what may be required is proof that the parties have lived as husband and wife. If they have the reputation among their friends and relations as having been lawfully (i.e. on the basis of custom and repute) married the law presumes that they were living together on the basis of a valid marriage contracted by them.

From 1877 onwards increased attention was given to facilitate registration by the appointment of provincial and district registrars of marriages. Ordinance No. 19 of 1907 created in addition to these officers the very important office of marriage registrar.

> The governor may with the advice of the Executive Council...divide the several provinces of the Island into such and so many divisions for the purpose of the registration of marriages as shall appear expedient, and such divisions or any of them at any time he may, with like advice, amend, alter or abolish (Section 6). The Registrar-General may... appoint one or more persons to each such division, who shall be called Registrar of Marriages... (Section 7)

These officers were also in addition registrars of births and deaths. They were unpaid officers, though they received a commission. It was a coveted job, and soon marriage registrars were within the reach of practically every village in the low country, so that registration of marriage became in the twentieth century almost universally practised in the low country. In contemporary Madagama the villagers perceive registration of marriage as a legal requirement which interestingly enough, is *not* the legal position. Ironically the situation is reversed in contemporary Kandyan law. According to Kandyan law, registration *is* necessary for the legal validity of a marriage though most Kandyan villagers, especially in the remoter areas, hardly ever register their marriages.

Some social problems arising from the Roman-Dutch law

The Roman-Dutch law not only transformed the inheritance rules of the society but also created several social problems. We shall highlight briefly two interrelated problems, one arising from the practice of marriage registration, and the other from the law of divorce.

In contemporary law, registration gives legal validity to a marriage, but absence of registration does not prove the absence of legal marriage. Irrespective of the law, contemporary Madagama folk do not perceive registration in this manner for they regard absence of registration as rendering a marriage *legally* invalid, though acceptable from the point of view of village norms. Superficially one may explain the discrepancy between the actual law and its perception by saying that proof of marriage may be difficult for villagers to advance. Actually it need not be difficult to prove these unions as marriages since they are recognized by everyone as such on the village level. Moreover, the villagers are simply unaware of the law relating to proof of marriage through custom and repute.

More convincingly one could argue that acceptance of registration as a legal requirement of marriage was due to several ordinances, since repealed, which in fact made it a prerequisite. That these ordinances had effects on the behavioural level is seen in the numerous marriages registered in *thombos* as early as 1848 (though there may have been other motivations, of which we have no information, prompting people to register marriages). The fact that father and son registered their 'marriages' on the same day suggests that even at this early date a distinction was being made between acceptability of marriage on the village level and in formal law. Furthermore, registration *in general* is important in law in contexts outside of marriage. Deeds when they are registered give a transaction validity in law over non-registered notarial deeds. Registration of deeds is practically universal among villagers today. Registration of births and deaths is compulsory, and actually practised by Madagama folk. If registration is perceived as extremely important in one context, there is sufficient reason for Madagama folk to generalize it to the context of marriage.

While we could account for the contemporary, near universal practice of marriage registration, and the belief that it is a prerequisite for the legality of marriage, it does not explain why a social problem should necessarily arise from this situation. This has to do with motivational issues associated with the inheritance of property. For if registration is perceived as a legal requirement, then non-registered marriages are legally invalid. The offspring of such non-registered marriages could have no legal rights in the estate of their parents. Heirs next in line may be motivated to exclude them by invoking the legality of registration. In the four cases we have of exclusion of offspring of non-registered marriages, none contested the action in court for everyone perceived registration in the manner stated. In contemporary marriages the problem is less acute for most people register their marriages. It is in respect of marriages contracted in *earlier generations*, a generation or two back, that the issue becomes important. The typical situation is where a member of generation FA^4 or FA^5 has been widowed and then remarried. If one of these marriages is unregistered, the heirs of the registered marriage deny the rights of the heirs of the unregistered one to inherit the parental estate. P. M. G. Elias' wife's second marriage (pp. 84–5) and those of P. M. G. Elaris' heirs from his two marriages are cases in point (p. 81).

Speculators interested in buying shares may resurrect these problems in their own interest as occurred in the latter case. The threat of the dispossession of 'unregistered heirs' in the event of the partition is also present. P. M. G. John (p. 73) states that his father's father's second marriage was unregistered. Therefore he argues that the present heirs to that estate, P. M. G. Derenis and P. M. G. Podi Nona, are not legally entitled to the two shares of $\frac{1}{36}$ they now own. He does not contest their rights now but may do so, he says, in the event of partition. The importance of speculative interests in the threat of dispossessing 'unregistered heirs' is seen in another statement of John. Dingi Appu's daughter Baru Hamy, according to John, had not registered her marriage to V. Adiriyan. On Baru Hamy's death the share reverted to her sister Loku Hamy, who generously gave it back to her sister's husband. Thus legally, says John, Adiriyan could not have sold the share as he did. It should legally belong to Loku Hamy's heirs. These facts are in fact false because we know that Baru Hamy's marriage was registered. However, John's statement shows how the wish to dispossess unregistered heirs is rooted in a motivational context, here the hope of buying the share from the present heirs of the registered marriage.

Even more serious is that of 'desertion'. The problem could be summed quite simply by stating that an act that would have been construed as 'divorce' in the traditional system is, according to the Roman-Dutch law, converted into one of 'desertion'. A case of desertion cannot be reconverted to a 'divorce' owing to the considerable expense involved in court action; and the difficulty of obtaining divorce under the law. The problem can be comprehended in a case like the following one. A man marries a woman who dies, he remarries (registers) but his second wife leaves him. Traditionally this act would be tantamount to divorce. The man takes a third 'wife'—but the third marriage legally has perforce to be a bigamous one if registered, or of simple concubinage if unregistered.

In the case of the latter the offspring of the 'union' would be illegitimate, and not entitled to the parents' estate. This is exactly what happened in the case of Elaris (branch *U*, see p. 81). The problem need not be very important on the level of social action, but for the fact that the 'legitimate heirs' may deny the rights of the 'illegitimate heirs', or may sell their property to a speculator, as happened in the aforesaid case. Under traditional law these problems cannot arise because 'desertion' would be viewed as divorce, and subsequent 'concubinage' would be a legally valid marriage. We have five cases of persons deserting a spouse and 'running away' (as the Sinhalese would phrase it) with another. This creates a whole series of problems pertaining to illegitimacy of children and conflict over inheritance rights.

CHAPTER 6

GENEALOGY AS A CHARTER OF RIGHTS

In this chapter we shall attempt to illustrate the general proposition that in this type of land tenure system a genealogy is a 'charter of rights'. Since the data for Ihala Madagama particularly suit our purpose, we shall present these data in some detail utilizing Pahala Madagama to a lesser extent, mainly for 'controlling' the scanty evidence from Ihala Madagama.

Partition proceedings had been instituted in Ihala Madagama in September 1956 by two non-resident speculators in respect of the paddy fields only; not for the *goḍa iḍam*. When we were there in 1961 no final decree had yet been given. Such court delays are a major problem in Ceylon and are confined not only to partition proceedings. We thus had two systems of land tenure: Pahala Madagama which was functioning more or less adequately on the basis of the traditional *taṭṭumāru* scheme, and Ihala Madagama where the traditional system was doomed to end with the implementation of a court decision on partition. Owing to the partition proceedings that were going on it was almost impossible to get accurate information on the genealogical devolution of shares in this hamlet. However, the 'misinformation' given in the genealogical charters presented by individuals had a great deal of sociological relevance, for it was possible to treat the genealogies as charters of rights and the different charters as expressing a dialectic of conflicting claims.

IHALA MADAGAMA HAMLET: THE DATA

We propose to handle the data in the following manner. We shall initially present the plaintiffs' charter of rights. This charter is elicited from the plaintiffs' libel or plaint which has to state, according to the law of partition, the devolution of shares in the common (Ihala Madagama) estate and a list of all shareowners with the (approximate) shares they hold. Any statement or observation *we* wish to make is included in parentheses. Against the plaintiffs' charter we shall pose the genealogical charters of several selected residents of the hamlet, some of whom support the partition action, and others who oppose the action.

The Ihala Madagama *yāya* consists of about twenty-three acres of paddy land. According to the plaintiffs' charter they were originally owned by four ancestors of the present *vāsagama* members. No information about earlier ancestors is available. In order to make the data of the two hamlets comparable we shall assume a hypothetical ancestor preceding the generation above that mentioned by the plaintiffs. This will equalize the two hamlets in respect of 'generations'. The equalization of generations is not guesswork but based on inter-hamlet marriages. Thus for purposes of comparison and control, the generation of the hypothetical Founding Ancestor of Ihala Madagama will be referred to as FA^1. The data will deal with generations FA^1 to FA^6.

The plaintiffs' version is represented in Fig. 19. The four original ancestors are I. M. G. Silappu, I. M. G. Balappu, I. M. G. Lokuappu and I. M. G. Edirihamy, each owning $\frac{1}{4}$ share of the *gama*. The plaintiffs' version of the devolution of shares of each ancestor will be posed against that of resident villagers, to elucidate the dialectic of conflict. It is necessary to follow carefully the statements of informants in relation to the kinship chart in Fig. 19 and the other charts presented.

The person directly responsible for filing partition was the first plaintiff Panangala Liyanage Peter, speculator, owning the largest number of shares in the *gama*. He was supported by the second plaintiff, and other outside shareholders, most of them kinsmen of the plaintiffs. When partition was filed almost all of the villagers were opposed to it, but soon after, clear-cut factions developed based on (*a*) interests in the *gama*, whether large or small; and (*b*) on traditional enmities within the Ihala Madagama *vāsagama*. I. M. G. Kartelis and Jasin Gamage Handy who were hamlet residents with the largest shares supported the plaintiffs. I. M. G. Amaris who had cultivated a large area of paddy land prescriptively, and whose prescriptive rights were denied by the plaintiffs' charter led the opposing faction. Traditionally there was enmity between I. M. G. Amaris and I. M. G. Kartelis, who, while being neighbours, never spoke to each other. Most of the resident villagers with small shares in the estate supported Amaris' faction. One close supporter was I. M. G. Ortina, married to Tavala Gamage Abeysinghe Bastian, whose claims to Ihala Madagama shares were also denied by the plaintiffs' charter, and Mavita Gamage Singho Appu, Amaris' sister's husband. Resident and non-resident *vāsagama* members without shares were generally indifferent to the partition, although their sympathies lay with the resident shareholders. The opposing faction was weak since the plaintiffs belonged to a powerful and wealthy kin group (*peläntiya*) from which was recruited the village headman in charge of Madagama, residing in neighbouring Lelwala, the resident village of the plaintiffs. In addition the plaintiffs had the support of the two wealthiest in-resident shareowners in Ihala Madagama, I. M. G. Kartelis and J. G. Handy. Amaris' anti-plaintiffs faction had little financial support, and in order to hire a defence lawyer Amaris had to mortgage practically every single immovable property he owned, including his house, and borrow profusely from his daughters' husbands. Of the anti-plaintiffs faction Amaris was the only person able to attend court regularly, the others could ill-afford the costs of transport to the District Court in Galle. Though there was traditional enmity between the leaders of the two factions, the major factor in the formation of the factions was in respect of what individuals stood to gain or lose if the plaintiffs' charter was accepted by the court. For example, there was a deep underlying enmity between I. M. G. Kartelis and J. G. Handy over earlier share speculation, yet these were submerged in a temporary alignment since both stood to gain by the plaintiffs' charter. But for the leadership of I. M. G. Amaris, of the anti-plaintiff faction, it is quite likely that the plaintiffs would have won their case without much delay. Most of the other villagers owned minute shares and were so poor, and depended for their existence on government *badu iḍam* that they could hardly have put up an opposition front. Amaris was the only person in the opposition who prescriptively enjoyed a large area of paddy land, and had refused to acknowledge the 'legal' rights of P. L. Peter, plaintiff (who had bought some of the shares which Amaris was enjoying prescriptively). As far as the plaintiffs were concerned Amaris was the only effective spearhead of the opposition and a bitter enemy.

We shall take the inheritance of each of the four ancestors separately. The plaintiffs' version will be presented first, and several charters counterposed against that of the plaintiffs.

ANCESTOR: SILAPPU, $\frac{1}{4}$ SHARE OF 'GAMA'

Plaintiffs' charter

I. M. G. Silappu had an only son, Ades, on whom devolved the share of $\frac{1}{4}$. In 1865, Ades by deed no. 10600 sold $\frac{1}{16}$ share to Elias Gunawardene. Elias Gunawardene's share of $\frac{1}{16}$ was inherited by his son Y. C. Buddhadasa Gunawardene, who sold it to first and second plaintiffs Panangala Liyanage Peter and Charles Rubasin Gunawardene in 1920, by deed no. 1737. The remaining $\frac{3}{16}$ share belonging to I. M. G. Ades devolved on Ades' two sons Endiriye and Ediriappu, who thus owned $\frac{3}{32}$ each.

Endiriye $\frac{3}{32}$. Endiriye's only daughter Nimal Hamy inherited this share. In 1920 (deed no. 1691) she sold this to two sons I. M. G. Romis and I. M. G. Uporis in equal shares. I. M. G. Uporis died childless and his share went to his mother and four siblings, who jointly sold this to P. L. Peter, first plaintiff in 1922 (deed no. 2603). Of this P. L. Peter sold $\frac{1}{32}$ to first defendant Leelawati (his daughter).

Ediriappu $\frac{3}{32}$. Ediriappu sold $\frac{1}{16}$ of his share to David Rubasin Gunawardene (father of second plaintiff) and I. M. G. Simandiris alias Simon (his son) in 1888, deed no. 2896. In 1930 David Rubasin Gunawardene sold his share to second plaintiff Charles Rubasin Gunawardene (deed no. 5916). On the death of Ediriappu, his three children Endiris, Simandiris alias Simon, and Davith inherited. They jointly sold their entire shares to Kariyawasam Godage Nandoris (a speculator from Gigummaduva) in 1924, deed no. 3410. This was inherited by his wife Jayasundera Hitcho Nona, second defendant, and four children—Wickremanayake, Gunawantha, Dharmapala and Piyasena, defendants three to six.

The charter that we pose against the plaintiffs' is that of I. M. G. Amaris, who stands to lose most by the partition action. Both charters are agreed on some aspects of the genealogy. Amaris agrees that Silappu had $\frac{1}{4}$ of the estate; his only son was Ades, who had two sons Endiriye and Ediriappu. However, there is considerable difference in genealogies beyond that point, and continuous differences in share allocation.

Amaris' charter

Amaris denies that Silappu sold $\frac{1}{16}$ share to Elias Gunawardene. In which case Silappu's son Ades inherited this share *in toto* (not $\frac{3}{16}$ as asserted by the plaintiffs); this share in turn devolved on Ades' two sons Endiriye and Ediriappu who had $\frac{1}{8}$ each (not $\frac{3}{32}$ as stated by plaintiffs). Amaris is not interested in the devolution of Endiriye's share because this does not affect his rights. He neither contradicts nor affirms it. He is, however, explicit that his

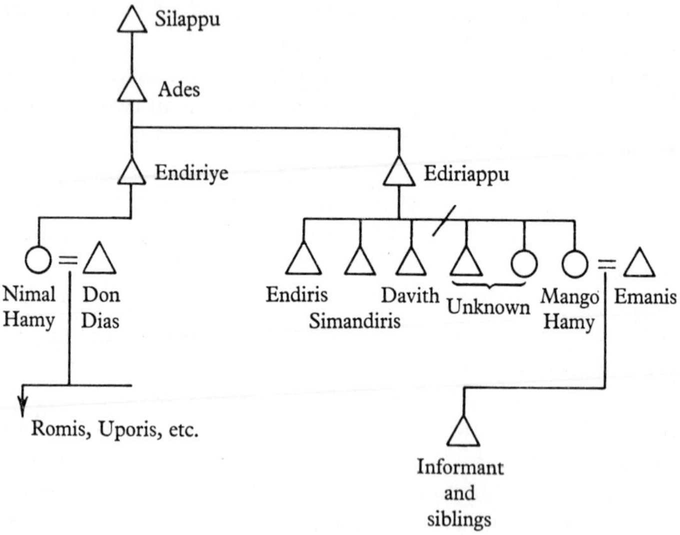

Fig. 20. Amaris' charter.

mother's father Ediriappu had $\frac{1}{8}$ and not $\frac{3}{32}$ as stated by plaintiffs. Furthermore, he adds three extra children to Ediriappu—his own mother and two siblings. Each sibiling had $\frac{1}{48}$ share. Thus the three siblings mentioned by the plaintiffs could have sold $\frac{1}{16}$ only if Ediriappu owned $\frac{1}{8}$; if he had owned $\frac{3}{32}$ as plaintiffs state, these three could have sold only a share of $\frac{1}{64}$ to the speculator K. G. Nandoris. Amaris asserts that his mother had $\frac{1}{48}$ and her two extra siblings $\frac{2}{48}$ jointly. Since the two siblings had left the village, his mother enjoyed these shares too prescriptively. It is in fact correct that Mango Hamy did enjoy these rights prescriptively, but the two extra 'lost' siblings are confirmed by none of the genealogies we have. We think this an invention to justify certain prescriptive rights enjoyed by Amaris. The three sons of Ediriappu whose shares were bought by the speculator K. G. Nandoris had left the hamlet—Simandiris at Balapitiya, a 'distant' town on the West Coast, Endiris in Colombo, and Davith in nearby Ambelegedera. Their shares were enjoyed prescriptively by Amaris' mother Mango Hamy (deceased). The shares, however, were sold in 1924 by these three brothers. The only way in which the prescriptive rights could be justified genealogically and legally is to oppose three other siblings against the three who sold the shares. These three other siblings are Amaris' own mother Mango Hamy, and two 'invented' siblings who are 'lost'.

A further problem arises at this point. While it is plausible to assume that I. M. G. Amaris invented two new siblings of his own mother, he could surely not have invented his own mother! If so why is this woman omitted from the genealogical charter of the plaintiffs? Her existence is certainly recognized by the plaintiffs elsewhere in their charter. In order to explain this we have to 'delve' into the past of Ihala Madagama hamlet.

I. M. G. Mango Hamy was the adopted daughter of I. M. G. Ediriappu; her genitor was a well-known Ayurvedic physician of the area, Don Mendiris Ediri Wickreme. Don Mendiris Ediri Wickreme belonged to the Karawa caste in a West Coast town, and practised his profession in the Madagama area, probably around 1860. He was a highly respected person, a famous physician and notorious womanizer. He had several mistresses both in Madagama and in neighbouring villages—a traditional attribute of high status. When children were born he used to give them for adoption to various families. One such family was that of Ediriappu. We do not know whether Ediriappu's wife too was a mistress of his. In any case Mango Hamy was certainly one of the physician's illegitimate daughters. However, Mango Hamy's was a clear case of adoption; she took the *vāsagama* name of her adopted father and lived with him.

This fact is implicitly recognized by the plaintiffs when they refer to her elsewhere in their charter as Madagama Gamage Mango Hamy. Further evidence for adoption exists. Mango Hamy's 'brother' Simandiris we said left the hamlet and resided in Balapitiya. Simandiris' daughter married his 'sister' Mango Hamy's son Theneris, who had learned Ayurvedic medicine from his mother's genitor Don Mendiris. Theneris lives uxorilocally in his wife's village in Balapitiya, and practises medicine there. This is a clear case of cross-cousin marriage, which once again suggests that Simandiris recognized Mango Hamy as a sister. Above all we have the statement by Mango Hamy's son Amaris that his mother's father is indeed I. M. G. Ediriappu. Yet she is excluded from the plaintiffs' genealogy. What could be the reasons for this exclusion?

It is obvious that if Mango Hamy's existence is genealogically recognized it must alter the plaintiffs' charter in one of two ways:

(*a*) If the share owned by Ediriappu was $\frac{3}{32}$, Mango Hamy is entitled to one-fourth of this, which automatically reduces the share of the three male siblings. They therefore could not have sold $\frac{1}{16}$ ($\frac{2}{32}$) to the speculator but much less, since a portion of this has to be allocated to the sister.

(*b*) If indeed they sold $\frac{1}{16}$, and the existence of Mango Hamy was recognized, it would confirm the opposition charter of Amaris which states that Ediriappu owned $\frac{1}{8}$ share (and not $\frac{3}{32}$) and did not sell his shares to any outsider. The dilemma could be resolved by amputating Mango Hamy from the genealogical charter. But equally important is the *rationale* for doing this. It may well have been the case that Mango Hamy, being a female, did not inherit any property at this generation level (FA^5). Yet Mango Hamy resided at marriage in the hamlet and there is traditional basis for her inheriting a share. Furthermore, her son claims she did; and the plaintiffs could hardly deny her right under the current Roman-Dutch law, which they themselves often employ in allocating shares in their charter. Thus under both customary and formal law Mango Hamy has a right to inherit Ediriappu's estate. The more important *rationale*, asserted by the pro-plaintiffs faction, is that Mango Hamy was an illegitimate daughter of Don Mendiris Ediri Wickreme and that Ediriappu was not her 'pater'. This is false, but the grounds for this assertion, according to the imperfect evidence we have, seem to be as follows. Mango's genitor was Don Mendiris, the 'genetrix', his mistress Walakulu Gamage Edo Hamy. Don Mendiris had apparently two other children, Jimoris and Girigoris, from this mistress. The plaintiffs are treating Mango as a sister of Jimoris and Girigoris and a daughter of Don Mendiris' mistress, rather than a daughter of Ediriappu, which she was by adoption, and public recognition. The plaintiffs are also using the fact that proof of adoption would never, or could never, be sucessfully advanced by Amaris, particularly since Mango Hamy 'married' a prohibited relative, her 'father's brother'.

ANCESTOR: BALAPPU, $\frac{1}{4}$ OF 'GAMA'

Plaintiffs' charter

On the death of Balappu his sons Baby Appu and Babappu inherited $\frac{1}{8}$ share each.

Babappu $\frac{1}{8}$. Babappu had seven children who inherited $\frac{1}{56}$ each.

(1) I. M. G. Don Dias $\frac{1}{56}$. On his death his wife Nimal Hamy and four children sold this share of $\frac{1}{56}$ to first plaintiff P. L. Peter in 1922.

(2) I. M. G. Davith $\frac{1}{56}$. Davith sold this share in 1881, deed no. 1527, to Panangala Liyanage Suaris, who, in 1905, no. 10922, sold it to his two sons, P. L. Uporis and P. L. Peter, who in turn jointly sold it to seventh defendant Jayawardene Jinadasa.

(3) I. M. G. Udaris $\frac{1}{56}$, inherited by his sons Ernolis, Siyaneris and Jandoris, eighth, ninth, and tenth defendants.

(4) I. M. G. Ujati $\frac{1}{56}$, devolved on his two children Laiso and Somaris, eleventh and twelfth defendants.

(5) I. M. G. Emanis $\frac{1}{56}$. On his death his wife I. M. G. Mango Hamy and four children, Ortina, Amaris, Theneris and Juli Hamy, inherited the share. Mango Hamy sold her share ($\frac{1}{112}$) to thirteenth defendant Mavita Gamage Singho Appu (her son-in-law) and (her son) I. M. G. Amaris, eighteenth defendant, in 1953, deed no. 815. (Each gets $\frac{1}{224}$. The rest would go to four children equally, $\frac{1}{448}$ each.)

(6) Daughter of Babappu $\frac{1}{56}$. She died and her husband S. G. Pedris sold the share to P. L. Uporis in 1925. S. G. Pedris and an only son are also dead.

(7) I. M. G. Laiso Hamy $\frac{1}{56}$. She and her husband W. A. Pedris sold this share of $\frac{1}{56}$ to P. L. Uporis in 1925, deed no. 318, and he in turn sold it to seventh defendant, Jayawardene Jinadasa.

Baby Appu $\frac{1}{8}$. On the death of Baby Appu, this share of $\frac{1}{8}$ devolved on his two sons, Mathes and Uporis (each getting a share of $\frac{1}{16}$).

Mathes ($\frac{1}{16}$). The plaintiffs' charter simply states that Mathes sold his share to Wickreme Aracchige Diyonis. He in turn sold $\frac{1}{72}$ share to Mavanana Hettige Obiyes (Mathes' daughter's husband). This was inherited by Obiyes' sons, M. H. Tevenis, M. H. Girigoris and M. H. Appu Singho, nineteenth, twentieth and twenty-first defendants. (Each would have shares of $\frac{1}{216}$.) The rest of his inheritance ($\frac{14}{288}$, presumably) was sold back to Mathes by Diyonis. This was inherited by his children Odiris Arnolis—twenty-second defendant, Samel—twenty-third defendant, and Siyadoris, Adara Hamy, Hinni Hamy and Yayapath Hamy—twenty-fourth defendant. (Each person here is entitled to $\frac{2}{288}$ share, which is assumed but not stated in the charter.)

Odiris' share was inherited by his daughters Ortina and Karlina—jointly $\frac{2}{288}$. Siyadoris sold his share (of $\frac{2}{288}$) to the twenty-first defendant M. H. Appu Singho (his sister's son) in 1940, deed no. 1270. Adarahamy also sold her share to M. H. Appu Singho in 1946, no. 3505. Hinni Hamy married M. H. Obiyes (father of Appu Singho) and this share was inherited by her children, M. H. Appu Singho, M. H. Tevonis and M. H. Girigoris. (Each gets $\frac{1}{432}$.) *Uporis* ($\frac{1}{16}$) sold his share to Kariyawasam Godage Nandoris (speculator) and this was inherited by his wife and children, who in 1942 jointly sold the share to the twenty-seventh defendant, I. M. G. Kartelis.

Against the plaintiffs' charter of rights regarding the inheritance of Balappu, we shall pose several charters. Owing to the highly controversial nature of the several charters we shall deal with the inheritances of Balappu's two sons, Baby Appu and Babappu, separately.

Balappu's son Baby Appu

Pro-plaintiffs charter of I. M. G. Kartelis

The genealogical charter presented by I. M. G. Kartelis is basically in agreement with that of the plaintiffs. However, he admits that at least one part of the plaintiffs' genealogy has been forged, namely the very portion pertaining to his own ancestors. It was not possible for us to get from I. M. G. Kartelis the exact nature of the forgery, or the motives for the forgery. In presenting his own genealogy Kartelis pretended complete ignorance of all the ancestors above his grandfather's (I. M. G. Uporis') generation. The reason for his feigned ignorance was due to his reluctance to contradict the plaintiffs' charter which he has identified with his own interests. The point which I. M. G. Kartelis asserts with certainty, and also the point at which his charter begins, is that his grandfather I. M. G. Uporis and his brother I. M. G. Mathes each had $\frac{1}{16}$ share of the *gama*. Uporis sold his share to a speculator from Gigummaduva, K. G. Arnolis (a brother of Kariyawasam Godage Nikulas who settled down in Pahala Madagama). K. G. Arnolis' share devolved on his son K. G. Nandoris, whose widow and children inherited the share. I. M. G. Kartelis 'created trouble' demanding that they sell it back to him. Arnolis' widow filed action in court and Kartelis was fined Rs. 80. But Kartelis, undeterred, continued to create trouble (*āravul*), till he compelled the widow and her children to sell the share to him cheaply for Rs. 300. 'Created trouble' means that he cultivated an area of $\frac{1}{16}$ of the estate by force, against the wishes of the owners. But he too rationalized the means adopted:

(*a*) he said that the descendants of an ancestor have a moral right to buy back the share, asserting traditional norms of the revocability of deeds;

(*b*) that his father's father Uporis was 'cheated' of his inheritance, a common explanation, but one justifying the resort to 'creating trouble' for redeeming the estate from those who have defrauded his ancestor.

Anti-plaintiffs charter of I. M. G. Ortina

Notice an important difference in this charter as compared with that of the plaintiffs and of I. M. G. Kartelis. A woman Anada Hamy, daughter of Baby Appu, and sister of Uporis and Mathes has been introduced into the opposition charter. This woman is totally absent in the pro-plaintiffs charters. What is the importance of this woman for the two factions? According to Ortina, I. M. G. Baby Appu had $\frac{1}{8}$ of the *gama*. He also had two sons and a daughter, Anada Hamy, ignored by the pro-plaintiffs charters. This daughter was given $\frac{1}{32}$ share by her father on the occasion of her marriage. Her husband resided uxorilocally. In the next generation there was a cross-cousin marriage between Anada Hamy's daughter and her brother's (Mathes') son I. M. G. Odiris. Informant (I. M. G. Ortina) and a sister I. M. G. Karlina are offspring of that union. Anada Hamy's other sons and daughters are scattered and 'unknown', except K. V. Handy Singho, the son of a daughter. Ortina claims that the share of $\frac{1}{32}$ given to Anada Hamy devolved on to K. V. Handy Singho, on herself (Ortina) and on her sister Karlina. The informant is illiterate and cannot specify the actual shares that have devolved thus, but she has been working a sowing area of 10 k as Anada Hamy's share. Of this 5 k goes to Anada Hamy's daughter Augustina and through her to her son K. V. Handy Singho; and 5 k to the other daughter Podi Hamy and through her to her daughters Ortina and Karlina. Ortina works all these

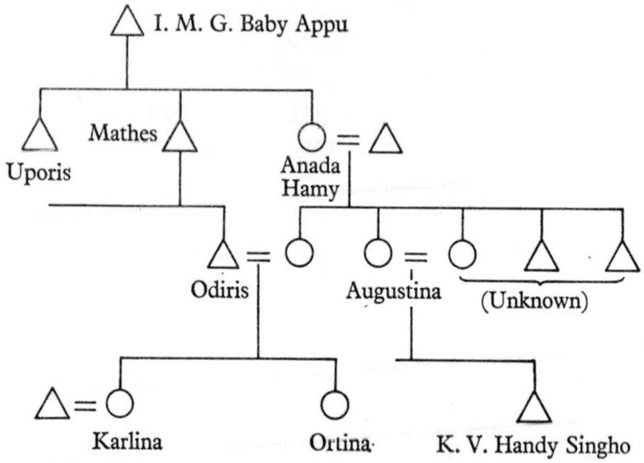

Fig. 21. Anti-plaintiffs charter of I. M. G. Ortina.

shares, but recognizes the others' rights with periodic 'gifts'. No one disputed their rights until partition was filed. If Ortina is right, the two daughters of Anada Hamy should have technically $\frac{1}{32}$. In fact 10 k in the Ihala Madagama estate of 320 k sowing area comes to about $\frac{1}{32}$. It would be correct to say that Anada Hamy's descendants have been cultivating a sowing area roughly consonant with their claims.

A neutralist charter: Mavanana Hettige Appu Singho

Mavanana Hettige Appu Singho is connected matrilaterally to the Ihala Madagama *vāsagama*. Though he belongs to the same subcaste he is an upwardly mobile person and has taken to share speculation. As far as the Ihala Madagama estate is concerned, his shares are not too large, and he avoids openly entangling with either faction in the dispute. His presentation of the case is shown in Fig. 22.

Baby Appu, he agrees with the pro-plaintiffs charter, had only $\frac{1}{8}$ of the estate. He also had a daughter Anada Hamy, he agrees with the anti-plaintiffs faction; but she got only a share of $\frac{1}{72}$ and not $\frac{1}{32}$ as Ortina states. This gives the sons Uporis and Mathes $\frac{1}{18}$ each, and not $\frac{1}{16}$ as asserted by plaintiffs. This share of $\frac{1}{18}$ was sold to K. G. Nandoris and not $\frac{1}{16}$. So that I. M. G. Kartelis who bought back the share of $\frac{1}{16}$ was getting more than he deserved, which was $\frac{1}{18}$.

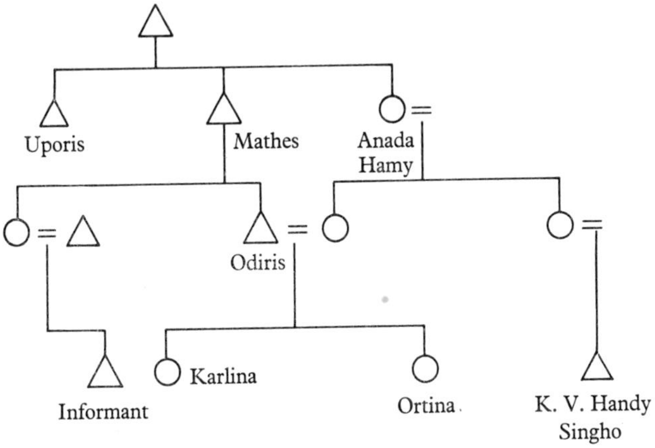

Fig. 22.

There is not the slightest doubt that Anada Hamy was a daughter of Baby Appu and a sibling of Uporis and Mathes. Before we examine the implications of the amputation of this woman from the plaintiffs' charter and that of I. M. G. Kartelis, let us consider the case of the other brother Mathes. According to the pro-plaintiffs charters he possessed $\frac{2}{32}$ share of which $\frac{1}{72}$ eventually went to his son-in-law M. H. Obiyes and thence to his three sons, and the rest to seven children in shares of $\frac{2}{288}$ each.

Ortina, we noted earlier, has already asserted that Baby Appu had $\frac{1}{8}$ of which $\frac{1}{32}$ was given to Anada Hamy, her mother's mother, and $\frac{3}{64}$ each to Uporis and Mathes. Since Mathes had seven children each should get $\frac{3}{448}$, which includes the share of her own father I. M. G. Odiris, Mathes' son. Ortina cannot calculate the share herself but she works a sowing area of 3 k for the share owing to Odiris, which in a total sowing area of 320 k, yields a fraction of $\frac{1}{107}$, which is slightly more than she is technically entitled to. The devolution of shares to I. M. G. Ortina is depicted in Fig. 23.

According to Appu Singho, Mathes had $\frac{1}{18}$ and not $\frac{2}{32}$ since Baby Appu gave Anada Hamy, the daughter, a share of $\frac{1}{72}$. He sold

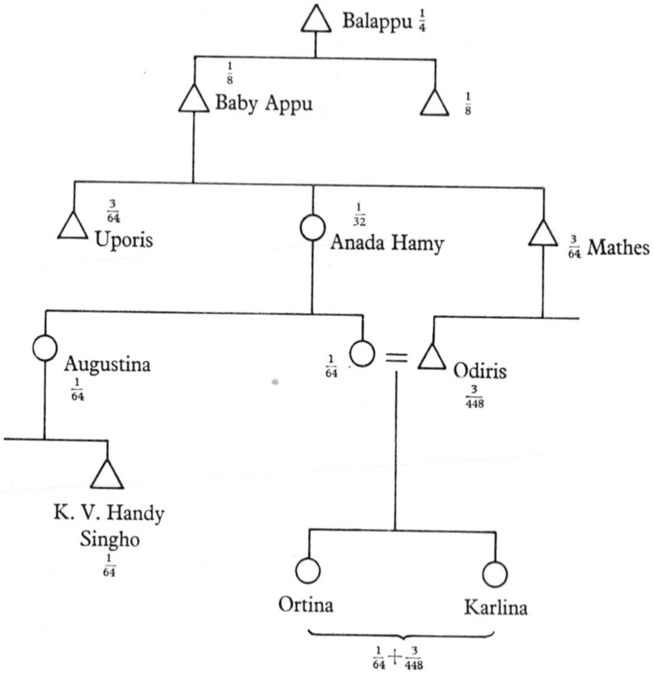

Fig. 23.

this share to Wickreme Aracchige Diyonis of Weliwitiye, and not $\frac{1}{16}$ as stated by the plaintiffs' libel. M. H. Obiyes, his son-in-law, and the father of our informant bought $\frac{1}{72}$ back from Diyonis. The rest was bought back by Mathes, who thus had a share of $\frac{3}{72}$ which devolved in intestate succession to the seven children in shares of $\frac{1}{168}$ each.

The informant is literate and knows his elementary mathematics, so that he could work the exact shares as depicted in Fig. 24. Of these several shareowners, two—Adarahamy and Siyadoris—have left the village and have sold their shares to our informant. The rest either work their shares or give them on lease.

I. M. G. Amaris, the leader of the anti-plaintiffs faction, had no direct share interest in Mathes' inheritance. Yet he too presented a charter in which he asserted that Baby Appu had $\frac{1}{8}$ of the estate, but all children, including the daughter Anada Hamy, had equal shares of $\frac{1}{24}$. He would thus give Anada Hamy a larger share than any of the others involved in the case. The motive for giving such a large share must be seen in the context of the enmity between

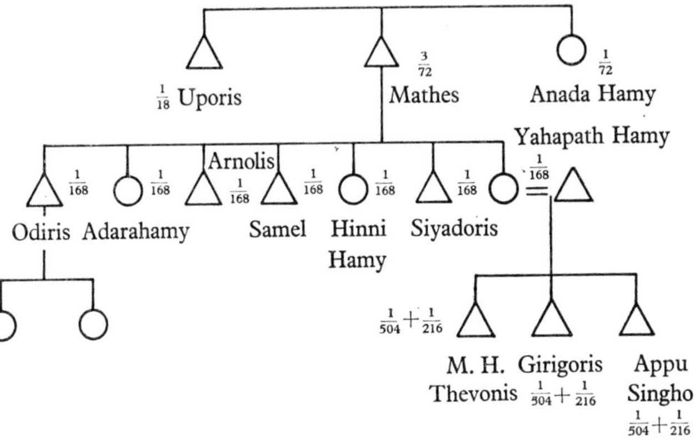

Fig. 24.

him and I. M. G. Kartelis. By giving Uporis $\frac{1}{24}$ share he has diminished the claims of his enemy Kartelis who claims $\frac{1}{16}$ for Uporis. Kartelis has a *rationale* (which the plaintiffs too use whenever it is advantageous for them) for giving Anada Hamy an equal share in the contemporary general law of intestate succession.

The several genealogical charters posed against the descendants of Babappu's son Baby Appu illustrate the dialectic of conflict which emerges when we treat genealogies as charters of rights. One dramatic contrast is the amputation of the woman Anada Hamy from the plaintiffs' charter, and her inclusion in the opposition. The omission by the pro-plaintiffs' is deliberate, for the inclusion of a female sibling with a share would diminish the rights of the male siblings Uporis and Mathes. According to Ortina's charter Anada Hamy got a share of her father's estate as dowry; nothing unusual in this generation level, where female inheritance *inter vivos* was noted even in Pahala Madagama. The plaintiffs not only deny that she got a share, but deny her actual existence. Whether Anada Hamy's share was $\frac{1}{32}$ as Ortina says, or $\frac{1}{72}$ as the neutralist M. H. Appu Singho states, it diminishes the share of Uporis. This would mean that Kartelis' own shares will be diminished since I. M. G. Kartelis bought back the share of Uporis from the speculator K. G. Nandoris. It is quite likely that Anada Hamy received some share, for her descendants (Ortina, Karlina, K. V. Handy) had been continuously cultivating a sowing area proportionate with her share.

Balappu's second son, Babappu

Balappu the ancestor under consideration had a second son, Babappu, according to the plaintiffs' genealogy, who inherited $\frac{1}{8}$ of the *gama*. When we pose Amaris' charter against that of the plaintiffs', the contrasts are very great. Amaris' charter denies that Babappu (whom he calls Baby Hamy) belonged to the same section of the *vāsagama* as Balappu: he belonged to a different one (see Fig. 25).

In Amaris' version, a sibling of Baby Hamy alias Babappu (according to the plaintiffs' version) named Baba Hamy was lost and this share devolved on our informant. We reject this implausible story and for purposes of comparison accept the plaintiff's version, particularly since both agree that Babappu or Baby Hamy had $\frac{1}{8}$ of the estate which devolved on seven siblings at $\frac{1}{56}$ each. Amaris also admits that all the shares were sold as the plaintiffs assert. If so, why invent a fictitious sibling of his father's father who was lost and whose share miraculously devolved on informant, through his father? Once again, we believe this involves the great contradiction between prescriptive ownership and legal share ownership. Babappu had seven children, who included two females who resided virilocally after marriage, probably at the turn of the century. The shares of the female siblings were enjoyed by the in-resident males, probably Emanis, and later prescriptively by his son Amaris. Actually we do not believe that in this case the females were given any share by their father at all; they married virilocally and it is most unusual for females of this generation (FA^4) to inherit on intestate succession. (We have no case of such inheritance in the Pahala Madagama estate.) But they were entitled to inherit according to *contemporary* Roman-Dutch based law, which was the generally accepted law when they sold their shares to speculator P. L. Uporis in 1925. In other words, the speculator bought shares which these females were, according to traditional norms, not entitled to inherit. In one case (Baby Nona, or simply 'daughter' according to the plaintiffs) the shares were sold on the death of the woman by her husband, who had no sentimental or other interest in the village. When these shares are sold (including probably the share of an outresident male Davith who sold his in 1881 to the first plaintiff's father), the prescriptive usufruct of the land by

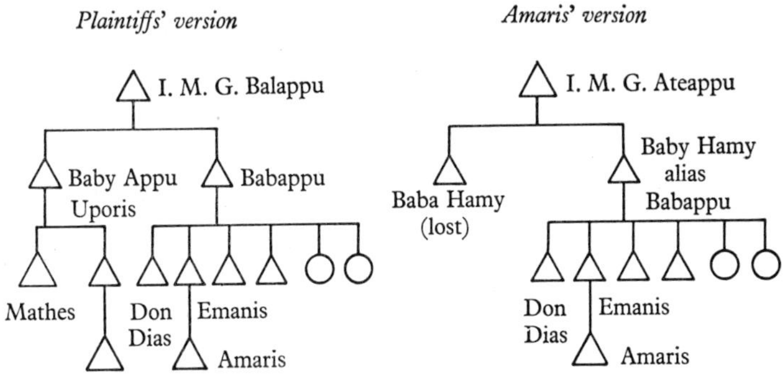

Fig. 25.

Emanis is undermined. One way to 'legalize' or legitimize the prescriptive ownership as a *legal* ownership of shares is to invent a new ancestor—in this case rather crudely by inventing a sibling of Babappu who was lost and whose share devolved on the in-resident males.

Of Babappu's share, all except that of three sons was sold to the plaintiffs—these being Emanis' share which devolved on his wife and children as stated by the plaintiffs, and the shares of Udaris and Ujati. Udaris ($\frac{1}{56}$) left the village to live uxorilocally in Mederipitiya in the Ratnapura District. He is now dead but his sons periodically visit the village to give the share on lease.

Ujati $\frac{1}{56}$. Ujati had three sons and a daughter. Two sons settled in distant Latpandura and Paiyagala respectively, while a daughter Laiso married a man from Hiniduma and lived virilocally. Their sons who left the village have no contact with their relations here.

One son, Semaris lives on a *badu iḍam* in Kahambiliyawalakada, adjacent to the hamlet. He pays his sister a token payment of rice whenever the latter visits him.

ANCESTOR: EDIRIHAMY—$\frac{1}{4}$ OF 'GAMA'

Plaintiffs' charter

This share of $\frac{1}{4}$ was sold by Edirihamy to Maddegama Vidane Aratchi (village headman) who in turn sold it to Don Mendiris Ediri Wickreme. Don Mendiris sold $\frac{1}{8}$ share to K. A. Charles Appuhamy in 1890, He in turn sold it to K. A. Girigoris Appuhamy, on whose death the share devolved on N. P. Katrine Jayasekere and children Dharmadasa, Nela, Vimala, and Sita (all of Colombo). In 1949, deed no. 1979, these people sold the share to thirty-second defendant Jasin Gamage Handy. The remaining $\frac{1}{8}$ share was sold by Don Mendiris in 1898, no. 6583, to Ihala Madagama Gamage Mango Hamy and Walakula Gamage Edo Hamy (her genetrix) in equal shares (that is, $\frac{1}{16}$ each). Mango sold her share in 1921, no. 2246, to P. L. Peter, first plaintiff. Edo Hamy ($\frac{1}{16}$) had three children, Mango Hamy, Jimoris and Girigoris. In 1953 Mango Hamy sold her share ($\frac{1}{48}$) to Mavita Gamage Singho Appu (her son-in-law) ($\frac{1}{96}$), thirteenth defendant, and I. M. G. Amaris her son ($\frac{1}{96}$), eighteenth defendant. Jimoris sold his share ($\frac{1}{48}$) to Endiri Wickreme Thevonis and Ihala Madagama Gamage Juanis in 1931 ($\frac{1}{96}$) each. (Thevonis is Juanis' wife's brother.) Girigoris sold his share in 1946, no. 7163, to Ediri Wickreme Thevonis ($\frac{1}{48}$) and this was inherited by Mavita Gamage Kristina, thirty-third defendant, and five children, Podi Hamy, Bala Hamy, Baby Hamy, Don Diris and Simon, thirty-fourth to thirty-eighth defendants (that is, E. W. Thevonis had shares of $\frac{1}{48} + \frac{1}{96} = \frac{3}{96}$. His wife Kristina was entitled to $\frac{3}{192}$ and the other $\frac{3}{192}$ was divided among five children.) On the death of Juanis this share devolved on his sons, I. M. G. Kartelis ($\frac{1}{192}$) and I. M. G. Nandoris ($\frac{1}{192}$), thirty-ninth and fortieth defendants.

Amaris' charter

We could get only confused and contradictory information from Amaris on this ancestor. He denies practically all the transactions claimed by the plaintiffs as attempts to defraud him. He admits that a share was sold to K. A. Charles Appuhamy, and was bought by J. G. Handy in 1949, but this original transaction was a 'fraud'. The remaining share was given to his mother, I. M. G. Mango Hamy, by her genitor Don Mendiris as a dowry; not half of it as plaintiffs assert. Walakula Gamage Edo Hamy, her mother's genetrix got none, and hence the 'sons' of the genetrix could not have sold their shares to I. M. G. Juanis and Ediri Wickreme Thevonis, as asserted by the plaintiffs.

The crux of the issue we feel is again the question of prescription against 'legal' share ownership. The plaintiffs claim that Edirihamy sold the share of $\frac{1}{4}$ to the village headman of Madagama who in turn sold it to the notorious physician Ediri Wickreme Mendiris. Mendiris sold a share of $\frac{1}{8}$ to total outsiders, who lost interest in the hamlet or its shares, till these heirs were resurrected in 1949 by J. G. Handy. Up till 1949, and as far as *goḍa iḍam* is concerned up until the present day, a large portion of this share was prescriptively enjoyed by Mango Hamy, and her son Amaris. Amaris, however, cannot easily explain this prescriptive ownership as legal ownership of shares in terms of a genealogical charter. Hence his charter is confused and contradictory, simply a barefaced denial of the plaintiffs. The charter, the details of which we omit here, is an attempt to give legal justification for the prescriptive usufruct of the property which Handy bought in 1949, and partly enjoyed by Amaris till then. Amaris asserts that he is sure that Handy will be deprived of his share at partition, and that his property will be restored to him (a futile and vain hope, we think).

ANCESTOR: LOKUAPPU (ALIAS ADRIS, ALIAS MATHES)—$\frac{1}{4}$ OF 'GAMA'

Plaintiffs' charter

I. M. G. Lokuappu sold $\frac{1}{8}$ of his share in 1877 (deed no. 1226) to Elias Gunawardene. He, in turn sold $\frac{1}{12}$ to P. L. Suaris in 1892. In 1905 Suaris sold this share to plaintiff P. L. Peter and P. L. Uporis ($\frac{1}{24}$ each). On the death of Uporis his widow Jayawardene Cicily Hamy ($\frac{1}{48}$), twenty-eighth defendant, and children Somapala and Wijesena (jointly $\frac{1}{48}$), twenty-ninth and thirtieth defendants, inherited it. The remaining share (of $\frac{1}{24}$) continued to be owned by Elias Gunawardene, on whose death it devolved on his son

Dharmapala Buddhadasa Gunawardene, who in 1920 sold the share to the plaintiffs Charles Rubasin Gunawardene and P. L. Peter ($\frac{1}{48}$ each).

Lokuappu had $\frac{1}{8}$ share left. He sold $\frac{1}{24}$ to P. L. Suaris, on whose death the share devolved to P. L. Peter, first plaintiff ($\frac{1}{48}$), and P. L. Uporis ($\frac{1}{48}$); the latter inherited by the widow of Uporis ($\frac{1}{96}$) and her two sons ($\frac{1}{96}$ jointly).

Lokuappu had $\frac{1}{12}$ still with him. He sold this to Nikulas Amarawickreme Gunawardene (son of Elias Gunawardene) in 1879. Nikulas sold $\frac{1}{24}$ to P. L. Peter, plaintiff, and Charles Rubasin Gunawardene in 1896 ($\frac{1}{48}$ each). The remaining $\frac{1}{24}$ was sold to his son Edwin Gunawardene in 1928, no. 1737.

None of the anti-plaintiffs faction are actively concerned with this share; some of them deny that there was such an ancestor, or that he had a share as large as $\frac{1}{4}$. Almost all say that it was either lost to the hamlet by 'force' or 'fraud'. The reasons for not presenting clear claims here is fairly obvious since most of the shares went very early to the plaintiffs and were actually cultivated or given on lease by them.

Genealogy as a charter of rights: 'amputation', 'attribution', and 'extension'

Of crucial importance to understanding both the *taṭṭumāru* and share market systems is that a genealogy is a charter of rights in this kind of system. Shares in *pravēni* are based on a genealogy: one's share is a share or part of a share that originally belonged to a *vāsagama* ancestor. Ancestors are important in so far as they provided a charter depicting how and when a particular individual obtained his 'share', and the manner in which his share is to be implemented in the *taṭṭumāru* scheme. A genealogy is a legitimation or validation, as in Weber's or Malinowski's usage, of an individual's right to *pravēni* property. If this were the case the genealogy a person would hold or affirm would contain a charter of his rights to the *vāsagama* estate. In situations where conflicting claims to shares would arise we would expect conflicting genealogical charters of rights (as in the cases presented earlier). Thus 'amnesia' in respect of an ancestor or of patrilateral female relations has structural relevance for it may enhance the rights of some individuals while it diminishes the rights of others. In Pahala

Madagama one of the constantly reiterated genealogical facts was statements about female siblings of one's ancestors who are 'lost', or 'unknown'. We know that in fact this is not the case, for the specified kinswoman may be very much alive, and known to the informant. In respect of the genealogical charter such a kinswoman is 'unknown', because genealogical recognition of her, that is, the inclusion of her in the charter, may be a threat to the informant's own inheritance.

This technique of omitting relations we call *genealogical amputation* or *excision*. An amputated genealogy gives an individual a set of rights he would not have if the genealogy had been complete. For a rather simple illustration see Fig. 26.

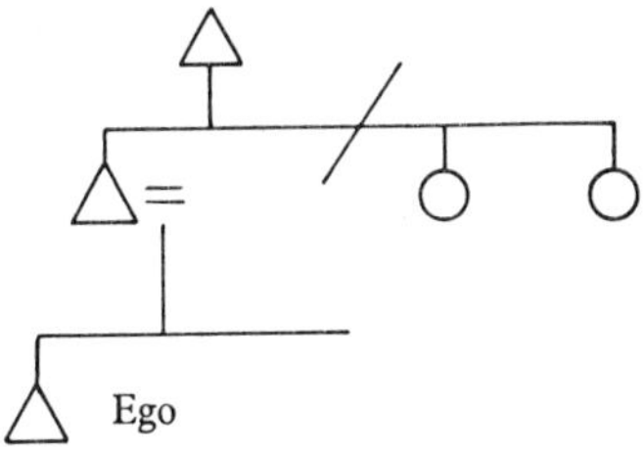

Fig. 26.

Ego in the above diagram has amputated his father's sisters from his genealogy; this means that he stands to inherit his grandfather's estate intact. The opposite technique is also important in the strategy of share speculation. This technique we have called *attribution*; a person may attribute to the genealogy of another, what that other person may deny or refuse to recognize. Thus if I am interested in buying Ego's share in the above chart, I may buy two-third's share of Ego's grandfather's estate from his father's sisters and thus compel Ego to recognize the relations he had amputated. A rather straightforward but common mode of amputation would be to lop off a kinsman or ancestor from the genealogy and deny that he or she ever existed (for example, the denial of Anada Hamy by the plaintiffs). Cases of 'genealogical amnesia' belong to this category, as when I. M. G. Kartelis 'forgets' his ancestors above his father's father's generation, so as to conform his charter with the plaintiffs'.

Genealogical *extension* summarizes the processes which result when for certain purposes a person invents a new kinsman, as illustrated by I. M. G. Amaris' clumsy attempts. Such extensions generally occur in the upper reaches of the genealogies which cannot be easily verified. These techniques, which result in the enhancement of the rights of one person and the reduction of the rights of a person genealogically opposed to him, are a part of the strategy of share speculation in the share market, the subject of the next chapter.

CHAPTER 7

THE SHARE MARKET

Creation of a share market

The *taṭṭumāru* system is based on ownership of land in undivided shares: traditionally, according to our model, proliferation of shares would be the exception rather than the rule. The shares in the estate of any hamlet could today be viewed as a 'share market'. The creation of a share market is a function of scarcity of land and the generational increase of people, combined later on with bilateral inheritance. With bilateral inheritance, and uxorilocal marriage arrangements for men, there also developed absentee shareowners, that is, men and women who own shares in the *vāsagama* estate, but do not live in the village and have no 'cultivation interests' in the land. There emerged thus a group of people who could 'sell' their shares, if they wished to, since they had no economic interest in retaining them. With the increasing fractioning of shares village residents too have to manipulate the share market in order to consolidate shares into workable units. Finally, there is the rise of speculation in shares, which is more a modern development absent or minimally present in the traditional system.

'Share speculation' refers to the buying and selling of shares in the 'share market'. Share speculation is modern in the sense that it presupposes a fairly developed 'cash economy', and a notion of 'investment'. 'Investment' in shares does not have the same denotation as in contemporary economic theory, for the motive for investing money in shares need not be due to rational economic thinking with the intention of maximization of 'profits'. For example, the prestige motive may be more important than the economic one, as we shall later show. 'Investment' is, however, based on rational action, that is, action in which goals are achieved by a careful consideration of the means. It is not rational *economic* action in a Weberian sense because the goals sought may not be primarily economic and the means not necessarily based on a criterion of technical efficiency. Thus rational action as we use it, refers to the achievement of goals through a 'calculation' of the means employed, unlike traditional action where the means is unequivocally predetermined by custom. The concept 'speculation' involves rational action in this sense, for there are several means for achieving the goal (buying shares): 'speculation' implies that the choice of means is rationally calculated with an intention of achieving the end. A 'speculator' is a person who buys, sells and otherwise manipulates shares in the share market. His rise is also a function of British rule and a development of a cash *oriented* economy. British rule created a class of Sinhalese officials in the nineteenth century who had access to cash, either directly through a salary, or indirectly through 'commissions' and other means like tax farming. In the twentieth century, practically everyone was involved in a cash economy, and there was a broadening of the number of people with a surplus of cash for investment in shares, as for example, boutique keepers, villagers with cash crops planted in their gardens or cash earned through selling of labour, and a general expansion of a class of village officials paid by the crown—headman, registrars of marriages, coroners, overseers and non-government 'officials' like notaries, office bearers of Rural Development societies and village committees. Speculators are persons who because of the availability of cash could manipulate the means in order to buy and sell shares in the market. It should be noted that the emphasis of the speculator is on buying rather than selling, which is a point of difference with the stock market. Investment in general is mostly limited to investment in land, generally in shares.

In-residents and out-residents

In the preceding section we have illustrated two major propositions. First, genealogies are charters of rights and, secondly, posed genealogies of different individuals claiming shares in the same *gama* express a dialectic of conflict. A third point which was implicit in the preceding account of Ihala Madagama is the strategy of speculation based on self-interest directed towards a carefully considered goal, that of buying and consolidation of shares in a share market. The term 'strategy' also implies 'choice': the goals of speculation are reached by a judicious and rationally calculated choice of means. Yet while the goals justify the means, it does not justify the adoption of *any* means. In general, though not always, the means have to be at least normatively *rationalized* or *justified*, either through legal or moral norms.

We shall now consider in more general terms the normative and sociological framework within which the strategies of share speculation takes place. The normative framework is relatively easy to understand and could be summed up by saying that with the introduction and acceptance of Roman-Dutch law, a multiplicity of norms come to govern action (the means) while the older legal norms of marriage continue to operate, however modified, as moral norms. The sociological framework—the framework of statuses and roles—is, however, more complex and needs careful elucidation. Our illustrations will be from both Ihala Madagama and Pahala Madagama, the latter will be used as a means of 'controlling' the evidence we have from the former.

Two useful terms will be initially defined. 'In-residents' refer to those members of the hamlet who own shares and reside in the hamlet, while 'out-residents' are those who own shares yet live outside the hamlet in other villages. An important sociological problem pertains to that of female out-residents. In Pahala Madagama we noticed that no female inherited shares on intestate succession up till and inclusive of generation FA^5. At generation FA^6 bilateral inheritance based on Roman-Dutch law is accepted. We therefore concluded:

(*a*) that persons in FA^4 generation acted according to traditional jural norms, so that their descendants in FA^5 received shares in accordance with those norms.

(*b*) in generation FA^5 the Roman-Dutch law of inheritance was beginning to be accepted so that their descendants at generation FA^6 inherited shares bilaterally according to that law. However, it must be noted that while the Roman-Dutch law was not accepted in decision making in generation FA^4, yet formally it was the general law of the country, and in generation FA^5 and below people were marrying according to the general law (except for a few who may have married *binna* according to Kandyan law). At generation FA^6, all out-residents, both males and females, are clearly recognized as entitled to shares bilaterally. Yet the old jural norms operate as moral norms, for out-residents, both male and female, are expected to renounce their 'cultivation interests' in the soil, while laying legal claim to their shares. The persistence of older jural norms as contemporary moral norms have a firm economic basis, for it is obvious that small shares could hardly be worked profitably unless they are consolidated with other shares belonging to the same *taṭṭumāru* subsection. This is possible if out-resident siblings renounce cultivation interests in the soil. Their legal claims to share ownership is recognized by the in-resident who gives periodic 'gifts' of rice or fruits as token acknowledgement of their rights. The distance of residence may also be an important factor. If the out-residents live close to the hamlet in neighbouring *badu iḍam* or villages, these token acknowledgements would often take place during visits. If the out-residents live in close proximity to the village they may even enjoy the produce of the *goḍa iḍam*, but not the paddy fields. Once again there is an economic basis for this, for while the enjoyment of fruit trees in *goḍa iḍam* is economically feasible, it is not so for paddy lands. Thus in Pahala Madagama, P. M. G. Gunadasa claims $\frac{1}{80}$ share of his father's inheritance while his six siblings (four of whom are out-residents) get only $\frac{1}{480}$. It is economically useless for the out-resident siblings to cultivate the paddy land, but one male sibling Gnanadasa living in *badu iḍam* on the outskirts of the hamlet enjoys the produce from the *goḍa iḍam*. Such uses are rare, and almost unheard of for females. In general out-residents receive token acknowledgement of their legal rights from in-residents. It is recognized, however, that they could, if they wished to, enjoy the produce of the *goḍa iḍam*.

These facts we have stated pose two problems in respect of out-resident females.

(1) Females could not inherit shares on intestate succession (except in *binna* marriage, in which case they become in-residents, or if there were no male heirs) at generation FA^4 or FA^5. Yet the general law of the country during these generation levels stipulated bilateral inheritance. Furthermore, when these women become older, the older jural rules have been supplanted behaviourally by the bilateral rules of inheritance. Hence *in principle* they could, if they wished to, retroactively assert their rights to shares which they did not possess at the time they were married.

(2) In generation FA^6 the problem is simpler. Here females clearly have legal and moral rights to shares, though out-residents are expected to relinquish their cultivation interests in the soil. But once again *in principle*, there is no reason why they should not put their shares to economic use by asserting cultivation interests, or selling their shares for cash. Assertion of cultivation interests is

a practical impossibility with small shares, but this is not the case with a cash sale.

These two problems respecting out-resident females have serious implications for in-residents as well as for share speculators (and share speculation even on the village level). For in-resident males there is a constant fear that a sister, on the instigation of her husband, would sell her land to outsiders. This was voiced constantly in Pahala Madagama, which has the more stable land tenure system. Another fear was that sisters will accept their roles as long as the parents are alive, but would sell their shares after the parents died. These fears we believe are rationally grounded in experience, not simply in Pahala Madagama, but from villagers' knowledge of other hamlets. In Pahala Madagama itself there was one such case of a female sibling selling to an outsider—this is the case of P. M. G. Agoris whose sister sold her shares, at the instigation of her husband it was said, to K. H. Karu, an outside speculator, contrary to the wishes of her brother who wanted to buy it for less than what was offered by the speculator (see p. 71). But most informants expressed the fear. The case of P. M. G. John (branch *B*) is instructive here. He has 'no connexions' with his sister who lives in Tavalama, a few miles away, whereas he is in contact with another sister residing in Panangala twelve miles away. The reason is that at this generation level (FA^6) females inherit bilaterally, though John states that they did not in his case. His fear is that his sister in Tavalama would assert her rights (and has probably attempted to do so). If so this would seriously diminish his own estate.

That such fears are well-grounded are quite apparent when we consider the genealogical charters of Ihala Madagama.

(1) *Generation* FA^4. In this generation it was most unlikely for females to inherit on intestate succession. Yet the five males and two females of Babappu, according to the plaintiffs inherited bilaterally. Actually what happened was that the two females married virilocally at the turn of the century. They had no interest in the village and sold their property in 1925, when bilateral norms had been fully accepted, to P. L. Uporis, speculator. In one case the out-resident female died, and the share was sold by her husband in 1925.

(2) *Generation* FA^5. Mathes had four sons and three daughters. One daughter married Mavanana Hettige Obiyes in the nearby

village of Mavanana. Two other daughters were out-residents and their shares were enjoyed prescriptively (or probably they got no share at the time they married) by the brothers. In the next generation FA^6 when bilateral norms were in force one female sold her share to M. H. Obiyes' son Appu Singho, speculator, in 1946.

The position regarding out-resident males is more or less the same, except that even traditionally they had their share of the estate, which they could resume if they decided to become in-residents. But as out-residents they and their descendants also were expected to renounce their cultivation interest in the soil. But males even more than females regularly tend to sell their shares to outsiders or residents. If the males were resident in *badu iḍam* near the hamlet they were generally averse to selling their shares. The reason is simple. Share ownership gives citizenship to a village, and is important (we shall show later) for the self-esteem and self-worth of a male. The loss of prestige involved in living in government *badu iḍam* is compensated by having shares in the natal hamlet. But for out-residents who have married uxorilocally, or neo-locally resident in cities, the position is different. Such out-resident males have been absorbed permanently into their wives' families, or in the cities where they live, and often have severed ties with the hamlet. They have less compunction in selling. But even here it is wrong to assume that they sell their land as soon as they leave the hamlet. On the contrary, land is sold long after these persons have left the hamlet and have stabilized themselves elsewhere. In Pahala Madagama several people who married uxorilocally and settled down in their wives' villages ended up by selling their shares eventually—P. M. G. Karo, P. M. G. Juanis (branch *B*, see pp. 72–3); P. M. G. Owinis, P. M. G. Eranolis, P. M. G. Elaris (branch *U*, pp. 78, 81, 88). As is evident from the charters posed in the preceding chapter the position is the same for Ihala Madagama. Thus out-residents, both male and female, are a fertile source for buying shares by the share speculators.

The phrase 'sold their shares' in reference to out-residents is somewhat misleading because it suggests that initial action was taken by the out-resident. Very often the out-resident is deliberately sought by a speculator, or if the out-resident wants to make a good cash sale he may contact a wealthy speculator himself. Such action illustrates the rationality of share-speculation, for genealogically crucially located out-resident kinsmen are sought after for their shares. In the actual hunt for such out-residents the rational calculation of means is important; the speculator deliberately exploits the contradiction between moral norms and the law in order to achieve his ends. There is a deliberate hunt for out-resident kinsmen who have left the hamlet. Consider for example the two females in generation FA^4 mentioned earlier. The rationality of such action is based on the speculator's awareness of the contemporary bilateral law, which could be retroactively utilized to give legal shares to out-resident females who either had never owned the shares if they were located in generation FA^5 and above, or had long abandoned any interest in the hamlet, or both. Earlier we made the statement that these females could *in principle* retroactively assert rights they did not possess at time of marriage: to implement what is possible in principle must at least depend on the awareness of the contradiction between the legal and moral complexity of the situation by the out-resident females. It is highly doubtful whether they comprehend the situation thus. The position is different with the speculator, who can implement in action what existed in principle from the point of view of these out-resident females.

The rationality of share speculation through the manipulation of means governed by contradictory norms is manifested in respect of another problem we highlighted in Ihala Madagama. Many out-residents have left the village to reside elsewhere and their rights have simply lapsed. In-residents have enjoyed these rights prescriptively, but such prescriptive usufruct is challenged when speculators hunt for these 'lost' kinsmen and buy their shares. These situations pose a contradiction between prescriptive usufruct and the law.

Prescription and the law

The irony of the situation in which villagers are placed lies in the contrast between the contemporary law of prescription and the actual perception of the law by the villagers. Traditionally prescription was generally recognized in law; hence the saying that after thirty years the devil himself can become a *pravēni* owner. The contemporary law based on Prescription Ordinance 22, of 1871 is even more liberal.

In Ceylon, proof of undisturbed and uninterrupted possession by a defendant...that is to say a possession unaccompanied by payment of rent or produce, or performance of service or duty, or by any other act by the possessor from which an acknowledgement of a right existing in another person would fairly and naturally be inferred, for ten years previous to the bringing of such an action, entitles the defendant to a decree in his favour with costs. (Pereira 1894:267)

Possession of a third of a century gives prescriptive title against the Crown (Balasingham, vol. III, part II, 1929:123). However, the villagers we interviewed perceived the situation differently. From their point of view a shareowner whose claims have lapsed, still has the legal right to resume control of his property at any time, or sell it to any person who would resume such control. The situation is analogous to the villagers' attitude to the registration of marriages which they believe is necessary for the legality of marriage. In both cases the inviolability of the written document is never questioned. A good example of this is the shares sold by Babappu's two daughters of generation FA^4. These shares were sold to P. L. Uporis in 1925 but they were enjoyed prescriptively up till 1961, when we were in the field, by Amaris, of the anti-plaintiff faction. However, in the partition case Amaris does not attempt to justify his case by the law of prescription. Instead he tries to legalize his prescriptive usufruct by manipulating the genealogical charter. Another instance is the share of $\frac{1}{8}$ sold by Don Mendiris Ediri Wickreme to outsiders in 1890. These outsiders lived in Colombo and had no interest in the hamlet whatever: their rights had lapsed totally. Yet when J. G. Handy bought these shares in 1949, about half a century later, Amaris, who had prescriptive usufruct of a portion of it, made no attempt to defend his prescriptive rights in law. Part of the acceptance of legal ownership against prescriptive ownership is that speculators have bought shares, and owing to their influence and power have succeeded in enjoying them. (Even villagers engaged in speculative activity may have done so.) Moreover, there is the difficulty of proving prescription in the *taṭṭumāru* scheme of undivided shares. If a speculator had even a single share in the *taṭṭumāru* system he could claim he was in possession of the *whole* property, since the length of the field is traversed. When such a person buys extra shares he could claim 'possession' by virtue of the earlier share enjoyed by him. We think speculators, and their partition lawyers for certain, are quite aware of this. The position is slightly different in respect of *goḍa iḍam*, for the *taṭṭumāru* scheme does not operate here. Instead villagers have enclosed larger areas of land than their shares would entitle them to and have planted fruit trees and built houses thereon. Prescriptive ownership would be less difficult to prove here, and hence the reluctance of lawyers to file partition in respect of such land (as in the Ihala Madagama case). But even here prescriptive title may be 'interrupted', and hence invalid. Such 'interruptions' to 'continuous and peaceful enjoyment' of the property, could arise in several ways.

(*a*) An out-resident may have practically renounced his interests in the *vāsagama* estate, yet periodically may have had his rights recognized by the in-residents who pay token acknowledgement of his rights. Or the out-resident may actively assert these rights himself periodically.

(*b*) When a share speculator buys a share from out-residents he may not cultivate the land (*goḍa iḍam*) himself but may either occasionally pick a coconut, or compel the in-resident to pay a token payment which undermines the prescriptive rights of the in-resident according to the law.

Finally, of course, even if the in-resident villagers were fully aware of the law of prescription they would have little chance of proving prescriptive title against wealthy speculators able to hire able lawyers. We predict that the plaintiffs in the Ihala Madagama case will eventually file partition for the *goḍa iḍam* once they have won their case for the paddy lands (and we have not the slightest doubt they will win their case in both instances). Sociologically speaking, the buying of shares from out-residents is tantamount to 'eviction' of in-residents who have enjoyed these shares prescriptively. The most glaring instance of this is I. M. G. Amaris who cultivated prescriptively about a $\frac{1}{8}$ share, but is left with less than $\frac{1}{56}$ according to the plaintiffs' charter even if he were to enjoy prescriptively the shares of two out-resident siblings.

It seems justified to say that speculative action takes place within a framework of contradictory norms brought about by the introduction of the new laws. We have noticed from the partition genealogies that out-resident siblings—particularly female siblings—posed a threat to the in-residents. This would explain an interesting feature of genealogies presented in Pahala Madagama, where informants constantly abstain from recognition of the existence of female siblings and their offspring in the upper reaches of the genealogies—they are 'lost', 'unknown', or 'no connexions' are maintained with them. The comparison with Ihala Madagama suggests that excision of females from the charters of Pahala Madagama informants are grounded in well-founded apprehensions. They pose a constant threat to in-residents. Their resuscitation would diminish in-resident rights, and they are therefore excluded from the charters.

The hunt for out-residents and 'lost' shareowners

The importance of out-residents prompts a hunt for such persons by those interested in buying shares, whether speculators or hamlet in-residents. The strategy of the hunt once again illustrates the rationality of share speculation. We shall present a few cases.

(*a*) *P. M. G. Elaris* (*branch U FA*[5]), *Pahala Madagama*

Elaris owned $\frac{1}{40}$ share of the *gama*, and resided there in 1901 with his first wife, who died childless. He married for a second time, and also lived in the village, but soon after marriage his second wife deserted him. He 'married' again for the third time, a woman from Talangalle. After his death, Ediri Wickreme Thevonis and Senanayake Dasilige Ernolis, speculators, bought Elaris' shares from his second wife and her children. The rationality of these several procedures was apparent from our interviews with the buyers. The whole question rested on the legality of Elaris' several marriages according to the contemporary general law, for there is no doubt that 'desertion' by the second wife would be tantamount to divorce according to traditional law. But according to the contemporary law, calculated Thevonis and S. D. Ernolis, the second wife was legally married to Elaris and entitled to sell his share on his demise. So they bought the share which they now enjoy. In 1957 P. M. G. Hovis got interested in Elaris' share, and calculated differently. He assumed, erroneously, that Elaris was not married legally to the second wife who deserted him but to the third wife with whom he lived uxorilocally. Thus he bought Elaris' share from this source. Hovis, however, does not enjoy the property allocated to this share, but at the time of buying he was banking on an eventual partition suit which he hoped would rebound in his favour as regards this share. In addition, Hovis bought an extra share of $\frac{1}{120}$ from Elaris' 'wife' and children. This was a share unreckoned by the earlier speculators, and probably unknown to the seller. What was this share? If one glances back to the data on the inheritance of Babappu (branch *U*) the following pertinent facts emerge.

We had noted that Babappu's share of $\frac{1}{8}$ was distributed in the manner depicted in our account (pp. 79–83). On the death of Babappu's wife Ano Hamy or Baba Hamy, her share was enjoyed by her daughter P. M. G. Nonno. Probably a verbal transaction without contemporary legal validity had taken place. Hovis is well aware of its legal 'invalidity'. If invalid, the mother's share should devolve on her three children equally in which case each gets $\frac{1}{120}$ share. This theoretically probable share of $\frac{1}{120}$ was what Hovis obtained from Elaris' third wife and descendants. Once again Hovis was hoping that in case partition was filed in the future he stood a chance of getting it. It is interesting to see what Hovis actually did with the shares he bought. Having bought them cheaply he sold one portion ($\frac{1}{120}$) to his mother's eldest brother's son, and mortgaged the other share ($\frac{1}{40}$) to Panangala Liyanage Upalis for Rs. 100. It cost him only Rs. 50 to buy these shares originally from Elaris' 'widow'!

Other cases from Pahala Madagama which illustrate the rationality of share speculation are the vicissitudes of P. M. G. Eranolis' share (p. 88) and P. M. G. Gunadasa's transactions with his half-sister Pelensina (p. 83).

(*b*) *Case of Jasin Gamage Handy, Ihala Madagama*

Jasin Gamage Handy we noted (p. 160) bought $\frac{1}{8}$ share originally belonging to Edirihamy, who had owned $\frac{1}{4}$ of Ihala Madagama. In 1884 Edirihamy sold $\frac{1}{8}$ to the village headman of Neluva residing in Maddegama and he in turn sold it to Don Mendiris Ediri Wickreme who gave $\frac{1}{8}$ to his mistress and illegitimate daughter Mango Hamy and sold $\frac{1}{8}$ to Kahaduwa Aracchige Charles Appuhamy of Galle. He in turn sold it to his brother in Colombo. None of these outside owners actually worked the share, or even laid claim to it. It was worked prescriptively by Mango Hamy and later by her son Amaris. However, by some chance I. M. G. Kartelis got to know of this share available in Colombo. It was a good chance of buying a share and settling a score with his enemy, Amaris. But he had no money, so he asked J. G. Handy, son of a man who settled in Madagama, to buy it 'jointly' with him. Handy was recently back from the British naval base at Trincomalee on the east coast where he had worked and had saved a large sum of cash. Kartelis' suggestion was that Handy should buy the share for both, and Kartelis would pay him later. But Handy had other ideas. His classificatory mother's brother P. M. G. James (branch *U*) had a son Francis, a harbour worker in Colombo. P. M. G. James suggested that Handy should contact his son, who in turn would contact the shareowners (whose name and address Handy had obtained from Kartelis). This he did and Handy, P. M. G. James and Francis (in 1949) went to Colombo armed with a pot of curd and treacle—traditional symbols of amity—and plenty of cash. The whole transaction cost Handy Rs. 1435—and his friendship with I. M. G. Kartelis. But with the Ihala Madagama partition case Kartelis and Handy rallied together—for mutual self-interest—to side with the plaintiffs. Both cases illustrate very well the systematic quest for 'lost' kinsmen or shareholders, the taking of chances and pitting one's own acumen against one's opponents. Other cases of hunting for shareowners and double-crossing one's opponents are: (*a*) Hovis buying the share of Appu Singho by outsmarting Gunadasa (p. 78); (*b*) I. M. G. Nandoris' and Kartelis' buying of P. M. G. Eranolis' share (p. 88).

Anomie and rational action

We have described some of the strategies of share speculation; the strategies are typically employed by outside speculators, but not confined to them exclusively, for villagers too consolidate shares through share speculation. We shall not deal with the most obvious strategy of speculation—simply buying shares from in-residents who are in need of cash. Speculators are generally the wealthy men of the area. Villagers in urgent need of cash either mortgage their property to them or sell it. We were interested in the more complex strategies of share speculation, strategies which illustrate the rationality governing action in the share market. These several strategies have the consequences we noted, for the genealogies are altered in a manner designed to further the interests of the individuals concerned. Thus the end results of various strategies in respect of genealogies was conceptualized as genealogical amputation or excision, genealogical attribution, and genealogical extension. These words are suggestive of the rationality of the processes which we have conceptualized here. These processes could be quite complex, as we have shown, and in most instances could hardly occur in the traditional land tenure system, where the laws of inheritance and marriage constituted a publicly accepted system of jural norms. For example, if the norms state that females cannot inherit the patrimonial estate under certain defined circumstances, the question of amputating them in order to deny them these rights would seem a meaningless and tautological procedure. The opposite processes resulting in genealogical attribution could also hardly occur traditionally, so that, for example, recognition of females in a charter is certainly not going to change the jural norms of the society. These processes could occur only when alternative (even contradictory) norms appear, for example, norms which state that the same females have the right to inherit. In the share market these alternative and contradictory norms are largely the result of the introduction and acceptance of the laws of inheritance and marriage derived from the Roman-Dutch law, conflicting with the traditional jural norms which have considerable significance in social action. This is the classic acculturation context of 'anomie', where introduced and indigenous norms are in conflict.

On the face of it, it would seem unusual to have rational action that we said characterized share speculation in the context of anomie. 'Anomie' is generally defined as a condition of normlessness. It is here defined as 'a condition producing a multiplicity of norms governing social action, often contradictory in nature'. The distinction is one between 'simple anomie' and 'acute anomie'. 'Simple anomie refers to a state of confusion in a group or society which is subject to conflict between value systems, resulting in some degree of uneasiness and separation from the group; acute anomie, to the deterioration and, at the extreme, the disintegration of value systems, which results in marked anxieties' (Merton 1957:163).

Anomie is often said to produce social disorganization and confusion but this need not necessarily be the case with 'simple anomie'. It is necessary also to specify the system which is characterized by anomie, for it is quite likely that one system (like a land tenure system) may have anomic conditions specific to that system, whereas universalistic norms characterizing the larger social system (for example, Buddhist norms) may not be anomic. Even Durkheim in *Suicide* was speaking of a special kind of anomie specific to the primary groups he was interested in. Anomie may produce confusion in certain areas of social action, but may not do so in other areas within the same system. However, if anomie need not always produce confusion and chaos, it generally introduces a lack of predictability in behaviour, inevitable when social action is governed by a multiplicity of norms. One consequence of anomie is, however, clear, especially in the acculturation context where there is a clash between indigenous and introduced norms. *Anomie always increases the range of norms governing action, and undermines the rigid means-goal connection governing traditional action.* It thus makes possible a greater manipulation of means, and a greater normative rationalization or justification of means.

Anomie in the land tenure system of Madagama is relevant for understanding the manipulation of means in the share market system, which is a subsystem of the contemporary land tenure system. Speculators are interested in buying shares which now become a goal of action. The means for achieving the goal is now defined by a multiplicity of norms: greater choice of norms is possible from the available range, and hence a greater choice of means for achieving goals. For example:

(*a*) the speculator may find it worthwhile to explore traditional moral norms to buy shares;

(*b*) he may find these ineffectual in achieving the goals and he may by-pass them; he may say that the new legal norms are more important than the older moral norms and may rationalize his conduct on this basis. The legal norm may be converted ('rationalized') into a moral norm. A condition of anomie could then produce a greater plasticity of means so that means could be rationally weighted or manipulated in order to achieve the goal. Share speculation as rational action has to be viewed against a framework of anomie.

Partition: the end of the land tenure system and the share market

We have said earlier that the loss of the structural prerequisite spells the eventual demise of the *taṭṭumāru* system, and with it the sociological significance of *vāsagamas*. There occurs a continual fractioning of shares, so that the subsection system becomes unworkable. In such an eventuality opportunity is available in the general law for any co-sharer to put an end to the system of undivided shares by filing a partition suit. The Partition law of 1863 provided an opportunity up to 1951 for any co-owner to file partition. Partition when instituted under the Ordinance of 1863 constitutes the end of the *taṭṭumāru* system: each co-owner is given a permanent area of land co-ordinate with the share he owns. Each person from now on works his own demarcated portion of land, which is permanent and 'safe' title. There can be no rotation of plots, and the old egalitarian ideology is ended. It is also the end of the share market. Both systems, based on undivided shares, cannot exist after partition. The Ordinance of 1863 was superseded by the Partition Act of 1951 (Act no. 16 of 1951). The Ihala Madagama partition suit was filed in 1956 under the 1951 Act. Though the new partition law was designed to cure the evils of the old, the remedy came too late for most villages in the Sinhalese low country where partition had already taken place under the Ordinance of 1863. Since we are interested in the effects of partition on Ihala Madagama as well as in its impact on traditional land tenure in general, we shall consider initially the Act of 1863.[1]

The Partition Ordinance No. 10 of 1863

This ordinance has been described by a leading authority as 'a piece of patchwork, ill-drawn and wanting in uniformity of language . . . the number of supreme court decisions on its various sections is a sad commentary on its shortcomings. Most of the difficult points have now been finally settled by judicial decision, and the ordinance fulfills with tolerable satisfaction, the object for which it was intended' (Jayawardene 1925:xxxi). The weaknesses of the ordinance are highlighted in Jayawardene's work; and we shall not be concerned with these. Rather we shall deal with those aspects of the Ordinance relevant for our purposes.

One of the fundamental features of the partition law is that any one co-owner might compel a partition or sale of the property. The plaintiff filing partition has to state in his libel or plaint the extent of the shares and interests of all the co-owners, of mortgages if any, and a general description of the property including improvements made by any co-owner. Otherwise the plaint could be set aside for fraud. Thus all co-owners are parties to a partition suit.

Furthermore, any co-owner can compel partition even if all the other co-owners are opposed to it. Costs in partition suits are apportioned among all the co-owners, *pro rata*. It is also possible for a person who is not in possession of the property and whose title is in dispute to institute partition proceedings. In all cases the court must not proceed on admission but must require evidence in support of the titles of all parties. Summons have to be served on the defendants, and if they cannot be found, upon the person or persons in actual possession of the property, or if there are no such persons, as the court may direct (Pereira 1894:206–9).

> If the defendants be in default the court may proceed to *exparte* hearing; and in that case, if the plaintiff's title be proved give judgment on default decreeing partition or sale as the court may deem fit. If the defendant appear and dispute any material allegation in the libel, the court must proceed to examine the titles of all parties interested, and decree a partition or sale according to the application of the parties, or as the court may deem fit. (Pereira 1894: 209–10)

A tremendous duty is cast on the judge to ascertain the actual owners of the property, since partition title is final and conclusive 'against the world'.

> If during the hearing certain persons are named to the court as proper parties to the suit on account of their having interests in the land entitling them to actual possession, the court may call in aid the provisions of Section 18 of the civil procedure code in order to give such persons an opportunity to establish their claims... (Pereira 1894:210–11)

When a partition is decreed the court generally issues commission to a person agreed to upon by the parties, or, if they cannot agree, to a person named by the court to carry out the effect of the decree.

> The commissioner must after thirty days notice proceed in the presence of all parties concerned, if they appear, to make the partition according to the ascertained proportions of the several owners and with reference to the value of any improvements made thereon and the party by whom they have been made, and in conformity with any special directions in the decree; and make his return to Court. (Pereira 1894:211)

The commissioner is often the surveyor who surveyed the land on behalf of the court. When the commission's return has been received the court gives notice to all parties and then, after a summary hearing of the parties, enters final judgement. If the shares are small and partition impractical, the court appoints a commissioner for the sale of the property. The commissioner has to put up the property for sale first among co-owners at the appraised value, and if no sale is forthcoming for them, put it up to public auction to the highest bidder. A sale may be cancelled for misconduct among co-owners, as for example, if it was proved a co-owner bought the property on behalf of an outsider (Pereira 1894:212). Commissioners are allowed remuneration from a deposit to be made in court (by a plaintiff). The person making the deposit recovers the sum from each of the co-owners *pro rata*.

The 'decree' is binding on all, unless a defendant satisfies the court that summons had not been served on him, or the proceedings had been grossly irregular. In which case proceedings are taken *de novo*. Once a 'final decree' has been entered by the court the case cannot be opened up, so that 'persons owning interests in the land partitioned, whose title has by fraudulent collusion between the parties been concealed from the court in the partition proceedings, are not entitled on that ground to have the decree set aside, their only remedy being an action for damages' (Pereira 1894:213).

The Act of 1951 introduced several procedural and a few substantive changes in the law of partition. For our purposes the more significant substantive changes are the following.

(1) The right of appeal to the Supreme Court, even after final decree has been given (see 68), was unequivocally stated in the Act of 1951.

(2) Section 26 allows the judge in his interlocutory decree to make the following orders: (*a*) order for the partition of the land; (*b*) order for the sale of the land in whole or in lots; (*c*) order for a sale of a share or portion of the land and a partition of the remainder; (*d*) order that any portion of the land representing the share of any particular party only shall be demarcated and separated from the rest of the land; (*e*) order that any specified portion of the land shall continue to belong in common to specified parties or to a group of parties; (*f*) order that any share could remain unallotted.

Thus it is possible under the new law for any co-owner or owners to enjoy certain portions of the land in common. But it is doubtful whether in practice this would mean much, for small shares are likely to be sold on the orders of the court. In any case the provisions of the Act of 1951 puts an end to the traditional and tenure system, for the *yāya* treated as a unit estate is partially or wholly broken up into smaller demarcated units.

The law of partition is directly related to the ends of speculative activity. The speculator buys shares in the estate of any given *vāsagama*. These shares will often be from different sections or subsections in the *taṭṭumāru* scheme, and each share may be quite small, though added up they may amount to a large share in the gross. In the actual cultivation of the fields small shares scattered in different subsections are often unworkable so that they may have to be left fallow, or given out on *andē* lease. The consolidation of scattered shares and their representation in a single cultivable area of land is not possible in the traditional scheme. Such an arrangement is possible only through partition. At partition all the scattered shares are added up and the individual is allocated a permanent, demarcated single stretch of land in proportion to the gross share he owns. From the point of view of the speculator this has important implications. Scattered shares in the *taṭṭumāru* scheme can be economically worthless, but worthwhile from the point of view of prestige and power motives. The speculator extends his control over a hamlet, according to the traditional feudal model of prestige and power. With partition, however, economic interests can be *combined* with prestige and power interests, so that, after partition decree, allocation of a single stretch of permanently demarcated land with secure title permits the individual to put the land to better economic use. He need not leave the land fallow for there will always be demand for a single and large cultivable area of land by villagers. If the speculator lives close to the hamlet from which he bought shares, he may cultivate it himself. Or if he decides to give it on *andē* lease he may get an economically satisfactory *bin havula*, rather than the formal acknowledgement of suzerainty he would otherwise receive. The law of partition therefore gives the speculator an opportunity to consolidate his holdings in a manner not possible traditionally. Some of the speculators interviewed had partition in view explicitly; in buying scattered shares they were rationally calculating the possibility of plot consolidation through eventual partition proceedings.

The position regarding partition is quite different as far as the resident in a hamlet holding small shares is concerned. The villagers are well aware of partition as being unfavourable to them from their knowledge of partition proceedings in nearby villages. Partition proceedings had taken place in Pahala Madagama hamlet between two brothers P. M. G. Hovis and P. M. G. Seetin over a plot of *sinnakkara* land cultivated with rubber by their father P. M. G. James. While we were there the wealthiest resident shareowner of Pahala Madagama hamlet, P. M. G. John, was seriously weighing the possibility of instituting partition proceedings for the Pahala Madagama estate. Resident shareholders (and even non-residents) have a vested interest in retaining their shares. It gives them 'citizenship' in the hamlet and enhances their self-image through the fiction of being independent landowners. Shares, however small, are important from the point of view of the prestige, dignity and self-esteem of a villager. Economically too it is better for a peasant to juggle shares in a single subsection, through *andē* or by cultivating fallow land, for he has only to make a nominal acknowledgement of an outside shareholder's right to the property. As far as *goḍa iḍam* is concerned he has a decided advantage, for he can generally use an area of land larger than he is technically entitled to. Small shares are generally likely to be sold at partition on the orders of the court due to their minuteness or difficulty of partibility. Finally the small shareowner is a poor peasant who is compelled to pay for defence lawyers, if he is interested in contesting the action, and also the costs of partition proceedings such as surveyors' and commissioners' costs, which he can ill afford. Peasant indebtedness is a general consequence of partition.

The provisions of the partition law are largely to the benefit of the speculator and large shareowner. Though small shareowners (that is, most villagers) are opposed to partition, a non-resident speculator with hitherto no cultivation interest in the soil could institute partition action. Education, knowledge of the law, and capacity to hire a partition lawyer are also on the side of the speculator, whereas most villagers cannot afford to attend the District Court located in the provincial capital of Galle, thirty-six miles away. Since sale of small shares is likely to ensue, speculators have the financial capacity to buy these shares. One of the frequent complaints among the villagers in the low country is that commissioners are partial towards wealthy and influential speculators who get the best plots of land for their shares.

Since villagers can financially ill-afford to be present in court and defend their interests adequately, the possibility always exists for plaintiffs to present inaccurate or fictitious statements of claims. Even if villagers realize that they have been defrauded, they can do very little about it after the final decree has been granted, at least under the Ordinance of 1863 unless they file suit for damages—an almost impossible procedure for any villager to adopt.

The calculation and miscalculation of shares

The precise calculation of shares is one of the impressive aspects of the data presented to us in respect of both Ihala and Pahala Madagama. This is most impressive when we compare it with the clumsier attempts made by Indian villagers in Baden-Powell's work. The difference in sophistication here is a function of literacy. Indeed, while the majority of Madagama residents are literate there are a few (with a primary school or secondary school education) quite capable of working out the fractional shares involved. Speculators and those with speculative interests in the two hamlets (like P. M. G. John, P. M. G. Hovis, I. M. G. Kartelis, J. G. Handy) were able to correct the anthropologist's own ventures into arithmetic! But it must not be assumed that when an illiterate, or poorly educated villager sells his shares, he works out the mathematics himself—this is done by the buyer who has the requisite ability, or on advice readily available in the village. The calculation of exact shares—analogous to a book-keeping mentality—is once again an aspect of the 'rationality' of share speculation. Several instances of this 'rationality' have been noted in our data. Here we shall illustrate with an interesting example from the share speculator Panangala Liyanage Peter. In his charter the plaintiff P. L. Peter states that I. M. G. Nimal Hamy had $\frac{3}{32}$ share from Silappu's inheritance—this was sold by her and her children to P. L. Peter in 1922. The charter also states that Nimal Hamy's husband had $\frac{1}{56}$ share (Babappu's inheritance) which was also sold to the plaintiff in 1922 by Don Dias' widow Nimal Hamy and her children. The charter implies that the two sales were separate. In fact the shares were not sold in the manner stated. On the death of Don Dias the family fell into debt and Nimal Hamy and her children sold both shares ($\frac{1}{56}$ and $\frac{3}{32}$) to P. L. Peter in a lump. The deed records that twenty-five shares of $\frac{1}{224}$ each were sold to P. L. Peter in 1922, an exact working out of the arithmetic involved. But instead of stating $\frac{25}{224}$ as one would have expected the deed records twenty-five shares of $\frac{1}{224}$. The reason for this curious phrasing we feel is that it permits the speculator to manipulate the shares more flexibly. For instance, he could give a few shares of $\frac{1}{224}$ as dowry to a daughter, or gifts to a son-in-law, if the occasion arose.

Related to the rationality involved in the exact calculation of shares is the case of *rational miscalculation.* Share miscalculation does not reflect an incompetence in arithmetic, but a deliberate strategy of speculation. The logic of miscalculation is based on the assumption that while undivided shares in an estate could be precisely calculated and cultivation interests allocated on this basis, they need not be precisely stated in a deed of transfer, particularly when the parties involved in the transaction 'know' each other. The share could be slightly increased in the deed to enhance the interests of the parties involved in the transaction. We have several cases of this, some of which we have omitted from the data presented by us. A good example is the case of P. M. G. Nikulas (branch *B*) who transferred his share of $\frac{1}{9}$ to his children in 1916, though the deed records a transfer of $\frac{1}{6}$. The 'miscalculation' is carried right through by Nikulas' heirs (see pp. 70–1). In the actual *taṭṭumāru* scheme Nikulas' heirs enjoy only a share of $\frac{1}{9}$; hence the miscalculation may seem useless. But such miscalculations have potential uses:

(*a*) if the actor wants to sell the share to an outsider he could get a larger price for the share;

(*b*) in the eventuality of partition such a strategy may rebound to the actor's advantage. Other cases of rational miscalculation are where bogus deeds are given as P. M. G. Nandiris' deed to D. L. S. Weerawardene (p. 88) and P. M. G. Jayaweera's deed to K. G. Nikulas (p. 86).[2]

A superb instance of rational miscalculation could be elicited from the charter of the plaintiff in the Ihala Madagama case. According to the law, the plaintiff's libel has to state not only the exact devolution of shares in the property, but also the shares (approximately) that all the shareowners are legally entitled to. A list of the shareowners and their shares appears in the conclusion of the plaint. However, an interesting discrepancy appears between the shares allocated to the various shareowners in this list and the shares they are stated to own *according to that section of the*

Table 13. *Partition share list of plaintiffs*

Name	Share allocated in charter (approx.)	Whether correctly calculated or not
Plaintiffs		
1. P. L. Peter	1132/4032	1038/4032
2. Charles Rubasin Gunawardene	420/4032	Correct
Defendants		
1. P. L. Leelawathi	126/4032	Correct
2. Jayasundere Hitcho Nona	126/4032	Correct
3. K. G. Wickremanayake	—	—
4. K. G. Gunawantha	126/4032	Correct
5. K. G. Piyasena	—	—
6. K. G. Dharmapala	—	—
7. Jayawardene Jinadasa	216/4032	Correct
8. I. M. G. Ernolis	—	—
9. I. M. G. Siyaneris	72/4032	Correct
10. I. M. G. Jandoris	—	—
11. I. M. G. Laiso	72/4032	Correct
12. I. M. G. Somaris	—	—
13. Mavita Gamage Singho Appu	60/4032	78/4032
14. I. M. G. Ortina	—	—
15. I. M. G. Amaris	36/4032	Correct
16. I. M. G. Theneris	—	—
17. I. M. G. Julie Hamy	—	—
18. I. M. G. Amaris	36/4032	78/4032
19. M. H. Thevonis	56/4032	Approx. correct
20. M. H. Girigoris	—	—
21. M. H. Appu Singho	84/4032	Approx. correct
22. I. M. G. Arnolis	—	—
23. I. M. G. Samel	84/4032	Approx. correct
24. I. M. G. Yahapath Hamy	—	—
25. I. M. G. Ortina	28/4032	Approx. correct
26. I. M. G. Karlina	—	—
27. I. M. G. Kartelis	252/4032	Correct
28. Jayawardene Cicily Hamy	126/4032	Correct
29. P. L. Somapala	126/4032	Correct

Table 13 (*cont.*)

Name	Share allocated in charter (approx.)	Whether correctly calculated or not
30. P. L. Wijesena	—	—
31. Edwin Gunawardene	$\frac{168}{4032}$	Correct
32. J. G. Handy	$\frac{504}{4032}$	Correct
33. Mavita Gamage Kristina	$\frac{63}{4032}$	Correct
34. E. W. Podi Hamy	—	—
35. E. W. Bala Hamy	—	—
36. E. W. Baby Hamy	$\frac{63}{4032}$	Correct
37. E. W. Don Diris	—	—
38. E. W. Simon	—	—
39. I. M. G. Kartelis	$\frac{42}{4032}$	Approx. correct
40. I. M. G. Nandoris	—	—
Total	$\frac{4018}{4032}$	
Difference	$\frac{14}{4032}$	

plaintiffs' own charter which records the devolution and *exact* share transactions that are supposed to have taken place in Ihala Madagama. What is important to realize is that if the plaintiffs win their case, land will be allocated permanently to individuals on the basis of the plaintiffs' final share list. It would have been simple for the court bureaucracy to check the list against the statement of share devolution; but this procedure is not undertaken in the badly understaffed court bureaucracies. The following columns in Table 13 will illustrate the discrepancy: the first column gives the list of share owners, the second the shares they are allocated according to the plaintiffs' reasoning, the third, how far this accords with the section in the charter which deals with the exact devolution of shares. We have calculated the exact shares various shareholders are entitled to according to the information in the plaintiffs' charter and have stated in the third column how our calculations accord with the plaintiffs' list. If the two figures are exactly correct, we include the word 'correct'; if there is a minor error we state 'approximately correct'. Any significant discrepancy is included in column 3.

The plaintiffs have left unaccounted a $\frac{14}{4032}$ share. This is nothing unusual because the defendants claim that the shares are allocated approximately (*samānava*) and not with mathematical exactness.

The calculations for all the shareowners are approximately correct except for three 'miscalculations'.

(1) The first plaintiff is entitled to $\frac{1038}{4032}$, yet he has allocated to himself a larger share of $\frac{1132}{4032}$, a difference of $+\frac{74}{4032}$.

(2) I. M. G. Amaris is entitled to $\frac{78}{4032}$ yet he is allocated only $\frac{36}{4032}$, a difference of $-\frac{42}{4032}$.

(3) I. M. G. Amaris' brother-in-law, Mavita Gamage Singho Appu closely associated with Amaris in fighting the plaintiffs is given $\frac{60}{4032}$ when he too is entitled to $\frac{78}{4032}$, a difference of $-\frac{18}{4032}$.

The losses of both Amaris and his brother-in-law amount to $\frac{60}{4032}$. Note how skilfully the plaintiff (the first plaintiff was actually the leader) has diminished the shares of enemies who fought actively against him; not too much to attract attention of the court, and not too little from the point of view of the defendant's concerned. He has reduced the shares of the two defendants by $\frac{60}{4032}$ and then added to this the $\frac{14}{4032}$ unaccounted for in the charter, which gives a sum of $\frac{74}{4032}$. This $\frac{74}{4032}$ the first plaintiff adds to his own share so as to give him the sum of $\frac{1132}{4032}$ he has claimed is legally due to him! If of course he is questioned by the court there is always the argument that the shares were calculated approximately, rather than exactly.

CHAPTER 8

THE IDEAL SCHEME IN CONTEMPORARY APPLICATION

The ideal scheme delineated in an early chapter is simple in structure: but we pointed out that the norms of the ideal scheme in all its symmetry cannot be implemented in reality, owing to the complexity of the empirical facts. The complexity of the empirical situation resulted in the freezing of the Pahala Madagama *taṭṭu-māru* scheme at two generation levels, the third generation from the founding ancestor (FA^3) for branch *B* and the fourth (FA^4) for branch *U*. This is the permanent and publicly recognized scheme: other arrangements, inevitably required by the continuing fractioning of the original estate as one progresses down the genealogical series, would be private arrangements between individuals which have to be accommodated within the public scheme. We described the implementation of the ideal scheme in generation FA^4: the norms of the ideal scheme could be satisfactorily translated in terms of the complexities of the empirical situation of that generation. We shall now show how the ideal scheme is applied in contemporary Pahala Madagama where the empirical situation shows an extreme complexity, not manifested in generation FA^4. When we compare the empirical situation in generation FA^4 with the contemporary one, at least two sets of facts stand out.

First, a change in inheritance from an agnatic emphasis of generation FA^4 and earlier, to the strictly bilateral pattern of the contemporary kinship system. The successful operation of the traditional land tenure system greatly depended on the congruence between the norms of the land tenure system and the inheritance rules of the society. Although there was no perfect congruence between the two, there was sufficient normative consonance to enable the land tenure system to function with considerable efficiency. We noted that the land tenure model calls for patrilineal inheritance and patrilocal residence for males, and the inheritance laws in their actual operation tend to favour the patrilineal devolution of property rights and a patrilocal aggregation of male kinsmen. In contemporary Madagama there is a marked lack of fit between the two systems, for while the ideal model is still governed by patrilineal norms, the rules of inheritance have become strictly bilateral. This two way pull is a major source of tension in the system: the norms of the ideal type are in conflict with the bilateral inheritance laws of the society, and these inheritance laws are in turn in conflict with earlier existent legal norms, which while having no contemporary legal validity, have considerable moral significance for Madagama residents.

Secondly, there is a marked change from the relatively small number of shares in generation FA^4 which facilitates the operation of *taṭṭumāru*, to the extraordinary proliferation of shares today, with its attendant problems pertaining to the accommodation of private arrangements within the public scheme. These two sets of facts make the implementation of the ideal scheme in contemporary Pahala Madagama a difficult task involving considerable strain. But since the ideal scheme *is* the basis for the operation of the contemporary land tenure system, we shall attempt to show how it is done, and describe further the structural sources of strain in the system.

As is evident from Fig. 27 the total area of paddy land is divided into two permanent *geographical* divisions—*ihala kaṭṭiya* and *pahala kaṭṭiya*—each geographical division containing five named fields of varying sizes. The *ihala kaṭṭiya* consists of a total sowing area of 132 (approx.) kurini, while *pahala kaṭṭiya* has 136 (approx.) kurini. In the agricultural season of *yala* 1961, which we shall describe, branch *B* was allocated the Pahala Kattiya, while branch *U* had the Ihala Kattiya. We shall describe the organization of the fields and the operation of *taṭṭumāru* scheme in respect of each branch.

Initially one could have certain 'expectations' regarding the relative normative stability of the two branches. If we are correct about our propositions regarding the major sources of strain in the system—the lack of fit between the land tenure model and the inheritance laws and the increasing proliferation of shares—we could expect branch *B* to show a greater stability than branch *U*, for the latter shows extreme fractioning, and controversies over property rights between kinsmen. This is indeed the case, for branch *B* is far more stable than branch *U* in respect of land tenure.

The Pahala Madagama paddy lands (*maḍa iḍam*) consisted of an area of about eighteen acres, divided into named fields of unequal size, most of which were contiguously located, except the field of Udagaldeniya which is located on the Mavanana road. We are, however, interested in neither the geographical nor the agricultural aspects of land tenure, but in its sociological aspects. The villagers

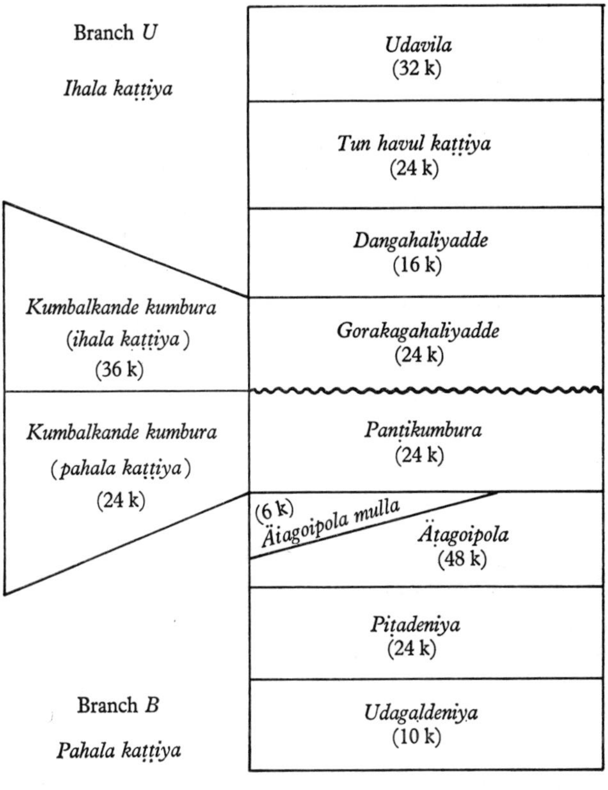

Fig. 27. Formal representation of Pahala Madagama Yāya.

themselves treat the whole of the *maḍa iḍam* as if it were one contiguous block, consisting of a total 'sowing area' of twenty-two 'bags' (*malu*) of paddy or, according to the smaller village unit of measurement, 264 k (actually it is slightly more). The villagers do not calculate in terms of acres in actual cultivation, for in view of the unequal distribution of fertile and infertile plots, such calculations do not make economic sense. Calculations in relation to 'sowing area'—that is, the number of kurini of paddy that is sown—is more feasible since this could be accommodated into the *taṭṭumāru* scheme with its equalitarian norms. The above chart indicates the manner in which the fields are treated for purposes of *taṭṭumāru.*

BRANCH 'B': ORGANIZATION OF 'TAṬṬUMĀRU'

Branch *B*, owing to its relative stability, has considerable success in the empirical implementation of the *taṭṭumāru* scheme. In *Yala* 1961, we pointed out, it was the turn of branch *B* to work the fields in the geographical division, the *pahala kaṭṭiya*. Accordingly, the *taṭṭumāru* scheme frozen at generation FA^3 has to be applied—thus the *pahala kaṭṭiya* has to be divided into three equal units representing the subsection shares of Dingi Appu, Lokuappuve and Balappuve. Since the whole stretch actually consisted of a sowing area of 136 k, each ancestor would be entitled to about 45 k. The mathematics of the scheme cannot be strictly followed, for consideration has to be paid to the practical layout of the fields. In branch *B* the organization of the tenurial arrangements is performed in three steps.

Step 1

The first step is the allocation of fields to the three subsection ancestors, Dingi Appu, Lokuappuve and Balappuve.

Dingi Appu is allocated the field named *äṭagoipola*, minus the *mulla* or corner of the field. The reason is that *äṭagoipola* has a sowing area of 54 k which is much more than the area (45 k) that Dingi Appu is entitled to. Hence the corner, consisting of 6 k, is excluded, and Dingi Appu allocated 48 k.

Lokuappuve and Balappuve are allocated the rest of the *pahala kaṭṭiya*, but since they are viewed as a single jointly cultivating sibling unit, the *taṭṭumāru* fiction of two equal parts need not be empirically implemented. However, this fiction is important when the time comes in the following year to rearrange the subsections within the *kaṭṭi*; and also when, after a period of four years, the *kaṭṭi* themselves have to be alternated.

Step 2

Step two in the process is to make 'private arrangements' within the public scheme. According to our genealogies Dingi Appu had two daughters, Loku Hamy and Baru Hamy, who owned $\frac{1}{12}$ *pangu* each (see p. 74). The present owners of these shares find it practical to reorganize the field in terms of these two earlier shares. This is a private arrangement through consultation among the present owners of Loku Hamy's and Baru Hamy's shares, and is of no importance for the shareowners of the other subsections. Thus the field *äṭagoipola* is in turn divided into two equal 'portions', an upper and lower (also called *äṭagoipola ihala kaṭṭiya*, upper portion, and *pahala kaṭṭiya*, lower portion). Baru Hamy is allocated *äṭagoipola* upper portion consisting of 24 k sowing area. Loku Hamy is allocated *äṭagoipola* lower portion also consisting of 24 k sowing area. These private arrangements are quite important for the subsection sharers, and statements of the following type are frequent: 'I am working Baru Hamy's share this year', '*X* and *Y* are jointly working Loku Hamy's share'.

Similar private arrangements are made in respect of the two shares of Lokuappuve and Balappuve, who according to the 'model' have to be allocated two subsections. According to our genealogies this 'polyandrous pair' had three sons, Juan Appu, Odiris and Adonis. The present shareowners of these persons in turn have their own private arrangements within the public scheme, so that the fields allocated to Lokuappuve-Balappuve are further subdivided into three equal portions. All three parts have a sowing area of 88 k *in toto*. The allocation of fields is as follows:

Juan Appu is allocated the field named *panṭikumbura* with a sowing area of 24 k.

Odiris is allocated *kumbalkande kumbura pahala kaṭṭiya* plus *äṭagoipola mulla* (corner), with a sowing area of 30 k.

Adonis is allocated *piṭadeniya* and *udagaldeniya* with a sowing area of 34 k.

Note that if the allocation of sowing areas is performed mathematically each person above should have about 30 k, but this is not possible since the mathematics have to be accommodated to the geographic location of the fields. Hence Juan Appu has been given the field *panṭikumbura* which has only a sowing area of 24 k, and Adonis is allocated two fields with a much larger sowing area.

However, Juan Appu is compensated, for *panṭikumbura* is a fertile field with a larger yield, whereas Adonis has a larger area with poorer fields. These arrangements have been graphically presented in Fig. 28.

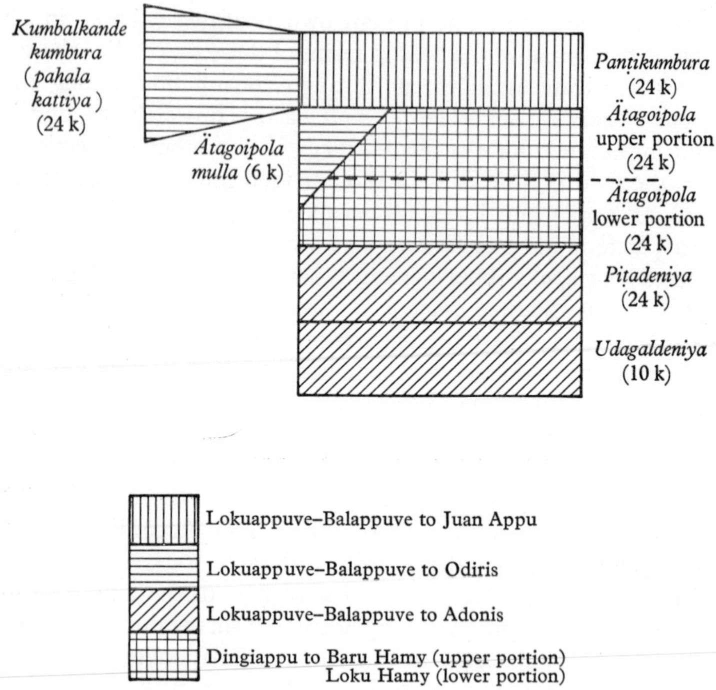

Fig. 28. Branch *B*: representation of fields.

Step 3

The organization of tenurial arrangements is in terms of a genealogical reference: according to the ideal model the genealogical reference is to the 'subsection ancestors' of generation FA^3, to whom three subsections are allocated. The genealogical reference in step 2 is to the offspring of these subsection ancestors, but this genealogical reference we noted is not part of the public charter. None of these ancestors are of course alive, but they are important in the tenurial organization. Step 3 of the process is where the present owners of the genealogical ancestors of step 2 organize *their* tenurial rights, *within the limits imposed by step* 2 of the process. We noted in step 2 that fields were allocated to the five descendants of the three subsection ancestors of FA^3. For example, regarding Dingi Appu's inheritance, Baru Hamy has the upper portion of *äṭagoipola* field and Loku Hamy the lower portion. In step 3, the present owners of the original share belonging to Baru Hamy will organize their shares *within* the upper portion of *äṭagoipola*, while the present owners of Loku Hamy's original share will organize their shares within the lower portion of *äṭagoipola* field. These are private arrangements between the present shareowners of these ancestors: one group of shareholders may not be interested in the private arrangements of the other group. Thus the present shareowners of Baru Hamy's original $\frac{1}{12}$ share may organize their shares in any manner they like, independent of the manner in which owners of Loku Hamy's share organize theirs. This is contrasted with step 2 where the division of *äṭagoipola* (allocated according to the model to Dingi Appu) into two portions has to have the consensus of *both* Baru Hamy's and Loku Hamy's shareholders. In summary we could say that step three concerns the private arrangements within the private arrangements performed in step 2.

Dingi Appu: subsection ancestor. Field: äṭagoipola

The field *äṭagoipola* is divided into two equal portions, allocated to the two daughters of Dingi Appu, subsection ancestor. In practice the owners of the shares may or may not cultivate the fields. The two portions of the field are actually worked in the following manner.

Äṭagoipola upper portion—Baru Hamy

Present shareowners	Share	Number of kurini technically entitled to
S. D. Boris	$\frac{1}{36}$	8
Madarasinghe Aron	$\frac{1}{36}$	8
K. G. Senaratne, Don Arnolis' son	$\frac{1}{36}$	8

Äṭagoipola lower portion—Loku Hamy

Present shareowners	Share	Number of kurini technically entitled to
P. M. G. John's wife	$\frac{1}{24}$	12
P. M. G. John	$\frac{1}{48}$	6
Epa Seneviratne	$\frac{1}{48}$	6

Äṭagoipola upper portion

P. M. G. Arnolis. He works the share owned by S. D. Boris on a share cropping basis (*andē*). The 'actual sowing area' he works is 8 k which is what Boris is technically entitled to.

P. M. G. Singho Appu. Singho Appu works the share owned by K. G. Senaratne of Mavanana: the actual sowing area is once again 8 k. Singho Appu had sold his own share in the *gama* to D. L. S. Weerawardene with the (informal) agreement that the latter would sell it back to him. This Weerawardene refused to do, and Singho Appu compensates by working the share owned by Senaratne, which he has obtained on *ukas*, or mortgage, about six years ago for Rs. 25. The contract is however an informal one, having no legal validity.

Kankanan Gamage Piyadasa. Piyadasa is the son of Kankanan Gamage Don William of our genealogies, who owns shares in the *gama* and is connected affinally and consanguineally with the Pahala Madagama Gamage *vāsagama*. Piyadasa works an actual sowing area of 8 k obtained on *andē* from his mother's brother Madarasinghe Aron, the owner. However, *andē* here is merely a 'fiction' for in fact Piyadasa does not give a share of the crop to his uncle.

Thus the shares are owned by non-resident outsiders but they are actually worked by citizens and residents of Pahala Madagama. The field (*äṭagoipola* upper portion) is, however, not subdivided further in practice for all three persons cultivate it in co-operation, jointly contributing labour, time and seed paddy, and jointly sharing the *asvänna* (yield at harvest). This form of contract between such co-operative cultivating teams is known as *asvänna havula*, or *asvänna bedīma* (share or division of crop). It is pertinent to note the kinship relations of the contracting parties: P. M. G. Arnolis, an adopted member of the *vāsagama*, is classificatory 'son' (*puta*) of P. M. G. Singho Appu, and classificatory cross-cousin (*massinā*) of K. G. Piyadasa. K. G. Piyadasa is a classificatory *bǟna* ('sister's son') of P. M. G. Singho Appu.

Äṭagoipola lower portion

P. M. G. John. He cultivates an actual sowing area of 12 k. The share belongs to his wife. He also cultivates 6 k for the $\frac{1}{48}$ share coming from his father, P. M. G. Abaran.

Kankanan Gamage Piyadasa. He works the $\frac{1}{48}$ share owned by

Epa Seneviratne on *andē*. His actual sowing area is 6 k. Both P. M. G. John and K. G. Piyadasa work the fields jointly and share the yield (*asvänna*) John getting ¾ of the yield and Piyadasa ¼. Note once again that the outsider does not work the field but gives it on *andē*—in this case a small token money payment—even though the hamlet is a mile and a half from the owner's house. The kinship relationship between the two cultivators is classificatory uncle and nephew (*māma-bāna*).

Subsection ancestors: Lokuappuve-Balappuve
Odiris, Juan Appu, Adonis, sons of Lokuappuve-Balappuve

Odiris is allocated the field named *kumbalkande pahala kaṭṭiya* (24 k), and *äṭagoipola* corner (6 k) (*mulla*) yielding a total sowing area of 30 k.

The following are the contemporary shareowners.

Kumbalkande pahala kaṭṭiya—Odiris, 24 k

Present shareowners	Share	Number of kurini technically entitled to
P. M. G. John	$\frac{1}{36}$	6
Epa Seneviratne	$\frac{1}{36}$	6
P. M. G. Derenis (including sister's share)	$\frac{2}{36}$	12

Äṭagoipola mulla—Odiris, 6 k

Present shareowners	Share	Number of kurini technically entitled to
P. M. G. John	$\frac{1}{36}$	1½
Epa Seneviratne	$\frac{1}{36}$	1½
P. M. G. Derenis (and sister)	$\frac{2}{36}$	3

In practice once again outsiders have given out their fields to residents of the hamlet. The fields were actually cultivated thus:

Kumbalkande pahala—24 k

P. M. G. John. He works his own share which comes to a sowing area of 6 k.

Kankanan Gamage Piyadasa. He works the share owned by Epa Seneviratne, amounting to 6 k.

Panangala Vitanage Piyasena and P. M. G. Ariyapala (son of P. M. G. Theris). These two people, classificatory cross-cousins, work the share owned by P. M. G. Derenis, as the latter does not live in the hamlet, but resides in a government agricultural 'colony'. These two have the fields on *andē* from the owner on a *bin havula* basis—that is, 'share for soil ownership'. For cultivation purposes the paddy field is divided into two parts—P. M. G. John and K. G. Piyadasa jointly work one half, while P. V. Piyasena and P. M. G. Ariyapala the other. Each pair shares the *asvänna* (yield) at harvest. As far as this field is concerned the two pairs of cultivators did not swap the two parts of the field in this season (*maha*). The reason is that *kumbalkande pahala kaṭṭiya* field is uniformly fertile and requires no private biannual plot rotation arrangements.

Äṭagoipola mulla—6 *k*

P. M. G. John. John works 1½ k sowing area he is entitled to. Working such a small area is uneconomical so he jointly cultivates it with his classificatory *bāna*, *K. G. Piyadasa*, who works the share owned by Epa Seneviratne on *andē*.

P. V. Piyasena and P. M. G. Ariyapala. They jointly work the share of P. M. G. Derenis. Once again the *äṭagoipola* corner is divided into two parts, the pair John-Piyadasa working one, and Piyasena-Ariyapala, the other. But this field is *not* uniformly fertile: thus John-Piyadasa pair had the fertile lot in *yala*; last *maha* they had the infertile lot, while Piyasena-Ariyapala had the fertile field.

Panṭikumbura—Juan Appu 24 *k*

Present shareowners	Share	Number of kurini technically entitled to
K. H. Karu Hamy's heirs	$\frac{1}{54}$	4
V. K. Somaris	$\frac{1}{54}$	4
D. L. S. Weerawardene	$\frac{1}{81}$	2·7
K. H. Karu Hamy's heirs	$\frac{1}{81}$	2·7
P. M. G. Theris	$\frac{1}{81}$	2·7
P. M. G. Podi Singho	$\frac{3}{108}$	6
Edirisinghe Andiris' heirs	$\frac{1}{108}$	2

Actual cultivation by:

P. M. G. Arnolis. He cultivates his father's (P. M. G. Podi Singho's) share of 6 k jointly with *P. M. G. Ariyapala* (son of Theris, the owner), who cultivates a sowing area of 6 k when he is entitled to only 2·7 k.

Edirisinghe Ariyapala. He cultivates a sowing area of 6 k when he is technically entitled to 2 k from his late father's share.

It is obvious that as far as *panṭikumbura* is concerned there is 'encroachment' by actual cultivators. The reason is that it is not worth while for wealthy entrepreneurs like V. K. Somaris and D. L. S. Weerawardene to work their shares. Moreover, the shares are too small or, for some other reason, cannot be given on *andē* either; hence they leave their plots fallow. The late K. H. Karu's share was generally cultivated on a *karamāru* basis by his sons, but this season it too was left fallow. If a field has been left fallow the custom is that the person cultivating the neighbouring plot could encroach *on a part* of the fallow field. He has to, however, obtain prior permission of the owner, or if questioned by the owner state, 'Your share is still there'. However, one cannot encroach on the *whole* of a neighbour's plot: this would require an *andē* contract. Thus P. M. G. Ariyapala has encroached a sowing area of 3·3 k of D. L. S. Weerawardene's plot, and Edirisinghe Ariyapala an area of 4 k of K. H. Karu's. In practice whole encroachments occasionally occur, especially in branch *U* where considerable *anomie* prevails.

P. M. G. Arnolis and P. M. G. Ariyapala, classificatory parallel cousins, the former an 'adopted' member of the *vāsagama,* jointly cultivate their plots, while Edirisinghe Ariyapala cultivates his separately. No private rotation agreements are feasible since much of the land is uncultivated by the owners, and the present cultivators have only small shares in the field.

Udagaldeniya and Pitadeniya—Adonis 34 *k*

Present shareowners	Share	Number of kurini technically entitled to
P. M. G. Karaneris	$\frac{1}{36}$	8·05
P. M. G. Punneris	$\frac{1}{36}$	8·05
P. M. G. Hitcho Hamy	$\frac{1}{36}$	8·05
P. M. G. Karlina	$\frac{1}{36}$	8·05

This section is owned by members of the *vāsagama* who do not reside in the village. They have thus given away their shares for cultivation on *ukas* or *bin havula* to the following residents of Pahala Madagama.

P. M. G. John. He cultivates P. M. G. Karaneris' share which he has obtained on *ukas* on the basis of informal contract rather than on notarial deed. The rest—*Edirisinghe Sumanapala, P. M. G. Nandiris, K. G. Piyadasa*—have theirs on *andē* for share of the produce (*bin havula*). There is no private plot rotation here because the whole length of field is cultivated jointly by all. Kinship ties between the four are as follows:

P. M. G. John is *māma* (mother's brother) to Edirisinghe, who is John's son-in-law's brother.

P. M. G. John and P. M. G. Nandiris are classificatory brothers.

K. G. Piyadasa and P. M. G. Nandiris are classificatory mother's brother and sister's son (*māma-bāna*).

K. G. Piyadasa and E. Sumanapala are classificatory cross-cousins.

E. Sumanapala and P. M. G. Nandiris are classificatory mother's brother and sister's son (*māma-bāna*).

BRANCH 'U'

The same principles of field allocation are observed in respect of branch *U*. We shall present in brief the situation here. Step 2 of the process described for branch *B* is eliminated because there was only one heir in generation FA^3, and the *taṭṭumāru* scheme was frozen at FA^4 generation. There were, as we noted earlier, four subsection ancestors to whom the fields were allocated in the following manner. The total stretch consisted of five named fields with a total sowing area of 132 k: *udavila* (32 k), *tun havul kaṭṭiya* (24 k), *dangahaliyadde* (16 k), *gorakagahaliyadde* (24 k), *kumbalkande ihala kaṭṭiya* (36 k). Thus theoretically each ancestor was entitled to a sowing area of 33 k each. As far as branch *U* was concerned the discrepancy between the sowing area each subsection ancestor was technically entitled to and that which was actually cultivated was greater than for branch *B*. But the difference in the *size* of subsections is of no consequence for branch *U*, which consists of four subsections on a four year rotation scheme, unlike branch *B* which has *three* subsections on a four year scheme. Each subsection ancestor in branch *U* has to cultivate during the four years all four sections, irrespective of their sowing area strength. Thus branch *U*, which had *ihala kaṭṭiya* for *yala* 1961, could make better use of the 'natural' layout of the fields in the actual organization of *taṭṭumāru*, so that fields need not be arbitrarily carved out (like the 'corners' of branch *B* fields).

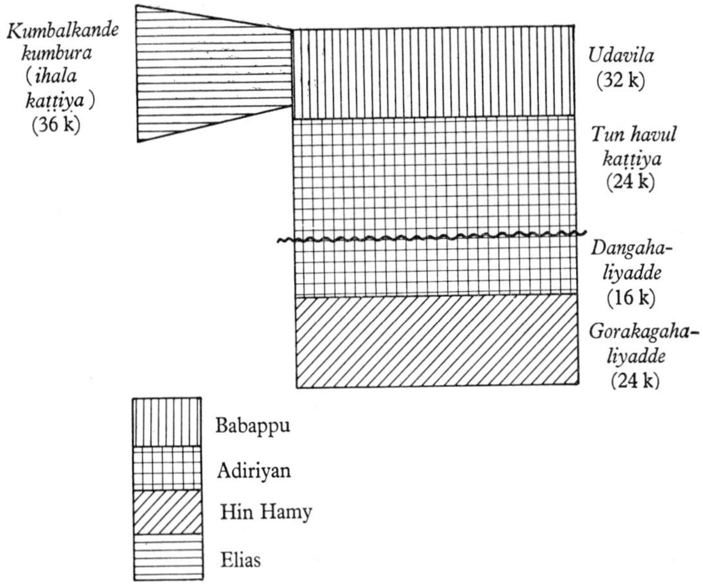

Fig. 29. Branch *U*: representation of fields.

Step 1. The fields were allocated to the four subsection ancestors in the following manner:

Babappu	*udavila* (32 k)
Adiriyan	*tun havul kaṭṭiya* (24 k) and *dangahaliyadde* (16 k)
Hin Hamy	*gorakagahaliyadde* (24 k)
Elias	*kumbalkande kumbura ihala kaṭṭiya* (36 k)

Step 2. Here the private arrangements of the present shareholders have to be co-ordinated with the public scheme implemented in stage one of the tenurial organization process.

Subsection ancestor: Babappu. Field: udavila

Present shareowner	Share	Number of kurini technically entitled to
P. M. G. Gunadasa	$\frac{1}{80}$	3·02
Gunadasa's six siblings each have $\frac{1}{480}$	$\frac{1}{80}$	3·02
Madarasinghe Aron	$\frac{1}{80}$	3·02
E. W. Thevonis (also claimed by P. M. G. Hovis)	$\frac{1}{80}$	3·02
P. M. G. Nonno	$\frac{1}{80}$	3·02
Senanayake Dasilige Pitchoris	$\frac{1}{80}$	3·02
Kankanan Gamage Podi Hamy (P. M. G. Gunadasa's wife)	$\frac{1}{80}$	3·02
Kankanan Gamage Podi Nona (Godapita Gamage Diyonis' wife)	$\frac{1}{80}$	3·02
Kankanan Gamage Don William (and mother—P. M. G. Wimala Hamy)	$\frac{2}{80}$	6·04

In the actual cultivation of the fields some of the problems seen in branch *B* are better highlighted here, for here even more than in branch *B* non-residents who own shares find it hardly feasible economically to cultivate the minute sowing area they possess. Thus Madarasinghe Aron, and P. M. G. Nonno and E. W. Thevonis do not work their shares—since the land is left fallow they are worked by K. G. Don William and K. G. Podi Nona (or rather her husband G. G. Diyonis), both resident cultivating shareowners. As regards S. D. Pitchoris' share an interesting arrangement prevails. This share ($\frac{1}{80}$) is given on *andē* to P. M. G. Gunadasa who has in addition the following: $\frac{1}{80}$ belonging to him; $\frac{1}{80}$ to his wife; he also cultivates the $\frac{6}{480}$ ($\frac{1}{80}$) owned by his six siblings, who find it economically impossible to cultivate individually the small portions each possesses. Gunadasa has a servant-patron relationship with the Senanayake Dasilige 'family' whose rubber plots in the Pahala Madagama *goḍa iḍam* he looks after, and often works as paid labourer on their plantations elsewhere. Thus while technically Gunadasa has the $\frac{1}{80}$ share on *andē* he in fact does not pay either in produce or cash to Senanayake Dasilige Pitchoris. Yet it is formally and publicly recognized as an *andē* contract: and Gunadasa formally acknowledges the master-servant relationship by taking a gift of betel to the Senanayake Dasiliges every New Year. However, P. M. G. Gunadasa does not cultivate the total portion himself; he finds it more economical to work for the Senanayake Dasiliges on their plantations. He therefore gives some of this to P. V. Piyasena (married uxorilocally to a daughter of P. M. G. Nandiris) on *andē* (*bin havula*) basis. But in this case Gunadasa takes his pound of flesh (which is $\frac{1}{5}$ of the produce). Thus the actual cultivators of *udavila* are the following:

P. V. Piyasena (8 k) on *bin havula* from P. M. G. Gunadasa
P. M. G. Gunadasa (8 k)
G. G. Diyonis (8 k)
K. G. Don William (8 k)

Kinship relationship: all four are classificatory cross-cousins.

Subsection ancestor: Hin Hamy. Field: gorakagahaliyadde (24 *k*)

Present shareowners	Share	Number of kurini technically entitled to
Senanayake Dasilige Boris	$\frac{1}{16}$	12
D. L. S. Weerawardene	$\frac{1}{48}$	4
P. M. G. Theris	$\frac{1}{48}$	4
K. H. Karu's heirs	$\frac{1}{48}$	4

Once again Senanayake Dasilige Boris' share of $\frac{1}{16}$ is given formally on *andē* to P. M. G. Gunadasa, his servant. Gunadasa cultivates a sowing area of 6 k, and gives a sub-*andē* contract of 6 k to P. V. Piyasena. They cultivate separately. P. M. G. Ariyapala cultivates his father's (P. M. G. Theris') share plus the share owned by D. L. S. Weerawardene. Note that Weerawardene's share originally belonged to Theris' brother Singho Appu but owing to the strained relation between them the latter does not cultivate it on *andē*. However, this does not prevent his brother's son from doing so. Karu's share is cultivated by his son K. H. Ariyadasa. Ariyadasa and P. M. G. Ariyapala work the fields jointly and share the *asvänna* on a two to one basis.

Subsection ancestor: Elias. Field: kumbalkande kumbura ihala (36 *k*)

Present shareowners	Share	Technically entitled to sowing area of
D. L. S. Weerawardene	$\frac{1}{32}$	9 k
K. G. Amarapala (of which $\frac{1}{64}$ also claimed by his *massina* P. M. G. Nandiris)	$\frac{1}{32}$	9 k
Ihala Madagama Gamage Kartelis	$\frac{1}{32}$	9 k
Ihala Madagama Gamage Nandoris	$\frac{1}{32}$	9 k

The 'anomic' situation prevalent here owing to conflicting share claims is manifested also in the cultivation of the fields. D. L. S. Weerawardene, the absentee owner, has given his share to P. M. G. Nandiris, from whom he bought it originally, on *andē*. But note that this could be disputed by Nandiris' siblings at any time. Nandiris also works the disputed area of 9 k which is claimed by Amarapala for his $\frac{1}{32}$ share. While Nandiris only claims $\frac{1}{64}$ of this, he actually works the whole area since Amarapala, who is a younger man without strong kinship support in the village, wants to avoid a direct clash with his more powerful cousin. But Amarapala had filed a court case when we were there. What the outcome was we do not know. Of the shares owned by the two brothers, I. M. G. Kartelis and I. M. G. Nandoris of Ihala Madagama hamlet, the whole sowing area of 18 k is worked by the elder brother Nandoris, without any compensation for the younger, who was actually instrumental in carrying out the transactions involved in buying these shares.

Subsection ancestor: Adiriyan. Field: tun havul kaṭṭiya (24 *k*) *and dangahaliyadde* (16 *k*)

Once again we notice that the non-residents own a number of these shares, and as usual they do not cultivate them. One reason for non-cultivation should be quite apparent now. Given the existence of the *taṭṭumāru* scheme of subsections, the problem of accommodating small shares becomes acute and an economically fruitless one for non-residents. For example, P. M. G. Semaris

Present shareowners	Share	Technically entitled to sowing area of (approx.)
S. D. Sumanapala	$\frac{4}{112}$	9 k
P. M. G. Seetin	$\frac{1}{112}$	3 k
P. M. G. Podi Nona	$\frac{1}{112}$	3 k
P. M. G. Jinadasa	$\frac{1}{112}$	3 k
P. M. G. Hovis	$\frac{1}{96}+\frac{1}{96}$	6 k
P. M. G. Semaris	$\frac{1}{96}$	3 k
P. M. G. Sumana *et al.* (4 shares of $\frac{1}{384}$, that is)	$\frac{1}{96}$	3 k
P. M. G. Wimala Hamy (son K. G. Don William)	$\frac{2}{96}$	6 k

is entitled to a sowing area of 3 k—it is utterly unprofitable for him to cultivate this tiny sowing area. S. D. Sumanapala has 9 k sowing area, which is quite reasonable, but consider what happens when he moves to another subsection in a subsequent year and is allocated a small field like *gorakagahaliyadde* which will give him a sowing area of only 6·8. This is of little economic significance for a wealthy man like S. D. Sumanapala. So he leaves it fallow and Hovis, who traditionally cultivated it, works this portion as usual. One could frame this in general terms: the smaller the sowing area of a field the greater the problem of accommodating fractional shares ('private arrangements') within it. Thus, in actuality Hovis cultivates 15 k, his own share and Sumanapala's which is lying fallow. Godapita Gamage Diyonis works his wife's portion and that of P. M. G. Jinadasa of Colombo which lies fallow; P. M. G. Seetin works his own and P. M. G. Semaris' which is also fallow. Seetin, however, acknowledges an *andē* contract with his father's brother Semaris, which is only to be expected since his uncle lives in a nearby village. G. G. Diyonis and P. M. G. Seetin, 'cross-cousins' (the former married to Seetin's sister), jointly cultivate a sowing area of 18 k and share the produce. The remaining area of 3 k belongs to Sumana and her sons, but is worked by P. M. G. Nandiris by force, the *rationale* being that Nandiris' deceased son-in-law Sirisena was Sumana's son. Nandiris, however, has no legal or moral right to this share.

It is immediately apparent from the preceding presentation that the traditional *taṭṭumāru* scheme provides the basis for the contemporary allocation of shares, in spite of extreme share fractioning. However, from the evidence we have, more startling and unpopular conclusions can be drawn about 'agrarian economics' in South and South-East Asia. First, we hold that the fractioning of shares does not lead to an uneconomic subdivision of fields. Secondly, the system of undivided shares, as long as a *taṭṭumāru* type system continues to function, *actually prevents the subdivision of fields*. Thirdly, a multitude of shareowners does not imply a multitude of cultivators, so that fields are not cultivated in an uneconomic manner. Since all these conclusions are contrary to the current opinion about Asian agriculture, it is worth examining them in more detail.

Though most authorities make a distinction between undivided shares and subdivision of lands, there is an undemonstrated assumption that the latter is in some way caused by the former. Farmer, reviewing some of the trends in agricultural economic policy in Asia has this to say:

> ...There was a great deal of discussion in Ceylon in the 1920's on ways and means of preventing not only subdivision but also the passing of holdings into the possession of a number of heirs...In many Asian rice growing countries where subdivision has not been condemned and restricted already, recommendations for its control are being made. Thus, in the World Bank report on the economic development of Malaya, it is stated that, as in other Muslim countries, laws of inheritance cause minute subdivision which is well attested by land registers in many parts of the Federation, and this subdivision combined here with scattering 'leads to uneconomic holdings, concealed unemployment, increased indebtedness, reduced productivity of the land...and in general has a disintegrating effect on an agricultural community.' The report goes on to recommend Federal legislation similar to that already in force in Kelantan, where no parcel of land less than the prescribed minimum may be subdivided or held in undivided shares...
>
> (Farmer 1960:226)

In a recent paper an economist argues that in Ceylon 'the problem appears more serious when we realize that the process of subdivision of the physical unit of cultivation is being carried further with each generation though possibly not to the same extent as in the case of ownership' (Arulpragasam 1961:62). One of the perennial themes of administration reports and political debate is the serious economic ills of shareownership, and subdivision.

In his paper Farmer has shown quite convincingly that the subdivision of land is not the great economic and social evil it is often thought to be. Here we shall attempt to show that the laws of inheritance are not the prime cause of subdivision, as long as land is held in undivided shares. Whenever subdivision occurs it is only temporary, for in the next season the group of cultivators may decide to work a larger unit. The present units cultivated are all economically feasible for labour intensive small scale agriculture.

In spite of the proliferation of small undivided shares there are techniques for overcoming the subdivision of fields.

(1) *The pooling of shares*, whereby shares within a single subsection are pooled together by an individual or group. Since each subsection incorporates one or several fields, the fields themselves need not be subdivided into small 'parcels'. Share pooling is effected by mortgages of shares of absentee owners, or obtaining shares on *andē* lease.

(2) *Crop sharing, or asvänna havula.* A group of individuals cultivate a single field, and divide the produce in proportion to the share(s) they own, obviating the necessity for the subdivision of fields.

The advantage of the share system in the economics of paddy cultivation lies in the fact that shares are 'floating'; they are not shares in a specific permanently marked out area of land, but in rights in an estate. A proliferation of small shares which we noted for our hamlet in 1961 has one effect: such shares are economically worthless unless pooled with other shares in the same subsection. People owning small shares, particularly absentee owners, are willing to lease them to cultivators on a nominal or token acknowledgement of the owner's rights. Sometimes owners leave their land fallow, which permits in-resident cultivators opportunity to 'encroach'. None of these conditions could exist with the end of the share system. The Partition Ordinance was partly designed to combat the evils of undivided ownership. In fact, partition of land inevitably produces subdivision of fields. Since partition has the effect of consolidating the shares of absentee landlords (especially those of outside speculators) scattered in various subsections into a single permanent holding, it gives the landlord a firmer economic hold on the hamlet. He need no longer give his land on nominal lease; he can actually cultivate it himself or give it on a share cropping or cash basis profitable to him. Once land has been partitioned, or in any other condition where the share system does not operate, the laws of inheritance may produce subdivision of the *land*, in contrast to the former mode where inheritance laws produced fractioning of *shares*.

The fractioning of shares inevitably springing from the loss of the structural prerequisite of the system in combination with inheritance laws, produces a multiplicity of owners, over fifty in our hamlet in 1961. But the actual cultivators are restricted in number. Nine persons cultivate the fields allocated to branch *B* and ten to branch *U*. We believe that the near equal distribution of cultivators in the two *kaṭṭi* is not fortuitous. It makes good economic sense. The average per person is slightly less than an acre. Peasants cultivate land when it is practical to do so; the ownership of a share does not presuppose cultivation of land. Share ownership has primarily to do with prestige motives; cultivation with economic *and* prestige motives. Nine persons seems a satisfactory number that a *kaṭṭi*, treated as an extended cultivation unit of nine acres, can take. In terms of the whole stretch of paddy land (*yāya*, that is, both *B* and *U*) the number of cultivators is only sixteen, since several persons who cultivate the one also cultivate the other. The average for the actual *cultivated* stretch is well over an acre per person.

In case averages are misleading we shall present in the following table the sowing area cultivated by each individual in respect of the whole stretch.

Fourteen kurini constitute an average sowing area of one acre; about nine persons cultivate a sowing area of an acre or more. Of this number, three cultivate well over two acres, and three less than two acres, but more than one. Six persons cultivate an area of less than an acre. Of the six at least three cultivate paddy land elsewhere too—E. Sumanapala in Ihala Madagama, K. H. Ariyadasa in Mavanana, P. M. G. Hovis in Panangala. One person, K. G. Don William, in fact enjoys more than 8 k, because his unmarried son K. G. Piyadasa cultivates 30 k, which goes for 'family' consumption. Thus in fact only two people cultivate a sowing area of less than an acre (14 k). While none of the above are self-sufficient in terms of rice, our evidence suggests that:

(*a*) peasants cultivate in economically feasible land units;

(*b*) most persons cultivate a reasonably large sowing area *in toto*, though none are self-sufficient;

(*c*) the number of cultivators depends not on the number of owners but on the capacity of the land. Regarding the last we may suggest that the actual number of cultivators for the whole stretch has been more or less constant from at least 1909 to the present day. If we were right that fourteen 'families' cultivated the fields in 1909, in 1961 it is only fifteen! There has been no material increase or decrease in terms of yield either—then, as well as now, the yield remains about fivefold. Furthermore, though the majority have their fields from absentee owners, hardly any part of the produce is given to them (except in one case where in-resident P. M. G. Gunadasa has given an *andē* lease to in-resident P. V. Piyasena).

Table 14. *List of cultivators and sowing area of the Pahala Madagama fields yala 1961*

Name of cultivator	Total sowing area (k)
P. M. G. John	34
K. G. Piyadasa	30
P. M. G. Nandiris	27½
P. M. G. Ariyapala	21½
P. V. Piyasena	21½
I. M. G. Nandoris	16
P. M. G. Hovis	15
P. M. G. Arnolis	14
G. G. Diyonis	14
P. M. G. Gunadasa	14
P. M. G. Seetin	9
E. Sumanapala	8½
P. M. G. Singho Appu	8
K. G. Don William	8
E. Ariyapala	6
K. H. Ariyadasa	4

Several contrasts have to be noted though. Before 1909, it can be assumed that *chena* cultivation provided a subsidiary source for paddy and other grains. In recent times there has been only sporadic *chena* cultivation. More importantly, the number of cultivators the fields can hold has to do with the economics of cultivation. It does not tell us about landlessness and 'agrarian unrest' at all.

Ever since 1909, population pressures and land shortage have created in the area a large number of peasants who cultivate no paddy at all. These people work as hired labourers, in tea and rubber plantations, in the plumbago mine nearby and in the Neluva tea factory. The problem would have been acute had not the government stepped in and eased the situation by granting Crown land on permanent lease to 'landless' villagers. These lands are called *badu iḍam*. It is outside the scope of this work to discuss *badu iḍam*, except to state that from 1931–65 practically every villager has been given two to three acres of *badu iḍam*. *Badu iḍam* are generally cultivated with cash crops and provide an important source of income for peasants. For our purposes what is important is that *badu iḍam* was totally contradictory to the traditional mode of village expansion through founding a *gama*. In *badu iḍam* a strictly limited area of land is given to single individuals. More drastically, according to the law, these lands could only be alienated to a single successor. This typical governmental solution to the so-called invidious inheritance laws in Asian societies is bound to create increased dissension in the family and conflict between siblings. In a system of primo or ultimogeniture, the prospective rights of siblings are clearly defined in relation to the birth order. But in the present law pertaining to *badu iḍam* this is not the case and one could predict conflict between siblings, and between parents and children over inheritance of this type of property.

CHAPTER 9

THE IDEOLOGY OF STATUS AND THE FORMATION OF 'PELÄNTIYA'

TYPES OF CONTRACT AND THE IDEOLOGY OF 'ANDĒ'

In the preceding discussion three kinds of contractual arrangements between cultivators have been noted: (*a*) co-sharing (*asvänna havula*), (*b*) share cropping (*andē*), and (*c*) mortgage (*ukas*). If viewed in terms of dyadic relationships co-sharing involves an equalitarian relationship between the co-operating individuals, whereas *andē* implies an unequal one, the owner having a higher prestige than the cultivator. In Madagama, he may also have a higher social rank. Mortgage like *andē* implies an unequal relationship and it is considered demeaning for a person to mortgage his lands, for it is an index of his temporary loss of status as an independent landowner. *Ukas* could be of two types: where an individual is indigent and asks a wealthy person for a sum of money against the mortgage of his property, or where a resident villager asks a wealthy 'absentee landlord' for a mortgage of the latter's property. It is the former that is disprivileged, not the latter which is only technically *ukas* but is in fact viewed as a favour done to the mortgagee by the mortgagor. This type of mortgage is not common: it is really a conversion of an *andē* relationship from a share cropping to a cash basis, providing the mortgagee with a greater amount of security and permanency of tenure than in *andē*. This form of mortgage contract we shall for convenience call '*andē-ukas*', a combination of *andē* and *ukas* type contracts.

We have at our disposal thirty-one cases of mortgages contracted on notarial deed on record from 1918 to 1960. Of these, twenty-four cases were with 'outsiders': land was mortgaged to people who had no direct cultivation interest in the land and were not village residents. Of these twenty-four all except two mortgage contracts were with non-*vāsagama* mortgagees—the two cases being contracts with P. M. G. Semaris who, though a *vāsagama* member, was a wealthy man living in Miguntenne, and not concerned with the economic aspect of the contract. The rest were cases where the mortgagee was a village resident, in which case the economic or cultivation interest is predominant. Furthermore, seventeen of the twenty-four contracted with 'outsiders' were with members of two closely related dominant 'lines'—the Panangala Liyanage, and Senanayake Dasilige 'lines'. In summary, twenty-four of thirty-one cases are mortgages contracted with wealthy non-residents, not primarily interested in the cultivation or use of the mortgaged property.

Ukas or mortgage was traditionally an important means of raising loans in Sinhalese society at exorbitant rates of interest (D'Oyly 1929:62). In contemporary Madagama, however, almost all the mortgage contracts recorded stipulate 'the right of possession in lieu of interest' (*polimara ukas*). Thus land sales due to foreclosure of mortgage were rare. Most people manage to redeem their mortgage pledges eventually, and when in a few cases people actually sell their mortgaged property, this is not due to 'foreclosure of mortgage' but for purposes of raising cash. The mortgagee hardly enjoys the produce of the land which is in his possession. When the mortgagee is a resident, the paddy fields are generally given back to the owner on an *andē* basis, or if the owner is himself an absentee it is given to another tenant or left fallow. As far as *goḍa iḍam* is concerned, the mortgagee may occasionally pick a few arecanuts from the trees; otherwise he rarely enjoys the produce of the land, unless the mortgaged property should contain an important cash crop like rubber. This is, however, rarely mortgaged. I know only of one case of a rubber plot being mortgaged. Picking an occasional fruit from the tree is more often a public symbolic act rather than one solely springing from economic motives: it is an assertion of one's temporary 'overlordship of the domain'. Most cases of *ukas*, as far as Pahala Madagama is concerned, are disguised *andē* contracts—except that in the former the 'landlord' is only a temporary owner of the property. The mortgagee in these cases is, however, interested in eventually obtaining a permanent ownership of the property, so that a true *andē* relationship could be established. Both *ukas* and *andē-ukas* generally result in an *andē* type relationship: except that in the former the mortgagor is viewed as being in a subordinate position whereas in the latter he is in a superordinate one. In *ukas* the mortgagee takes upon himself the roles of landlord temporarily. In *andē-ukas*, the mortgagor is the landlord giving out his property on 'lease' to a resident cultivator: the landlord, being wealthy, could terminate the 'lease' at will.

The case of I. M. G. Kartelis v. Don Haramanis Rubasin Gunawardene

P. L. Peter (whose sister's son is Don Haramanis Rubasin Gunawardene, headman for Madagama village living in Lelwala) is an absentee owner of a considerable extent of Ihala Madagama *pravēni*. I. M. G. Kartelis, an influential Madagama resident and village leader, obtained Peter's share on *andē-ukas*, for Rs. 300. But Kartelis was not acting as humble tenant: a highly ambitious and upwardly mobile man he was aspiring to become prominent himself. Such aspirations by resident villagers are a threat to the 'family' (*pelāntiya*) of the headman and his uncle, who decided to pay back the money and redeem the mortgage. But I. M. G. Kartelis refused to accept the money, for he wanted to continue enjoying the lease. Ultimately the headman had to instruct his lawyer to send a cheque for Rs. 300 to Kartelis, and compel him to acknowledge receipt of the money.

'ANDĒ'

If *ukas* can be viewed as disguised *andē* type contracts, it is of considerable importance to understand the latter. Structurally viewed *andē* is a share cropping arrangement between the owner of the land and the person cultivating it. *Andē* means 'half': in this case the landowner receiving half the produce from the cultivator. In traditional parlance *andē* was merely one type of share cropping arrangement. *Oṭu*, for example, was another kind where less than half was given to the landowner, depending on the nature of the soil, etc. (Brohier, vol. 1, 1950:6; see also Codrington 1938 and Bertolacci 1817 for other types of share cropping contracts). In contemporary Madagama, as probably elsewhere in Ceylon, *andē* is the general term used for all share cropping arrangements, the portion given to the landlord being known as *bin havula* (soil share). Generally speaking the theory is that the *bin havula* will depend on the labour, time and amount of seed, paddy and fertilizer supplied by the landowner. In Madagama generally, the absentee landlord has no economic interest in paddy cultivation and does not materially assist the tenant in any way. A quite different system prevails in Pul Eliya where the landlord is often a peasant himself and generally involved in the production process (Leach 1961:249–51). In Madagama, only a token payment is given to the landlord, which is simply a formal acknowledgement of rights of ownership. Sometimes even this is waived if the absentee landlord is a wealthy kinsman, so that P. M. G. Seetin gives nothing to his father's brother, nor K. G. Piyasena to his mother's brother. But even here the landlord's rights have to be recognized, so that when a peasant wants an *andē* contract from a wealthy landlord, he has to offer the latter a *bulat hurulla* (a sheaf of betel leaves) and worship him. It is also customary for the tenant to visit the landlord with a *bulat hurulla* every New Year. However, when the *andē* landlord is a Pahala Madagama resident, and a cultivator directly interested in the agricultural production process a strict contractual arrangement as that prevalent in Pul Eliya obtains. Thus P. M. G. Gunadasa has an *andē* relationship with P. V. Piyasena: the latter gives Gunadasa an exact one-fifth share of the produce.

It must not be construed from this account that landlords are uninterested in the economic aspect of the *andē* contract. There are for example, economic factors that inhibit the landlord from taking a strict share of the produce. The landlords own small shares, and cultivating these shares in terms of the *taṭṭumāru* scheme is difficult, as pointed out earlier. The gross yield of the crop is so small in this region that it is not often worth while for a landlord to demand his share. Moreover, the landlord's presence at harvest is required if a strict apportionment of the crop is to take place, and this is not easy if the landlord is not a village resident. Even when a tenant gives the landlord a token portion of the produce he would make an apologetic statement of the following sort: 'This year was a bad harvest.' 'The birds devastated a good part of my crop.' 'The drought (or rain) made my paddy grains hollow (*bol*).' These statements are never taken literally: they are an 'apology' for not giving the landlord the amount theoretically due to him. Finally, it must be remembered that the poorer peasants themselves are only partially dependent on the paddy fields for their subsistence. They are partly motivated to cultivate the fields for the prestige and dignity associated with the role of peasant cultivator. It also minimizes the indignity of having to substantiate one's income by selling one's labour for hire in the nearby tea factory and plumbago mine. But while it is true that there are factors that militate against a landlord obtaining his due portion, even if he was seriously interested in it, this still begs the question. The crucial issue is why should wealthy landlords in the first place be interested in buying these small scattered shares in outside villages, or invest their money in mortgage contracts, when they are aware of the economic worthlessness of the transactions? The answer obviously is that motives more powerful than economic ones are at work, motives pertaining to power and prestige. The control over tenants, while economically of little importance, enhances the status of individuals and families in the power structure of the region. It is to this ideology of power, derived from traditional feudal norms still possessing great vitality and contemporary relevance, that we must now turn.

The ideology of *andē* and *ukas* is simply an aspect of the wider normative ideals pertaining to prestige, power and authority in the society. On the level of social structure *andē* (share cropping) and *ukas* (mortgage) are common to many societies; but here we are interested in the 'attribution of meaning' to these social relationships, that is, their normative or cultural structuring within a single society. On one level these norms have to do with the rights, duties and obligations of each member of an interacting dyad: but this does not exhaust the content of the norms, for there are values governing *andē* and *ukas*, which transcend the dyad, and are a part of a wider set of norms that govern a whole class of similar types of social relations in the society. The class in this instance groups together certain types of dyadic social relationships characterized by inequality in terms of prestige, power and authority: ego is viewed as superior to alter in terms of these three values. We are interested in exploring the norms that govern this class of relationships, for we believe this will lead us to view better the political relationships in the society, and especially the problem of status mobility and the motives for land speculation in the village.

The norms of *andē* discussed hitherto are derived from Sinhalese feudalism. While the social structure of feudalism is no more, the norms pertaining to power, prestige and authority are derived from feudalism, and provide ideals for emulation by the people. To describe Sinhalese Feudalism is outside the scope of this work and accounts of it are available elsewhere (D'Oyly 1929; Pieris 1956; Hayley 1923). In order to highlight the problem succinctly from the point of view of our work, we shall consider feudalism in terms of a dyadic relationship. We have 'reduced' the complex feudal ideology of power and prestige into a relationship between an interacting *ego* and an *alter*. The 'dyadic reduction' of feudalism is basically a relationship between landlord and tenant—known in Indian sociology as a *jajmani* relationship. The former owns the land and the latter cultivates it. The landlord is released from direct physical involvement in the agricultural production process; the latter is tied to it. A complex network of rights and duties are associated with this relationship, but these too could be reduced to the central idea of service (Hocart 1950): the tenant renders service to the lord, and the lord in turn has prescribed jural rights over his tenant. The relationship is an unequal one; the landlord has a higher rank (and may belong to a higher caste or subcaste) than the tenant. The social distance between the two is symbolized by ceremonial. The type of ceremonial is indicative of the relative statuses of the members of the interacting dyad, the higher the status of landlord relative to the tenant, the greater the elaboration of ceremonial.

Power, prestige and authority were (and are) typically perceived in traditional Sinhalese society in these terms: an unequal relationship between landlord and tenant governed by rights, duties and the performance of ceremonial. Status aspiration in any society is not conducted in a vacuum but in relation to an ideal (or ideals) however vague and tenuously held it may be. Such an ideal was available in Sinhalese feudalism, in the relation between landlord and tenant most conspicuously manifested in the upper hierarchy of the feudal political system. Another powerful ideal for emulation is the Buddhist order of monks: but here there is a sharp cleavage between prestige and power, the status of the monk carrying high prestige but very little power and authority in respect of the lay order. By contrast feudal norms provided an ideal for status aspiration which *combined* prestige, power and authority in a single scheme of relationships. The high point in the institutionalization of the 'feudal dyad' is the relation between king and subject.

In Sinhalese theory the king was *bhūpati* 'lord paramount of the soil of Lanka' or *bhūpala* 'protector of the earth'. All landed property is conceived as derived from him, and reverts to him on its escheat (Brohier, vol. 1, 1950: 1; D'Oyly 1929:46; Pieris 1956:43–5). Knox writing in the seventeenth century said: 'The country being wholly his, the King farms out his lands not for money but for service' (Knox 1681:168). Thus, the king is supreme landowner and all his subjects are tenants of different types: all owe services to him without exception.[1] These services were called *rājakāriya*, or *royal duty*. But the services were not of a kind; they varied with the social status of individuals or groups performing them, and the nature of the contract between king and subject. The non-performance of services rendered the lands *purappāḍu*: 'escheated to the crown'. Similarly treason was a violation of the social contract between king and subject, and confiscation of property was one of its consequences. As supreme owner of the soil the social distance between king and subject was extremely great: abject ceremonials of obeisance and prostration symbolized this social distance (D'Oyly 1929:4–5; Andrews 1917). The king in theory owned all land, but in fact had direct managerial control of only a part. These estates were called *gabaḍāgam* (royal villages or estates): the tenants of these estates owe special *rājakāriya* to the king. For our purposes what is most relevant are those royal villages whose tenants enjoyed their lands on condition of cultivating the king's *muttettu*, that is, the special area of the estate which had to be gratuitously cultivated by the tenants and the produce delivered to the royal storehouses (*gabaḍā*).

Royal lands or *gabaḍāgam* when granted to individuals were known as *nindagam* (Pieris 1956:60 ff.). These lands were given to the officers of the crown, the *radala* aristocrats, as perquisites of office. The dues and services that were formerly paid to the crown were now payable to the lord, or *gamladda* (owner of a *gama*). The land was often given by the king on a written grant (*sannasa*) and the lord had to pay a fee initially on his appointment as grant holder. He had also to acknowledge the formal overlordship of the king by paying him his annual respects (*däkum*: literally 'seeing'), generally consisting of a unilateral payment of gifts and the performance of obeisance. As in the case of *gabaḍāgam* certain classes of tenants had gratuitously to cultivate the lord's *muttettu*, which consisted of a fifth or sixth of the estate according to Pieris (1956:53). D'Oyly mentions two forms of *muttettu* tenure:

First *ninda muttettu* which is sown entirely and gratuitously for the benefit of the proprietor, grantee or chief by other persons (*nilakārayō*) in consideration of the lands which they possess; and second *anda muttettuva*, which is sown by anyone without obligation, on the usual condition of giving one-half of the crop to the proprietor.

(D'Oyly 1929:54)

Anda muttettuva then is simply a version of the *andē* contract, where a half-and-half share cropping contractual relationship exists between tenant and absentee owner. But it is no ordinary contract—it is associated with feudal overlordship. Pieris records the continual struggle during the Kandyan period among *nilakārayō* to acquire *pravēni* title which 'conferred heritable title in perpetuity' (Pieris 1956:44). Acquisition of *pravēni* title implies ownership of property unmediated by suzerainty to an overlord, and the compulsory performance of services contractually required of the tenant. The *nindagama* tenants had a double contract, with two landlords requiring two kinds of services—one, service to the king which all citizens had to render, and the other, to the lord of the village. This double contract diminished their rights of ownership in the lands, and gave them an inferior status *vis-à-vis* groups who had only a single contract to the king, namely, *rājakāriya* which is in fact a privilege right of citizenship.

Sharpe classifies the services due to the *gamladda* (lord) into two broad types. First, labour, which involved the cultivation, care and safe delivery to the *valauva* (manor) granary of the *muttettuva* harvest. Secondly, honorary attendance on the lord on public occasions to carry the lord's insignia of office like flags and *sesat* banners, and on domestic occasions in the lord's *valauva* (see Pieris 1956:54). Not all tenants had to perform both types of services. However, the caste or subcaste status of the tenant was related to the kind of service he had to render, services of a menial kind being considered more demeaning than attendance on the lord as a member of his retinue. The concept of *pirisa* or *sēnāva*, 'host', the number of persons the lord could muster, and that of *pirivara*, 'retinue', were of extraordinary importance in the ideology of feudalism, for *pirivara*, and *senaga*, *sēnāva*, or *pirisa* provided an index of the prestige, status and power of the lord. The *pirisa* consisted of a series of dyadic relationships centrifugally located in the lord. The lord was the hub or pivot (role centre) from which a multiplicity of unequal dyadic relations radiated. Dickson (1870) presents an ideal picture of these dyadic role relationships located in the landlord as role centre.

On the estates of the chiefs and large landowners (*nindagam*) the services...are of the greatest possible variety. Chiefs and *mudiyanselā* perform various honorary services. (*Goigama*) tenants cultivate the home farm (*muttețțu*), accompany their lord on journey, take their turn in duty at the manor house (*valauva*). *Durē* tenants carry baggage and the lord's palanquin while the Vahampure carry the palanquins of the ladies of the family and also provide for the service of the kitchen; and though there is a complete absence of equality and system in the remuneration given for domestic services, all such services are provided for with the utmost care. A chief with several villages will draw his cook or his bath boy for two or three months a year from one village, from another for four months, and a third for one month, etc., carefully arranging to have one throughout the year. There are the potters to make the tiles and supply earthenware; the smith to clean the brass vessels, and repair and make agricultural implements; the cunam weaver (*kinnarayā*) and the outcaste *rodiyā*, who buries the carcasses of animals that die on the estate, and supplies ropes, etc., made of hide and fibres. Others supply pack bullocks for the transport of the produce of the fields, and for bringing supplies of salt and cured fish from the towns on the coast.

(Quoted in Pieris 1956:64)

These several tenants performing services constituted the landlord's role-set (Merton 1957:106–20). The basic characteristic of this role-set was the structural uniformity of the role relationship between the members of the role-set (the 'role others') with the role centre in the landlord. The basic structural similarity in these role relationships was its inequality: a superordination-subordination relationship. All the role others of the landlord performed service to him—though there were variations in degree and type of service dependent on the social status of each 'role other'. The symbols of status and prestige were also of the same type—ceremonials symbolizing the social distance between the two, manifested in obeisance and ritual. The totality of the role others constituting a lord's role-set is his *pirisa*, *senaga* (host) or *pirivara* (retinue). In everyday social and economic life the *pirisa* or *pirivara* is not manifested as a unified group, but there are special occasions when the lord's *pirisa* is formally assembled.

(*a*) *Processional events.* On state visits or state duties the lord would be accompanied by his *pirivara*. Several Western observers have commented on this phenomenon. The strength, display, panoply of the *pirivara*, and the mode of travel of the lord (whether in palanquin, on elephant or foot—all being minutely regulated) indicated the power of the lord.

(*b*) *Rites of passage* at the landlord's house where the tenants will gather and assist in the proceedings.

(*c*) *Däkum*, '*respects*'. The tenants of the lord all gathered together on certain occasions to pay *däkum* or respects to him—consisting of a unilateral payment of gifts. One special occasion for *däkum* is pertinent for our purposes. This is during the Sinhalese New Year in April which is a special occasion for paying visits to respected kinsmen and superiors in Sinhalese society. On this day the tenants pay obeisance to the lord, by presenting him with a *bulat hurulla* or sheaf of betel leaves, and worshipping him. The whole role-set is brought together to the role centre on this occasion. All these are occasions for the formal 'cultural performance' of the everyday role relationships between landlord and tenant.

It should be remembered, however, that the landlord could be of several grades, some more powerful than others. Since land given to a lord was a perquisite of office, landlords of this type were feudal office holders. This implies that minor office holders were themselves members of the role-set of a major office holder. For example, a *vidāne* (a village 'headman') or a *liyanna* (a scribe) may have several tenants cultivating his estate (*gama*) but he has in turn to pay *däkum* to his overlord who may be *disāva* or provincial governor. There are limits (*sīma*) to the power of each landlord: each landlord represents a role centre, one greater (commanding a larger radius of dyads) than the other. Each centre is a repository of power and authority: the ultimate repository of power is the king. The chiefs pay *däkum* to him and acknowledge him as their overlord. Since he is owner of all the soil of Lanka, he is the overlord of all: all citizens render service, or *rājakāriya* generally devoted to public works and military services. These services are qualifications of citizenship, as pointed out earlier. But there is a limit (*sīma*) even to the power of the king. For though he is viewed as a deity or *bodisatva*, he himself is under the overlordship of the Guardian Deities of the Island, to whom he has to pay formal obeisance during certain religious rituals.

The phenomenological implications of our dyadic reduction of Sinhalese feudalism is great: power, prestige and authority is perceived by the Sinhalese as overlordship of an estate (*gama*) and its inhabitants, and its associated ceremonialism. The extreme phenomenological importance of this notion of power is manifested in the fact that the allocation of power roles among the respective deities of the pantheon is modelled on this pattern. The feudal idiom of the Sinhalese pantheon has been described elsewhere in detail (Obeyesekere 1962), suffice it to state here that deities too have their areas (*sīma*) of special jurisdiction, and minor gods owe service to the major gods, and constitute their retinue (*pirivara*), while the demons and inferior spirits are the *pirisa* (host) of the major gods. In rites of propitiation of gods, the *kapurāla* (priest) and his assistants perform the same kind of obeisance and homage paid to the overlord or king. In processions where the insignia of the gods are paraded, their human attendants constitute a retinue, carrying flags, palanquins, banners and other attributes of feudal authority and power. Above all these deities is the Buddha himself, who is generally depicted in legends and paintings as accompanied by a *pirivara* of *dēvās*. In sermons about the life of the Buddha, contemporary monks constantly refer to an arrival or departure of the Buddha as *pirivarāgena*, 'accompanied by a *pirivara*'. Similarly Mara, the arch enemy of Buddha, is depicted with his hosts, *senaga*, attacking the Buddha. In sociological terms the *pirivara* or *pirisa*, as stated earlier, constitute the role-set of the landlord: each role other involved in an unequal dyadic relationship with the landlord as role centre.

Gods and kings are the ideal phenomenological representations of this notion of power. Kings are often viewed as gods, and gods viewed as kings (ultimately both viewed as parental figures). We would understand better the notion of *chakravarti* 'world ruler', so important in Indian and South-East Asian political thinking, in this light. If the king, as ruler of Ceylon, is the highest concrete embodiment of the feudalistic notion of power, then it follows that the ideal king should be a ruler of the whole world—that is, a *chakravarti*. Similarly, if the Guardian Deities have supernatural control over the whole Island, and Sakra over the Buddha *sāsana* (the Kingdom of Buddhism), then it follows that the Buddha's power should be limitless, beyond all *sīma*, which is indeed how he is represented (Obeyesekere 1962). It is interesting to note the legend of the Buddha birth in this respect, for it is stated that when Siddharta was born the court astrologers prophesied that he would either be a *chakravarti* or a Buddha—both representing the extreme phenomenological dimensions of this notion of power. The term *chakravarti* appended to the name of South Asian kings, often rulers of petty principalities, has been treated by scholars as an example of the Indian predilection for flowery metaphor. On the contrary, given these notions of power, it is a legitimate and natural aspiration for any king. Indeed it is a legitimate aspiration for the ordinary citizen, whose perceptions of power are also based on these norms. So that one of the popular *prārtanas*, or rebirth wishes attached to acts of Buddhist piety, is to be born as a *chakravarti* (or a god) in a future birth. This fantastic wish, uttered by poor contemporary peasants, indicates on the one hand the relevance of the *chakravarti* ideal for them but more importantly what the ideal represents—authority and power viewed as control over territory (land, *gama*, 'estate') and persons tied to it, a *pirivara* or *pirisa* paying homage to the lord.

The *chakravarti* wish of the peasant shows clearly the importance of these power norms for the ordinary villager, for since he himself performed *rājakāriya*, the peasant was directly involved in the traditional power structure of the society. More importantly in relation to the social structure of the hamlet the feudalistic ideas of *muttețțu* and *pirivara* have their direct sociological counterparts. The *muttețțu* we noted was the special area cultivated gratis by the tenants for the lord: in the hamlet there is a special area cultivated gratuitously by the peasants for the officer known as the *gamarāla* (literally 'village head'). Leach (1961) says that under the traditional system the *gamarāla* was the person to whom the *nindagama* has been leased by the overlord, while others (Pieris 1956; Codrington 1938) emphasize the tax collecting role of the *gamarāla*. *Gamarālas*, however, not only existed in *nindagamas* but also in villages which were, like those in Hinidum Pattu, 'free'. Hence it is likely that their major duty was tax collection and mobilization of *rājakāriya* services and organization of *tațțumāru* arrangements, with little or no police or jural rights and duties. A part of the village *gama* or estate was cultivated gratuitously for the *gamarāla*: this analogue of the lord's *muttețțu* was known as the *gamvasama* (Codrington 1928), or *elapātha* (Leach 1961; Ievers 1899). The tax collecting role of the *gamarāla* is now defunct though a modified version of the office is found in the Nuwarakalawiya district (Leach 1961:148–55). It is of no importance in contemporary Madagama, though the constant references in folk tales (Parker, vol. I, 1910; vols. II, III, 1914) indicated their traditional importance in this region. In our genealogies the heads of the two branches are called *gamarālas* (for example, 'Upe appu *gamarāla*'). The office of *gamarāla* was reconstituted by the British as 'headman', appointed by the government, and having clearly defined police and administrative duties. Though today no special field like the *elapātha* is reserved for the headman, villagers cultivate his fields for him, and perform other types of gratuitous services.

The *pirivara* also has its analogue in the village, on the level of caste and kinship. If the village is a *goigama* one like most villages in our area, then members of lower castes form a structural analogue of the *pirivara* of the lord. Sometimes members of the lower castes may be fields on leasehold by a particular family for services rendered, or they may be given payment in kind—a portion of the produce of the fields. Interaction between a person of *goigama* caste and a low caste displays the same unequal dyadic structure of feudalism: service, homage, land ownership (or payment by grain) are the constituent elements of the relationship. These role others of a *goigama* caste can constitute a kind of retinue, which like the landlord's retinue is formally mobilized on special occasions like rites of passage, and village and domestic rituals. On the level of kinship, the structural analogue of the *pirivara* or *pirisa* is the *nǟ pirisa* or 'kinship following'. A large *nǟ pirisa* is indicative of a person's influence, affluence and power. The *nǟ pirisa* is not simply a kindred which exists simply as an aggregate by virtue of consanguinity (Freeman 1961:192–220). It refers to those kinsmen who could be actively mobilized by an individual. Every individual in this sense has a *pirisa*, at least a few kinsmen who are his active supporters or following. Affluent individuals have large *nǟ pirisas* whose extent, strength and unity, are manifested on formal ritual occasions. It is in relation to the building up of *nǟ pirisas* that affinity assumes importance in the society.

The usurpation of patronymics and honorifics

In a society in which power was so finely institutionalized in a complex network of unequal relationships, one would expect validations of superordinate status to take various forms. One form is through patronymics and honorifics. These are of considerable importance, and traditionally kings and chiefs had several of these appended to their names as titles. Some of the names of Kandyan kings were in fact honorifics (like Kirti Sri Rajasinghe, Vimala Dharma Suriya). Dutch governors exploited this national weakness to the full by prolific use of honorifics in their dealings with kings and chiefs, and the British who came after them began to realize quite early that medals, titles and honorifics associated with office were an easy reward for faithful service. Traditionally, however, these titles were firmly guarded against usurpation. Like these titles there were a whole range of personal pronouns used to address people according to their rank: *umba, numbu, tō, oyā, tamusē, tammunānse,* and so forth. Even the term 'yes' has two applications: *ow* when one says 'yes' to people of the same or lower status and *ehē* or *ehemai* when one is replying to a superordinate, while *ehē svāmīni* ('yes lord') is used for a monk, or king. In the seventeenth century there was a special class of patronymics known as *paṭabändi nama, paṭa* meaning 'strap' and *bändi* meaning 'tied'. The terms came from a ceremony of 'knighting': the king tied a silken strap around the forehead of a recipient of title. Though originally these were not hereditary titles, there developed in later Kandyan times a whole subcaste of *mudiyanse* people (*mudiyanse* implying *paṭabändi* title) recruited from the middle ranks of the *goigama* who gradually constituted a bureaucratic *élite* in Kandyan society.

> Most *paṭabändi* names indicate that they were originally conferred for conspicuous military exploits (for example Jayasuriya or 'Sun of Victory', Vickramasuriya or 'Sun of Conquest') and the possession of several such names marked a person of distinguished lineage. Scions of a man honoured with a *paṭabändi* title such as Suriyasekera Mudiyanse would convert it into a patronymic and call themselves Suriyasekera Mudiyanselage, 'descended from Suriyasekera Mudiyanse'.
>
> (Pieris 1956:173)

This resulted in a spread of *paṭabändi* titles in Kandyan society. These *paṭabändi* names were quite different from the Sabaragamuva and low country *vāsagamas* we have described. Though they may be affixed to a *vāsagama*, the latter, like the Kandyan *gedera* described by Tambiah, is associated with an estate, while the former need not be. Thus Leach is wrong when he says the *vāsagamas* are of no importance in Pul Eliya: the so-called Pul Eliya *vāsagama*—Raja Guru Mudiyanselage, 'descendants of a Mudiyanse who was teacher to the King'—is simply a *paṭabändi* name usurped by Pul Eliya folk to boost their prestige. There are no *vāsagamas* of the type we have described in the Nuwarakalawiya district (Leach 1961:3).[2]

With the three streams of foreign conquest, the prohibition against assuming patronymics and titles associated with rank was lifted, and there was a mass 'usurpation' of these honorifics particularly among the dominant *goigama* (and a few of the *karāva*) caste. With Portuguese conquest, a new set of prestigious titles were introduced, chiefly Don and Señor. Villagers all over the Sinhalese low country lapped up these names so that Don was a very popular personal name among 'respectable' peasants, the 'model' for such usurpation being the name of the last Sinhalese king of Kotte who, as a converted Catholic, called himself Don Juan Dharmapala. Señor was thoroughly indigenized and converted to 'Singho', as is evident from Madagama names. The Portuguese era was also important for it provided lower castes, who dared not usurp *paṭabändi* titles, an opportunity to take over Portuguese 'surnames'—so that Perera, de Silva, De Mel, Salgado were most popular with the *karāva* and *salāgama* castes and Fernando with both *karāva* and the washer (*radava*) castes. The Dutch period introduced no new honorifics but with the British a new 'prestige trend' could be observed. This was the conversion of *paṭabändi* names into surnames after the British practice, and the use of English 'Christian' names (for example, David, Charles, etc., in our genealogies). By late British times 'Don', 'Señor' had been pejorated: prestige was associated with *paṭabändi* surnames, usurped by the Western-educated bureaucratic intelligentsia. *Goigama* villagers sometimes changed their *vāsagama* into surnames but more often chose surnames that belonged to influential Sinhalese families either in a region or nationally, for example, Senanayake, Wickramasinghe, Wijewardene, Weerasekera, Gunawardene of our genealogies.

The usurpation of patronymics by peasants led to their pejoration. Thus 'Don' and 'Singho' are no longer prestigious. Even foreign names like Perera, de Mel, etc., and English 'Christian' names are currently looked upon with disfavour. The use of English type surnames has probably come to stay. An interesting case of pejoration is the traditional title given to *goigama* caste people—*appu*. *Appu* which was a term of respect in Kandyan times lost its aura and was linked with *hāmi* ('lord') so that *appuhāmi* became a common honorific attached to 'respectable' peasants in British times. *Rāla* was a highly respectable term; now it is combined with *hāmi* and *rālahāmi* is used as a term of address to village headmen, registrars of marriages, coroners, police constables, etc. The simple term *appu* or *rāla* is no longer prestigious and is used for 'ordinary' peasants. It would be disrespectful to use these terms for any 'official'.

The motives for the usurpation of honorifics is clearly seen in relation to our earlier argument—it is an emulation of a position of power, prestige and authority by persons who were traditionally debarred from such positions. But while it is easy to emulate these 'titles', it is far less easy to acquire the other privileges associated with title—large 'estates' and *pirisas*. Hence honorifics, without these other supports are constantly subject to pejoration. Within recent years *paṭabändi* names, which were generally *goigama* prerogatives, arc being acquired by non-*goigama* castes, as a glance at the local newspapers indicates. It is very likely therefore that *paṭabändi* surnames within a few years will be as common as Jones and Williams in American or English society. At present, however, name-changing is a necessary though not sufficient condition for status mobility.[3]

POWER, PRESTIGE AND THE 'PELÄNTIYA'

A large part of the Ihala Madagama *gama* has, we noticed, passed from the hands of members of a *vāsagama* to outsiders having several different *vāsagama* names. These outsiders are closely related to one another and belong to a kinship group, which we will later describe as a *peläntiya*. We refer to the share owners shown below.

The only other group of outsiders with significantly large shares are the widow and children of K. G. Nandoris, speculator from Gigummaduva, who jointly own $\frac{1}{16}$ of the *gama*. These people are not related to the persons mentioned below. The plaintiffs and their kinsmen thus own $\frac{2274}{4032}$ of the *gama*, or well over half. In other words a closely related kin group (*peläntiya*) has during a period of about eighty years come to 'control' a *gama*, which originally belonged to a 'free' peasant *vāsagama*.

1. Panangala Liyanage Peter	$\frac{1132}{4032}$ or $\frac{1038}{4032}$	over $\frac{1}{4}$ of the *gama*
2. Charles Rubasin Gunawardene	$\frac{420}{4032}$	about $\frac{1}{6}$ of the *gama*
3. Panangala Liyanage Leelawati, daughter of P. L. Peter	$\frac{126}{4032}$	$\frac{1}{32}$ of the *gama*
4. Jayawardene Jinadasa, brother-in-law of Panangala Liyanage Peter	$\frac{216}{4032}$	$\frac{3}{56}$ of the *gama*
5. Jayawardene Cicily Hamy (wife of Panangala Liyanage Uporis) and	$\frac{126}{4032}$	$\frac{1}{32}$ of the *gama*
6. two sons Panagala Liyanage Somapala and Wijesena	$\frac{1}{126}$	$\frac{1}{32}$ of the *gama*

If we look at Pahala Madagama, about 40 per cent of the estate is controlled by outsiders but scattered among a number of them. The prominent shareowners here are Senanayake Dasilige Pitchoris ($\frac{1}{80}$) and his brother's son S. D. Boris ($\frac{1}{16}+\frac{1}{32}$), who jointly own little less than $\frac{1}{10}$ of the *gama*; and D. L. S. Weerawardene, Registrar of Neluva, who owns shares of $\frac{1}{32}+\frac{1}{68}+\frac{1}{81}$. The Senanayake Dasilige family (*pavula*) own considerably more of Pahala Madagama *goḍa iḍam*, and at times owned more shares than they do today. One share of $\frac{1}{32}$ which S. D. Boris owns was actually 'sold' to him by Panangala Liyanage Peter in 1946. The speculative activities of the Senanayake Dasilige *kānḍaye* (group) are still going on and it would be correct to characterize them as the dominant outside speculators in Pahala Madagama. This will come out clearly if we look at the mortgage transactions. Of the thirty-one transactions of mortgages we have collected for Pahala Madagama, eleven were contracted with Senanayake Dasilige Pitchoris, six with Panangala Liyanage Peter (and one with Rubasin Gunawardene); that is, eighteen out of thirty-one mortgage transactions were with the Senanayake Dasilige or Panangala Liyanage *kānḍaye* (group). Thus three outside groups dominate the two hamlets—the Senanayake Dasilige 'group', the Panangala Liyanage 'group', and the Rubasin Gunawardene 'group'. The three groups seem to have three different *vāsagama* names, but in no sense are they discrete *vāsagamas*, of the type we described for Ihala and Pahala Madagama. Transcending their *vāsagama* identities, on which they themselves do not place much emphasis, are the complex nexus of kinship ties that link these groups together and transform them into a single kindred type kin group, the *pelāntiya*. In order to elucidate the structure of *pelāntiyas* we shall describe three of them stratified on an ascending order of prestige. The first *pelāntiya* we shall describe is the one referred to above, the *pelāntiya* made up of families belonging to three lines—the Senanayake Dasilige, the Panangala Liyanage, and the Rubasin Gunawardene lines. The second is a more powerful and prestigious *pelāntiya* in the region; and finally we present an even more prestigious *pelāntiya*.

Pelāntiya No. 1. In Fig. 30 the darker triangles and circles represent some of the members of the *pelāntiya* from the point of view of an Ego in the *pelāntiya* located in the fifth generation depicted in the chart. The members of the *vāsagama* line are included in plain ink. All the kinsmen depicted here could ideally be a *nā̈ pirisa* of any powerful member of the *pelāntiya*. For purposes of analysis and description of the kinship bonds that interrelate the *pelāntiya*, we shall initially make distinctions between the following terms: *vāsagama*, '*vāsagama* line' or 'status line', *pelāntiya*, and *nā̈ pirisa*. A *vāsagama* is a corporate hamlet of the type described for Ihala and Pahala Madagama. A 'status line' is simply a group of patrilateral kinsmen bearing a common 'surname'; thus status lines could be *vāsagama* names that have lost their involvement in a corporate hamlet due to the changes we have depicted, or any other patrilateral aggregate of kin bearing a common name. A *pelāntiya* is a group of kinsmen of several status lines, selectively chosen on the basis of 'status honour', reflected in a 'common style of life' based on traditional feudal values, pertaining to incumbency in office, with its attendant accoutrements of power and authority, such as control over an estate or *gama* and a retinue or following (*pirisa*). A *nā̈ pirisa* are all the kinfolk any Ego could effectively summon for certain purposes like *rites of passage*, and always includes members of one's *pelāntiya*, and some members of the *vāsagama* and status lines with which one is connected through consanguineal or affinal links.

The *pelāntiya*, like any kindred group, is not named, since its range may vary with the genealogical location and status of Ego. But a person when referring to his *peläntiya* may make a statement like the following: *api Rubasin Gunawardene peläntiya* 'we are of the Rubasin Gunawardene *peläntiya*'. This does not mean that a *peläntiya* is a single status line. It arises out of an attempt to refer by name to a group, which not being descrete, simply cannot be named. For example, the current village headman of the Neluva division Don Haramanis Rubasin Gunawardene may say that he belongs to the Rubasin Gunawardene *peläntiya*, but on elaborating his statement would always include members of the Senanayake Dasilige and Panangala Liyanage status lines, and always exclude some members of these lines. The term *vāsagama* may be used by individuals today to denote any status line, so that the headman generally would say that he is of the Rubasin Gunawardene *vāsagama*, but may qualify it by adding *api pelänti kārayō*, 'we belong to a *peläntiya*'. Empirically the term *peläntiya* refers to several of these status lines linked together through affinal exchanges (Senanayake Dasilige *peläntiya* × Rubasin Gunawardene *peläntiya* × Panangala Liyanage *peläntiya* = *peläntiya*). When reference is made to a *peläntiya* a man would rarely use the first person singular, but rather the plural—*apē peläntiya* ('our *peläntiva*') not *magē peläntiya* ('my *peläntiva*'). At any point in the historical development of a *peläntiya*, the group must minimally include select members of a man's own status line plus at least one status line with which the former is affinally linked. In dominant *peläntiyas* even the affines of one's affines may be included in one's own *peläntiya*. Thus dominant *peläntiyas* may consist of several status groups linked together by direct or indirect affinal links and opposed status-wise to the peasant subcastes of the region. The *peläntiya* members view their relationship to the latter as a master–servant, or a patron–client one. In the *peläntiya* charts we have drawn we have only depicted a significant section of each *peläntiya*. They do not by any means include *all* those whom Ego would consider members of his *peläntiya*.

In Fig. 30 some members are alive while others would have been considered dead members of the *peläntiya*. One of the interesting features of a *peläntiya* is how easily the offspring of a member of a *peläntiya* can be dropped off the *peläntiya* list, though retained as a member of the *nā pirisa*. In order to elucidate some features of the *peläntiya* and *peläntiya* formation, we shall describe how three different *vāsagama* lines, through affinal exchanges converged into a *peläntiya* by the fifth generation.

The first link up is between two lines—that of the Rubasin Gunawardenes and the Panangala Liyanages—as Fig. 31 indicates.

The first affinal link up occurs in generation 2 where Don Andiris Rubasin Gunawardene marries Panangala Liyanage Punchi Nona. Since it is the first step in *peläntiya* formation, we must sketch some of the background history of the two lines. The Panangala Liyanages were originally an offshoot of a *vāsagama* line from the village of Panangala. One member of this line settled in the village of Lelwala, where the Rubasin Gamage *vāsagama*

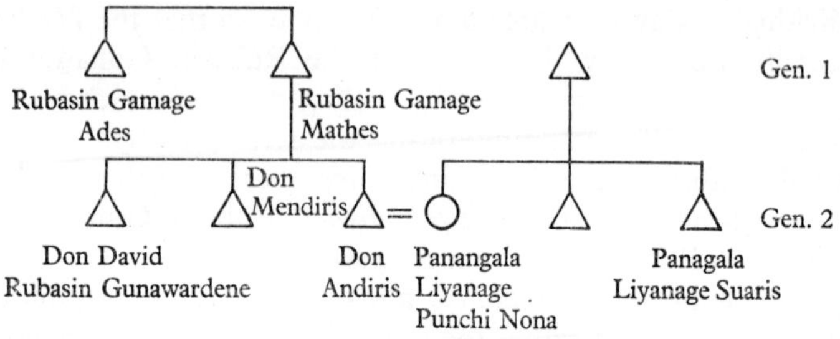

Fig. 31.

was located. We know nothing of the man who first resided there; one son, P. L. Suaris, was quite wealthy and there is some evidence that he was a minor official. Their subcaste designation, *liyanagē* (scribe), suggests that they were of a higher subcaste than the *gamagē* folk among whom they resided. By contrast, note the original subcaste status of the sibling group who in generation 2 call themselves Rubasin Gunawardene: in generation 1 they were Rubasin *Gamagē* folk, the subcaste term *gamagē* has the same status connotation as that of the present villagers in Ihala and Pahala Madagama. Thus originally (in generation 1 of our chart) the Rubasin Gunawardenes were Rubasin Gamage people, belonging to a *vāsagama* owning shares in a hamlet in the present village of Lelwala. They were 'ordinary cultivators'. How did the inferior *gamagē* acquire a *paṭabändi* ('knighthood name', 'title') of Gunawardene in a single generation? The sons of Rubasin *Gamagē* Mathes acquired government office—and with the acquisition of office they converted the *gamagē* subcaste term to the Gunawardene *paṭabändi* title as befitting their new status. Moreover, the title Gunawardene was used in a non-traditional manner, not *before* one's personal name as it was done traditionally, but after the personal name, emulating here their white superiors of the colonial 'raj' that supposedly 'conferred' this title on the family. 'Adopted the title' would express the reality, 'the title was conferred upon' would express the fiction, in accordance with traditional feudal norms of 'conferring' *paṭabändi* names by the king. Don David Rubasin Gunawardene was police officer of the whole Hinidum Pattu (*kostapäl*, 'constable', *araççi*) and later registrar of marriages. It was likely that he became a Protestant (at least formally) and hence probably the reason for getting office from the British. Registrars of marriages at that period were generally Protestants, and even now the family home of the Gunawardenes is called *palliye gedera* (literally 'church house'). The second brother Don Mendiris was a village headman for thirty-five years. The third Don Andiris had no office but compensated this lack by marrying P. L. Punchi Nona, sister of the speculator P. L. Suaris. This established an alliance between the two families.

P. L. Suaris and Don David, *massinās*, entered into speculative activities and bought shares in Ihala Madagama, and in other villages in the area. In other words, a *peläntiya* was started, and members of the *peläntiya* began to establish control over estates, or *gama*, by buying shares. This aspect of *peläntiya* formation is important, for the simple reason that office in the colonial bureaucracy was not associated with *nindagama*, which were perquisites of office in both Kandyan and Dutch times. While formal *authority* over a *gama* was not available as a perquisite of office to these new native officers, they compensated by acquiring *power* (informal authority) over a *gama* by buying shares. They also gave up direct involvement in the agricultural production process, by giving their land on *andē* lease, or employing villagers to cultivate it, sometimes gratuitously, as is often done even today for headmen. We can now summarize several processes involved in *peläntiya* formation:

(*a*) change of name from low subcaste to higher, generally *paṭabändi* status, with the acquisition of office;

(*b*) emancipation from the agricultural production process;

(*c*) strategic marriages so as to enlarge the *peläntiya*;

(*d*) control and power over villagers in a *gama*, as a substitute for formal traditional authority over it.

One of the problems involved in *peläntiya* formation is the continuing maintenance of its 'status honour'. Fundamentally the problem involves two things: not to revert back to the subcaste status of free peasants or cultivators involved in the agricultural production process, and to retain within the *peläntiya* as many offices as possible. Both are perilous possibilities for newly formed *peläntiyas*. The first, unless accompanied by considerable wealth is dependent closely on the second. But attainment of office was no easy task, for these jobs were limited and there was a continual power scramble for them among various *peläntiyas*. Hence one of the phenomena one notices repeatedly is the elimination of

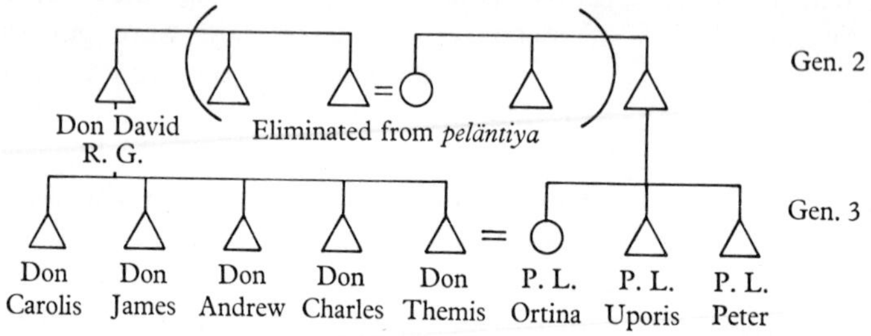

Fig. 32.

families who have lost their status honour from the *peläntiya*, though they may be retained within the *nā pirisa*. Thus in generation 2, Rubasin *Gamagē* Ades and his son Rubasin *Gamagē* Adris, and the brother of Panangala Liyanage Suaris are eliminated from the *peläntiya*. In generation 3, Don Mendiris' and Andiris' sons reverted to cultivator status and are eliminated, in spite of the fact that they have the *peläntiya* name, and that their respective fathers originally belonged to it. The case of the latter is interesting for Don Andiris married Panangala Liyanage Punchi Nona: yet they are rejected. The alliance between the Panangala Liyanage and the Rubasin Gunawardene lines is rebuilt in generation 3 through the alliance between the two families who managed to retain their status honour—the daughter of P. L. Suaris marries the son of his partner in speculation, Don David Rubasin Gunawardene. Formally viewed from the point of Dravidian kinship theory, this would be a case of classificatory cross-cousin marriage, which perpetuates in the second generation the alliance created in the first (Dumont 1957). From the point of view of *peläntiya* formation the strategy of the marriage lies in the fact that the members who contracted the cross-cousin marriage in the earlier generation were eliminated from the *peläntiya* (together with others unable to retain their status honour) in the next generation. Instead an alliance was freshly created between the two families who did retain it (Fig. 32).

Let us consider the distribution of offices among the members of the *peläntiya*, consisting of these two families, in the third generation.

Family of Don David Rubasin Gunawardene

Don David Rubasin Gunawardene's sons managed to hold a few offices. Don Andrew Rubasin Gunawardene married into a wealthy family in Galle and resided there in order to educate his children. He has powerful affinal relations including a member of Parliament. One of his daughters is a trained teacher, one son a business man, while the rest attend good high schools in Galle. His brother Don Carolis held office as *pattuva rālahāmy* (the chief headman for Hinidum Pattu) but his sons also 'degenerated' into 'cultivators', without title. In fact some of them are not cultivators but own small village shops and are engaged in petty business activities, and hence labelled as 'cultivators'. Don Charles turned out best, for he was a headman for seven years and registrar of marriages, a coveted post, for thirty-nine years. His children too have done extremely well. Don Themis had no office but he married Suaris' daughter, as we noted earlier; his son Don Haramanis is present village headman of Neluva Division (which includes Madagama).

Family of Panangala Liyanage Suaris

Of Suaris' two sons, P. L. Uporis was village headman of Neluva —a post he got owing to the influence of Don David Rubasin Gunawardene and his father's wealth. He contracted a marriage with Jayawardene Cicily Hamy of a wealthy *peläntiya* from distant Deniyaya. On the death of his father-in-law he took his wife's brothers, who were minors, into his custody, and according to one of them (J. Jayawardene Jinadasa) defrauded them of their inheritance. His brother P. L. Peter married from a *peläntiya* in neighbouring Mavanana, the Senanayake Dasilige; with this marriage there was a further expansion of the *peläntiya* by including members of the Senanayake Dasilige *peläntiya* (see Fig. 33).

By this marriage three status groups converged into a *peläntiya*. The direct link was between the *peläntiya* segments of the Panangala Liyanages and the Senanayake Dasiliges. But there was an indirect connexion already between the Rubasin Gunawardenes and the Senanayake Dasiliges, for Don Charles Rubasin Gunawardene married a woman Madde Kariyakaranage Podi Nona, whose father's classificatory sister married Senanayake Dasilige Don Diyes de Silva, the father-in-law of P. L. Peter. The new alliance resulted in greater control over *gamas* by the *peläntiya* for

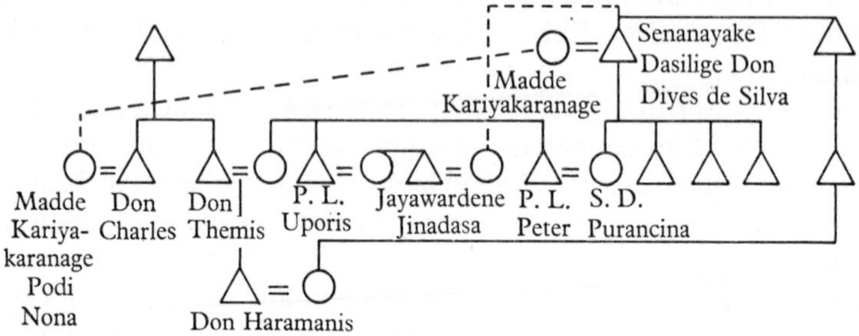

Fig. 33.

the Senanayake Dasiliges were speculators with shares in Pahala Madagama and other hamlets. By this time members of the *peläntiya* had control of about half Ihala Madagama, and a considerable part of Pahala. Meanwhile P. L. Uporis planted his indigent brother-in-law J. Jayawardene Jinadasa in Ihala Madagama to look after the *peläntiya* 'interests'. He married him off to a moronic woman connected by a classificatory link to the dominant Senanayake Dasilige group (indicated by broken lines). He was also given $\frac{3}{56}$ share of the *gama*.

In the next generation Don Themis' only son Don Haramanis Rubasin Gunawardene became village headman of Neluva; that is, he took over the job from his mother's brother, P. L. Uporis. His first marriage was with his mother's brother's (P. L. Peters') wife's male parallel cousin's daughter, Senanayake Dasilige Gunawati. We had noted that the link-up between the Rubasin Gunawardene and the Senanayake Dasilige segments had been indirect: through this classificatory cross-cousin marriage a direct linkage was established, further tying together the whole *peläntiya* in a network of kin relationships. In this generation, as with earlier generations, the sons of *peläntiya* folk who had degenerated into cultivators are excluded from the *peläntiya*. This leaves only three families of the earlier generation of Rubasin Gunawardenes in the *peläntiya*—the powerful family of Don Andrew residing in Galle, the family of Don Charles Rubasin Gunawardene, second plaintiff in the Ihala Madagama partition case, and that of Don Themis married to P. L. Ortina. The case of Don Themis is singularly interesting for it illustrates the importance of office in the *peläntiya*. Don Themis had no office, but his son became village headman owing to the influence of his brother-in-law, the previous headman. Don Themis, while being a member of a *peläntiya*, does not hesitate to work in the fields, though his son is headman. The son treats the father who lives with him with scant respect, often openly contemptuous and rude. It is as if the son himself considers the father a 'cultivator', unworthy of the status honour of the *peläntiya*, though formally belonging to it.

In this generation important social changes have taken place in the country. Educational opportunities have greatly expanded, and families of wealthy *peläntiyas* were educating their children to occupy the increasing number of new offices available. Thus Charles Rubasin Gunawardene's children were all well off—teachers, clerks in government service, students boarded in Galle high schools, etc. (see Fig. 30). One daughter, Ratnaveli, married Delavakkada Liyanage Weerawardene, the brother of D. L. S. Weerawardene, marriage registrar of Neluva, the other dominant shareowner in Pahala Madagama. The Weerawardenes belonged to a more powerful *peläntiya*, traditionally opposed to the Rubasin Gunawardenes. At this point the wealthiest family of the *peläntiya* gives a woman to another dominant *peläntiya* in the region also controlling several *gamas* in the area. The *peläntiya* is still viable and continues to expand, increasing its control over neighbouring hamlets.[4]

THE EFFECTIVE 'PELÄNTIYA' AND IDEAL 'PELÄNTIYA'

Following Leach's distinction between an ideal and effective *pavula* (Leach 1961: 105–7) it would be worth while making a distinction between an ideal and effective *peläntiya*. The chart we have drawn mostly contains members of the effective *peläntiya* and only few members of the ideal *peläntiya*. The effective *peläntiya* consists of those *peläntiya* kinsmen resident in their respective villages, actively co-operating in maintaining the *peläntiya* status and furthering its interests by buying shares in other hamlets and endeavouring to keep offices within the *peläntiya*. The ideal *peläntiya* would include members of the effective *peläntiya* as well as those out-resident patrilateral and affinal *peläntiya* folk. However, unlike the Pul Eliya ideal *pavula*, the members of the ideal *peläntiya* are crucially important for the status honour of the *peläntiya*. They formally assemble at rites of passage, particularly weddings and funerals, and their presence adds to the prestige and grandeur of the *peläntiya*. In Fig. 30 the family of Don Andrew Rubasin Gunawardene, the wealthy Galle resident, would be members of the ideal *peläntiya* of the in-resident Rubasin Gunawardenes. From Don Andrew's point of view his effective *peläntiya* would be his powerful affinal kinsmen, whereas his ideal *peläntiya* would include the Rubasin Gunawardenes of Lelwala. However, it is quite likely that Don Andrew's effective *peläntiya* kinsmen, who as we said includes a member of Parliament, may not consider the Rubasin Gunawardenes of Lelwala as members of *their peläntiya*, but rather members of their *nā̆ pirisa*. Hence *peläntiyas* are mutually overlapping rather than discrete groups, though from the point of view of any family there may be some cut-off point. Unlike the kindred the *peläntiya* is family centred, rather than ego centred. Any discreteness in the *peläntiya* emerges from the point of view of a family, or a group of families dependent on the closeness of their genealogical location—for example, the families of two brothers, or two *massinās*.

STRATIFICATION OF 'PELÄNTIYAS': 'PELÄNTIYA' NO. 2

In the Hinidum Pattu there were several *peläntiyas* of the type described above, each *peläntiya* competing with the other in the scramble for office. As noted earlier, the *peläntiya* continually contracts or expands, the expansions often due to marriage alliances between isogamous *peläntiyas*. Each *peläntiya* controlled a certain area; it controlled offices within an area, and shares in *vāsagama* hamlets in the area. The strength of the *peläntiya* was dependent on:

(*a*) the area and extent of control, which is manifested in the lateral spread of the *peläntiya* through its marriage alliances;

(*b*) the quality of the offices controlled, that is, the status and prestige associated with office;

(*c*) the prestige of its ideal *peläntiya*; the non-resident patrilateral and affinal kin, who indirectly bring prestige to the *peläntiya*. (For example, a member of Parliament or a member of the Ceylon civil service belonging to an ideal *peläntiya* can assist the effective *peläntiya* in the village to get coveted offices.) The *peläntiya* we described had control over Ihala and Pahala Madagama, Mavanana and Lelwala and other hamlets both in terms of shares and offices. The offices they held were however not the highest in status—generally the post of village headman or *vidane āraççi* or registrar of marriages.

There were other *peläntiyas* which had larger control of offices and hamlets. *Peläntiyas* tend to be stratified according to the power, prestige and control they had over office and *gama*. In order briefly to illustrate the *status stratification* of *peläntiyas* we shall present selected portions of another *peläntiya* stratified higher than the one described earlier. The portion of the *peläntiya* we shall now present is seen from the family focus of Delwakkade Liyanage (D. L. S.) Weerawardene, registrar, Neluva, the other dominant shareholder in Pahala Madagama. Weerawardene's *peläntiya* had been traditionally opposed to the Rubasin Gunawardenes, but with the stabilization of the latter *peläntiya* a marriage was, we noted, contracted between Don Charles Rubasin Gunawardene's daughter and D. L. S. Weerawardene's officeless younger brother. Whether the marriage will actually result in a political *alliance* between the two *peläntiyas* only later events can tell. At the moment, in spite of the marriage, the *peläntiya* of D. L. S. Weerawardene is higher than the Rubasin Gunawardene's. Indeed, D. L. S. Weerawardene speaks with open contempt about his brother's affinal kin, and refuses to recognize them as his *peläntiya* kinsmen.

According to their origin myth the Delwakkade Liyanage status line originated in the following manner. The founder of the line was a keeper of the land records (*lekammiti*) in the Kandyan Kingdom. He settled down in the village of Baraniwela in the Hinidum Pattu. He had four sons, three of whom settled in three different villages in Hinidum Pattu, and one resided in the paternal village of Baraniwela. They were the founders of the four status lines of the *liyanage* (scribe) subcaste in the northern part of the Hinidum Pattu, thus:

Neluva village	Neluva Liyanage line
Habarakada village	Habarakada Liyanage line
Dellawa village	Dellawa Liyanage line
Baraniwela village	Baraniwela Liyanage line

The myth neatly explains the original unity of the *liyanage* subcaste in this area. Two of the four lines—Baraniwela Liyanage and Neluva Liyanage—degenerated to the level of cultivators and intermarried with them. Branches of the other two lines moved from their original villages into other villages over which they established control—thus one branch of the Habarakada Liyanages settled down in Mavita, while a branch of the Delwakkada Liyanages settled down in Neluva. Several families among these branches enhanced their status and were converted into the *peläntiya*, presented in Fig. 34.

Thus D. L. S. Weerawardene's (our Ego's) paternal great grandfather was simply a Delwakkada Liyanage man of Dellawa who settled in Neluva. However when this man's son got a coveted office he too changed his name into an impressive *paṭabändi* one: Don Stanislaus de Silva Wijewickreme Weerawardene, not one but *two* Sinhalese *paṭabändi* names (Wijewickreme, literally 'overpowering grandeur', and Weerawardene, literally 'overflowing strength') plus, of course, the usual Portuguese 'Don'. Don Stanislaus' son married a female from a powerful branch of the original Delwakkada Liyanage people in Dellawa, who also after receiving government office had changed their name into Abeygunawardene. A daughter married a member of the Habarakada Liyanage family settled in Mavita. Thus a new *peläntiya* was created. The alliance was repeated in the next generation in the identical form—a male from the Delwakkada Liyanage Weerawardene group married a woman from the Delwakkada Liyanage Abeygunawardene group; a female from the Delwakkada Liyanage Weerawardene group married a male from the Habarakada Liyanage group (the latter meanwhile had adopted the name of Jayatilleke).

The contrasts with the *peläntiya* described earlier are important—none of the lines here are *gamagē* subcaste lines or *vāsagamas* originally, unlike the original inferior Rubasin Gamage and Dasilige in the former *pelāntiya*. This *pelāntiya* in other words had traditionally been of higher subcaste status. The Weerawardene *pelāntiya* also dominate office and *gama* over a larger area—Neluva, Mavita, Batuwangala, Dellawa, Habarakada. The area would be even still larger if we had presented the whole *pelāntiya* rather than a portion of it. There is also, as a glance will indicate, a larger concentration of offices, some of these the most coveted from a prestige point of view—justice of the peace, coroner, postmaster and headmaster of village schools. The term 'landed proprietor' indicates a *pelāntiya* member without office but owning fairly large landed properties, emancipated from agricultural work, and practising the 'style of life' of the *pelāntiya*. These large landed proprietors are very influential members of the *pelāntiya*; they often have extensive rubber or tea plantations, rather than shares in a *gama*. But they too have their retinue or following—the paid labourers who work on these plantations. It may well be that the *pelāntiya* just described will merge with the earlier *pelāntiya* if the strategic marriage contracted is cemented by further alliances.

STATUS STRATIFICATION: 'PELÄNTIYA' NO. 3

The *pelāntiya* discussed above does by no means represent the highest in the status hierarchy of *pelāntiyas* in the Hinidum Pattu. There is at least one *pelāntiya* in the northern region of the Hinidum Pattu that is of an even higher status. A section of this *pelāntiya* is depicted in Fig. 35.

Villagers in the area often assert that the Wijenayakes are the only 'real' (*niyama*) *pelāntikarayō* in the area. When questioned as to what is meant by 'real' they would state that they are the only group whose male members are addressed *hāmu*, whereas members of the other *pelāntiyas* are addressed as *rālahāmy* (if an office holder) or *mahatmayā* (if a non-office holder). The term *hāmu* is an abbreviation of *hāmudoruvo* (lord) the traditional form of address to members of the feudal *radala* caste. In the contemporary Sinhalese low country the full term *hāmodoru* is generally reserved for Buddhist monks, and a few high 'officials' like Judges and Government Agents. The less prestigious abbreviation *hāmu* is used for laymen of high *pelāntiya*. The question arises as to how the

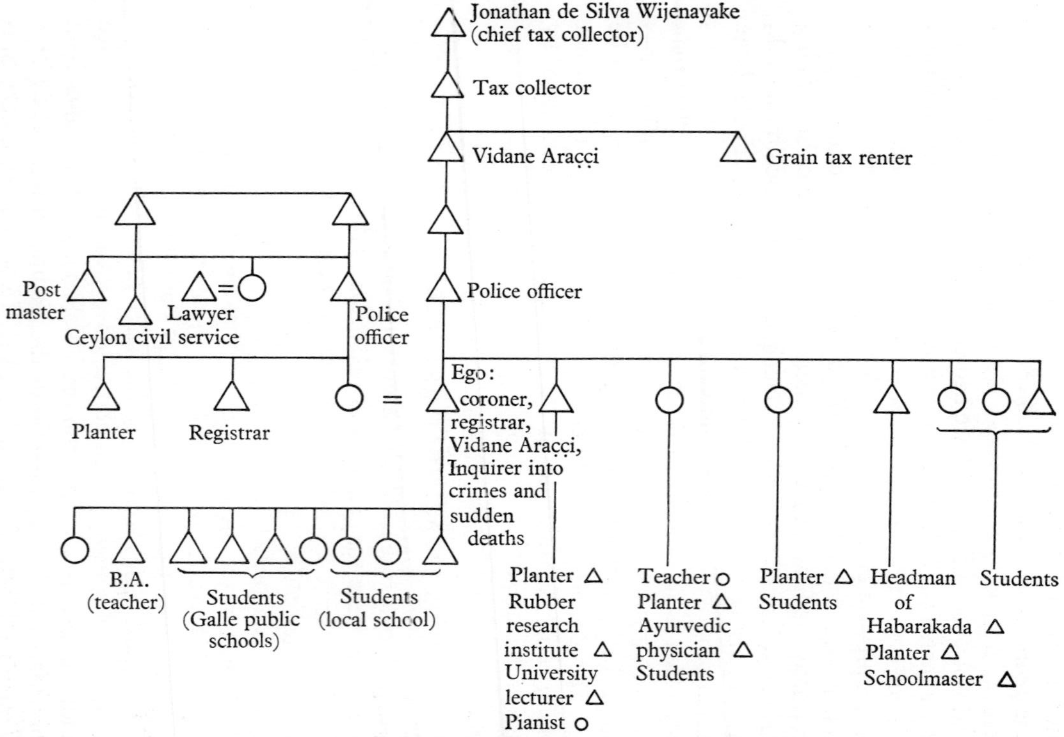

Fig. 35. *Peläntiya* (section) of the Wijenayakes.

Wijenayakes became the closest approximation in the Sinhalese low country to the traditional feudal aristocracy in the status structure of Hinidum Pattu.

Looking at the *peläntiya* names in the above chart, it is impossible to guess their origins. No *vāsagama* name is prefixed to their completely English-style surnames. However, the 'founder' of the *peläntiya* was a Habarakada Liyanage man, which meant that this *peläntiya* was originally a branch of the Habarakada Liyanage line. When the 'founder' of the *peläntiya* became chief tax collector for Hinidum Pattu, he changed his name into Wijenayake. The subcaste designation of *liyanage* was completely excised, and a *peläntiya* got started. Since the founder was a holder of a very prestigious office, the *peläntiya* he created was a high one, whose descendants were entitled to be addressed as *hāmu*. The *peläntiya* also was able to own vast areas of land in the Hinidum Pattu. For example, the Ego of our chart owns approximately the following landed properties in the Hinidum Pattu.

Table 15. *Lands owned by Ego of Fig. 35*

Name of village	Highland (acres)	Lowland (acres)
Habarakada	100	80
Tavalama	20	6
Mavanana	8	3
Gigummaduva	4	6
Ambelegedera	3	2
Neluva	1	1
Dellawa	1	1
Total	137	99

This extreme affluence had several important consequences. (*a*) Several members of the *peläntiya* could board their children in good public schools in Galle, and give them an education that could fit them for important bureaucratic posts in the government, rather than 'village' positions. Members of other *peläntiyas* were doing the same thing but this group had an early start being office-holders for six generations. Thus there are Wijenayakes who hold office of Government fiscal agent, forest officer, university lecturer, school teacher, etc. (*b*) Though some members held important 'local' offices—this was not the desired goal. The ideal was bureaucratic positions in the national administration. (*c*) The realization of this goal in any significant sense had one important implication. Power over hamlets in the region was reduced, for persons serving in the national administration had often to settle down in cities and contract marriages with persons of similar status outside the local region. Thus *peläntiyas* of the third type have high prestige in the region; but their power becomes systematically reduced by the gradual ejection of office-bearing males from their native villages. Some of these out-resident males may not have direct interest in their *peläntiya* property and may either sell it or give it on lease. When these processes continue for some time the *peläntiya* as a status group of kinsmen having control over office and *gama* and practising a certain style of life, breaks up into smaller discrete 'familial' groupings structurally though not normatively similar to the *pavula* described by Leach. In the *peläntiya* we have just described these processes have not yet occurred. But we suggest that this is a common process that occurs in respect of prestigious *peläntiyas* in the Sinhalese low country.

The last point is a very important one though it leads us to a problem largely outside the scope of this work. However it is worth brief mention. Historically we believe that the major portion of the so-called 'Sinhalese urban middle class' manning white collar bureaucratic jobs in government and mercantile employment and constituting a national *élite* originated from *peläntiyas* of the type we described for our region. Up to the time of National Independence (1948), entry into these envied positions were based on an expensive English education in 'colleges' modelled on the English public school. As far as the major part of the *goigama* caste population of the Sinhalese low country were concerned access to these jobs through an English education was a financial impossibility, except for members of *peläntiyas*. Hence *peläntiyas* had probably a crucial role in the formation of a 'middle class', or a 'national bureaucratic *élite*'.

THE 'PELÄNTIYA' STYLE OF LIFE

The *peläntiyas* we noted are based on the feudal aristocratic ideal of power and authority based on office and control over a *gama*. But the feudal aristocracy was a hereditary one, whereas the *peläntiyas* of Hinidum Pattu were non-hereditary. Retention of a family in the *peläntiya* depended on its wealth, affluence and access to office, in its ability to maintain the 'status honour' of the *peläntiya*. The 'status honour' of the *peläntiya* is manifested in its 'style of life', which could be summed up briefly as one of conspicuous display. This conspicuous display is manifested in everyday contexts as well as in ceremonial ones. In everyday life, the style of living of the *peläntiya* member must be in marked contrast to the *gamagē* subcaste among whom he lives. His house is almost without exception a brick or stone structure, with a tile roof, plastered and whitewashed walls, cement floors, good furniture. The verandah or the front of the house is where 'visitors' are received. It generally consists of two kinds of furniture—large chairs on which the *peläntiya* folk sit and benches and stools for non-*peläntiya* folk. A near patrilateral kinsman who has fallen from the *peläntiya* state often sits on the bench, if there are no lower subcastes or castes present. A *peläntiya* man has always open house; ideally like Chaucer's Franklin, it should 'snow' 'in his house of mete and drinke'. Villagers who come there are served tea, or a rice meal (depending on the hour of arrival). Visiting *peläntiya* folk and government officers on circuit are fed with lavish extravagance.

Villagers, we noted, address *peläntiya* folk as *rālahāmy* if an office holder, or *mahatmayā* if a non-office holder. *Peläntiya* members do not cultivate their own fields. They are either given on lease (*andē*) or cultivated gratuitously by villagers if the *peläntikaraya* is a headman, or villagers are hired as paid labourers. All the persons who are under the 'control' of the *peläntiya* member constitute his *pirisa*, or 'following'. The *pirisa* in turn is constituted of those who are kinsmen (*nā pirisa*) and those who are not. The *nā pirisa*, though internally differentiated, is distinguished from the inferior subcastes who are in the pay of or owe *andē* service to the *peläntiya*. These 'servants' of the *peläntiya* are the analogue of the traditional feudal lord's retinue of servants. They pay formal homage to the *peläntikaraya* (member of a *peläntiya*) on Sinhalese New Year's Day by worshipping him and offering him betel leaves. In exchange the *peläntikaraya* may give a small cash present, or a sarong, or other item of clothing. The number of 'servants' paying homage to a *peläntiya* member is an index of the prestige of the individual member, and brings credit to his *peläntiya*.

The strength, unity and prestige of the *peläntiya* as a whole is manifested most clearly in *rites of passage*, particularly marriage and funeral rites where the whole *nǟ pirisa* is assembled, and the 'tenants' convened. The latter and low status kinsmen may perform menial tasks—constructing *pandals* and other temporary but imposing ornamental structures. These occasions are clear vindications of the status honour of the *peläntiya*.

We shall not describe these ceremonial occasions here, except to state that they are occasions of lavish display where the status honour of the *peläntiya* is asserted and vindicated. It is on these occasions that the distinctions between the *peläntiya* and the rest of the *nä pirisa* are observed—*peläntiya* members have special privileges, whereas non-*peläntiya* kinsfolk may be excluded from them. For example, in weddings only *peläntiya* folk are generally invited to the wedding trip to the bride's house (*gamanaṭa yǟma*); they may be invited to partake of exclusive feasting arrangements from which the rest of the kin group are barred. Such distinctions are required to maintain the separateness of the *peläntiya*, and vindicate to the 'public' its ideal of exclusiveness.

'PELÄNTIYA' AND STATUS GROUP

We have used the terms 'status honour', 'status group', 'status stratification', in our description of the *peläntiya*. The terms are derived from Max Weber's brilliant study of 'status groups'. A *peläntiya* in our view is a 'status group', and is in structure fundamentally different from the corporately organized *vāsagama*. Weber opposes status groups with social classes; the latter are formed on an 'unambiguously economic interest, and indeed those interests involved in the existence of a market' (1958: 182); whereas status groups are formed on the basis of a common ideology.

In contrast to classes, *status groups* are normally communities. They are, however, often of an amorphous kind. In contrast to the purely economically determined 'class situation' we wish to designate as 'status situation' every typical component of the life fate of men that is determined by a specific, positive or negative, social estimation of *honour*. This honour may be connected with any quality shared by a plurality and, of course, it can knit to a class situation: class distinctions are linked in most varied ways with status distinctions...But status honour need not necessarily be linked with a 'class situation.' On the contrary, it normally stands in sharp opposition to the pretensions of sheer property. (1958:187)

Weber describes the bonds that tie the status groups together as one of status honour, manifested in behaviour as a *style of life*.

In content status honour is normally expressed by the fact that above all else a specific style of life can be expected from all those who wish to belong to the circle. Linked with this are restrictions on social intercourse (that is, intercourse which is not subservient to economic or any other business's of 'functional' purpose). These restrictions may confine normal marriages to within the status circle and may lead to complete endogamous closure. (1958: 187–8)

The status honour of the group is dependent on the maintenance of its style of life; those who cannot live up to the expectations of the group are sloughed off. We notice this in *peläntiya* formation, where those who belong to the *peläntiya* in one generation, owing to their inability to maintain the style of life of the *peläntiya* may be eliminated from it in the next. Hence the 'amorphous' nature of these groups that Weber observed. The amorphousness of *peläntiyas* is mostly manifested in the process of formation; once they are stabilized they become less amorphous, as with traditional hereditary aristocracies. *Peläntiyas* could hardly be continuously stable for, as pointed out earlier, there is a limited number of offices to be divided among several *peläntiyas*. It is almost inevitable that some members fall off. In principle, when there is stability the unity of status groups is maintained by endogamy. Such endogamy is rare for the *peläntiya* in process of formation; however, an isogamous pattern of strategic marriages is important for linking several status groups together into a single *peläntiya*. These isogamous marriages are reinforced by cross-cousin marriages between the status groups. Indeed one could say that what is important in *peläntiya* formation is not a special type of marriage pattern, like cross-cousin marriage or isogamous marriage, but rather the *strategy* of marriage. By strategy we mean (once again) the utilization of a marriage 'rule' or 'type' for a specific purpose or goal, in this case the furtherance of *peläntiya* interests. In this sense even hypergamous or hypogamous marriages can be successfully employed. In a situation like this it is senseless to talk of a theory of cross-cousin, or any other type of, marriage rule; what is at issue may rather be a theory of status group formation. The *utilization* of the rules in the strategy of marriage highlights the importance of choice in the pursuance of recognized and desired ends. The strategy of marriage—the choice of rules—is at variance with the marriage ideology of the *peläntiya*. Ideally the members of a *peläntiya* would constantly reiterate the norm of endogamy; it is correct, they say, that marriages should be within the *peläntiya* or between like *peläntiyas*. Here is a situation where the ideology is at variance with the empirical situation—the empirical situation requires a strategic utilization of marriages, the ideals require an endogamous or isogamous 'closure'. However, there is no real paradox here for the ideal is projected into a 'not-yet-realized-goal' of a stable *peläntiya*; the reality expresses the attempts to reach the goal.

The style of life of privileged status groups involves generally certain characteristic features according to Weber. There is a 'monopolization of ideal and material interests' such as the attempt at monopolization of 'office' in *peläntiyas*, and attempts to have a monopoly of the share market. Furthermore,

> the decisive role of a 'style of life' in 'status honour' means that status groups are the specific bearers of all 'conventions'. In whatever way it may be manifest, all 'stylization' of life either originates in status groups, or is at least conserved by them...Quite generally among privileged status groups there is a status disqualification that operates against the performance of common physical labour. (Weber 1958:191)

In the case of the *peläntiyas* the 'model' for status emulation in status group formation is the traditional aristocracy. Hence the style of life of the *peläntiya* is an aristocratic style. The attributes of its status honour are (*a*) incumbency in office; (*b*) control over 'estates'. The vindication or expression of status honour is the style of life of the *peläntiya*. This vindication of 'honour' in a specific life style is manifested in emancipation from the agricultural production process, and conspicuous 'display', both ceremonial and non-ceremonial, as we have noted earlier.

One major theoretical qualification must be made in respect of Weber's notion of status group. The view that status groups are formed on the basis of an ideology can be misleading if taken literally. As Norman Birnbaum pointed out Weber deals with psychological variables in social analysis, though these variables are rarely explicitly formulated (Birnbaum 1953). In his discussion of status groups we feel that Weber assumed though never made explicit an antecedent psychological (motivational) variable. The word 'status' in concepts like 'status honour' and 'status group' has two connotations:

(*a*) status as ideology,

(*b*) status as motive (e.g. power and prestige needs). Underlying the ideology are the power and prestige motives of individuals which are the instigators of action in status group formation. Thus motive and ideology in combination are probably the crucial variables in status group formation.[5]

CHAPTER 10

KINSHIP, RESIDENCE AND LAND TENURE

We shall not discuss kinship behaviour or terminology *per se*, but some aspects of it in relation to land tenure and the share system. However, it is necessary to present the formal terminological system. The Sinhalese have what Dumont calls the Dravidian type terminological system, or Iroquois according to Murdock. The terminology is presented in Fig. 36 based on Yalman (1962:557). The unique features of the terminology are as follows:

(*a*) the terminology is classificatory;

(*b*) parallel cousins are distinguished from cross-cousins; the former equated with sibling and the latter with brother- or sister-in-law;

(*c*) father's brother is distinguished from mother's brother; the former is the equivalent of mother's sister's husband;

(*d*) mother's sister is distinguished from father's sister; the former is the equivalent of father's brother's wife, and the latter of mother's brother's wife;

(*e*) since terminology-wise, a cross-cousin is always married to a parallel cousin or sibling and vice versa, the offspring of any terminological sister is distinguished from a terminological brother;

(*f*) there can be no terminological category of affines in the system; all affines are converted into consanguineal kinsmen, by converting wife's siblings into cross-cousins, and their parents into mother's brother and father's sister and so on.

The neatness of the terminological system has attracted many anthropologists—Morgan, Rivers, Lévi-Strauss, Murdock, Dumont, to mention a few. The most recent exposition comes from Yalman. Yalman's 'hypothesis' commits the fallacy of deducing behavioural regularities from a terminological system. According to him the *function* of the terminology is to 'regulate marriage and sexual relations inside bilateral and largely endogamous "kindreds"'. It is difficult for us to see how a terminology regulates marriage in this sense. Regulation of marriage is done by human

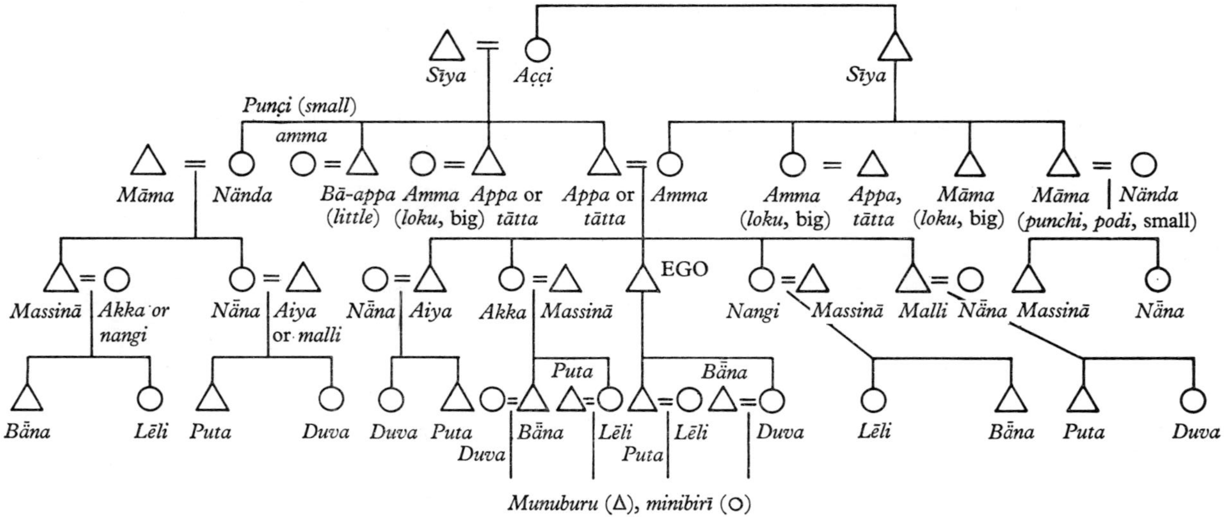

Fig. 36. Sinhalese kinship terminology

agents in an action context. Yalman goes on to say that the terminology implies 'a prescriptive bilateral cross-cousin marriage rule. In this respect the terminology is highly systematic, and all the terms imply bilateral cross-cousin marriage, and such marriage is essential if the categories of kinship are to be kept in order' (Yalman 1962:548). To assume that such marriages are essential if the categories of kinship are to be kept in order, is to imply that Sinhalese get married in order to keep their kinship categories in proper shape. This is an empirical, not a prima facie theoretical issue. Empirically there is no *prescriptive rule* enforced in action unanimously by the Sinhalese. It is true that all marriages are between cross-cousins in the terminological sense, even marriages with total strangers, who after marriage are designated as consanguines. But a hypothesis that states that all marriages are between cross-cousins in the terminological sense is impossible of refutation and is no hypothesis at all. In fact it is questionable whether one could use the term 'prescription' to marriages between non-kinsmen who are, *after the event*, designated as kinsmen.

Yalman relates the terminology to the kindred structure and this in turn to land rights.

> Women carry the property claims with them upon marriage to their husbands. If these are outsiders, then theoretically the control of land also passes to outsiders. In the Sinhalese case rights in land are not in fact allowed to leave the kindred with the woman. She is either married to a relative close enough that the property does not leave the close circle or, if she marries an 'outsider', he is assimilated into the family, and again the land remains within the 'kindred'. (Yalman 1962:551)

Aside from the facts which are quite different in Madagama, Yalman's structural categories are impossible of disproof. If a woman marries a close relative, land is retained within the kindred; if she marries an outsider he is assimilated into the kindred through the terminological system, and land is once again retained in the kindred. In fact, Yalman commits the same error that he attributes to Lévi-Strauss, who insisted on the exogamic principle in Kariera kinship, and to others who infer from the Kariera-Dravidian terminology a patrilineal system, or a matrilineal one. Yalman introduces a bilateral 'pigeon-holing' system. The question as to what type of kinship behaviour is consonant with the terminology depends surely not on terms viewed in the abstract by the anthropologist, but on the *values*, if any, associated with the terminology in the behavioural context. Thus it is possible to use the terminology empirically in various ways—in lineages, or bilaterally as in Yalman's data, or in a *vāsagama* structure associated with exogamy in Madagama. It is not possible *a priori* to predict behaviour or the type of social system from the set of terms alone.

Though Dumont, Yalman and others assert that the Sinhalese kinship terminology is based on an assumption of prescriptive systematic bilateral cross-cousin marriage, such an inference could hardly be made from the behaviour and verbalizations of Madagama folk. Madagama people do not believe that cross-cousin marriage is prescriptive (or act as if they did), or even preferred except under certain circumstances. On the level of conscious motivation marriage in Madagama could best be seen as a *game* or *strategy*. It involves a set of decisions and choices individuals make after weighing the circumstances of each case. These decisions operate within certain limits. Outside of the incest taboo within the nuclear family marriage must be within one's *varige* or 'kind', either endogamously or between isogamous subcastes. It should occur outside the *vāsagama*; preferably between members of the same generation; never between parallel cousins and those who in the terminological system are addressed as parallel cousins (*aiya*, *malli*, *nangi*, *akka*). The restriction on parallel cousin marriage becomes lax when the relationship is between distant classificatory parallel cousins. We have several cases of these marriages which will not be discussed here.

The ideology of marriage is that between kinsmen (*nǟyo*). When one excludes prohibited kinsmen, these *nǟyo* would generally include persons one addresses as *nǟna* or *massinā* (cross-cousin) in the actual or classificatory sense. Each individual has a number of such kinsmen in a society where the nexus of bilateral kin ties has a large areal spread embracing about a dozen hamlets in the region. The particular *nǟya* (singular) one marries depends on decisions and choices made about each case. According to the formal ideology, it is good to marry *nǟyo* because the persons and their families (*pavula*) are already known to each other. The marriage strengthens the relationship between these families.

If ideally isogamous marriages should be between *nǟyo*, it follows logically that the closer the *nǟyo* the more preferred the marriage relationship. What could be logically inferred is behaviourally real for Madagama folk. It is in this regard that the concept *ävässa* is so crucial in the ideology of marriage. *Ävässa* means 'essential', 'close', and *ävässa nāyo* are already closely related kin. One's parallel cousins, mother's sisters, father's brothers, grandparents, as well as one's immediate cross-cousins are *ävässa*. The Sinhalese marriage preference is for *ävässa nāyo*. If one excludes prohibited and disapproved marriage partners, the *ävässa nāyo* whom one could marry must inevitably be one's immediate cross-cousins. Only in this sense could one say that cross-cousin marriage is the 'preferred' form of marriage in Sinhalese society.

Ävässa nāyo must be in the context of the Sinhalese marriage inevitably an *ävässa nāna* or *massinā* (immediate female or male cross-cousin). Such marriages the villagers say practically unanimously are good, precisely because they are between close kinsmen; it brings about *samagiya* ('concord', 'unity') between the two families (*pavula*). Since these marriages are essentially marriages of 'sentiment', giving a dowry to the man is not at all incumbent, though it may freely be given. Sometimes *ävässa* may include cross-cousins once removed, if such cross-cousins are members of a larger *pavula*, in Leach's sense of the term (as for example, the cross-cousin marriage between P. M. G. Gunadasa and K. G. Podi Hamy described later on). Generally *ävässa* marriages are between immediate cross-cousins.[1]

All marriages (*hira*) outside of *ävässa* marriages, are viewed simply as marriages between *nāyo* or *nā pavul* (related families). Such marriages are inevitably between classificatory cross-cousins in the terminological sense. Even marriages between classificatory parallel cousins are converted fictionally into classificatory cross-cousin ones. These marriages are never viewed as *ävässa*, they are marriages between *nāyo*. There is thus a crucial distinction between *ävässa* and non-*ävässa* marriages, even though all such marriages are terminologically between cross-cousins. In marriages between non-*ävässa nāyo* dowry is almost always given. A dowry is not a legal requirement and in no way legitimates the marriage as does the African bride price; it is a payment in cash or kind, which gives dignity to the woman, and a symbolic recognition of the fact that she could depend on her family of orientation in time of need.

The distinction between *ävässa* and non-*ävässa* marriages is of some sociological importance in cognatic kinship systems, when contrasted with classic unilineal systems. In unilineal systems, cross-cousin marriage creates alliances between groups exchanging women, irrespective of the harmonic or disharmonic character of the groups. In a situation where two or three (or more) lineages exchange women, the distinction between classificatory and immediate cross-cousins are not important from the point of view of interlineage alliances. In cognatic societies, like the Sinhalese, where unilineal lineages are absent, classificatory cross-cousin marriages have different kinship implications from true cross-cousin marriages. True or immediate cross-cousin marriages build up alliances between families, intensifying the close consanguineal ties that existed in the previous generation. Classificatory cross-cousin marriages bring together families that were loosely related in the previous generation. In true cross-cousin marriage, a close consanguineal tie between a brother and a sister, is followed by a close affinal tie in the following generation. In classificatory (non-*ävässa*) marriages a loose consanguineal tie between a terminological brother and sister is followed by a close affinal tie in the next—the looseness of the consanguineal tie is dependent on the degree of closeness of the classificatory siblings in the kinship system. In *ävässa* marriages two families get together and build up a closely knit larger *pavula*. The Sinhalese of Madagama have a saying that marriages between distant relations or between persons previously unrelated are for *lābe* or profit. What they mean by this is that (*a*) such marriages may involve large dowries; (*b*) it gives an individual or family a new set of kinsmen. *Ävässa* marriages by contrast are marriages of sentiment—they do not involve a dowry, they do not extend the range of kinsmen but rather they intensify already existent close consanguineal ties.

MARRIAGE AND SHARE CONSOLIDATION

Cross-cousin marriage had traditionally little implication for property consolidation. With bilateral inheritance being accepted as the norm, and consequently females inheriting shares, cross-cousin marriage had different implications for property consolidation. For example, a brother *X* and a sister *Y* now have equal shares in the paternal estate; in the next generation the estate becomes fractioned further through the inheritance of their respective children. One of the mechanisms by which shares could be consolidated is through the marriage of the son (or daughter) of *X* with the daughter (or son) of *Y*. Cross-cousin marriage, however, is not the only manner in which property consolidation could occur, for *any* male with shares in the *vāsagama* estate could marry any shareowning female and thus bring about property consolidation. Thus share consolidation through marriage cannot be viewed simply as a 'function' of a special type of marriage rule like cross-cousin marriage, but rather as a *special strategy* of marriage, arising out of the changed social context where women have begun to inherit shares. In this case share consolidation through marriage makes no strategic sense unless (*a*) both partners reside in the hamlet, and (*b*) the shares are worth consolidating—minute shares are not of much use. In fact, all the cases of 'marital share consolidation' we have resulted in the consolidation of shares which added up were economically fruitful, and eventuated in both partners residing in the same hamlet. We suggest that an important motive in contracting such marriages is to bring about share consolidation.

Marital share consolidation—branch U

Case no. 1

Cross-cousin marriages (classificatory) between:

(*a*) K. G. Siyadoris and his father's sister's husband's brother's daughter, P. M. G. Wimala Hamy;

(*b*) P. M. G. Gunadasa and his father's cross-cousin's (male—K. G. Siyadoris') daughter, K. G. Podi Hamy;

(*c*) K. G. Podi Nona (female) and P. M. G. Derenis of branch *B*.

Terminologically all these are marriages between cross-cousins (*nǟna* and *massinā*) yet none of them between immediate cross-cousins.

In an earlier chapter we noted that P. M. G. Babappu who owned $\frac{1}{8}$ of the *gama* sold his share to his wife's brother Kankanan Gamage Adris. K. G. Adris in turn transferred this share *inter vivos* to three of Babappu's children, to Babappu's wife Ano Hamy, and to one of his own sons in shares of $\frac{1}{40}$, in 1914. His son died childless and this share of $\frac{1}{40}$ devolved on K. G. Adris. About two years later Adris arranged a marriage for his son K. G. Siyadoris to P. M. G. Wimala Hamy, Adris' brother-in-law's brother's daughter. He also transferred to Siyadoris $\frac{1}{80}$ share of the *gama*. This marriage was a strategic merger, for Wimala Hamy already owned $\frac{1}{96}$ share of the *gama*, and also effectively enjoyed the $\frac{1}{96}$ share belonging to her 'lost' sister. After marriage Siyadoris resided in his wife's hamlet. But this is not a traditional *binna* type marriage, for uxorilocal residence in the present case is a part of the whole

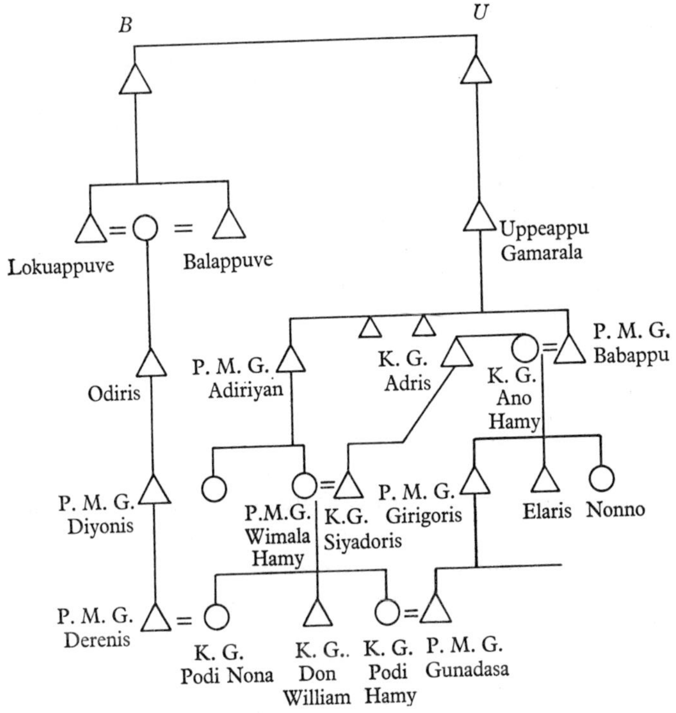

Fig. 37.

strategy of share consolidation through marriage. It is not a case of a landless villager residing in his wife's hamlet. On the contrary it is a merger between two persons owning shares in the same estate: residence in the same hamlet is required if the merger is to be effective. It is also a case of a non-*vāsagama* male having shares in the *vāsagama* estate and strengthening his 'citizenship' in the hamlet by marrying a *vāsagama* member.

K. G. Siyadoris' daughter Podi Hamy married her classificatory cross-cousin P. M. G. Gunadasa, Babappu's son's son. Podi Hamy was given $\frac{1}{80}$ of the *gama* by her father; this was legally transferred to her much later. Gunadasa owned $\frac{1}{80}$ of the *gama*; the marriage once again was a strategic union leading to share consolidation. Notice also the pattern of residence which was neither traditional *dīga* nor *binna*. Both were hamlet residents owning shares and residing in the same hamlet after marriage, a situation that could not arise out of the conditions in the ideal model. To speak of a 'residence rule' in this situation seems sociologically meaningless.

A daughter of K. G. Siyadoris, Podi Nona, married P. M. G. Derenis, son of P. M. G. Diyonis of branch *B*. The kinship connexion before marriage between the two parties was vague and indirect. It was a cross-cousin relationship only in the sense that any cross-cousin of a member of branch *U* would be considered a cross-cousin of a member of the same generation in branch *B*. To view this a cross-cousin marriage makes little sense. In this case the important factor is the strategic merger between two persons owning shares in the same estate. P. M. G. Derenis owned $\frac{1}{36}$ of the *gama* and Podi Nona received $\frac{1}{80}$ from her father: both resided in the Pahala Madagama hamlet after marriage. If one examines the three marriage strategies described, one is impressed by the fact that no true cross-cousin marriages were contracted by the parties concerned. At the same time the fact that cross-cousins (classificatory or actual) possess shares does not mean that they would marry.

The type of marital share consolidation we have considered arises out of the pressures created by land shortage combined with female inheritance of *pravēni* shares. The consolidation of shares does not lead necessarily to the consolidation of property, unless the shares are in the same *taṭṭumāru* subsection. Even if the consolidated shares are in different *taṭṭumāru* subsections, the cultivation of these shares becomes economically feasible for in-resident couples.

Case no. 2

The strategy of marriage leading to share consolidation comes out even more dramatically in two cases from Ihala Madagama where the marriages were between 'forbidden' kinsmen, namely classificatory father's brother and brother's daughter (Fig. 38). The marriages presented in this figure violate accepted Sinhalese kinship norms; the marriages are between two members of the same *vāsagama*, and also between classificatory 'father' and 'daughter' in the terminological system. It was difficult for us to get detailed information about these marriages from informants owing to the partition proceedings. It could well be that we were being presented with an amputated genealogy and that one generation has been omitted in I. M. G. Babappu's genealogy. Even if this were the case and the two couples were members of the same generation the marriages would be between two parallel cousins of the same *vāsagama*. We are fairly certain that these marriages were indeed between classificatory 'father' and 'daughter'. For the marriage of I. M. G. Mango Hamy with her 'father' I. M. G

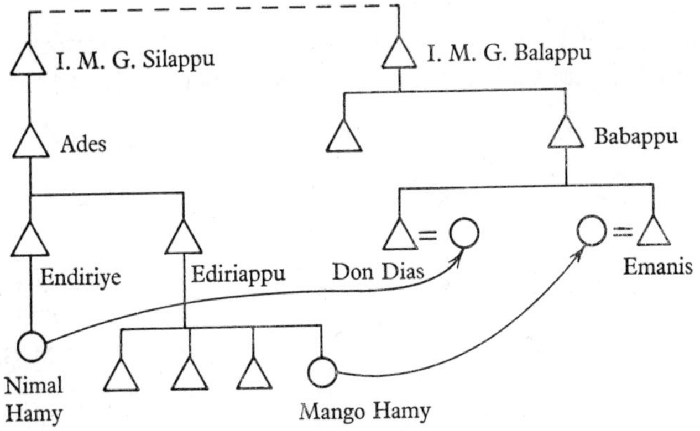

Fig. 38.

Emanis, there is a *rationale* in that she was her father's adopted daughter, her genitor and genetrix being Don Mendiris Ediri Wickreme and his mistress. Thus though she belonged to the *vāsagama*, her 'blood' was not that of her adopted parents. The ideology of 'blood' as Leach has correctly pointed out is very important in Sinhalese custom, and may have been used in this case to override kinship and marriage norms (Leach 1961:74). Regarding the marriage of I. M. G. Nimal Hamy with her classificatory father, I. M. G. Don Dias, we have no evidence about adoption. In any case we do not doubt there was some 'rationalization' for this marriage. Probably they were considered descendants respectively of the two unrelated males who supposedly founded the hamlet and hence without direct 'blood connection'. But in spite of any 'rationalization', there is also no doubt about the general disapproval of marriage between such close *vāsagama* kinsmen, leading to a radical reorientation of kinship relationships.[2] We therefore infer that one of the motives for these marriages is consolidation of substantial shares owned by both husband and wife. Though these would be the conscious motives (strategic choices) there may well have been unconscious oedipal motives at work too (we have one case of father-daughter incest in Pahala Madagama hamlet). These two marriages led to the consolidation of $\frac{1}{56}$ share of Don Dias with $\frac{3}{32}$ of Nimal Hamy; and $\frac{1}{56}$ of Emanis with $\frac{1}{48}$ of Mango Hamy.

Case no. 3

Marriage of P. M. G. Podi Nona with her classificatory cross-cousin Godapita Gamage Diyonis of Mavanana. This is a case of

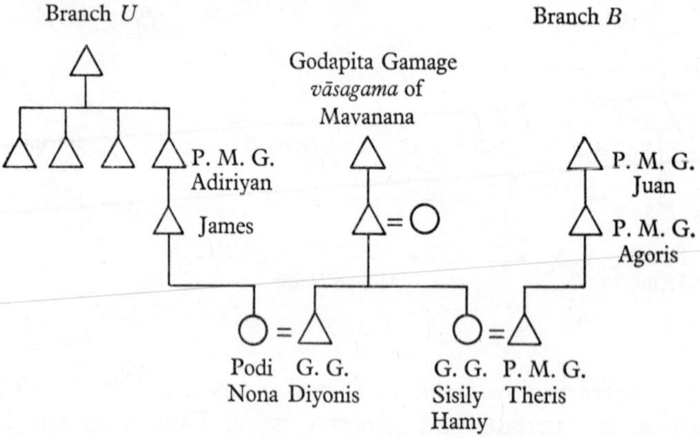

Fig. 39.

classificatory cross-cousin marriage, though it would not be viewed as a cross-cousin marriage by the villagers. It will be viewed as a marriage between kinsmen (*nǣyo*). However, terminologically the relationship between the two is *massinā-nǣna*, for one of G. G. Diyonis' sisters married P. M. G. Theris of branch *B*, a classificatory parallel cousin of P. M. G. Podi Nona. This marriage strictly speaking does not involve share consolidation, because G. G. Diyonis has no shares in the Pahala Madagama estate, though his wife has $\frac{1}{112}$ share. However, Diyonis has a small share in his own village Mavanana, which is adjacent to the Pahala

Madagama hamlet. He lives uxorilocally with his wife; this permits him to enjoy his wife's share of the estate, as well as his own situated a few hundred yards away from his wife's, in the next village. While this is not a case of share consolidation it illustrates the factors that precipitate the formation of these marriage relationships—namely, general unavailability of land so that one attempts through marriage strategies to enlarge one's estate. In this case, though the property is located in two different hamlets the married pair can enjoy both properties owing to the closeness of their location.

IMPLICATIONS OF CHANGE FOR THE KINSHIP SYSTEM

Bilateral inheritance has two major implications for kinship behaviour, first the change in the structural position of sisters and brothers-in-law (*massinā*); and secondly, open conflict between brothers over inheritance. We shall deal with these two problems separately.

According to traditional laws of inheritance *dīga* married sisters do not own shares in the *gama*, whereas brothers do. The relationship between brother and sister is expected to be an amicable one; that between sister's husband and wife's brother one of friendliness and co-operation. In part this was due to the fact that *dīga* married sisters do not inherit the patrimonial estate and were not competitors with the brothers for the *pravēni* inheritance. With changed inheritance rules, sisters became competitors with their brothers in a manner that could not occur traditionally. Traditionally sisters could inherit only on *binna* marriage; they are then analogous to male siblings structurally, their husband's having an inferior role in the households. In the changed situation, virilocally married daughters who were often out-residents began to inherit shares. This introduced the several sources of tension described earlier between brothers and sisters. Furthermore, it changed the structural role of brother-in-law (*massinā*). Unlike the traditional *binna* married husband, who had an inferior status in the wife's household, the contemporary virilocally married woman's husband has managerial control over the wife's property, and if she dies intestate, has claim to half her property, the other half devolving on the children. In several instances we noticed that the husband was directly or indirectly instrumental in selling the wife's *pravēni* shares. The fear that the husband would induce the wife to do so is pervasive in the village.

Kinship relations with the brother-in-law have changed considerably from traditional behaviour; his position is analogous to that of a male sibling, and the element of reserve and formality that characterized the latter relationship, also tends to govern the former. However, this is not universal, there being still cases of traditional 'joking' behaviour between in-laws, particularly those who are not perceived as a threat to one's inheritance. But these cases are becoming increasingly rare; the general attitude between in-laws being one of reserve. In some cases the formality and reserve between *massinās* turn into open conflict, resulting in severance of kinship relations. We have over half a dozen cases of such severed relationships, for example, the relationship between Godapita Gamage Diyonis and his *massinā* P. M. G. Hovis; between P. M. G. Singho Appu and his sister's husband.

We feel that these changed kin relations have resulted in a significant change in kinship terminology. Brothers-in-law who were addressed as *massinā* in the traditional system are now addressed as *aiya* or *malli* (elder or younger sibling, parallel cousin), and sisters-in-law addressed traditionally as *nǟna* are now generally addressed as *akka* or *nangi* (elder or younger sister, parallel cousin). We do not agree with Leach that these were traditional alternate modes of address. In Rambadeniya, an isolated Kandyan jungle village where we once worked, the forms of address and reference were consistently *nǟna* and *massinā*. In the more urban areas in the Sinhalese low country, cross-cousin marriage too has practically died out. Further researches are required to validate the conclusions we have drawn regarding changes in terminology.

If the relations between *massinās* were traditionally cooperative and amicable, the traditional relationship between male siblings was one of reserve and formality. Structural changes have altered the relationship between *massinās* in the contemporary kinship system; similar changes have also affected drastically the relationship between brothers. The structural variable that has brought about changes in kin behaviour is not bilateral inheritance, but the changes in residence patterns due to land shortage. The problem was highlighted in an earlier chapter, and is equivalent to the situation in which virilocally married sisters are placed.

Traditionally brothers were aggregated in a single hamlet whose residents had ancestral or *pravēni* shares in an estate or *gama*. In the context of change due to land shortage brothers move out residing uxorilocally, neo-locally, or otherwise. *What* pushes male siblings out is land shortage; *where* they move out would depend on individual circumstances. These out-residents pose constant problems to in-resident siblings, for the latter expect the former to 'abdicate' their interests in the village, so that in-resident siblings could enjoy the shares of out-residents prescriptively. In fact we noted that brothers, like sisters, may sell their shares to outsiders. When this happens, or threatens to occur, the relationship between brothers is severed. Sometimes final severance may not occur but an extremely strained relationship may prevail instead. For example, P. M. G. Uruveris, resident in Mavanana, sold the paddy shares in the Pahala Madagama estate to a shopkeeper Epa Seneviratne in preference to his in-resident brother P. M. G. John who wanted to buy these shares himself. Uruveris and John 'speak' to each other, but the latter was not invited on the occasion of the marriage of Uruveris' son. A case of total severance of relationship between brothers is that of P. M. G. Hovis and P. M. G. Seetin. P. M. G. Hovis resided initially in his hamlet, then lived uxorilocally in his wife's village where he had considerable property. His father P. M. G. James had planted one acre and thirty perches of rubber in land which he had bought from the Crown. In 1952, Hovis persuaded his father to give him half this property on deed. When his father died Hovis had one-half of the plantation, and the rest was diffused among the other siblings, but effectively controlled by the only in-resident sibling P. M. G. Seetin. Since Hovis resided uxorilocally, Seetin continued to enjoy the *whole* property. Hovis repeatedly asked his brother for a regular 'rent', but Seetin refused and once insulted him by saying, 'Your lands are in Panangala', that is, his wife's village. In 1957 Hovis filed a partition suit, which was granted by the District Court.

Other cases of total or partial severance in sibling kin relationships are between P. M. G. Gnanadasa and P. M. G. Gunadasa; I. M. G. Amaris and his brother. In general whenever an out-resident sibling has sold his share to outsiders, it creates a rift between the in-resident and out-resident siblings concerned. To sum up, in the traditional land tenure system where a brother resided in the hamlet and worked shares in a *gama*, the kin relations were formal and reserved. They belonged to the same ideal *pavula*, as Leach would say. Land shortage precipitating new residence patterns put a further strain on these already formal relationships, so that partial or total severance of sibling kin relationships tended to take place.

RESIDENCE PATTERNS AND CHANGES IN HAMLET STRUCTURE

There has recently been in the anthropological literature some controversy regarding the adequacy of conventional 'rules of residence' (Goodenough 1956; Fischer 1958; Barnes 1960). We shall not enter into this controversy except to explicate our own view in relation to a single case study, Madagama. Let us enumerate some of the conventionally accepted meanings of 'residence'.

(1) First, there is a view of residence by Murdock and others as a jural rule—hence a formal 'rule of residence'. Alternatively a rule of residence is seen as an 'institution'. For example, Dunning says, '...if explicit structural linearity is lacking, a greater emphasis might normally be placed on other social institutions, one of which is residence rules' (Dunning 1959:806).

(2) In contrast with a jural rule there is the actual pattern of residence for a whole society, that is, the practice of residence irrespective of normative or jural sanction.

(3) Residence, as Fischer and Barnes view it, is the way individuals or couples are classified. This too deals with actual practice.

We are not interested in residence as jural rules, for reasons which will soon be clear. We shall also make no qualitative distinction between the residence profile of a society and the residence pattern of individuals or couples. We suggest that for dynamic analysis it is better to view 'residence' in terms of statistical trends, rather than jural or institutional norms. Where we have stable statistical trends, or where social change is at a minimum, we can speak of the 'dominant' and 'normal' patterns of residence in a society. Thus a 'normal residential pattern' is a 'stable statistical trend' where people marry under conditions of relative social stability. This normal trend may or may not be jurally sanctioned by the society. In any case what is most useful from an analytical point of view are the factors that produce or cause the 'stable statistical trend'. Thus these trends are end-products of structural or motivational variables, which are the cause of the trends. For example, ten societies may show a drift from uxorilocality to virilocality, but it is possible that the conditions that produce the 'drift' may in each case be different—changes in ecology, land tenure, prestige system, etc. If indeed the 'rule' is a function of such variables a formal taxonomy of residence may be of limited use unless the taxonomic scheme is geared to deal with the underlying 'dynamics'. It is true, as Murdock (1949) pointed out, that *some* change of residence is a function of the incest taboo. It is then possible to produce an exhaustive set of combinations as he has done in 'World Ethnographic Sample'. However, the mere production of combinations may not be useful, unless one is aware of the variables producing them. Assuming that such key variables exist—for example, variables *X*, *Y*, *Z*—we say that a pattern of residence is caused by *X*, *Y*, *Z*. When *X*, *Y*, *Z* change, or new variables *A*, *B* are introduced, there are bound to be changes in that residence pattern. The greater the varieties of changes introduced the greater the variability of residence patterns, producing Fischer's 'anomalous' types of individual residence. In principle there need be no distinction between individual and societal patterns of residence—the latter is a formulation of statistical regularities from a sample of individual cases. A distinction can however be made between individual and idiosyncratic cases. For example, a cripple living in a predominantly neo-local set up may be compelled to live uxoripatrilocally, that is, in his wife's father's house. Such idiosyncratic cases may not be sociologically significant. It must finally be mentioned that it may not be possible to isolate all the factors that cause residential patterns: but even if necessary and sufficient conditions cannot be set up, we may be able to formulate necessary *or* sufficient conditions.

If one ignores underlying structural or motivational variables and focuses on place and form of residence of each individual or couple *per se*, one may end up in the terminological morass that threatens residence classification. Thus Ayoub and Lieberman clutter up the prevailing confusion by 'patricipient residence', 'matricipient residence', 'fratricipient residence' and 'other cipient compounds' (1962:162); while Carrasco compounds the confusion with more compounds—patridomestic patrivicinal, neo-domestic avuncuvicinal, patripropinquous, patrilonginquous! (Carrasco 1963).

In order to elucidate the structural precipitates of residence we shall employ as few terms as possible. Table 16 gives the data on residence from Pahala Madagama hamlet. Data pertain to resident patterns of males and in-resident females.

Table 16. *Residence pattern of Pahala Madagama hamlet, 1790–1961*

Branch and generation	In-resident males (husband, patrilocal; wife, virilocal)	In-resident females (wife, patrilocal; husband, uxorilocal)	Men reside in wife's village (uxori-local)	Men live elsewhere (neo-local and other)
'*B*'FA^2–FA^4	7	1	0	0
'*U*'FA^2–FA^4	5	0	0	1
'*B*'FA^5 and after	10	1	7	5
'*U*'FA^5 and after	12	9	4	6

We consider land to be the major structural variable that determines the pattern of residence. Up to generation FA^4 (inclusive) there are only two cases of 'deviation' from the pattern ('stable statistical trend') of male in-residence (patrilocal residence, *dīga* marriage). The period is roughly up to 1880. One case of 'deviation' was where a female Baru Hamy married *binna* in the absence of male heirs, and the other P. M. G. Hin Hamy who had to leave the village owing to 'eviction' during the Grain Tax crisis. After generation FA^4, there are increasing pressures on land due to the operation of the Grain Tax and the other factors of change discussed earlier. One would expect therefore an increasing ejection of males and consequent out-residence. The choice of *place* of residence would depend minimally on availability of land or employment. The opportunity for obtaining land is restricted to (*a*) *badu iḍam*, (*b*) agricultural colonies, (*c*) marriage to a woman with land. Alternatively one may move out of the hamlet and seek non-agricultural employment in Colombo or in the larger cities. Though choice of residence is dependent on motivational factors, the structural variable that forces individuals to make choices is generally scarcity of land.

Formal classifications like 'neo-local and other' make little sense sometimes, for one cannot easily classify a person who alternates between two residences like a *badu iḍam*, colony, or wife's village and the parental hamlet. Equally difficult to classify are intravillage strategic unions. However, in practically all the cases we have the major structural variable that underlies residence patterns is land. This is true even in the case of in-resident females. Here a landless male from another village marries uxorilocally a female with land from the hamlet.

From generation FA^5 (inclusive) onwards land pressures push males out of their parent hamlet. After FA^5 (1880's) there are exactly twenty-two cases of out-residence for twenty-two cases of in-residence. About half the males in the hamlet since generation FA^5 leave the hamlet to take residence elsewhere, either in their wives' villages or in a new locality. Since before generation FA^5 the proportion was twelve in-residents to one out-resident, there is over 42 per cent increase in male out-residence!

The sociological implications of these migrations are very great particularly for the traditional corporate hamlet structure. These migrations destroy the relative homogeneity of the traditional hamlet. In the above table we have only recorded the members who initially left the hamlet to reside elsewhere. We have ignored their descendants. However, the descendants of these migrants introduce into their 'adopted' villages, in two or three generations, a group of kinsmen with their original *vāsagama* names. To illustrate take the case of, *X* a hypothetical hamlet. *X* was up to and inclusive of generation FA^4 a hamlet consisting of a homogeneous body of kinsmen, mostly members of a single *vāsagama*. As a result of population-land pressures, hamlet *X* is subject to intrusion by members of several alien *vāsagamas*, *a*, *b*, *c*, *d*, *e*. In the first generation it is only a single individual from an alien *vāsagama* that invades *X*, but in a couple of generations their numbers increase, so that *X* ceases to be a homogeneous (single *vāsagama*) hamlet. If these aliens have legitimated their position by buying shares from the hamlet *pravēni*, then further structural changes have occurred. Thus one of the major consequences of the ejection of males from their parental hamlets to new ones is the radical reorganization of hamlet structure. The problem is seen in Pahala Madagama itself. This hamlet which previous to generation FA^5 was a homogeneous one, is now 'heterogeneous', consisting of representatives of the following *vāsagamas*: Kankanan Gamage, Godapita Gamage, Halviti Gamage, Vanasinge, Jasin Gamage, Kariyawasam Godage. The situation is worse in Ihala Madagama. It is bound to be much worse in the more densely populated areas of the Southern and Western provinces. One conclusion can therefore be drawn from the above analysis: *the demographic variable, in combination with the relative lack of availability of land could alone produce radical changes in hamlet structure*. It is hence not surprising that hamlets of the old type hardly exist in most of the Sinhalese low country, except in relatively 'isolated' regions like the Hinidum Pattu.

'Anomalous residence' of P. M. G. Hovis

Land pressures create all sorts of 'anomalous' residence patterns. We have several cases of these but we shall use one example as an illustration.

We have included P. M. G. Hovis in the category 'neo-local and other'. Hovis married while his father P. M. G. James was still alive and in control of the ancestral property. After marriage Hovis lived one year in his natal hamlet, and then moved over to his wife's village in Panangala. He had obtained from his father-in-law a dowry of over one and a half acres of high land with 'safe title' (not in undivided shares). In addition his wife owned $\frac{1}{120}$ share of the Panangala *pravēni* jointly with four siblings. At the time of Hovis' marriage, his wife's siblings were minors and one of the motives of Hovis' father-in-law was to have a man to manage the estate. This Hovis did quite assiduously even at the expense of his wife's siblings. For example, his wife owned an acre of high land jointly with her siblings. Hovis planted this with rubber entirely for his own benefit.

Yet Hovis was entitled to land in Madagama too which he inherited at his father's death in 1954. When his father died Hovis started a pattern of alternating residence. He would live for a period in Madagama enjoying his substantial patrimonial inheritance while his wife and children would reside in Panangala. Though this pattern of alternating residence was by no means symmetrical villagers had a joke that Hovis' mode of residence left him no time to have sexual intercourse with his wife! By 1961 Hovis had practically sold his entire inheritance at Pahala Madagama, and was contemplating residing permanently in his wife's village.

CITIZENSHIP

When non-*vāsagama* persons enter the hamlet they stabilize their position by buying shares. Shares in *pravēni*, as Leach pointed out for Pul Eliya, confer 'citizenship' rights in the hamlet. In Madagama all persons who own shares in the *vāsagama* estate are considered 'citizens' of the hamlet. A person may belong to a certain *vāsagama* but if he does not own shares in the *vāsagama* estate he is viewed as having severed connexions with the *vāsagama*. Thus a person who marries uxorilocally or neo-locally may sell his *pravēni* shares but retain his *vāsagama* name. By selling one's share one has renounced one's citizenship rights in the hamlet. These rights pertain to cultivation of high and low land according to an agreed *taṭṭumāru* scheme, and traditionally involved rights to chenas, forests and wastes. They also probably entailed (traditionally) *rāja-kāriya* duties and payment of taxes. Above all, shares were important for the self-esteem of individuals in a society where ownership of land is an index of prestige and status. A person without *pravēni* share is a person without a *gama*, a worthless fellow. A vagrant is often described in Sinhalese as a 'person without a *gama* and a *geye* (house)'. To have a *gama*, that is, to be a citizen of a hamlet, one must have shares in it. The sociological significance of shares outweighs its purely economic significance.

The sentiment that *pangu* or shares make one a citizen of a *gama* (*gamē minissu*, 'people of the hamlet') is expressed in proverbial idiom as 'the right to pick a coconut from a tree in the hamlet'. A person in Hinidum Pattu living outside his hamlet but owning a minute share in it, when questioned as to why he does not sell his share may say, 'Well, when passing my hamlet (*gama*) I can stop there and pick a coconut off a tree to have a drink'. Translated this means that a share gives a person privileges and rights he can assert at any time, for example, the right to build a house on *pravēni* land irrespective of the size of his share. The idea of picking a coconut, jak, or arecanut from *pravēni* land is literally put into effect by small shareowners. Consider the case of P. M. G. Andiris' offspring. Andiris (branch *U*) owned $\frac{1}{96}$ of the *gama*; on his death his three daughters and a son inherited $\frac{1}{384}$ share each. The son, Pediris Singho, died and his family dispersed; one daughter Sumana resided in the hamlet while the others resided in their husbands' hamlets. Effectively the in-resident Sumana works the $\frac{1}{96}$ share of her father, but periodically her siblings or their children visit the hamlet and pick a few coconuts, arecanuts or jak-fruit. The economic value of these products is negligible but in doing this they are symbolically asserting their citizenship in the *gama*. Sometimes, as pointed out earlier, the in-resident may take the initiative and give 'gifts' to the out-resident, symbolically acknowledging the latter's rights in the *vāsagama*.

There are two ways of acquiring citizenship in a hamlet. One by birth, and the other by *naturalization*. The first is for persons with a *vāsagama* name, or the offspring of persons with shares in the *vāsagama* estate. The latter process is for outsiders seeking to establish themselves in the hamlet, particularly in the context of the migrations mentioned earlier. The process whereby an outsider is affiliated into the hamlet and becomes a naturalized citizen is well structured.

(*a*) The 'outsider' is generally 'conducted' into the hamlet through a bilateral kinship network. He is generally someone related to the hamlet however remotely.

(*b*) Once in the hamlet or before residing there, the person will buy *pravēni* shares and establish citizenship claims in the hamlet. This will permit him to build a house in the hamlet and cultivate its fields.

(*c*) Though a person is technically a citizen by virtue of share ownership his kinship connexions with the hamlet are weak and his position is not, in the kinship sense, stable. He will therefore try to establish kinship ties with families of other citizens, through affinity, and thus stabilize his position in the hamlet kinship structure. By this process he and his descendants cease to be outsiders. For even though they do not carry the *vāsagama* name, they are connected to the *vāsagama* through close bilateral kinship ties. A few cases of 'naturalization' will help illustrate these processes.

Cases of citizenship by naturalization

(I) *Edirisinghe Andiris*

He came from a neighbouring village Ambelegedera, dominated by a *vāsagama* of the Edirisinghes containing many powerful and wealthy people. However, the pressures that were driving out other people were at work here. He was one of eight siblings, five of whom were males. Though he had a share in the Ambelegedera estate which came to a 6 k cultivation area of paddy land, he was faced with a very typical problem, namely, that small shares were *effectively* controlled and worked by elder male siblings. So he decided to settle down in Pahala Madagama with his wife buying a share of $\frac{1}{108}$ from P. M. G. Karo. This made him a citizen of Pahala Madagama. These ties were stabilized in the next generation when one of the sons, Edirisinghe Ariyapala, married the daughter of the wealthiest member of Pahala Madagama, and a daughter married the wealthiest resident shareowner of Ihala Madagama, J. G. Handy.

It is interesting to note that Edirisinghe Andiris did not sell his inheritance in his village of orientation. He sold the high land, but the 6 k of paddy land is given out on *andē* by his youngest son Sumanapala. The reason is clear: while the Edirisinghes consider themselves to be Madagama citizens, they would also like to be affiliated with the higher status parent *vāsagama* of the Edirisinghes at Ambelegedera. One way of doing this is to maintain shares in the parental hamlet.

(2) *Jasin Gamage Vilian Singho*

We do not know the exact date in which J. G. Vilian Singho from distant Morawaka became a resident of Madagama. He probably came to Pahala Madagama about 1900 or later, as a young unmarried man of about twenty-six years of age.

We do not know why he picked Pahala Madagama, but one thing is obvious. The structural pressure due to land scarcity felt in Madagama was also being felt in Morawaka, so that villagers everywhere were being pushed out of their villages of orientation. It is no accident that Jasin Gamage Vilian Singho was one of ten siblings, seven of whom were males. In any case he bought from the government one acre of land (*sinnakkara*) and settled down in the hamlet. Note that he is of the *gamagē* subcaste like other Madagama villagers. He married Lanka Gamage Loku Etana, who is related to branch *U* of the *vāsagama*. The manner of marriage is interesting. Vilian Singho's wife's (Loku Etana's) mother's sister was the second wife of P. M. G. Adiriyan, branch *U*, FA^4. Loku Etana had been orphaned in early childhood and lived in Madagama with her mother's sister and husband. Vilian Singho, by marrying a poor propertyless orphan, gained kinsmen from the *vāsagama*, and stabilized his position. He was still in some sense an outsider for while he owned property adjacent to the hamlet, he had no shares. This was rectified in the next generation by his two sons Jasin Gamage Liveris and Jasin Gamage Handy. The eldest son Liveris bought a small area of high land from a member of branch *U*. A bachelor, ex-monk, and now practising shaman, he lives on this land with his ageing mother. The younger brother Handy left the village and sought employment in the British naval base in Trincomalee. He bought $\frac{1}{8}$ share of the Ihala Madagama estate in 1949 and two months after this married the daughter of

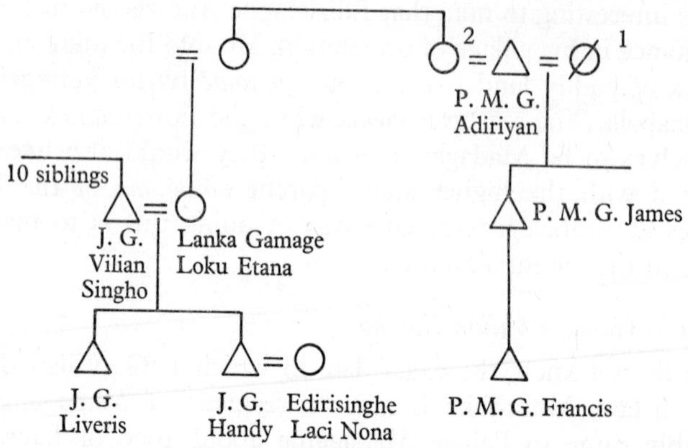

Fig. 40.

Edirisinghe Andiris. Thus of Jasin Gamage Vilian's two sons, one became a citizen of Pahala Madagama and the other of Ihala Madagama.

(3) *Kariyawasam Godage Nikulas*

The third important family of outsiders to acquire citizenship rights in Pahala Madagama was that of Kariyawasam Godage Nikulas. K. G. Nikulas' father had been a gaoler at the Galle prison. He had been a 'friend' of the Mudaliyar (Mudiyanse Hamaduruvo) of Hinidum Pattu who had given him some land at Hinidum Pattu; later he acquired considerable property on his own. However, Nikulas on the death of his father was posed with the same problem as Edirisinghe Andiris. As the youngest male of a family of eight children, he could not 'get along' with his elder brothers who controlled the property. He left his village of orientation and opened a boutique in Pahala Madagama. He married P. M. G. Vyanti Hamy of branch *U*, and probably gave her the money to buy a $\frac{1}{32}$ share of the *pravēni* from her stepbrother P. M. G. Jayaweera. After his wife's death he remarried H. K. Katrina. In the next generation his daughter by the first marriage married P. M. G. Nandiris, son of his wife's stepbrother.

Nikulas, like Edirisinghe Andiris, did not sell his shares in Gigummaduva. His son K. G. Amarapala periodically works a paddy field there. Once again the reason is that like the Edirisinghes at Ambelegedera the Kariyawasam Godages at Gigummaduva had done very well for themselves, and their poorer relation at Madagama wished to maintain some contact with the parent *vāsagama* through the share he owned.

(4) *P. M. G. Podi Singho and his siblings*

We noted that when P. M. G. Elias of branch *U* died his wife controlled the estate and remarried a man who lived with her in Pahala Madagama. The offspring of the second marriage took the *vāsagama* name of their mother's first husband rather than their father. The intention of the mother was probably to give these children rights in the *vāsagama* estate. However, when the two sons of the first marriage came of age, they took over their father's estate entirely, leaving nothing to their uterine step-siblings. Here is a case of 'adopted' *vāsagama* members without *pravēni* shares. All except two siblings left the hamlet for good; the two remaining consequently bought shares and thus established themselves as citizens. P. M. G. Vyanti Hamy bought shares from her stepbrother and P. M. G. Podi Singho bought shares in branch *B* from P. M. G. Karo Appu. This illustrates that kinship connexions (that is, *vāsagama* name) do not grant 'citizenship': the crucial factor is ownership of shares. The siblings who have no shares leave the village.

We have dealt with the three instances of total outsiders who have become citizens of Pahala Madagama by buying shares in *pravēni* and have stabilized their position by establishing kin ties with members of the dominant *vāsagama*. Both steps are essential if one is to be assimilated into the community. Since strictly speaking a citizen of a hamlet is a shareowner and a *vāsagama* kinsman, outsiders who come in must also own shares and at least become kinsmen of members of the *vāsagama*. We have no instances of any outsider in Pahala Madagama who performed one of these steps but not the other; both steps are necessary for full assimilation. We can illustrate with an example from Ihala Madagama, where an outsider becomes a citizen by buying shares from the *vāsagama*, but owing to the absence of kin ties with the *vāsagama* is not assimilated into the hamlet.

(5) *Jayawardene Jinadasa, a citizen by default*

Jayawardene Jinadasa is a poor man, though connected with a powerful *pelāntiya*. His father held the posts of fiscal and village headman. While he and his male siblings were all minors, his father had married off a daughter Cicily Hamy to Panangala Liyanage Uporis, the share speculator. According to Jayawardene, Uporis persuaded his father to give most of his lands to Uporis. On the death of the father, Uporis acted as guardian of the children.

The present lands in Ihala Madagama were gifted by Jayawardene's two *massinās*, P. L. Uporis and his brother P. L. Peter. The reason seems clear—Jinadasa was to act as caretaker of the extensive properties of the Panangala Liyanages in Ihala Madagama. Thus Jayawardene Jinadasa becomes a citizen by default: he is planted there by his wealthy kinsmen. He is also a fool, an utterly incompetent worker and no threat to them. Soon after Jinadasa was planted in Ihala Madagama a marriage was arranged for him, this time to an equally unwanted female of the Senanayake Dasilige *pelāntiya*. Senanayake Dasilige Podi Nona, a sloppy, inefficient, almost moronic woman was married off to the ineffectual Jayawardene Jinadasa. Jinadasa did not therefore establish any kin ties with Madagama folk, so that while he is a 'citizen', he is treated as an outsider. Jinadasa himself is not interested in allying himself with Madagama people. Living in the glories of his ancestral past, he talks of his father's greatness, and the fact that he (the father) had never 'touched' agricultural implements in his whole life. He talks of his powerful relations the Panangala Liyanages and Senanayake Dasiliges, even though he admits that the latter treat him with contempt. Despised by his relations, and held in pity and commiseration by the less prestigious Madagama folk, Jinadasa and his family remain an alienated and lonely group.

CHAPTER II

THE THEORETICAL AND METHODOLOGICAL BACKGROUND OF THE STUDY

We shall attempt here to place the study of Madagama in the tradition of anthropological writing. Historically this study leans on the theoretical work of Maine and his followers, qualified by contemporary social anthropological theory. Maine in his *Ancient Law* not only concerned himself with kinship theory, such as for example the study of corporate groups, agnation and cognation, the structure of the joint family and patripotestal authority, but more directly in our line of thinking, he concerned himself with the origin and structure of the 'hamlet', or what he called the 'village community'. He clearly recognized that the 'village community' or 'joint village' or 'Aryan village' was both a kinship group and a common property owning body. 'The village community of India is at once an organized patriarchal society and an assemblage of co-proprietors' (Maine 1907:272). Kinship as Maine correctly points out is inextricably linked with common rights in property.

Maine's conception of the village community is strictly analogous to our characterization of *gama*, which is on the one hand a collection of land holdings or an estate held in 'shares', and on the other hand the kinship collectivity of the hamlet. There is in both an ideology of common origin. Maine recognizes that this is fundamentally an *ideology*, which may be notoriously at variance with the actual facts of origin. 'The village community then is not necessarily an assemblage of blood relations, but it is either such an assemblage or a body of co-proprietors *formed on the model of an association of kinsmen*' (Maine 1907:275–6, italics mine). This 'domain' is held in common and administered by an elected manager or eldest agnate. The community provides for the management of the common fund and organizes its own internal government for the administration of justice and the apportionment of taxes and public duties (1907:273–4). From time to time outsiders may be incorporated into this theoretically homogeneous kin group. In North India the village communities were in fact formed by 'blood relations' but 'a mere purchaser of a share may generally, under certain conditions, be admitted into the brotherhood' (1907:274). In South India village communities have sprung not from one but from two or more 'families', so that the facts contradict the ideology. 'Indeed the occasional aggregation of men of different castes in the same society is fatal to the hypothesis of common descent...Yet in all these brotherhoods either the tradition is preserved or the assumption made, of an original common parentage' (1907:274).

Maine's interest was largely historical. In *Ancient Law* he was interested in the village community in order to discover the origins of property and ownership. In his later work (*Village Communities in East and West*, *The Early History of Institutions*) he was interested in discovering the original Indo-European proto-community. The stimulus for research on these lines was provided by the dramatic success of Indo-Aryan philological studies. As Maine suggested explicitly, what was required in juridico-sociological studies was the transference of the methodological biases of philology ('the comparative method') in order to discover the origins and evolution of the village community. Comparative studies, indicated Maine, establishes the identity of the Indian village community and the ancient European village, the former surviving much longer than the latter owing to India's relative isolation till British times (Maine 1876:103). As much as the study of Sanskrit has led to a reconstruction of the primitive Indo-European proto-language, so the study of the Indian village should lead us to reconstruct the Indo-European proto-village community. While this is only a distant goal, Maine describes what he considers to be main features of the hypothetical village community. The most important feature of the village community is the arable mark or the cultivated portion of the village domain. There are minute and multifarious rules governing the cultivation of the mark, but the ultimate sanction for their rules is authority, custom and chance rather than contract, specifically the obligations of kinship sanctioned by patriarchal authority (*patria potestas*). Associated with the arable mark is the waste or common land which in Teutonic Europe was mostly for pasture, but in vegetarian and agricultural India was potential arable land. The land was owned jointly by a body of kinsmen larger than the family, and the control of village affairs was in a council of elders which declared customary law. Contemporary examples of individual, rather than joint ownership of property, is due to the dissolution of ancient co-ownership, especially through the partition of inheritance (Maine 1876: 107 ff.).

Maine's work set up a tradition of sociological writing on the village community in India and Ceylon, as for example, Phear (*The Aryan Village in India and Ceylon*), Mayne (*Hindu Law and Usage*). Unfortunately much work written in this tradition was vitiated by an overreliance on the information in the Dharmashastras, a lack of detailed sociological information on existent communities, and a cultural evolutionary perspective. The general position is well summed up in the following quotation:

> The village referred to in Manu was, we can hardly doubt, the well known village community, the constitution and position of which are so important in the Hindu land system; the village is, in fact, the key to that system.

Or again:

> From the slight reference to it in Manu we have to pass by a long stride of centuries to what has been observed in such recent times as the period since British rule. It is from such observations, with the aid of analogies from similar institutions existing in modern times in other countries, that we have to construct the idea of the village community of Hindu times. (Phillips, quoted in Baden-Powell 1892: 106)

The quotation illustrates very well the theoretical and methodological biases of these scholars, typical of the intellectual ethos of the nineteenth century. There is first the social Darwinistic emphasis on origins, and in all the writers mentioned, a preoccupation with stages of development of the village from its 'Aryan' origins to its present day; secondly the uncritical use of the comparative method ('analogies from similar institutions') with its assumption that institutions which are contemporaneously similar had the same origin; thirdly the belief that present institutions are either adequate representations, or 'survivals', or degenerate forms of the Aryan prototype.

From the perspective of contemporary social science it is easy to dismiss these theories as naïve speculative fancies unrelated to the mundane empirical facts of social life. But to dismiss these theories offhand would be a mistake, for while the methodological assumptions of these scholars are largely discredited, they did not speculate in an empirical vacuum. There was in fact considerable evidence, however unsystematized it may have been, collected by British revenue officers and administrators from several parts of India, that *some* form of 'village community' consisting of kinsmen jointly owning property existed in this region. For revenue purposes, taxes were generally collected from the property owning corporation as a whole, rather than from individuals. The British civil service was so enamoured of the idea, that even non-communal villages were converted by the Administration, in whole provinces, into 'joint villages'. But while the British Administration was no doubt instrumental in the creation and diffusion of 'joint villages' where none existed before, the evidence suggests that such villages of indigenous origin already existed in many parts of India. This evidence is presented by Baden-Powell in his massive three-volume (and unfortunately neglected) study of the *Land Systems of British India* (1892), which is a collation and systematization of data pertaining to land tenure and land revenue administration gathered by generations of British civil servants. A summary of the evidence is available in the later and better known work by Baden-Powell, *The Indian Village Community* (1896).

Baden-Powell's work represented the first significant break through in the impasse reached in the study of the village community. Though addicted to dubious lineal evolutionary stages and an uncritical comparative method (1892:403, 406), Baden-Powell had very little sympathy with origin theories based on little evidence, and the facile explanation of present differences in village structure in terms of 'survival' or degenerate forms of an earlier pure type. Baden-Powell's scholarship, though firmly grounded in the nineteenth century, anticipates the empiricism of twentieth-century social science. The massive amount of data collated by him, though often lacking in the depth and detail that contemporary anthropologists would look for, illustrated forcefully the complexity of the empirical situation pertaining to the structure, composition and origin of villages, and their bases of solidarity. He takes exception to naïve origin theories: '...the identity of some forms of the Indian village with the Mark or tribal holdings in Ireland, is only "identity" in the sense in which German, Greek,

Lithuanian, and Latin tongues could be called "identical" with Sanskrit or Zand' (Baden-Powell 1892:174). As far as the universal prevalence in India of the joint village is concerned, the empirical facts do not in the least warrant such an assumption.

> The term community might, if not explained, be apt to mislead. It can be correctly used only with reference to the fact that in many villages families live together under a system which makes them joint owners; while in others the people merely live under similar conditions and under a sense of tribal or caste connection, and with a common system of local government. It cannot be used as suggesting any idea of having the land or anything else 'in common'. (1892:113)

The suggestion is that the village community represents at best one type of organized social life where the basis of solidarity lies in joint ownership of land: it does not exclude other bases of solidarity, nor does it include other types of communities organized on different principles. Moreover, 'joint ownership' does not involve the idea of possessing land 'in common', if by this is meant 'something of a communistic type as regards property in land'; and most certainly 'collective ownership has nothing to do with the social community of goods' (1896:3).

Baden-Powell classifies all the villages in India into two broad types—one that has no appearance of common or joint ownership which he names the *raiyatwārī* type; and a type in which some form of joint ownership prevails. Far from the joint village being the typical mode of organization of communities in India, the *raiyatwārī*, or non-joint type, constitutes the largest class of villages (1896:9–19). The one is not a derivative of the other, though the joint type may sometimes atrophy into a *raiyatwārī* type. While Baden-Powell says that any notion of a pure Aryan type is nonsense, the *raiyatwārī*, he suggests, contrary to popular opinion, is the typical 'Aryan' form of village organization before the Mogul conquest of India. By 'Aryan' he means a pre-Moslem type which is a synthesis of Indo-Aryan and Dravidian features (1892:144–65). According to him, the main concentration of joint villages is found in the Punjab, the North-west provinces and Oudh, whereas the rest of India, by and large, contains *raiyatwārī* types, or survivals of earlier joint villages. The view that the bulk of Indian villages are of the *raiyatwārī* type is confirmed by another nineteenth-century authority (Campbell 1881).

From the point of view of our thesis we are not so much interested in the *raiyatwārī* type as in the joint type described by Baden-Powell. Baden-Powell points out that the joint village is not of one uniform type, but takes several forms. In *Land Systems of British India* he discusses three forms of the joint tenure as the *zamindārī* type, the *pattidāri* type, and the *bhaiāchārā* type (vol. I, 1892: 158–61) previously discussed by Mayne (Mayne 1950: 305–309). These three types are somewhat revised in *The Indian Village Community*. Here he speaks of a joint village organized on a tribal basis (*bhaiāchārā*) and depending on a succession of joint heirs to an individual founder (*pattidāri*), and villages formed by families with no tribal and no aristocratic basis, or on voluntary association (1896: 3). Different principles of classification are adopted in other parts of the book (230 ff., 295 ff., 331 ff.) so that the typological distinctions are not always clearly maintained. However, he gives a reason for the proliferation of forms of joint tenure: basically this is due to differences in the *principle of sharing*. Thus different principles of division or partition of the estate may alone produce a variety of forms of joint tenure. But cross-cutting the different forms of tenure are features common to all villages of the joint type: (*a*) In all cases the village forms something like a unit estate. The adjoining waste is an integral part of the estate and at the absolute disposal of the owners. Partition of the waste, when it occurs, is based on the share system which operates in respect of arable land. (*b*) The modern land revenue administration (of Baden-Powell's time) treats the village as a single estate liable to one lump sum of revenue, distributed over holdings or among co-sharers according to their own principles of division. Joint responsibility for payment of revenue is assumed. (*c*) 'It is not at all necessary that the joint village should be actually held undivided. In some cases it is so held...Very often the arable is divided and the waste is not, either because it is more conveniently kept as a common grazing ground, or because it is not yet wanted for the extension of cultivation' (1896: 22). (*d*) The physical size of the land (estate) may vary from a few hundred acres to a few thousand, and this in turn may affect the organization of tenurial arrangements. (*e*) There are no headmen exercising police or juridical authority as in the *raiyatwārī* village; instead management of the joint estate is by a committee of heads of houses or *panchayat*. (*f*) In many cases the co-sharing proprietory body are of non-agricultural caste, or have established a landlord position over an earlier cultivating body. In which case the larger part of the land will be held by tenants, whereas the management will be by the proprietary body. (*g*) The proprietary body, especially if of one clan or one ancestor, is often desirous of excluding strangers. This gives rise to the custom of pre-emption where 'the intruding vendor must offer it at fair value to one of the existing co-sharers (usually in order of blood relation to himself), and then to the members of the same subdivision, before selling to any outsider' (1896:27).

Of the several forms of joint tenure described by Baden-Powell, two types are relevant for our analysis, because of the similarity in the 'principles of sharing' with the norms of our ideal model. These two forms of tenure are the *bhaiāchārā* type and the *pattidāri* type.

Bhaiāchārā principles of sharing

Bhaiāchārā tenure is where the village is based on a clan organization: either where an already existent clan has settled down and founded a village or where clans grow out of a family of settlers later dispersed over a wide area (1896:407) (typically found among north-west frontier tribes). Here the whole clan owns a territorially demarcated area of land or an estate. The head (ancestor) of the original family (or head of several families originally settled) 'own' the whole estate. In the second generation this total unit area is further subdivided among the sons of the founder, who form 'branches' of the clan: the original estate is divided into territorially demarcated 'primary divisions'. These are further subdivided in the generations of the founder's grandsons, and great-grandsons, who also have special territories within the larger estate allocated to them. These divisions are permanent: they are also named after the ancestor of each division. 'All later and now existing families belong to one or other of the thus established groups and subgroups, and take shares within the territory belonging to each: there are no new designations given to subsequent divisions' (1896:408). To use our own terminology the system is 'frozen' at a certain point for the purposes of land tenure. These territorial units may develop into hamlets or villages (1896:412). Solidarity is based on clan and kinship sentiment. Several of the major territorial units may have a common plan of cultivating the land, but nowhere is the clan as a whole a joint property owning unit. However:

> It is quite possible that groups of close kindred will cultivate their shares jointly; it being more profitable to do so than to split up the land into small severalty holdings [1896:409];

that is, joint cultivation could exist *within* the territorially demarcated permanent ('frozen') unit, but not *between* such units.

Shares within each permanent unit (that is, shares allocated after the freezing of the system) are assigned on one of two principles.

(1) There is a *per capita* distribution. Every man, woman and child was counted, and each household thus received the number of shares which the count of heads indicated.

(2) The ancestral shares were calculated according to the 'pedigree table', in descent from the heads of each permanent unit or branch (1896:409). Both modes of sharing are clearly illustrated in Baden-Powell (1896:410).

The pattidāri principles of sharing

The village based on the *pattidāri* principle of sharing is still closer to our ideal model. Here the estate originated with a single founder (or a group of siblings).

> In all this class of cases the principle of sharing is, or originally was, not one of 'democratic' equality of right in the area obtained, but one depending on the place in the table of descent from the founder or acquirer, the different heirs each taking the 'legal' share that belongs to him by the law or custom of inheritance [1896:29];

that is, the *per capita bhaiāchārā* principle did not obtain here. In the course of time, strict shares may have been forgotten or changed, and affinal kinsmen and 'helpers in time of need' may be admitted to shares, while in other instances shares may have been sold to outsiders, or all remembrance of correct fractional shares may be lost so that the village reverts to the *raiyatwārī* type.

Theoretically the unit estate belonged originally to a single founding ancestor. Then in the generation of the sons the estate is divided into *pattī* (structurally and linguistically the equivalent of our *kaṭṭi*), the number of sections dependent on the number of sons. Only in recently founded villages have the present villagers personal memory of *pattī* ancestors. The next grade of divisions within the *pattī* are often called *thok*, and then *tūlā* (or *tōlā*). At a certain point the system is once again frozen, and further subdivisions have no public character and are unnamed. Each *pattī*, section, or subdivision may have a *lambadar*, a manager of the section, probably the equivalent in Ceylon of the *gamarāla* (Leach 1961:166). The principles of sharing are diagrammatically represented by Baden-Powell (1896:31), and reproduced here (Fig. 41).

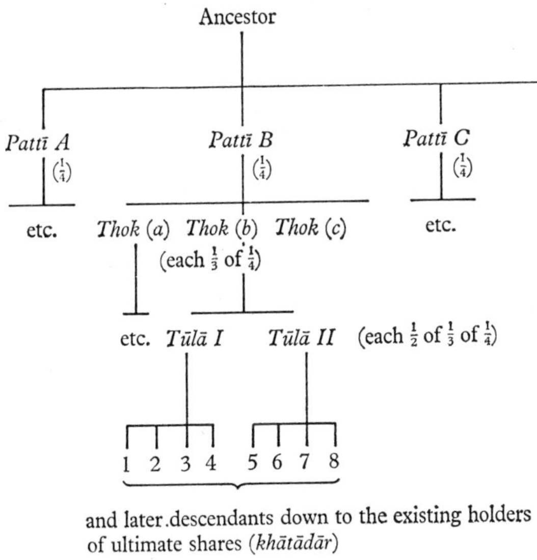

Fig. 41.

Baden-Powell calls villages that contain these principles of sharing, *pattidarī*, or 'ancestrally shared'.

> This principle (*pattidarī*...) is simply the result of the joint succession of all the heirs together. It is in villages of this class that it can be truly said that the village is the group which is held together *by the land* which it occupies 'in common'—that is, as joint heirs or co-sharers. It is also in villages of this class...that we hear of a person being a 4 *āna* sharer, that is, owning $\frac{1}{4}$ of the estate, or being a '2 *āna* 3 *pāi* 15 *kaurī*' sharer. (1896:30)

The theory is that the whole estate is treated as a rupee, and fractional shares calculated on the basis of monetary units. In Ceylon, with its higher standard of literacy, simple fractions are substituted for the clumsier rupee unit.

When Maine and Baden-Powell discuss the village community they do so through a 'model'. For example, Baden-Powell's discussion of the 'principles of sharing' is methodologically close to our 'model'. It is of the same methodological order as 'models' of patrilineal or matrilineal descent or unilineal descent groups that anthropologists talk about. What does the model contain? Our ideal model, like Baden-Powell's, contains a set of norms or principles regarding the ideal operation of land tenure and the mode of founding hamlets. A great deal of confusion exists in anthropological literature when writers assume that a descriptive model of kinship is a social structure or a set of sociological facts, rather than a set of principles which specify the manner in which the particular system should be organized. It is probably this fallacy that Leach points out when he makes a distinction between the ideal type and his statistical system (Leach 1961:9).

If the 'model' contains a set of principles, then one concern of empirical analysis is the manner in which these principles are applied. It would seem obvious that a strict logical implementation of our model (where complicating variables are eliminated) is impossible in reality for this would assume an isomorphism between model and data, implying a completely static, 'ideal' social structure. However, an ideal model such as ours has one use at least—it throws into relief the complicating variables that always exist in reality. Two types of variables of this sort exist—first those variables ('organizational changes') that pertain to traditional conditions for which the model was 'designed'; secondly those variables ('structural changes') to which the society has been subject, rendering the ideal model an anachronism.

Even in the most favourable traditional conditions the set of principles contained in the model cannot be applied without 'adaptation' to the existent social set up. These organizational adaptations employed in Pahala Madagama have been discussed by us. We shall give two examples of similar adaptations in other hamlets or villages of Hinidum Pattu.

(*a*) According to the principles contained in the model a hamlet is founded by an ancestor, and its residents are his descendants in the male line. Yet even for Ihala Madagama there is some evidence that the *gama* was founded by two persons from different villages. But divergence from theory is met by a 'fiction', so that the *vāsagama* descendants of these two people are viewed as if they were a single patrilineal aggregate. Similar 'fictions' are where non-*vāsagama* folk adopt the *vāsagama* name.

(*b*) In theory the name of the *gama* is the name of the founder as well as that of the hamlet. In many hamlets in the area this is the case. Take the contemporary 'village' of Mavanana. It actually contained several hamlets which now have converged into the modern village. Traditionally even at the time of the Grain Tax Mavanana was one hamlet in a cluster; it was 'owned' by members of the Mavanana Hettige *vāsagama*. Another hamlet was Godapitagama: the *vāsagama* name of the hamlet residents was Godapita Gamage. Similarly, the hamlet of Mavita nearby was the residence of Mavita Gamage people. Today these hamlets too have changed radically in character. Though this is the theory of hamlet formation it is indeed conceivable that a *gama* would be named after the *vāsagama* of the parent line. Thus there was a *gama* called Godagama in the present 'village' of Mavanana. As far as we know there are no Godagama Gamage people who are, or were, share-owners of Godagama. But the fact that it, like Godapitagama, was treated as a separate hamlet is evident from the Grain Tax register of Hinidum Pattu for 1882, which lists it as a separate 'hamlet' distinct from both Mavanana and Godapitagama. Such cases were, however, the exception rather than the rule in the Hinidum Pattu. In other areas in the low country the variation may have been greater.[1]

We have attributed to Maine, Baden-Powell and others the use of a methodological device which we have called an ideal model or type, or an indigenous model. What is the methodological status of such a 'model'? What we have called a model is not in the first place a 'theoretical model' in its scientific philosophical usage of a 'calculus of a theory'. It is also not an empirical system in the Parsonian sense of an existent social system in actual operation (or Leach's statistical system, or Weber's ideal type). It is based on a normative plan (an ideal) which the villagers hold. The informants make normative statements as to how the land tenure arrangements ideally and actually should be organized, and from these we construct a model of the system, namely a set of principles or rules and conditions for the optimum operation of the system in the absence of complicating variables. The empirical system we said always involves complicating variables. These complicating variables need not even be uniform for a particular region. In the villages environing Madagama certain cultural, demographic, genealogical, and economic variables may be differently weighted. It is precisely in this regard that the analytical construct we call 'an indigenous model' helps. By constructing a 'pure type', we were able to isolate the variables that make the actual system deviate from the pure type. It is also possible in principle to deduce hypothetical complicating variables, which in some cases may be empirically manifest.

Ours is a 'descriptive model' rather than 'theoretical model' or 'ideal type'. However, it is ideal in that it deals with pure conditions and is based on ideal norms (principles) villagers have of land tenure. Such a descriptive model differs from Weber's ideal type in two respects.

(*a*) A descriptive model such as ours is based on the cognitive plans of informants. The informants can recognize the substantive referents of the model which is not generally the case with Weber's ideal types.

(*b*) Our model is ideal in so far as it deals with principles or norms, whereas Weber was explicit that the ideal type does not deal with normative ideals in this sense (though both deal with pure conditions). In spite of the differences between the two types in formal structure and mode of construction, their methodological uses in research are similar. It will therefore be useful to compare the ideal type with the kind of descriptive model we have been employing.

An ideal type is sometimes confused with a hypothesis, theory, or a model (see Martindale 1959:58), though Weber was explicit that the ideal type was a methodological rather than a theoretical construct (1949:92).

The ideal typical concept will help to develop our skill in imputation in *research*: it *is* no 'hypothesis' but it offers guidance for the construction of hypotheses. It is not a description of reality but it gives an unambiguous means of expression of such a description. (Weber 1949:90)

Thus while hypotheses, theories, and models may deal with idealized events or pure conditions it does not seem useful to identify them with ideal types. Weber goes on to state thus:

An ideal type is formed by the one sided *accentuation* of one or more points of view and by the synthesis of a great many diffuse, discrete, more or less present and occasionally absent *concrete individual* phenomena, which are arranged according to those one sidedly emphasized viewpoints into a unified analytical construct (*Gedankenbild*). In its conceptual purity this mental construct (*Gedankenbild*) cannot be found anywhere in reality. It is a utopia. (Weber 1949:90)

By the terms 'one-sided accentuation' and 'one-sidedly emphasized viewpoint' we feel that Weber deals with the problem of construct criteria in the ideal type. There is a deliberate, *methodological* omission of empirically 'real' conditions from the ideal type. The elements ('parts', 'traits') of the ideal type are abstracted from and may even distort the social reality. The manner in which the elements are chosen and arranged is pragmatic, based entirely on the research problem which the ideal type is designed to elucidate. But the traits or elements obviously cannot be haphazardly organized; they have to be arranged 'into a consistent ideal construct by an accentuation of their essential tendencies' (Weber 1949:91). To put it differently, the elements of the type must have a logical or empirical 'fit'. Thus there is a superficial formal resemblance of an ideal type to a theory (a deductively interrelated body of laws) or a theoretical model; but with a difference. The ideal type is devoid of a *calculus*, it has no formal *nomological network*, though it must 'appear as adequate from the nomological standpoint' (Weber 1947:92); and the elements that form the type must be 'objectively possible' (1947:91). Nomological adequacy and objective possibility are quite important construct criteria. By the first term Weber meant that the type—its elements—must not flout any of the known laws of nature (Martindale 1959:70); in the second case the elements must also *in principle* be objectively (or empirically) possible (or realizable). For example, there is no natural reason why the pure conditions of the market are not objectively possible in principle. But while the substantive referents of the type are logically conceivable as empirical possibilities, they are not empirically *probable* for pure conditions do not exist in nature. Only type approximation is probable (Weber 1947:96). Hence the seemingly paradoxical nature of Weber's statement quoted earlier where he says that the ideal type in its conceptual purity is nowhere found in reality. By contrast a descriptive model like ours is closer to the social reality.

The relationship between the cognitions of individuals (or other empirical facts) and the ideal type is another aspect of type construction which Weber deals with, and is relevant to our own methodology. The gap between the ideal type and the cognitions of the masses is large. Ideas in the minds of informants are concrete and multifarious; 'it exists in the minds of an indefinite and constantly changing mass of individuals and assumes in their minds the most multifarious nuances of form or context, clarity and meaning' (Weber 1949:96). Empirically, for example, says Weber, the Christianity of the Middle Ages is many things including the feelings and cognitions of the masses, but for analytical purposes these are 'fused into an idea'. 'It is a synthesis which we could not succeed in attaining with consistency without the application of ideal type concepts' (1949:96). We too construct an idealized or purified model. But the descriptive model we employ by contrast with Weber's is closer to the cognitive map of individuals though not isomorphic with it. This is minimally the methodology that anthropologists adopt when they describe a named lineage or descent group (or our 'ideal model' of land tenure). The informants themselves have cognitions or cognitive plans; we rephrase these abstractly as part of the process of anthropological conceptualization. At this point the cognitive plans of individuals are converted into the descriptive model of the anthropologist. This, we repeat, is minimally what we do, for we may do other things in addition to this.

But ideal types or descriptive models, however constructed, are of little use unless they can generate hypotheses, institute comparisons, or facilitate causal analyses. For these purposes the ideal type must be geared to the research interests of the scientists. In terms of our ideal model of land tenure, we have eliminated complicating variables, so that we have a system in perfect equilibrium. We use the type for two major purposes:

(*a*) as a baseline for the traditional system and as a comparison with an empirical system of land tenure; and

(*b*) as a means for bringing into relief complicating variables that are always found in an operating system. Weber also justifies similar methodological uses for his ideal type. Regarding the first he says that the ideal type 'has the significance of a purely limiting concept with which the real situation or action is *compared* and surveyed for the explication of its significant components' (1949:92). The importance of the second comes out in his discussion of Gresham's law (1947:96), and of classical economic theory which he (erroneously we feel) considered to be an ideal type rather than a theory

(1947:90–112). In any case the ideal type of pure rational economic action has several methodological uses such as its comparison with the actuality, but more importantly for emphasizing non-rational variables. By

> ...throwing the discrepancy between the actual course of events and the ideal type into relief, the analysis of non-economic motives actually involved is facilitated. The more sharply and precisely the ideal type has been constructed, thus the more abstract and unrealistic in this sense it is, the better it is able to perform its methodological functions in formulating the clarification of terminology, and in the formulation of classifications and hypotheses. (Weber 1947:111)

The operations performed here are similar to what we do with our descriptive model. We have precisely and sharply, if more 'realistically' constructed our type: we place the data against the type and the complicating variables are thrown into relief. These variables are then analysed.

We do not share Leach's distrust of types as long as we know what we are doing with them. We do agree with Leach, however, in eschewing type construction for its own sake, or type reification. Our use of the model in the manner stated has permitted us to examine the structural changes that have overtaken the land tenure system of our village. This is rarely done in social anthropology, with its structural-functional bias. In social anthropology the emphasis is in general on 'static' synchronic analysis: this is a common criticism of structural-functional analysis. If diachronic analysis is conducted it is done in the manner of historical recounting (idiographically rather than nomothetically). We have adopted a method for isolating specific factors of change. Our emphasis is thus on massive, externally produced structural changes rather than internally produced organizational changes, to use Firth's useful distinction (Firth 1951:80–121). Though we do not deal with organizational change, we do show how the phenomenological referents of our model as manifest in the cognitive map of individuals are put to organizational effect. This we perform for two periods—the period up to *FA*[4] (chapter 2) and the contemporary scheme (chapter 8). Moreover, these massive changes are not specific to our village; since they are produced by external forces we have tried to assess the larger implications of these changes for Sinhalese society in general. Our assessment of the pan-Sinhalese effects of these changes are far from satisfactory, hampered as we have been by the unavailability of relevant documentary and field work data. But we believe that it is possible to assess the impact of these changes more precisely when we do eventually have access to such data.

We have demonstrated that drastic social changes have occurred in Madagama; similar if not identical changes have taken place elsewhere. Yet social anthropological studies in Ceylon have looked at Sinhalese social structure as if such changes had not occurred. Yalman has studied kinship, marriage and land tenure in a village in the Walapane Division (Yalman 1958: 1962). This is precisely one of the areas where the effects of the Grain Tax were acutely felt (see pp. 116–20). Yet in his analyses he speaks of the Sinhalese kindred, kinship, marriage and land tenure assuming that what he writes is applicable to Sinhalese society in general. Hardly any attempt is made to investigate whether Terutenne is Terutenne today because of important structural changes that have occurred in its social structure. Yalman's methodology is adequate if one is interested in studying Terutenne of 1958; in which case one can talk only of Terutenne kinship, etc., in 1958 not of *Sinhalese* kinship. A study of the social structure of Sinhalese villages calls for a study of change. It is difficult for us to believe that the changes in landownership in this area had no effects on the social structure of the villages. Fisher, writing of the adjacent Udukinda Division where similar changes occurred in the Grain Tax period, says that feudal relations between chiefs and villagers were severely strained; old loyalties had disappeared. 'This change of sentiment had been brought about by the fact that the chiefs had been largely concerned with the purchase of confiscated lands...' (S.P. IV, 1891:2). The villages have been invaded by Moslems and low countrymen and general signs of poverty in a once prosperous area are seen everywhere. 'In brief the old Kandyan Feudal system and village life have broken up and are rapidly disappearing' (S.P. IV, 1891:3). Surely in such a situation a diachronic assessment of changes is called for as a prerequisite for synchronic analysis?

The same methodological difference exists between Leach's study of Pul Eliya and our study of Madagama. Leach eschews diachronic analysis: he explicitly states that his is a study of Pul Eliya in 1954. The diachronic depth of his study merely leads up to the study of contemporary Pul Eliya. It is not designed to elucidate change. Yet it seems quite clear that Pul Eliya has undergone considerable changes. It is difficult for us to imagine the eradication of malaria not having had important implications for change—to use a simple example. Though Leach superbly deals with 'organizational' factors ('how people manipulate the system'), we find his statistical system a precariously equilibrated exchange model of society. This is no condemnation of the model, except that it is clear to us that the precarious equilibrium of Pul Eliya in 1954 is a product of several factors of change through generations which have been neglected in the analysis. Let me quote:

> The allegedly baneful and extortionate activities of the village trader are an important factor in bringing about a constant change in the economic status of particular households. From the social point of view this must be considered a positive function. Without some such equalizing mechanism the community would cease to be homogeneous in terms of economic class, and would probably disintegrate altogether.
>
> (Leach 1961:176)

Land in Pul Eliya falls often into the hands of Tamil or Moslem traders. But since these buyers are traders rather than cultivators they are likely to sell the land back at first opportunity to a local villager. Thus land always remains with the corporate *varigē*, though it may pass from one individual or compound group to another (Leach 1961:130).

The antecedents of this type of analysis come from Mauss through Lévi-Strauss. A system of social action is viewed as a series of reciprocal exchanges which keep it in equilibrium, contrary to Leach's own denial (Leach 1961:299). A change in the direction of exchange results in the disintegration of the system. Hence Pul Eliya society depends for its continuity on the Tamil trader: take him away and the society disintegrates. The whole system is pivoted on a single role (or its functional equivalent). It is highly doubtful whether a human community is that vulnerable. What in fact Leach does, we feel, is to compound two levels of analysis: (*a*) a system model of equilibrated exchanges; and (*b*) an empirical existent human community. The disappearance of the trader, as a unit in a system model, does not destroy the existent human community. The human community may change, readjust, and experience structural or organizational changes. A unilateral direction of exchange destroys not so much the community but the model.

If Pul Eliya society, according to Leach, depended for its continuity on its Moslem and Tamil traders, no such historical accident occurred in Madagama. Here, as in many other low country villages, the traders are Sinhalese. Furthermore, land sales were to wealthy outside kin groups (*pelāntiya*) interested in keeping the property themselves. Land leaves the hamlet kin corporation permanently, altering consequently the power structure of the society. The landlords are, however, much less extortionate than Pul Eliya ones. Says Leach:

> When *ukas* and *andē* contracts are examined individually the terms seem excessively onerous; how can the cultivator possibly afford to pay such rates of interest? But seen in the larger context of contractual relations between affinal kin we see that the economic burdens of indebtedness cancel out. What Peter owes Paul, Paul, for some quite different reason, owes to Peter. The residue of the total pattern is not an impossible burden of debt, but an extremely dense mesh of reciprocal indebtedness which binds together the members of the *varigē*. (1961:140–1)

In contemporary Madagama what is impressive is the unilateral direction of service, the lack of reciprocity in exchange relationships. What Peter owes Paul, Paul assiduously retains; Peter is thus left dependent on Paul. It is possible to stretch one's imagination and think of this too as an exchange relationship. One may say while Paul buys land from Peter, he retains title and ownership and allows Peter usufruct of it in exchange for formal homage. This would oversimplify the complexity of the social facts, for what is exchanged are items whose value and cathexes are radically different. Both Peter and Paul prize land ownership very highly: when Peter loses his land and retains a hazardous usufruct he has made a bad bargain. Moreover, at partition even this may go with the total 'disintegration' of the traditional land tenure system. But even if the land tenure system 'disintegrates' it does not involve the disintegration of the whole community. The society has changed, however radically. These changes do not come suddenly, but through a long period. For example, the Roman-Dutch law was first implemented in the 1830's: it seeped into the village about eighty years after. Moreover, with the radical changes that have come over the society since its founding new subsystems have come into existence—a *peläntiya*, a share market. They continue to exist as more or less viable social structures.

There is an important point of agreement between Leach's thesis and ours. Madagama too affirms the thesis that 'kinship is not a thing in itself' (Leach 1961:305). Such a position is entirely consonant with the intellectual tradition of Maine and his 'school'. This statement of Leach's indeed illustrates a fundamental point of agreement between Leach's thesis and ours and the whole tradition of writing we have mentioned. *Vāsagama* genealogies are viewed by us as charters of rights: conflicting genealogies represent a dialectic of conflict. Status groups like *pelāntiyas* if viewed as kinship units are not things in themselves. What holds the *pelāntiya* together is the ideology of feudalism which is articulated with the power and prestige motives of individuals. Kinsmen carrying the *pelāntiya* name are lopped off if they cannot retain the *pelāntiya* style of life. *Vāsagama* or *pelāntiya* kinship identity *per se* is of limited sociological significance. This thesis could be spelled out further in respect of *vāsagamas*.

In theory when a hamlet (*gama*) reaches a certain population load or peak, men may leave their parent hamlets and found new hamlets elsewhere. This may be the action of a single individual and his sons, a group of siblings, or probably any group of kinsmen. The important fact is that they conceive of themselves as founding and belonging to a theoretically exogamous 'patriline' within a subcaste, called a *vāsagama*. Present hamlet residents generally view their *vāsagama* as founded by a single ancestor. One could note at the very outset that this is very different from 'lineage fission' characteristic of many simple societies where kinship forms the structural base of the social system. In such societies the segmented unit forms part of a larger maximal lineage or a part of still larger unilineal organization of kinsmen like a clan. In the Sinhalese hamlets of Hinidum Pattu, where subcaste rather than clan or other maximal unilinear kinship units constituted the basis of social organization of the region, a different set of principles operates. When an ancestor leaves his parent hamlet and *vāsagama* and founds a new one he severs connexions with the former. He founds a new one which has no structural or terminological connexions with the parent line. It is not so much a fissioning of a lineage but the founding of a new *vāsagama* that has occurred. However, if kinship connexions with the parent line have been severed, the subcaste connexions are maintained, for when a person founds a new 'line' he retains his subcaste identity. His *vāsagama*, and the *vāsagama* of his descendants through the male line, as mentioned in chapter 2, is a conjunction of the newly founded 'patriline' and traditional subcaste name. The continuity of the subcaste is clearly more important than the continuity of unilineal groupings through time. It is the subcaste that establishes the status of the *line*, rather than the line in any significant way enhancing the status of the subcaste.

When we agree with Leach that 'kinship is not a thing in itself', we do not assume the lack of importance of kinship sentiment in social interaction. Unilinearity *per se* is not very important, even less important than with Indian Brahmin groups with their strong patrilineal ideology and patrilineal ancestor worship. Unilinearity is a framework for the organization of a landed estate (*gama*), the devolution of rights in respect of that estate, and the operation of its land tenure system. Furthermore, the 'line' is in theory synonymous with the name of the estate or *gama* which in turn may be synonymous with a residential group or hamlet. If the 'patrilineal line' denotes a named *gama* rather than a fissioned kin group, then it would seem desirable to give the newly formed *gama* a new name, rather than treat it as an extension of the old parent line (which may result in the confusion of property rights). Finally it should be noted that traditionally when a person founds a new *gama* he owes no jural obligation to his own kinsmen. His legal rights are vested in him by the feudal state or some traditionally constituted political authority representing the central government, or through prescriptive ownership after a period of time. The area of land (*gama*) which is legally his is a distinct structural entity requiring a new name rather than a duplication or extension of the *gama* and 'line' of his father in which he originally had residential and *pravēni* rights.

Thus it would seem that the name given to the 'line' is not based on kinship choices but on land rights. The name of the *gama* is the name of the 'line' rather than vice versa. The patrilineal name is simultaneously a kinship name as well as that of an estate but the name originated in respect of ownership of a landed estate rather than through kinship factors. In theory there could be no formation of a new named 'patriline' without an ownership of a *gama*. Once an estate or *gama* is founded patrilinearity is the framework for its organization and operation Thus the primary structural significance of unilinearity is that it provides a charter for the organization of rights in land. When the structural nexus between unilinearity and land tenure loses its importance the 'line' and *vāsagama* merge into 'a status line', that is, a unilineal classification of kinsmen with a vague ideology of common descent. It simply becomes an aggregation of individuals bearing a common name and has little sociological significance. This is what has happened in most part of the Sinhalese low country, so that it becomes easy for a sociologist like Ryan and an ethnologist like Raghavan to confuse these with clans and similar unilineal groupings.

Ideally a *vāsagama* is a corporate group of patrilineal kinsmen owning shares (*pangu*) in a *gama*. The corporate character of the *vāsagama* lies in its embodiment in an estate. Marriage and other factors, however, may result, even under traditional conditions in non-*vāsagama* members having shares in the *gama*. Thus though a *vāsagama* may ideally constitute a corporate hamlet, non-*vāsagama* kinsmen may become members of the hamlet by virtue of share ownership in the *gama*. It is here that the concept of *gamē minissu* (citizens of the *gama*) is important. *Vāsagama* expresses the ideal corporate structure of the hamlet, *gamē minissu*, the real corporate hamlet structure. Under the conditions of change we have described there are more non-*vāsagama* citizens in the corporate hamlet. Traditionally these would be in the main confined to *binna* married inlaws, and their descendants who could adopt the *vāsagama* name, as P. M. G. Singho Appu and his siblings did in branch *U*. When outsiders buy shares in the hamlet as they have done recently, they are also converted into affines through marriages with resident shareholders of the hamlet. To summarize, ideally a *vāsagama* is a corporation; in fact all those who own shares in the *gama* are members of a corporate hamlet (*gamē minissu*). Always, however, the *taṭṭumāru* scheme of land tenure is organized in reference to a *vāsagama* genealogy, and not the genealogy of non-*vāsagama* citizens of the hamlet.

We have described the structure of *vāsagamas*, previously undescribed for Ceylon. We have also shown the change in *vāsagamas* through the operation of the factors of change through time. As a result the power structure of the society changes too; new kin groups like *pelāntiyas* come into existence. We have described the structure of these previously unrecorded kin groups. These social changes also produce extreme share fractioning. Though share fractioning has been noted for South and South-East Asian societies ours is probably one of the most detailed, systematic studies of the subject. Share fractioning creates a share market. We have described the structure of the share market and its unique type of rational action, and special entrepreneurial and 'account book' mentality. This combined with the drastic residential changes due to the ejection of males from overcrowded hamlets have considerable implications, we feel, for economic development (or chaos) in the area. Though we have dealt briefly with kinship and marriage, these are largely in relation to changes in land tenure. A larger treatment of the subject though desirable would have been outside the scope of this work.

One would expect considerable social discontent to arise out of the conditions described in this book. This is indeed the case. But overt conflict is much less than the covert pervasive distrust or conflict that are manifest in social action. What impresses us is that in spite of tremendous social changes, there is a continuing normative rationalization of action. Even when individuals act in terms of self-interest, or when conflict between kinsmen occurs, action has to be normatively justified. Pure non-normative individualism occurs but rarely. This is not to say that action occurs smoothly and harmoniously. Conflict is endemic. We have illustrated some of the forms conflict takes in this society in previous chapters. Let us illustrate further a typical though extreme case of 'conflict' in respect of *goḍa iḍam* (high land).

In our work we have largely ignored the tenure of *goḍa iḍam*. One important difference in respect of undivided ownership of *goḍa iḍam* and paddy lands is that for the latter strict share implementation in cultivation (subdivision) is an economically impossible proposition. This is not always the case with *goḍa iḍam*. I have seen a single jak fruit divided into four or five portions distributed among shareholders in several villages in the Sinhalese low country (though not in Madagama). Even in Madagama conflict over *goḍa iḍam* was more common than that over *maḍa iḍam*. Let us illustrate with an example the type of conflict endemic in undivided ownership of *goḍa iḍam*. A few years ago the village headman of Neluva, whose *peläntiya* owned the largest number of shares in Ihala Madagama, felled five jak trees in an enclosed plot of high land (*koraṭu*) known as *baduwatte*. He wanted them for building purposes, but had hoped to divide them among the rest of the shareholders, he told us. This action offended I. M. G. Amaris and I. M. G. Kartelis, who retaliated by cutting down five jak trees each. When the small shareholders saw 'their' trees being felled by those who held large shares, they too started to hew down the remaining trees. Now there are no more jak trees left in *baduwatte*.

The point of the tale is that there is considerable social discontent in Madagama. Yet on the credit side the Rural Development Society of Madagama, under its energetic secretary built a new primary (grade) school entirely through village efforts, paid a teacher for a period of six months, and provided midday buns for its children. After its survival for six months the policy of the government is to take over a school founded by villagers. This the government did, and now Madagama has a village school with three teachers, including an English teacher (an affinal relation of the secretary of the Rural Development Society!). The Society also banned gambling and drinking in the village, with fair effectiveness. Though we would indeed question the unconscious motivations for such altruistic behaviour, we are nevertheless impressed by the capacity of norms to exercise constraints on social action.

This is where we disagree with Leach's generalization that the constraints of economics are prior to the constraints of morality and law. It is true that economic factors are crucial to the formation, maintenance and continuity of social systems. Since Marx and Weber we are aware of the causal importance of economics (*a*) in the formation of social systems, (*b*) as instigators of social action in any ongoing society. But a distinction has to be made between the formation of social systems and the causes of social action in any society. Social systems like classes, castes or *vāsagamas* may be structured primarily on an economic base; or on a basis of an ideology in conjunction with power motives, as with *peläntiya* type status groups. The *instigators* of social action may be primarily economic, or due to prestige and power motives, depending on the context of action. But whether instigated by primarily economic, prestige or power motives, social action is rarely a direct behavioural 'reflex' of these motives. In Madagama, in spite of the tremendous social discontent, action is constrained by morality and law. In spite of the existence of contradictory norms action continues largely to be conducted normatively. There has to be a continuous normative rationalization of action. Madagama lies near the huge tropical Sinharaja forest. Periodically elephants crash through the human barricades and ravage the crops ripening on green stalks of paddy. But the law of the jungle is outside the human pale. Fang and claw have been blunted by the normatively rationalized competitive ethos of the human social order.

APPENDIX

THE GRAIN TAX ORDINANCE OF 1878

PART I

4. THE word 'grain', when used in this Ordinance, shall mean such grain or produce as at the date of Part I of this Ordinance coming into operation is by law, custom or usage (whether general or local) subject to the payment of any tax, duty or share to Government.

The word 'paddy' shall include every description of paddy except what is commonly known as 'el-wi' or 'hill-paddy'.

The expression 'dry grain' shall mean and include every description of grain or produce other than paddy, which is subject, at the date of Part I of this Ordinance coming into operation to grain-tax.

The expression 'grain-tax' shall mean the tax, duty, or share due to Government in respect of grain grown in this Island.

Persons entitled to cultivate any land in 'tattumaru' shall be deemed for the purposes of this Ordinance joint owners of such land.

5. FROM and after the time when Part II of this Ordinance shall come into operation in any district there shall continue to be levied by and payable to Government such grain-tax as by law, custom or usage (whether general or local) was theretofore levied or payable; but the grain-tax due in respect of the produce of each field or parcel of land liable thereto shall be commuted either—

(1) For a fixed sum payable annually; or

(2) For a fixed sum payable in those years only in which the field or parcel of land produces a crop; or

(3) For a sum varying with the estimated value of the crop and payable in those years only in which the field or parcel of land produces a crop.

Such fixed sum payable annually is hereinafter termed 'annual-commutation'.

Such fixed sum payable in those years only in which the field or parcel of land produces a crop is hereinafter termed 'crop-commutation'.

Such sum varying with the estimated value of the crop and payable in those years only in which the field or parcel of land produces a crop is hereinafter termed 'grain-duty'.

Whether 'annual-commutation', 'crop commutation' or 'grain-duty' is to be paid in respect of the produce of any field or parcel of land, the produce of which is liable to grain-tax, and the amount of annual-commutation, crop-commutation or grain duty so payable, shall be determined in manner hereinafter appearing.

6. AS soon as the proclamation bringing Part II of this Ordinance into operation in any district at the future date therein mentioned shall have been published in the *Gazette*, it shall be lawful for the Governor to appoint for such district an officer or officers, not exceeding three in number, to be styled 'The Grain Commissioner' or 'The Grain Commissioners' of such district, and such Commissioner or Commissioners at any time or from time to time to remove and another or others to appoint in his or their place or respective places. The Governor may also diminish the number of Grain Commissioners for any district or districts. Such Commissioners shall hold their office during the Governor's pleasure and shall receive such remuneration as the Governor shall, with the advice of the Executive Council, determine.

Such Commissioner or Commissioners may employ any persons to act as his or their assistants or as assessors or valuators for the purpose of assisting him or them in carrying out the purposes of this Ordinance. Such assistants, assessors or valuators shall be paid such remuneration by the Government for their services as the Governor shall determine.

7. IN all cases of paddy cultivation it shall be optional with the owner of the land, the produce whereof is liable to grain-tax, to elect whether annual-commutation or crop-commutation shall be payable in respect of such produce.

Such election shall be made within such reasonable time as the Grain-Commissioner or Grain-Commissioners shall appoint in that behalf, and shall be final.

If no such election shall be made within the time appointed in that behalf, the Commissioner or Commissioners shall, with as little delay as possible, determine in which of the two modes above mentioned the grain-tax in respect of the produce of any land, as to which no such election has been made, shall be payable, and such determination shall be final.

When the land belongs to several owners who cannot agree as to the mode in which the grain-tax shall be payable, the Commissioner or Commissioners shall determine the same, and such determination shall be final.

Where in any case the ownership of any land is in dispute or doubtful, the Commissioner or Commissioners shall determine who is entitled to exercise the option of choosing the mode in which the grain-tax in respect of the produce of such land shall be payable, and such determination shall be final.

8. THE amount of annual-commutation payable in respect of the produce of any field or parcel of land may be determined by agreement between the owners of the land and the Commissioner or Commissioners, in which case such agreement shall be binding upon all persons then or thereafter becoming interested in the land.

If the ownership of the land is in dispute or doubtful, the Commissioner or Commissioners shall determine who is the owner of the land for the purpose of such agreement, and such determination shall be final.

If no such agreement can be entered into, the amount of annual-commutation shall be determined as follows:—

The Commissioner or Commissioners shall ascertain, with as much accuracy as practicable, the average annual yield of paddy of such field or parcel of land during the fourteen years next preceding the date of enquiry, or if the land shall have been brought into cultivation for the first time within such fourteen years, then during the time between the date of such first cultivation and the date of enquiry; and the value in money of the customary proportion due by way of grain-tax of such average annual yield, after a deduction therefrom of ten percent, shall be the annual-commutation payable yearly in respect of such field or parcel of land. PROVIDED that it shall be lawful for the Commissioner or Commissioners, in determining the amount of annual-commutation to take into consideration any exceptional circumstances which may reasonably be expected to reduce or to increase the average yield of the said field or parcel of land, and in such cases to reduce or to increase accordingly the rate of annual-commutation payable in respect of such field or parcel of land.

For the purposes of this section the average price of paddy per bushel prevailing in the district, in which the land is situated, during the fourteen years preceding the enquiry shall, so far as the same is ascertainable, be deemed to be the value of paddy per bushel.

9. THE amount of crop-commutation payable in respect of the produce of any field or parcel of land shall be determined as follows:—

The Commissioner or Commissioners shall ascertain, with as much accuracy as practicable, the average annual yield of paddy of such field or parcel of land in those years in which the land has produced a crop, during the fourteen years next preceding the date of enquiry. And the value in money of the proportion due to Government by way of grain-tax of such average annual yield shall be taken as the amount of crop-commutation to be paid in respect of the produce of such field or parcel of land.

For the purpose of this section the average prices per bushel of paddy prevailing in the district, in which the land is situated, during the seven years preceding the enquiry shall be taken as the value of paddy per bushel.

No field or parcel of land shall for the purpose of this section be deemed to have produced a crop in any year unless the yield for such year has been three-fold at least on the quantity of paddy sown.

If any question shall arise whether or not the yield of any field or parcel of land has in any year been three-fold at least on the quantity sown, the decision of the Commissioner or Commissioners thereupon shall be final.

10. IN case the owner of any field or parcel of land shall be dissatisfied with the determination of the Commissioner or Commissioners in respect of the amount of the annual-commutation or of the crop-commutation fixed in respect of such land under either of the two last preceding sections, such party may within one month after the date of the decision of the Commissioner or Commissioners appeal therefrom to the Government Agent of the province, in which the field or parcel of land in question is situated, who may give such relief in the premises to the party so appealing as such Government Agent may deem expedient; and the decision of the Government Agent, unless an appeal be taken therefrom to the Governor and Executive Council, within one month, shall be final. If the appellant should be dissatisfied with the decision of the Government Agent, an appeal shall lie therefrom to the Governor and Executive Council, whose decision thereon shall be final and conclusive. In any case where the Government Agent of the province or any of his Assistants may be acting as Commissioner under this Ordinance, an appeal, if taken within one month, shall lie from his decision to the Governor and Executive Council, whose decision shall be final and conclusive. In the event of any such appeal being taken as provided by this section, the entries in the register provided for by the following section shall, if necessary, be altered or amended in accordance with the final decision or order.

11. THE Commissioner or Commissioners shall enter in a register to be kept for each district to be brought under the operation of Part II of this Ordinance the following particulars, to be inserted in parallel columns:—

(1) The name of each field or parcel of land in such district, in respect of which annual-commutation or crop-commutation is payable, with such description as to secure identification;

(2) The name or names of the reputed owner or owners of such field or parcel of land;

(3) The proportion of the produce of each field or parcel of land heretofore due to Government by way of grain-tax;

(4) Whether annual-commutation or crop-commutation is thenceforth payable in respect of such field or parcel of land;

(5) The amount of annual-commutation or crop-commutation as the case may be, payable in respect of each such field or parcel of land.

There shall be a distinct folio or distinct folios for each village.

Each entry in the register shall be duly dated at the time of making the same.

The entries in such register shall be conclusive evidence for the purposes of this Ordinance of all the facts entered therein.

PROVIDED however that, if any person interested in any land mentioned in such register shall be aggrieved at the entry of the proportion of the produce heretofore due to Government by way of grain-tax, it shall be lawful for such person at any time within six months of the date of such entry or insertion to institute a suit against the Government in any competent civil court to have such entry or insertion amended or altered, and such court shall have power, subject to appeal to the Supreme Court, to make such order in the premises and to award such costs as the justice of the case may require.

PROVIDED also that it shall be lawful for the Governors acting with the advice of the Executive Council, at the instance of any party interested therein, to correct any error or defect in such register.

Such register shall be kept in the English language with each English word translated into its equivalent in the native language most prevalent in the district, and shall be open for inspection by all persons interested therein at all reasonable hours at the Kachcheri of the district in which the fields or parcels of land therein entered are situated.

Any person interested in any field or parcel of land entered in the register shall be entitled to a copy of the entry relating to such field or parcel of land, certified by the Government Agent or some Assistant to such Government Agent. And any copy so certified as aforesaid shall be admissible in evidence in any court in the same manner and to the same extent as the register would be admissible in evidence, if duly produced.

13. GRAIN-DUTY, unless commuted by special agreement, shall be payable in respect of the produce of all lands sown with dry grain. Within fifteen days from the sowing of any land with dry-grain, it shall be the duty of the owner or cultivator to give notice thereof and of the extent of the land sown to the Government Agent or some Assistant to the Government Agent of the province wherein the land is situated, or to some officer to be nominated by the Government Agent in that behalf, and such Government Agent or Assistant shall direct some headman, of rank not below a Muhandiram, Korala or Udaiyar, to make a fair assessment of the probable value of the crop when cut, and the share

due to Government by way of grain-tax shall be forthwith payable in money to the Government, and the Government Agent or Assistant Government Agent shall give a proper receipt for the same, when paid. Any person dissatisfied with the assessment of the headman shall be entitled to appeal therefrom to the Government Agent whose decision thereon shall be final. Any owner or cultivator of any land sown with dry-grain, who shall fail to give such notice of sowing as aforesaid shall be guilty of an offence and liable to a fine not exceeding fifty rupees.

It shall be the duty of the person receiving such notice to give a written acknowledgement of such receipt to the person giving the notice; and such written acknowledgement shall be the best evidence of such notice having been given.

In any prosecution under this section it shall be incumbent upon the defendant to prove that such notice was duly given, and not upon the prosecutor to prove that such notice was not given.

If no notice of the sowing shall have been given as hereinbefore required, and the crop shall have been cut without any assessment having been made as aforesaid, such Government Agent or Assistant as aforesaid shall direct some headman of the rank aforesaid to assess the grain-duty payable in respect of such crop; and such headman shall, after making such enquiry as he may deem necessary, make an assessment of such grain-duty; and such assessment shall be binding and conclusive for all the purposes of this Ordinance.

PART II

14. THE tax, duty or share due to Government in respect of grain shall be payable as hereinbefore provided, and shall not be farmed or rented from Government by any person or persons whomsoever.

16. THE annual-commutation or the crop-commutation payable in respect of the produce of any land shall be paid by the owner or the party for the time being in possession of the land to the Government Agent or some Assistant to the Government Agent of the province in which the land is situated, who shall give a proper receipt for the same.

The annual-commutation shall be paid on or before the thirty-first day of March in each year, unless the Governor, acting with the advice of the Executive Council, shall appoint some later date in each year for such payment in any specified district or districts, in which case it shall be payable on such later date; and the crop-commutation payable in respect of any land shall be paid each year as soon as the first crop of such land for the year shall be cut, but shall not be payable during those years in which the land does not produce a crop of paddy.

For the purpose of this section no field or parcel of land shall be deemed to have produced a crop, unless the yield shall be three-fold at least on the quantity of paddy sown.

PROVIDED always that no land shall be deemed to have produced less than three-fold on the quantity sown, unless due notice of a claim for exemption from payment of grain-tax in respect of such land shall have been given twenty-one days at least before the crop is cut to the Government Agent or Assistant aforesaid or to some officer appointed by such Government Agent or Assistant in that behalf. And it shall be the duty of the person receiving such notice to give a written acknowledgment of such receipt; and such written acknowledgment shall be the best evidence of such notice having been given.

Upon the receipt of such notice such Government Agent or Assistant or officer aforesaid shall after due enquiry determine whether such field or parcel has produced at least three-fold or not, and his determination shall be final.

18. IF the amount due for annual-commutation, crop-commutation or grain-duty is not paid, as soon as the same is due, either to the Government Agent or some Assistant to the Government Agent of the province in which the land in respect of the produce of which such annual-commutation, crop-commutation or grain-duty is payable, or to some collector authorized in writing by such Government Agent or Assistant Government Agent to collect or receive the same, it shall be lawful for such Government Agent, Assistant or collector to seize the land, in respect of which the annual-commutation, crop-commutation or grain-duty is due, or any crop or produce thereof, or any moveable property thereon, to whomsoever such land or moveable property may belong, anything in the Ordinance No. 6 of 1873, entitled *An Ordinance to prescribe the order in which the property of public defaulters may, in certain cases, be seized and sold*, to the contrary notwithstanding; and if the amount due on account of such annual-commutation, crop-commutation or grain-duty, together with the costs and charges payable under section twenty, shall not be sooner paid or tendered, to sell the property so seized by public auction at any time not less than twenty days from the time of such seizure. Such annual-commutation, crop-commutation, or grain-duty shall be a first charge upon the land in respect of the produce whereof the same shall be due.

26. THE annual-commutation or crop-commutation fixed or determined under the provisions of this Ordinance in respect of any field or parcel of land shall be revised by the Grain-Commissioner or Grain-Commissioners for the time being at the expiration of seven years from the date of the same becoming first payable, and thereafter at the ex-

piration of every seven years. At each such revision it shall be lawful for such Commissioner or Commissioners to increase or reduce the annual-commutation or crop-commutation payable in respect of any field or parcel of land, if any exceptional circumstances shall have arisen, which may in his or their opinion be reasonably expected to reduce or increase the value of the produce of such field or parcel of land or render more uncertain or less uncertain the probable yield thereof.

It shall also be competent for the owner of the land at any such revision to make his election whether annual-commutation or crop-commutation shall be thenceforth payable.

The revision of the Commissioner or Commissioners shall be subject to appeal to the Government Agent and his decision shall be subject to appeal to the Governor and Executive Council in the same manner and to the same extent and with the same effect as is provided for appeals by section ten.

Such revised annual-commutation or crop-commutation shall be duly entered in the register mentioned in section eleven, and shall become subject in all respects to the provisions of this Ordinance in the same manner as the annual-commutation or crop-commutation originally payable thereunder.

NOTES

CHAPTER 4, pp. 61–97

1 The position here is completely in accord with traditional law. Armour (1960:58–9) states that if a son recovers the family property sold by his father he is entitled to half-share only.

CHAPTER 5, pp. 98–143

1 The census of 1911 states that there were 26 families and 79 persons in Madagama, giving an average of about 3·0 per family. This seems hardly plausible. We do not know how the term 'family' was construed by the early Census enumerators. It is likely that they included old couples and single old persons in generation *FA* 4 as separate families. Our reconstruction that there were 14 families with 5·6 persons per family makes more sense.

CHAPTER 7, pp. 165–188

1 In 1926 the Government Agent Southern Province notes that 'Partition still forms the main subject of litigation. Partition cases are extremely dull and wading through the ramifications of pedigrees must in itself be a wearisome task. In one case the final division of land among the numberless co-owners is said to have resulted in fractions with a lowest common denominator of over 2,000,000. The use of the Court for the partition of lands as a hobby in this district appears to take the place of football grounds and picture palaces elsewhere.'

2 Similarly P. L. Peter transferred a share of $\frac{1}{36}$ to S. D. Boris. However, the records 'mistakenly' put it as $\frac{1}{32}$.

CHAPTER 9, pp. 211–247

1 The fact that in theory the King owned all land led early writers to distinguish between feudalism of the European variety, and authority stemming from 'allodial' possessions. In evolutionary perspective the latter, it was held, was anterior to baronial feudalism. In Europe the actual lords of the soil were the feudal lords. I think the distinction is a useful one, and the allodial base of Indian type feudalism is crucial to an understanding of the political basis of the caste system.

2 It is probable that the indiscriminate use of the term *vāsagama* was facilitated by the British who introduced the notion of a '*ge* name'. The erroneous notion that people of Ceylon had *ge* names was based on the fact that *vasāgama*, *gedera*, *paṭabändi*, and other types of 'surnames' often contained the suffix *ge*, which meant the genitive 'of' or 'belonging to' rather than the synonym 'house' (*ge*), as the bureaucracy conceived it. Since the low country *vāsagamas* were the most familiar type of '*ge* name', the two notions were fused into one by a process of bureaucratic logic.

3 See also Yalman (1961) for name changing in relation to caste.

4 Consider the extensive properties owned by five select members of this *peläntiya*. We include only those properties owned in village and hamlet *pravēni* lands; and by no means all.

Property owned by peläntiya folk in pravēni lands

S. D. Pitchoris	
Batuwangala	6 acres of tea and rubber; 24 k of paddy; 1½ acres of garden land; Many scattered shares
Mavita	2 acres of rubber
Danawala	5 acres of rubber; ⅛ of hamlet paddy lands
Ambelegedera	36 k paddy; 2 acres tea and rubber
Lelwala	20 acres of tea, rubber and paddy land
Talangalla	14 k paddy
Mavanana	72 k paddy
S. D. Boris	
Lelwala	7 acres tea and rubber
Danawala	1 acre *goḍa*
Neluva	7 k paddy
Madagama	72 k paddy; 3 acres rubber and 1 acre tea
S. D. Andiris	
Opata	1½ acres paddy and some garden; 2 acres rubber
Warukandeniya	3 acres rubber
Lelwala	3 acres garden; 7 k paddy
Danawala	1 acre garden
Batuwangala	6 k paddy
Neluva	14 k paddy
P. L. Peter	
Lelwala	220 k paddy; 6 acres rubber
Warukandeniya	*goḍa* and *mada*
Kadihingala	*goḍa* and *mada*
Pannimulla	42 k; 3 acres *goḍa*
Mavanana	7 k paddy
S. D. Theris	
Navalahena	4 acres rubber and tea
Ambelegedera	24 k paddy; 3 acres tea
Mavanana	28 k paddy; 1 acre *goḍa*

5 Weber's opposition between the economically determined class groupings and status groups has a much wider applicability. One could speak of groups formed primarily on an economic base and groups formed on a status (ideology cum motive) base. When rephrased in this manner the two notions link up remarkably well with Durkheim's 'organic' and 'mechanical' solidarity. The basis of solidarity of economically determined groups is 'organic'; that of status groups is 'mechanical'.

Notes

CHAPTER 10, pp. 248–272

1 *Avassa* is used in the sense employed by us in the Sinhalese version of the *Niti Niganduva*. The English version is vague owing to terminological difficulties.

2 Since these marriages are, to say the least, unusual it is worth considering whether there is traditional precedent for similar cross-genera-

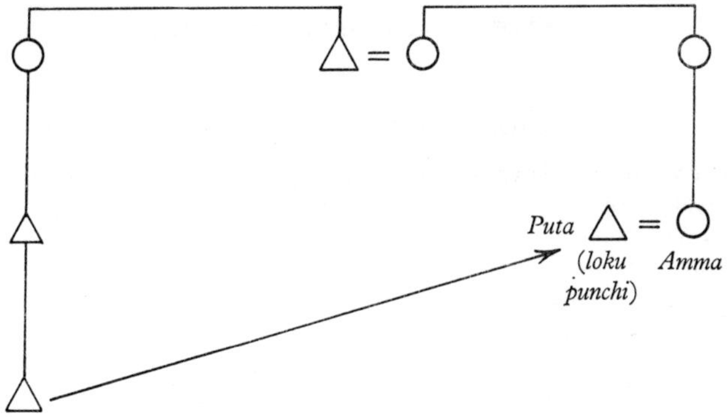

Classificatory mother–son marriage.

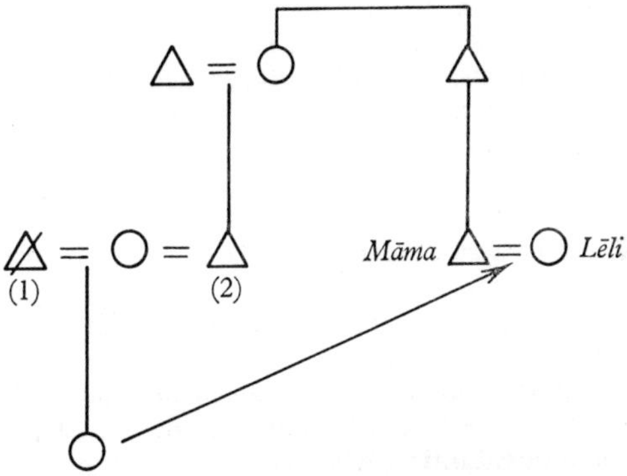

Classificatory mother's brother–sister's daughter marriage.

tion marriages. The Sinhalese version of the *Niti Niganduva* gives three cases of cross-generation marriages between kinsmen which are 'permitted' (*Niti Niganduva*, 1879:21–2). No details or qualifications are made regarding these marriages in the *Niti Niganduva* so that at best the conclusion that one can draw is that certain types of cross-generation marriages between kinsmen were 'permitted' traditionally.

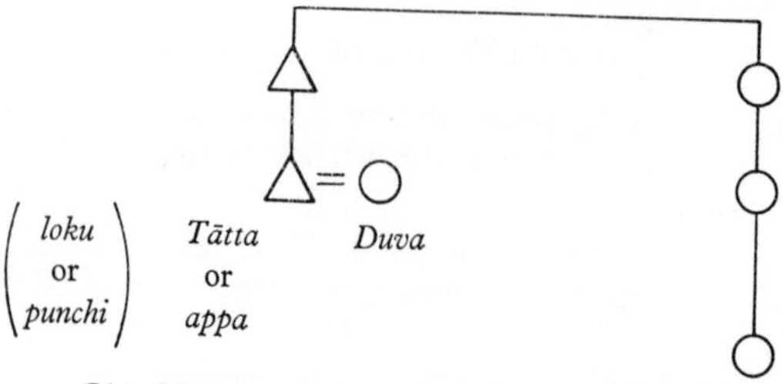

Classificatory father–daughter marriage.

CHAPTER II, pp. 273–296

1 The reason for this variation can only be an 'intelligent guess' owing to the scanty evidence regarding land tenure in other parts of the low country. We noted in chapter 1 that the type of land tenure system of Madagama was peculiarly suited to the ecology of Hinidum Pattu, and parts of the Western, Southern and Sabaragamuva Provinces adjoining it. Here the mountainous, undulating country with heavy rainfall was suited for the formation of *yāyas* (stretches of paddy field) of about fifteen to twenty acres in the valleys. Larger acreages could not be brought into cultivation owing to the nature of the physical terrain. It was thus conducive to the formation of small hamlets clustering around small *yāyas*. The terrain was not as steep as in the Kandyan Highlands, so that terraced fields did not exist; it was not completely flat and open as in the areas adjoining the coast in the low country. In the Kandyan area the physical terrain was such that the 'estate' perforce had to be small; thus the structural equivalent of the *vāsagama* is the Kandyan *gedera* described by Tambiah (1958). In the flat areas of the low country the *yāyas* could be much larger; *vāsagamas* also existed in the area. This could mean several things.

(*a*) The *vāsagama* was associated with a larger hamlet capable of holding more people or,

(*b*) the *yāya* was split into several 'estates' each associated with a separate vasagama, or

(*c*) each village contained several *vāsagamas* each *vāsagama* being associated with a separate 'estate' whether named or not.

These are some possibilities; whether they in fact prevailed or not we do not know. We do know however that most land in the low country was held in undivided shares; that some form of 'tattumaru' prevailed and that *vāsagamas* as named patrilateral aggregates existed and still exist today. The likelihood is that some modified form of the system in Hinidum Pattu prevailed in these areas too.

BIBLIOGRAPHY

Andrews, Robert (1917). 'Diary of an Embassy from the Government of Fort St. George to the Court of Candia in the Year 1795.' Ed. J. P. Lewis. *Journal of the Ceylon Branch of the Royal Asiatic Society*, vol. XXXVI, part III.

Armour, J. A. (1860). *Grammar of Kandyan Law*. Colombo.

Arulpragasam, L. C. (1961). 'A Consideration of the Problems Arising from the Size and Subdivision of Paddy Holdings in Ceylon, and the Principles and Provisions of the Paddy Lands Act Pertaining to them.' *Ceylon Journal of Historical and Social Studies*, vol. 4, no. 1, 51–70.

Ayoub Millicent, R. and Lieberman, S. (1962). 'Brief Communications.' *American Anthropologist*, vol. 64, no. 1, 162.

Baden-Powell, B. H. (1892). *Land Systems of British India*. 3 vols. Oxford.

——(1896). *The Indian Village Community*. London: Longmans.

Balasingham, K. (1929). *The Laws of Ceylon*, vols. I and III (part II). London: Maxwell and Sweet.

——(1933). *The Laws of Ceylon*, vol. II. London: Maxwell and Sweet.

Barnes, J. A. (1960). 'Marriage and Residential Continuity.' *American Anthropologist*, vol. 62, no. 5, 850–66.

Bertolacci, Anthony (1817). *A View of the Agricultural, Commercial and Financial Interests of Ceylon*. London: Penbury and Allen.

Birnbaum, N. (1953). 'Conflicting Interpretations of the Rise of Capitalism: Marx and Weber.' *The British Journal of Sociology*, vol. IV, June 1953, 125–41.

Brohier, R. L. (1950). *Lands, Maps and Surveys*, vol. I. Colombo: Ceylon Government Press.

Campbell, Sir George (1881). 'Tenure of Land in India' in *Systems of Land Tenure in Various Countries*. London: Cobden Club.

Carrasco, Pedro (1963). 'Brief Communications.' *American Anthropologist*, vol. 65, no. 1, 133–5.

Codrington, H. W. (1938). *Ancient Land Tenure and Revenue in Ceylon*. Colombo: Ceylon Government Press.

Dickson, Sir J. F. (1870). 'Reports of the Service Tenures Commission' quoted in Ralph Pieris (1956), *Sinhalese Social Organisation*, p. 64.

D'Oyly, John (1929). *Constitution of the Kandyan Kingdom*. Colombo: Ceylon Government Press.

Dumont, Louis (1957). *Hierarchy and Marriage Alliance in South Indian Kinship*. Occasional Papers of the Royal Anthropological Institute, London.

Dunning, R. W. (1959). 'Rules of Residence and Ecology among the Northern Ojibwa.' *American Anthropologist*, vol. 61, no. 5, 806–16.

Farmer, B. H. (1960). 'On Not Controlling Subdivision in Paddy Lands.' In *Transactions and Papers, 1960*, Publication No. 28. British Institute of Geographers, London, pp. 225–35.

Ferguson, A. M. and Ferguson, J. (1890). *Taxation in Ceylon: with special reference to the Grain Taxes: the important duty on rice balanced by a local excise levey; and the proposal to substitute a general land Tax.* Colombo: Observer Press.

Firth, Raymond (1951). *Elements of Social Organization.* London: Watts and Co.

Fischer, J. L. (1958). 'The Classification of Residence in Censuses.' *American Anthropologist*, vol. 60, no. 3, 508–17.

Fortes, Meyer (1953). 'The Structure of Unilineal Descent Groups.' *American Anthropologist*, vol. 55, no. 1, 17–41.

Freeman, J. D. (1961). 'On the Concept of the Kindred.' *Journal of the Royal Anthropological Institute*, vol. 91, part 2, 192–220.

Goodenough, W. H. (1956). 'Residence Rules.' *Southwestern Journal of Anthropology*, vol. 12, 22–37.

Government Reports and Enactments. Act No. 16 of 1951. An Act to Provide for the Partition and Sale of Land Held in Common and to Effect Consequential Amendments to Other Written Law.

Administration Report of the Government Agent, Western Province for 1868.

Administration Report of the Government Agent, Southern Province for 1870.

Administration Report of the Government Agent, Sabaragamuva Province for 1877.

Administration Report of the Government Agent, Southern Province for 1878.

Administration Report of the Government Agent, Southern Province for 1880.

Administration Report of the Government Agent, Southern Province for 1885.

Administration Report of the Government Agent, Southern Province for 1886.

Administration Report of the Government Agent, Western Province for 1886.

Administration Report of the Government Agent, Central Province for 1886.

Administration Report of the Government Agent, Central Province for 1887.

Administration Report of the Government Agent, Sabaragamuva Province for 1887.

Administration Report of the Government Agent, Uva Province for 1887.

Administration Report of the Government Agent, Western Province for 1888.

Administration Report of the Government Agent, Sabaragamuva Province for 1888.

Administration Report of the Government Agent, Southern Province for 1888.

Administration Report of the Government Agent, Western Province for 1889.

Bibliography

Administration Report of the Government Agent, Western Province for 1890.

Administration Report of the Government Agent, Southern Province for 1891.

Administration Report of the Government Agent, Southern Province for 1939.

Blue Book of 1888.

Blue Book of 1892.

Ordinance No. 12 of 1840. To Prevent Encroachments upon Crown Lands.

Ordinance No. 14 of 1840. For securing the Due Collection of the Duties or Tax upon Paddy and Dry Grain.

Ordinance No. 6 of 1847. An Ordinance to amend in certain respects the Law of Marriages, and to Provide for the better Registration of Marriages, Births, and Deaths.

Ordinance No. 10 of 1863. An Ordinance to Provide for the Partition or Sale of Lands Held in Common.

Ordinance No. 13 of 1863. An Ordinance to Amend in Certain Respects the Law of Marriages in this Island, and to Provide for the Due Registration Thereof.

Ordinance No. 29 of 1865. An Ordinance to Amend the Ordinance No. 14 of 1840.

Ordinance No. 5 of 1866. An Ordinance to Facilitate the Recovery of Moneys Due as Commutation of the Paddy Tax, and the Performance of Labour.

Ordinance No. 1 of 1867. An Ordinance Related to Claims to Forest, Chena, Waste and Unoccupied Lands.

Ordinance No. 22 of 1871. An Ordinance to Amend the Laws Regulating the Prescription of Actions.

Ordinance No. 15 of 1876. An Ordinance to Amend the Law Relating to the Matrimonial Rights of Married Persons with Regard to Property and the Law of Inheritance.

Ordinance No. 11 of 1878. An Ordinance to Make Provision for the Better Collection of the Tax, Duty or Share Due to the Government Upon Grain Grown in this Island.

Ordinance No. 2 of 1895. An Ordinance to Consolidate and Amend the Laws Relating to the Registration of Marriages other than the Marriages of Kandyans or Mohammedans.

Ordinance No. 2 of 1907. An Ordinance to Consolidate and Amend the Law Relating to Forests and the Felling and Transport of Timber.

Ordinance No. 19 of 1907. An Ordinance to Consolidate and Amend the Laws Relating to Registration of Marriages other than the Marriages of Kandyans or of Mohammedans.

Proclamation of 3 September 1801.

Proclamation of 30 December 1802.

Proclamation of 21 November 1818.

Regulation No. 9 of 1822.

Sessional Paper XVI of 1877.

Sessional Paper XII of 1880.
Sessional Paper XXXIV of 1880.
Sessional Paper XL of 1880.
Sessional Paper III of 1881.
Sessional Paper XXIX of 1889.
Sessional Paper VII of 1890.
Sessional Paper VIII of 1890.
Sessional Paper IV of 1891.
Sessional Paper II of 1892.
Sessional Paper III of 1892.
Sessional Paper XVI of 1959.

Hayley, F. A. (1923). *A Treatise on the Laws and Customs of the Sinhalese.* Colombo: H. W. Cave and Co.

Hocart, A. M. (1950). *Caste: A Comparative Study.* London: Methuen.

Ievers, R. W. (1899). *Manual of the North-Central Province, Ceylon.* Colombo: Government Press.

Jayawardene, A. St V. (1901). *The Roman Dutch Law as it prevails in Ceylon.* Colombo Daily News Press.

Jayawardene, A. St V. (1919). *The Law Relating to the Registration of Deeds.* Colombo.

Jayawardene, A. St V. (1925). *The Law of Partition in Ceylon,* Colombo, Ceylon Daily News Press.

Knox, Robert (1681). *An Historical Relation of Ceylon.* London: Richard Chiswell; 1958 Edition by S. D. Saparamadu, Ceylon: Saman Press.

Lawrie, A. C. (1898). *A Gazetteer of the Central Province of Ceylon.* 2 vols. Colombo: Ceylon Government Press.

Leach, E. R. (1959). 'Polyandry, Inheritance and the Definition of Marriage.' *Man.* Article 199. London.

——(1961). *Pul Eliya, A Village in Ceylon.* Cambridge University Press.

Lee, R. W. (1953). *Introduction to Roman-Dutch Law.* Oxford: Clarendon Press.

Lévi-Strauss, Claude (1953). 'Social Structure.' In *Anthropology Today.* Sol Tax (ed.). Chicago, Illinois.

Maine, H. S. (1876). *Village Communities in the East and West.* New York: Henry Holt and Co.

——(1907). *Ancient Law* (10th ed.). London: John Murray.

Martindale, Don. (1959). 'Sociological Theory and the Ideal Type.' In *Symposium on Sociological Theory,* pp. 57–92. Ed. Llewellyn Cross. New York: Harper and Row.

Mayne, J. D. (1950). *Hindu Law and Usage* (11th ed.). Madras.

Merton, Robert K. (1957). *Social Theory and Social Structure.* Glencoe, Illinois: The Free Press.

Modder, F. (1914). *The Principles of Kandyan Law.* London: Stevens and Haynes.

Murdock, J. P. (1949). *Social Structure.* New York.

——(1957). 'World Ethnographic Sample.' *American Anthropologist,* vol. 59, no. 4, 664–86.

Niti Niganduva (1880) *or the Vocabulary of the Law as it Existed in the Days of the Kandyan Kingdom.* Trans. T. B. Panabokke and C. J. R. Le Mesurier. Colombo: Ceylon Government Press.

Obeyesekere, G. (1962). 'The Buddhist Pantheon in Ceylon and its Extensions.' Paper read at the Chicago Seminar on Theravada Buddhism, Summer 1962. Reprinted in M. Nash (ed.), *Anthropological Studies in Theravada Buddhism.* Yale University Press, 1966.

Parker, H. (1910). *Folk Tales of Ceylon*, vol. I. London: Luzac and Co.

——(1914). *Folk Tales of Ceylon*, vols. II and III. London: Luzac and Co.

Pereira, J. C. W. (1894). *The Laws of Ceylon.* Colombo.

Pereira, J. C. W. (1913). *The Laws of Ceylon* (2nd ed.). Colombo: Ceylon Government Press.

Perera, S. J. (n.d.). *History of Ceylon for Schools.* Colombo: Associated Newspapers of Ceylon.

Phear, R. (1880). *The Aryan Village in India and Ceylon.* London: Macmillan.

Pieris, Ralph (1956). *Sinhalese Social Organization.* Colombo: University of Ceylon Press Board.

Pieters, Sophia (trans.) (1908). *Instructions from the Governor General and Council of India to the Governor of Ceylon 1636–1665.* Ceylon Government Press.

Raghavan, M. D. (1961). *The Karavas of Ceylon.* Ceylon: K. V. A. de Silva and Co.

Report of the Land Commission (1958). Ceylon Government Press.

Report of Paddy Statistics (1956). Monograph No. 9, Department of Census and Statistics. Colombo: Ceylon Government Press.

Sawers, Simon (1826). *Digest of Kandyan Law.* Colombo.

Tambiah, S. J. (1958). 'The Structure of Kinship and its Relationship to Land Possession and Residence in Pata Dumbara, Central Ceylon.' *Journal of the Royal Anthropological Institute*, vol. 88, part I, pp. 21–44.

Tennant, Sir Emerson (1848). *Report on the Finances and Commerce of Ceylon.* H.M.S.O.

Thomson, Justice H. B. (1866). *Institutes of Ceylon*, vol. 2. London: Trubner.

Turnour, G. (1826). 'Memorandum on Sabaragamuva Law.' Reprinted in John D'Oyly, *Constitution of the Kandyan Kingdom*, pp. 107–9. Ceylon Government Press, 1929.

Weber, Max (1947). *The Theory of Social and Economic Organization.* Glencoe, Illinois: The Free Press.

——(1949). *Methodology of the Social Sciences.* Glencoe, Illinois: The Free Press.

——(1958). *From Max Weber.* Oxford University Press.

Yalman, Nur (1958). 'The Analysis of Kandyan Marriage: Landlords, Labourers and Aristocrats.' Ph.D.thesis, University of Cambridge.

——(1962). 'The Structure of the Sinhalese Kindred: A Re-Examination of the Dravidian Terminology.' *American Anthropologist*, vol. 64, no. 3, 548–74.

INDEX

Sinhalese terms are printed in italics; the reference is to the page giving the meaning

Index

Index

Ibbagahawatte, 86
ihala kaṭṭi, 19
Ihala Kattiya, 190
Ihala Madagama, 8, 10, 13–14, 213, 226, 234, 237, 270, 272; genealogy, 32, 144–64; land sales, 106–7, 127, 129; marriages, 66, partition, 179, 235; rotation, 31–5, Figs. 6–9 (pp. 32–4)
India, 221, 273; Brahmin groups, 292; British rule, 276; land tenure, 40, 278–9; village community, 274–8
inheritance, 10–11, 105, 132–4, 250; bilateral, 259; examples, 70–88; Kandyan, 48, 52; Sabaragamuva, 52–5; Sinhalese, 37–49
in-residents, 166–71, 264–8
intestacy, 42–3, 132, 135

jajmani, 216
James, share, 76–7, Fig. 15 (p. 103), Fig. 18 (p. 136), 176, Fig. 40 (p. 270)
Jinadasa, J., citizenship, 272

Kahambiliya-walakada, 160
kaiya, 8
Kalutara, land sales, 122–3, 125–6, 130
kānḍaye, 227
Kandy district, 114, 117; land sales, 122, 126
Kandy, kingdom of, 5, 22, 110, 216, 218, 224; feudalism, 14–16
Kandyan highlands, 116; Hills, 3; law, 1, 6, 9–10, 48, 53, 62, 140; marriage, 6; titles, 224–5
kapurāla, 221
karamāru, 23
Karavas, 17, 225
kariyakaranagē, 15
kaṭṭi, 19
Kegalle, 112; land sales, 122, 126
kin group; ideal and effective, 235–6; status, 211–47; stratification, 236–42; style of life, 242–4
kinnarayā, 219
kinship system, 37–9, 44; terminology, 248–53, Fig. 36 (p. 249)
Knutsford, Lord (Sir Henry Holland, Sec. of State), 113–14
kolave, 5
koralē, 130
koraṭu, 294
Korelegama, 72
Koswatte, 3
Kotte, 225
Kukulu Korale, 4
kumburu, 19
Kurakkan, 4
kurini, 7
Kurunegala, 114
Kuveni, a demoness, 68

lābe, 253
land sales, in Ihala Madagama, 106–7, in Pahala Madagama, 107–8, Tables 9–12 (pp. 122–6); settlement, 100; shortage, 58–9, 210; tax, 109–11; tenure: alienation, 38–40; examples, 31–5; ideal model, 17–31, 55, 134; marriage, 55–60; systems, 8–11; *see* shares
Latpandura, 159
Law; *see* Kandyan, Roman-Dutch, Sabaragamuva, Sinhalese
Lelwala, 3, 75–6, 87–8, 102, 128–9, 146, 213, 236–7
liyanagē, 15
Liyanage line, 129, 227–30, Fig. 30 (p. 229), Fig. 31 (p. 230), Fig. 34 (p. 258), 241
Lokuappuve line, 26–9
Lokuappuve-Balappuve, inheritance, 63, 70–4, 161–2, 192–7, Fig. 37 (p. 255)

maḍa iḍam, 13
Madagama, general survey, 1–11, 13; marriages, 6; *see* Ihala Madagama, Pahala Madagama
maha, 7
mahanaḍuva, 49
mahatmayā, 243
Maine, Sir Henry, 273–5
malli, 260
malu, 191
Mara, 221
Maritime Provinces, 1, 49, 54, 109, 115, 118, 129–30, 138
marriage, 6, 10–11, 17, 42, 245; average age, 66; *binna*, 46–60, 85, 168, 255–6, 259, 264; British law, 62, 129; Christian, 139; cousins, 60, 248–53; *dīga*, 42–53, 56, 71–4, 83, 259, 264; examples, 62–9; Kandyan law, 6; registers, 6, 62, 65, 138–40, 166; Roman-Dutch law,

prostitutes, 79
Protestants, 130, 138, 231
provinces, 1–2
Pul Eliya, 3, 17, 101, 106, 113, 214, 225, 236, 267, 288–90
purappāḍu, 217

radala, 15
rainfall, 3
raiyatwārī, 277
rājakāriya, 16
Rakwana Hills, 3
rālahāmi, 226
Rambadeniya, 68, 260
Ratmalana, 77
Ratnapura, 159; land sales, 122–3, 126
rebirth, 222
renting system, 110–11
residence patterns, 262–6
roads, 5
rodiyas, 68
Roman-Dutch law, 54, 129–34, 137–8, 140–3, 150, 159, 167, 177, 290
rotation, 18–21, 31–5
rubber, 5, 100, 210
Rural Development Society, 295

Sabaragamuva, 1–2, 17, 100, 112; Grain Tax, 116; land sales, 122–7; law, 6, 49, 52–5
Sakra, 221
salāgama, 225
Salpiti, 118
samagiya, 252
sannasa, 217
santatiya, 13
sāsana, 221
schools, 5, 102
Seetin, share, 77–8
Semaris, share, 78
sēnāva, 218
shares, absentees, 10; alienation, 38; cropping, 71; market, 10, 165–88; pooling, 207; principles, 279–81; speculation, 75, 165–6, 170–1, 176, 178, 182; system, 61–97; *see* genealogy, land, partition, rotation
Siddharta, 221
Silappu inheritance, 147, Fig. 19 (p. 145), Fig. 20 (p. 148)
sīma, 220
Singho, Appu, share, 78; Podi, 271–2, Fig. 15 (p. 103); Vilian, 269–70
Sinhalese, culture, 36; feudalism, 14–16, 215–20; Grain Tax, 114; kinship, 38–9; law, 40, 52, 130
Sinharaja Forest, 3, 5, 296
sinnakkara, 269
Siyane, 118
slaves, 16
Southern Province, 1, 5, 17, 118, 122–3, 127
status, 211–47
Swarnamali, Princess, 68

Talangalla, 81
talipot, 44
Talpe Pattu, 1, 118
Tamils, 289–90
taṭṭumāru, 18, 35–6
Tavalama, 81, 102, 169, 241
taxes, land, 109–12; others, 108; *see* Grain Tax
tea, 5, 100, 210
terminology, 248–53
Tesavalamai Code, 130
thombos, 6
Torrington, Lord (Governor), 108
Trincomalee, land sales, 126; naval base, 176

Udugama, 5, 70
Udukinda, 117, 121, 288; evictions, 119
ukas, 211
upasaka, 80
Uva, 1, 115, 119, 121–2, 126; Grain Tax, 117

vāḍakarayo, 16
vagrant, 267
vahalla, 16
valauva, 218
vāsagama, 14
Veddhas, 68
vidāne, 220
vihara-gama, 14
Vijaya, King, 68
village community, 273–9

Wace, Herbert (Asst. Agent), 117
Walapane, 288; evictions, 119–120
Waste Land Ordinance, 99–100
Weber, Max, status group, 244–7; village community, 283–7